D1592821

# PAKISTAN

## BEYOND THE 'CRISIS STATE'

MALEEHA LODHI

*editor*

# Pakistan

*Beyond the 'Crisis State'*

Columbia University Press
New York

Columbia University Press
Publishers Since 1893
New York   Chichester, West Sussex
© Maleeha Lodhi and the Contributors, 2011

Library of Congress Cataloging-in-Publication Data

Pakistan : beyond the "crisis state" / Maleeha Lodhi, editor.
    p. cm.
  Includes bibliographical references and index.
  ISBN 978-0-231-70244-7 (cloth : alk. paper)
  ISBN 978-0-231-80012-9 (eBook)
  1. Pakistan—Politics and government—21st century. 2. Pakistan—Economic
conditions—21st century. 3. Pakistan—Social conditions—21st century.
  4. Pakistan—Foreign relations—21st century. 5. Pakistan—Strategic aspects.
  I. Lodhi, Maleeha.

  DS389.P3427 2011
  954.9105'3—dc22

                        2011002064

∞

Columbia University Press books are printed on permanent and durable acid-free
paper. This book is printed on paper with recycled content.

c 10 9 8 7 6 5 4 3 2 1

References to Internet Web sites (URLs) were accurate at the time of writing. Neither
the author nor Columbia University Press is responsible for URLs that may have
expired or changed since the manuscript was prepared.

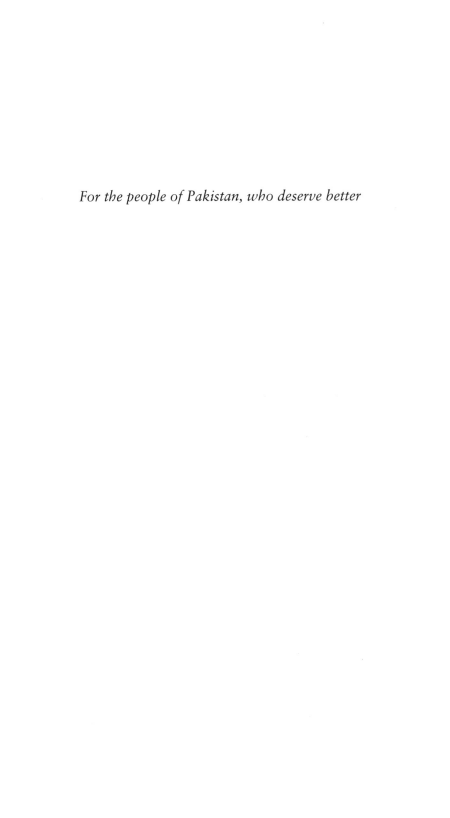

*For the people of Pakistan, who deserve better*

# CONTENTS

# ACKNOWLEDGEMENTS

The publication of this book was made possible by generous support from the Fellowship Fund for Pakistan, which enabled me to spend time at the Woodrow Wilson International Center for Scholars in Washington.

I am deeply grateful to my son Faisal Sharwani who helped me evolve the idea of this volume and who provided invaluable support throughout its preparation.

Special thanks are due to a number of other people: Munawar Noorani for his encouragement, Robert Hathaway for his intellectual guidance, Mustafa Hyder Sayed and Ben Sclafani for their cheerful research assistance, the publisher Michael Dwyer for working closely with me to shape this volume and Leilla Talebali for her dedication in bringing the manuscript to completion.

Finally, I owe special gratitude to many family members especially my brother Kamil Lodhi for offering extremely valuable ideas, comments and criticism during the process of this project.

# CONTRIBUTORS

MALEEHA LODHI twice served as Pakistan's Ambassador to the US (1993–1996 and 1999–2002) and for five years to the UK (2003–2008). She was a member of the UN Secretary General's Advisory Board on Disarmament Affairs from 2001–2005. Her extensive experience in diplomacy is matched by a career in the media. She is a founding editor of *The News*, Pakistan's leading English daily and editor of *The Muslim*. Currently a member of the Council of the London-based International Institute of Strategic Studies, she has been a Public Policy Scholar at the Woodrow Wilson Center in Washington (2009–2010) and a Fellow at Harvard University's Kennedy School (2008).

Dr Lodhi is the recipient of the President's award of Hilal-e-Imtiaz for Public Service. She also received an Honorary Fellowship from the London School of Economics (LSE) in 2004 and an Honorary Degree of Doctor of Letters from London's Metropolitan University in 2005. She taught Politics and Political Sociology at the LSE from 1980–85 and has also been a visiting faculty member at the National Defence University in Islamabad. Lodhi is the author of two collections of essays: *Pakistan's Encounter with Democracy* and *The External Challenge*. She received her PhD in Politics and BSc (Econ) from the LSE.

AYESHA JALAL is the Mary Richardson Professor of History at Tufts University where she teaches at the History Department and the Fletcher School. She obtained her BA in History and Political Science from Wellesley College, USA, and her doctorate in history from the University of Cambridge. Dr Jalal has been Fellow of Trinity College, Cambridge (1980–84), Leverhulme Fellow at the Centre of South Asian Studies, Cambridge (1984–87), Fellow of the Woodrow Wilson

Center for International Scholars in Washington, DC (1985–86) and Academy Scholar at the Harvard Academy for International and Area Studies (1988–90). Between 1998–2003 she was a MacArthur Fellow. She has taught at the University of Wisconsin-Madison, Tufts University, Columbia University and Harvard University.

Jalal's publications include *The Sole Spokesman: Jinnah, the Muslim League and the Demand for Pakistan* (1985 and 1994); *The State of Martial Rule: The Origins of Pakistan's Political Economy of Defence* (1990) and *Democracy and Authoritarianism in South Asia: A Comparative and Historical Perspective* (1995), *Modern South Asia: History, Culture and Political Economy* (1998 and 2011) co-authored with Sugata Bose, *Self and Sovereignty: The Muslim Individual and the Community of Islam in South Asia since c.1850* (2000) and *Partisans of Allah: Jihad in South Asia* (2008).

AMBASSADOR AKBAR AHMED is the Ibn Khaldun Chair of Islamic Studies, American University in Washington DC, the First Distinguished Chair of Middle East and Islamic Studies at the US Naval Academy, Annapolis, and a Non-resident Senior Fellow at the Brookings Institution. He has taught at Princeton, Harvard, and Cambridge Universities and is considered 'the world's leading authority on contemporary Islam' by the BBC. He has served in Balochistan and in north west Pakistan and was in charge of the administration as Political Agent in South Waziristan Agency. He has also served as Pakistan's High Commissioner to the UK and Ireland.

Ahmed is the author of over a dozen award-winning books, including *Discovering Islam*, which was the basis of the BBC six-part TV series called *Living Islam*. His plays, *Noor* and *The Trial of Dara Shikoh* have been staged and published. His most recent book, *Journey into America: The Challenge of Islam (2010)*, is an unprecedented study based on fieldwork of Muslims in America.

MOHSIN HAMID grew up in Lahore, attended Princeton University and Harvard Law School, and worked as a management consultant in New York and London. He is the author of two internationally bestselling novels translated into over twenty-five languages. The first, *Moth Smoke*, won a Betty Trask award, was a *New York Times* Notable Book of the Year, and was a finalist for the PEN/Hemingway award. The second, *The Reluctant Fundamentalist*, won several prizes including the Anisfield-Wolf Award and the Ambassador Book Award, and was shortlisted for many others including the Man Booker Prize, the James Tait Black Memorial Prize, and the International IMPAC Dublin Literary Award. He now lives in Lahore.

SHUJA NAWAZ is the first Director of the South Asia Center of The Atlantic Council of the United States in Washington DC. He is the author of *Crossed Swords: Pakistan, Its Army, and the Wars Within* (2008 and paperback 2009), *FATA: A Most Dangerous Place* (2009), and *Pakistan in the Danger Zone: A Tenuous US-Pakistan Relationship* (2010).

He is a graduate of the Columbia University Graduate School of Journalism, where he won the Henry Taylor Award. He was a television newscaster and producer with Pakistan Television from 1967 to 1972 and covered the 1971 war with India on the Western front.

He has worked for *The New York Times*, the World Health Organization, as a Division Chief for the International Monetary Fund, and a Director of the International Atomic Energy Agency, and has widely written and spoken on military and politico-economic issues on radio, television, and at think tanks. He was Editor of *Finance and Development*, the multilingual quarterly of the IMF and the World Bank.

SAEED SHAFQAT is the founding Director of the Centre for Public Policy and Governance at Forman Christian (College) University, Lahore. He obtained his PhD from the University of Pennsylvania, Philadelphia. He was Chief Instructor, Civil Services Academy of Pakistan (1988–2001) and Executive Director of the National Institute of Population Studies (2005–2007). Prior to that, he was Quaid-i-Azam Distinguished Professor and Chair (2001–2005), Pakistan Center at the School of International Affairs and Public Policy (SIPA), Columbia University and continues to be Adjunct Professor at SIPA.

His research articles on culture, politics, security, public policy, governance and civil service reform on Pakistan have been widely published. His books include: *Political System of Pakistan and Public Policy (1989); Civil-Military Relations in Pakistan (1997); Contemporary Issues in Pakistan Studies (2000, 3rd edition); New Perspectives on Pakistan: Visions for the Future (2007).* Currently, he is working on a monograph on 'Assessing the Dynamics of Pakistan-US Relations in the First Decade of the 21st Century'.

ZIAD HAIDER is a JD and Masters in Public Administration candidate at Georgetown Law and the Harvard Kennedy School. He previously served as a foreign policy advisor to US Senator Chris Dodd, professional staff on the House Committee on Homeland Security, and as a research analyst at the Henry L. Stimson Center's South Asia program. He was an American Society of International Law Fellow at the Human Rights Commission of Pakistan, researching governance reforms in Pakistan's tribal belt.

Haider has appeared as an expert commentator on South Asia in *Newsweek*, the *Associated Press*, and Al Jazeera and has written in the *Asian Survey*, *Far Eastern Economic Review*, *DAWN* (Karachi), and *Indian Express* (New Delhi), among other publications. A Fulbright Scholar in Malaysia where he studied Islamic law, he received his BA from Yale with distinction in Political Science. He is fluent in Urdu and proficient in Mandarin and French.

ZAHID HUSSAIN is an award-winning journalist and writer, a senior editor with *Newsline*, and a correspondent for *The Times* of London, *The Wall Street Journal* and *Newsweek*. He has also covered Pakistan and Afghanistan for several other international publications, including the *Associated Press* and *The Economist*. Hussain has authored two books: *Frontline Pakistan: The struggle with militant Islam* (2007) and *The scorpion's tail: The relentless rise of Islamic militants in Pakistan* (2010). The books have won widespread acclaim as seminal texts on the subject. He lives in Pakistan.

ISHRAT HUSAIN is the Dean and Director, Institute of Business Administration, Karachi and HEC Distinguished National Professor of Economics and Public Policy. He was Chairman, National Commission for Government Reforms (2006–08) and produced a comprehensive blueprint for governance reforms in Pakistan.

As the Governor, State Bank of Pakistan (1999–2005) he carried out the restructuring of the Central Bank and steered the Banking Sector reforms. He was awarded Hilal-e-Imtiaz for public Service. The *Banker Magazine*, London declared him the Central Bank Governor of the year for Asia in 2005 and the *Asian Banker Magazine*, conferred Lifetime Achievement Award in 2006.

Dr Husain served at the World Bank in various positions for over two decades including Director, Central Asian Republics; Chief Economist, East Asia and the Pacific; Chief Economist, Africa; Chief, Debt and International Finance Division.

He is the author of twenty-four books and monographs, more than twenty-five refereed journal articles and over 100 conference papers. His book *Pakistan: The Economy of an Elitist State* has received wide recognition.

Dr Husain received his Master's degree from Williams College and Doctorate in Economics from Boston University. He is a graduate of the Executive Development Program jointly organised by Harvard, Stanford and INSEAD.

MEEKAL AHMED graduated with a BA in Economics (Honors Comprehensive) from Georgetown University, Washington DC, after which he joined the Pakistan Planning Division in the President's Secretariat (1965). He held various positions including concurrently Chief of International Economics and Economic Research Section, Project Director of World Bank-assisted Technical Assistance Loans to Pakistan for policy research and analysis, which were subsequently embodied in World Bank Structural Adjustment loans to Pakistan, and Project Director of a USAID-funded project for developing feasibility studies in the field of manufacturing.

Dr Ahmed was sent on deputation by Government of Pakistan to the International Monetary Fund (IMF) in Washington DC in 1989 as Senior Advisor to Executive Director. While in the IMF, Dr Ahmed was promoted to Chief Economist, Planning Division. He retired from the IMF in 2005.

He has publications in academic journals in Pakistan and presently writes as an analyst for three English-language newspapers in Pakistan as well as for a quarterly journal and two websites on the subject of macroeconomic policy and structural reforms in Pakistan and Pakistan's prolonged interactions with the IMF.

MUDDASSAR MAZHAR MALIK is Co-founder and Executive Vice Chairman of BMA Capital. In addition, he serves as CEO, BMA Funds and is a member of the Executive Management Committee responsible for the overall strategy for the Group. In 2010, BMA was awarded Euromoney's Excellence Awards for being Pakistan's foremost investment banking firm. As a core member of the BMA Team, Muddassar has extensively advised large domestic and international groups on their investment programs in Pakistan.

He has also participated as a delegate at the World Economic Forum (Middle East) on two occasions and is committed to fostering entrepreneurship in Pakistan. He is a charter member of The Indus Entrepreneurs (Karachi Chapter) and is involved in supporting the MIT Enterprise Forum—Pakistan Chapter. He is also a Trustee for i-Care, Pakistan's first donor-advised charity foundation.

Malik received an MBA in Finance and Corporate Strategy from the MIT Sloan School of Management. He also received a BSc (Hons) in Economics and an MSc in Political Economy from the LSE, London.

ZIAD ALAHDAD, as Director of Operations, World Bank, helped manage the World Bank Institute and was a member of the Bank's seniormost management committees. He served as the chief of mission in Turkey and Romania. In Turkey, he managed the turnaround of one of the Bank's largest country portfolios. In Romania, he helped reverse the economic decline, securing Romania's path to European integration.

Alahdad helped manage the global Energy Sector Management Assistance Program and headed the Central and Eastern Europe Regional Energy Network, which provided analytical foundations for extensive energy investment. He managed operations in several countries including the Russia Oil Rehabilitation Project, the Bank's largest and first ever investment in Russia. He served as energy advisor in East Africa and Pakistan, and energy co-ordinator for Central Asia.

On retirement, Alahdad served as advisor to World Bank senior management. He is a board member of several think tanks including the Institute of Public Policy, Pakistan. He has authored several professional publications and lectured at the Woodrow Wilson Center, the Atlantic Council, Yale, Princeton and Georgetown Universities. He has advanced degrees in engineering (Shell Scholar, Loughborough University of Technology, UK) and management (Executive Education, Harvard Business School).

SHANZA NOORHASAN KHAN is the Executive Director of Strategic and Economic Policy Research, a private sector consulting firm in Islamabad, Pakistan. She has worked as a Poverty Research Associate at the Asian Development Bank, Islamabad, Pakistan and also served as a Junior Professional Associate at the World Bank. In addition, Khan has studied US macro-economic issues at the Federal Reserve Bank, Atlanta. She has recently consulted with the United States Agency for

International Development, Department for International Development, British High Commission, Aga Khan Planning and Building Service, GTZ, and Royal Netherlands Embassy Development Cooperation.

Khan focuses on both social issues and macro-economic analysis. Relevant to her development interests, her recent work has focused on Pakistan's poverty measurement and assessment of poverty lines, social protection, public-private partnerships, education and teacher training, assessing validity, credibility, and legitimacy of data. Khan holds a graduate degree in Public Policy from Harvard University, USA and an undergraduate degree in Economics from Emory University, USA.

MOEED W. YUSUF is the South Asia adviser at the United States Institute of Peace. Yusuf is engaged in expanding USIP's work on Pakistan to cover aspects that remain critical for the US and Pakistan to better understand the other's interests and priorities. His current research focuses on youth and democratic institutions in Pakistan, and policy options to mitigate militancy in the country. By training as a political scientist, he has worked extensively on issues relating to South Asian politics, Pakistan's foreign policy, the US-Pakistan relationship, nuclear deterrence and non-proliferation, and human security and development in South Asia.

Before joining USIP, Yusuf was a fellow at the Frederick S. Pardee Center for the Study of the Longer-Range Future at Boston University, and concurrently a research fellow at the Mossavar-Rahmani Center at Harvard Kennedy School. In 2007, he co-founded Strategic and Economic Policy Research, a private sector consultancy firm in Pakistan. Yusuf has also consulted for a number of Pakistani and international organisations including Sustainable Development Policy Institute (SDPI), Brookings Institution, UNESCO, Asian Development Bank, World Bank, Innovative Development Strategies, Sungi Development Foundation and Pugwash International. He has published widely in national and international journals, professional publications and magazines and writes regularly in the Pakistani press.

FEROZ HASSAN KHAN is a Senior Lecturer in the Department of National Security Affairs at the US Naval Postgraduate School, Monterey California. He is a former Brigadier in the Pakistan Army, with combat experience in command on active fronts and staff assignments in his military career. He last served as Director Arms Control and

Disarmament Affairs, in the Strategic Plans Division, Joint Services Headquarters. He represented Pakistan on numerous assignments in the United States, Europe, and Asia, assisting the Ministry of Foreign Affairs in multilateral and bilateral negotiations on nuclear arms control and international security issues.

He holds an MA in International Relations and Strategic Studies from the School of Advanced International Studies (SAIS), John Hopkins University, Washington DC. He has held a series of visiting fellowships at Stanford University, the Woodrow Wilson International Center for Scholars and the Brookings Institution in Washington DC.

He has widely participated in international and national conferences on strategic issues, international security; South Asia politics and security; nuclear non-proliferation and arms control issues. He has also written articles, book chapters in several reputed journals, newspapers and publications. He is currently writing a book, *Eating Grass: Pakistan and the Bomb* (forthcoming, 2011).

AMBASSADOR MUNIR AKRAM has had a long and distinguished diplomatic career including serving as Pakistan's Permanent Representative to the United Nations. His forty years experience in the foreign service, his two terms as President of the UN Security Council, and his numerous top-level contacts with world leaders give him a unique practitioner's perspective on international affairs, global issues and Pakistan's foreign policy. As Permanent Representative to the United Nations Ambassador Akram represented Pakistan in numerous United Nations bodies and international conferences, including the Security Council, the Economic and Social Council and the Conference on Disarmament and has written and negotiated a nuclear treaty with India. He is a prolific writer and has lectured widely on various strategic, political and economic issues.

AHMED RASHID is a Pakistani journalist based in Lahore, who has covered Afghanistan, Pakistan and Central Asia for a variety of publications since 1979. He is the author of the best-selling book *Taliban*. His most recent book is *Descent into Chaos: The US and the Disaster in Afghanistan, Pakistan and Central Asia*. His other books include *Jihad* and *The Resurgence of Central Asia*. He writes for the *Financial Times*, the *Washington Post*, the *New York Review of Books* and *BBCOnline* amongst other publications. *Foreign Policy* magazine chose him as one of the 100 Global Thinkers in 2009 and 2010. Rashid was educated at Malvern College England, Government College Lahore and obtained his degree in political science from Fitzwilliam College, Cambridge University.

SYED RIFAAT HUSSAIN is Professor and Chair of the Department of Defence and Strategic Studies at the Quaid-i-Azam University in Islamabad. Prior to this, he served as Chairman of the Department of Peace and Conflict Studies at the National University in Islamabad, and the Executive Director of the Regional Centre for Strategic Studies in Colombo, Sri Lanka. Professor Hussain has also taught at the Centre for International Security and Cooperation (CISAC) at Stanford University, California, USA, and has served as course director of the Foreign Service Academy in the Ministry of Foreign Affairs, Islamabad. He serves as a member of the editorial boards of many diverse publications, such as the *South Asia Journal* and the *National Defense University Journal and Regional Studies Quarterly*. He is a member of the Board of Governors of Pakistan Studies Centre, Karachi University.

Professor Hussain is the author of numerous books and publications, including *Afghanistan and 9/11: The Anatomy of a Conflict* (2002); *From Dependence to Intervention: Soviet-Afghanistan Relations During the Brezhnev Era (1964–1982)* (1994); 'Liberation Tigers of Tamil Eelam (LTTE): Shattered Quest for a "homeland"', in *Violent Non-State Actors in World Politics* (2009), and 'Pakistan's Changing Outlook on Kashmir', in *South Asian Survey* (2007). He received his PhD in International Studies from University of Denver, Colorado, USA.

# ABBREVIATIONS

| | |
|---|---|
| ACR | Annual Confidential Report |
| AG | Auditor General |
| AJK | Azad Jammu and Kashmir |
| ADB | Asian Development Bank |
| ANP | Awami National Party |
| AWAC | Airborne Warning and Control |
| BISP | Benazir Income Support Program |
| BJP | Bharatiya Janata Party |
| BLA | Balochistan Liberation Army |
| BoD | Board of Directors |
| BRIC | Brazil, Russia, India and China |
| C2ISR | Command and Control, Intelligence, Surveillance and Reconnaissance |
| CBMs | Confidence Building Measures |
| CCI | Council for Common Interest |
| CCP | Competition Commission of Pakistan |
| CEDAW | Convention on the Elimination of Discrimination Against Women |
| CENTCOM | US Central Command |
| CENTO | Central Treaty Organization |
| CJ | Chief Justice |
| CNG | Compressed Natural Gas |
| COAS | Chief of Army Staff |
| CPI | Consumer Price Index |
| CSP | Civil Service of Pakistan |
| DFID | Department for International Development |
| DGISI | Director General of Inter-Services Intelligence |

## ABBREVIATIONS

| | |
|---|---|
| DGER | Directorate General of Energy Resources |
| EIU | Economist Intelligence Unit |
| ESR | Education Sector Reform |
| FATA | Federally Administered Tribal Areas |
| FCD | Foreign Currency Deposit |
| FDI | Foreign Direct Investment |
| FoDP | Friends of Democratic Pakistan |
| FPSC | Federal Public Services Commission |
| GDP | Gross Domestic Product |
| GHQ | General Headquarters |
| GoP | Government of Pakistan |
| GRAPS | Gender Reform Action Plans |
| GST | General Sales Tax |
| GST | Goods and Services Tax |
| HDIP | Hydrocarbon Development Institute of Pakistan |
| HJI | Harakat-al-Jihad al-Islami (Movement of Islamic Jihad) |
| HuM | Harakat-ul-Mujahideen (Movement of the holy warriors) |
| IB | Intelligence Bureau |
| ICG | International Crisis Group |
| ICG | Indian Coast Guard |
| ICRG | International Country Risk Guide |
| IDBP | Industrial Development Bank of Pakistan |
| IEP | Integrated Energy Planning |
| IPP | Independent Power Producers |
| IJI | Islami Jamhoori Ittehad (Islamic Democratic Alliance) |
| ILO | International Labour Organisation |
| IMF | International Monetary Fund |
| IPDF | Infrastructure Project Development Facility |
| ISI | Inter-Services Intelligence |
| J&K | Jammu and Kashmir |
| JCO | Junior Commissioned Officers |
| JCSC | Joint Chiefs of Staff Committee |
| JeM | Jaish-e-Mohammad (Army of Mohammad) |
| JI | Jamaat-e-Islami (Party of Islam) |
| JUD | Jamaat-ud-Dawa |
| JUI | Jamiat Ulema-e-Islam (Party of Islamic Ulema) |

| | |
|---|---|
| KESC | Karachi Electric Supply Company |
| KP | Khyber Pakhtunkhwa (formerly known as the North West Frontier Province) |
| LEAPS | Learning and Educational Achievements in Punjab Schools |
| LeJ | Lashkar-e-Jhangvi (Army of Jhangvi) |
| LeT | Lashkar-e-Taiba (Army of Virtue) |
| LoC | Line of Control |
| LPG | Liquefied Petroleum Gas |
| MDG | Millennium Development Goals |
| MFN | Most Favoured Nation |
| MMA | Muttahida Majlis-i-Amal (United Council for Action) |
| MoU | Memorandum of Understanding |
| MQM | Muttahida Qaumi Mahaz (United National Movement) |
| MTDF | Medium Term Development Framework |
| MTFS | Medium Term Financial Strategy |
| MTOE | Million Tons of Oil Equivalence |
| NATO | North Atlantic Treaty Organization |
| NAVTEC | National Vocational and Technical Education Commission |
| NCA | National Command Authority |
| NCGR | National Commission for Government Reforms |
| NDS | National Directorate for Security |
| NES | National Executive Service |
| NFC | National Finance Commission |
| NGO | Non-Governmental Organisation |
| NIR | Net International Reserves |
| NMCC | National Military Command Center |
| NPA | National Plan of Action |
| NRO | National Reconciliation Ordinance |
| NSG | Nuclear Suppliers Group |
| NWFP | North West Frontier Province (currently known as Khyber Pakhtunkhwa) |
| ODI | Overseas Development Institute |
| OGDCL | Oil and Gas Development Company Limited |
| PAC | Pakistan Aeronautical Complex |
| PAEC | Pakistan Atomic Energy Commission |
| PAF | Pakistan Air Force |

| PATTA | Pakistan Afghan Transit Trade Agreement |
|---|---|
| PEPCO | Pakistan Electric Power Company |
| PES | Provincial Executive Services |
| PIA | Pakistan International Airlines |
| PICIC | Pakistan Industrial Credit and Investment Corporation |
| PML | Pakistan Muslim League |
| PML-N | Pakistan Muslim League (Nawaz Sharif group) |
| PMS | Performance Management System |
| PMSA | Pakistan Maritime Security Agency |
| PPP | Pakistan People's Party |
| PPP | Purchasing Power Parity |
| PRGF | Poverty Reduction and Growth Facility (of the IMF) |
| PSBR | Public Sector Borrowing Requirement |
| PSE | Public Sector Enterprise |
| PSEB | Pakistan Software Export Board |
| R&D | Research and Development |
| RAW | Research and Analysis Wing (India's premier security agency) |
| REER | Real Effective Exchange Rate |
| RGST | Reformed General Sales Tax |
| Rs. | Pakistani Rupee (also PKR) |
| SAARC | South Asian Association for Regional Cooperation |
| SAC | Sufi Advisory Council |
| SAFTA | South Asian Free Trade Area |
| SBA | Stand-By Arrangement |
| SDRs | Special Drawing Rights |
| SEATO | South East Asian Treaty Organization |
| SFC | Strategic Force Command |
| SMC | School Management Committee |
| SME | Small and Medium Enterprise |
| SMEDA | Small and Medium Enterprise Development Authority |
| SPD | Strategic Plans Division |
| SSB | Special Selection Board |
| SSP | Sipah-e-Sahaba Pakistan (Soldiers of the Prophet's Companions) |
| SUPARCO | Space and Upper Atmosphere Research Commission |
| TCF | Trillion Cubic Feet |
| TFP | Total Factor Productivity |
| TTP | Tehrik-i-Taliban Pakistan (Taliban Movement of Pakistan) |

## ABBREVIATIONS

| | |
|---|---|
| TVET | Technical and Vocational Education Training |
| UN | United Nations |
| UNICEF | United Nations Children's Fund |
| USAID | United States Agency for International Development |
| WAPDA | Water and Power Development Authority |
| WB | World Bank |

# INTRODUCTION

From the majestic Himalayan and Karakorum mountain ranges the Indus river winds down the plains of Pakistan for nearly a thousand miles to the Arabian sea. The banks of this river have been home to one of the world's oldest and greatest civilisations. The mighty river has been the country's lifeblood, animating much of its culture and history and helping to shape a distinctly Pakistani identity.

In the summer of 2010 it was the fury of the Indus river that unleashed itself on the country with devastating consequences. Engorged by heavy monsoon rain, the river system over-flooded and deluged large swathes of Pakistan—as much as a fifth of its land area—causing large-scale destruction and displacement. Twenty million people were affected by this calamity. And this at a time when Pakistan was struggling to cope with economic and security crises and reeling from the blowback of nine years of war in neighbouring Afghanistan that started with the US-led military intervention in 2001.

The floods exposed a paradox that lies at the heart of Pakistan's predicament today: that of a weak state and a strong society. As the government machinery foundered in responding to the situation, civil society, the business community, ordinary citizens and even the media, organised efforts to help the flood victims. The anaemic official response—notwithstanding the Army's effective rescue and relief efforts—contrasted sharply with the heroic actions taken by private charities and local communities.

What also mitigated the tragedy was the capacity for endurance of the afflicted, who set about rebuilding their homes and lives almost as soon as the waters receded and with remarkable dignity and an unfazed resolve to overcome the challenge.

1

Resilience has been part of Pakistan's story from the country's inception, obscured by the single-issue lens through which outsiders have lately viewed the nation. The prism of terror and extremism has deflected attention away from the strength and stability of its underlying social structures which have enabled the country to weather national and regional storms and rebound from disasters—natural and manmade.

Many foreign observers thought when the floods struck that this was one crisis too many which would finally tip Pakistan over the edge. But the country defied this doomsday prognosis as it had earlier ones.

While Pakistan has had to navigate multiple challenges, it has always been more than an entity that lurches from crisis to crisis. Its promising potential lies in a number of attributes: an able pool of professionals and technically trained people, a hardworking labour force, a growing middle class, an enterprising business community, an energetic free media, and a lively arts, literature and music scene. Pakistan's cultural plurality and open society are sinews of its strength. It has a significant industrial base, an elaborate infrastructure of roads and communication links, a modern banking system, a large domestic market and a thriving informal economy—factors that have averted a national breakdown even when in the throes of severe financial crisis. Its economic problems are rooted in poor state management, not Pakistan's economic fundamentals, which remain robust. It has managed—in spurts—to achieve high rates of economic growth, not nearly enough to keep pace with an exploding population, but sufficient to invest the country with several features of a modern nation.

Successive governments however have been unable to deploy these ingredients for success to unlock Pakistan's potential. Instead poor governance, rule without law and short-sighted leadership have mired the country in layers of crises that have gravely retarded Pakistan's progress and development.

It does not have to be this way. The country may yet escape its difficult first sixty-three years, resolve its problems and re-imagine its future. But doing so will need a capable leadership with the vision and determination to chart a new course.

This volume explores the path to a post-crisis state by identifying the policy responses that can bring about such an outcome. It is inspired by the belief that Pakistan's problems are soluble and its challenges can be overcome. And that Pakistanis themselves must reclaim their country by extricating it from the numerous challenges it faces.

Usually, edited books emerge from conferences. This book is the product of a 'virtual' conference—in cyberspace—that led to a meeting of minds among some of Pakistan's top practitioners and scholars, about the need to add a new dimension to the ongoing debate on 'Whither Pakistan'.

This collection offers a diversity of views and perspectives. But what binds all the distinguished contributors is their belief that Pakistan's challenges are surmountable and the impetus for change and renewal can only come from within, through bold reforms that are identified in the chapters that follow.

The issues discussed in the book cluster around the themes of governance, security, economic and human development and foreign policy, underlining the complex intersection of domestic and international factors that have shaped if not determined the Pakistan experience.

In the opening chapter of the volume Pakistan's leading historian, Ayesha Jalal, considers the country's current predicament in the light of a troubled past. She describes how a national paranoia has taken hold of the country, and identifies the lack of a critical historical tradition as the root of the problem. Her chapter argues that Pakistan can change course, in a strategic sense and also in terms of recasting its rational and emotional framework, if its people are allowed to delve into their history with open mindedness.

Award-winning novelist Mohsin Hamid represents the third generation of Pakistanis born after independence. His chapter offers an upbeat message of hope and sets out reasons for optimism about Pakistan. Its vastness, diversity, traditions of co-existence, and evolving democracy are identified as important assets. Furthermore, Pakistan has the resources to fund its own development and regenerate itself provided it chooses to increase its paltry levels of tax collection.

Dr Akbar S. Ahmed, author and anthropologist, seeks to establish that the nation's founder and his vision are central to today's debate about the nature and character of the Pakistani state. The debate has never been more intense between advocates of a modern, functional state, those demanding a theocratic state and still others urging a balance between the two. No voice is more important in this debate than that of Mohammad Ali Jinnah. Pakistan has yet to live up to the ideal set out in Jinnah's key speeches but his authority and legitimacy can still be used to translate this into reality.

My own chapter explores the intricate interplay between internal and external factors and examines Pakistan's tangled political past of governance failures, patronage-dominated politics and missed economic opportunities. The country must overcome five fault lines to chart a new, hopeful course. Socio-economic changes of the past decade or so have transformed the dynamic between state and society, created a larger, more politically assertive middle class and engendered a stronger, more 'connected' society. Once politics catches up with these changes the foundation would be laid for a functional and responsive state.

The next two chapters focus on the role of the country's most powerful institution, the military. Shuja Nawaz sets out the factors behind the Army's repeated political interventions and wide footprint in national life. He examines its complex relations with the civilian sector and changing internal dynamics to argue that civilian supremacy should be the goal.

Saeed Shafqat explores whether the military's hegemony may—or will—gradually give way to a party-led, representative system. He sees two paradoxical trends in the post-2008 election period: the continuity of the traditional political elite and the shift in the social composition of the military and civil bureaucracy. He concludes on a hopeful note by pointing to the emerging national consensus on restricting the political role of the military.

Turning to the role that ideology has played in Pakistan's evolution, Ziad Haider argues that religion has been used for multiple purposes including nation-building and security objectives. This has produced a blowback that now confronts the country with an unprecedented challenge. Pakistan's viability depends in large part on its ability to develop a new Islamic narrative that can be a force for progressive change.

Dr Ishrat Husain served until recently as the Governor of the State Bank. His vast experience informs a detailed consideration of how the civil service can be reformed and economic governance improved, without which, he argues, even well-crafted policies cannot be executed. He advocates building both formal and informal 'institutions of restraint' to ensure a system of checks and balances that can provide the essential pillars of good governance.

Pakistan's struggle against militancy and extremism is among its most daunting challenges. Award-winning journalist Zahid Hussain analyses how present efforts are at once containing and unintentionally incubating the militant threat and urges a number of measures to deal with the challenge more effectively and comprehensively.

Dr Meekal Ahmed is among Pakistan's top economists and has worked in various positions in the Planning Commission and the International Monetary Fund. From his overview of a troubled economic past Ahmed draws important lessons. Pakistan, he reasons, needs a regime-change in economic policy-making and implementation of key reforms to place the economy on a viable footing and realise the country's economic potential.

Muddassar Mazhar Malik offers a private sector perspective on economic competitiveness. He evaluates Pakistan's potential from the angle of what gives or can give it a competitive advantage to position it in the global economy. In a forward-looking assessment he sets out the factors that need to be addressed to evolve a strategy for Pakistan to emerge as a successful economy.

The crisis in Pakistan's energy sector is today the single greatest impediment to economic recovery. Ziad Alahdad investigates what it will take to turn this sector around. He argues that the lack of a coordinated policy has contributed to the problem. He shows how the right policy approach can help to address Pakistan's seemingly insurmountable energy deficit and pave the way for economic revival.

Moeed Yusuf and Shanza Khan make the case that education is critical to Pakistan's recovery. They argue that education, which lies at the heart of Pakistan's challenges, should be regarded as a strategic priority not just a development objective. The next decade should act as a corrective period to put in place policies to ensure full education access to all. The authors enumerate both short- and long-term measures that are required to achieve this.

Feroz Hassan Khan, a former Brigadier in the Pakistan Army relates the story of the country's nuclear quest. He details how the development of a covert capability took shape in response to the competing threat from India over four decades and reflected the effort to address its severe security predicament. In explaining the role of nuclear weapons in Pakistan's national security he argues that on at least five occasions since the mid-1980s a conventional war with India was averted.

Munir Akram focuses on the range of strategic challenges that Pakistan now faces. In a tour de force the internal threat from militancy, the country's interests in Afghanistan, a pervasive challenge from India and post 9/11 relations with the US are all assessed from the perspective of Pakistan's strategic decline as a consequence of multiple factors including economic weakness, domestic discord and strategic confusion. Akram brings his experience in Pakistan's diplomatic service to bear on the critical question of how the country can reverse its political, economic and diplomatic marginalisation in regional and global power relations.

Internationally renowned author Ahmed Rashid examines the complex issue of Afghanistan against the backdrop of a faltering US-led war effort, NATO countries looking for the exits and Pakistan's controversial policies. He assesses the possibilities for peace talks to end the long conflict and argues that Pakistan's stance will be critical to the outcome: whether the region descends into chaos or moves towards a negotiated settlement that ensures an orderly withdrawal of Western troops from Afghanistan.

Turning to relations with India, Dr Syed Rifaat Hussain appraises in the final chapter how efforts to forge a durable peace between the nuclear neighbours have fared against the backdrop of their continued rivalry over Kashmir. Highlighting the fragility of the Pakistan-India peace process, he argues that lasting peace requires an amicable settlement of the Kashmir dispute. India's rising influence as a global power and the Indo-US strategic partnership are not only aggravating Pakistan's security dilemmas but also discouraging New Delhi from seeking durable rapprochement with Pakistan.

The concluding note sets out what needs to be done to address Pakistan's systemic and fundamental challenges to set the country on to a course beyond a 'crisis state' and guarantee its long-term stability. It identifies the critical priorities on which a national consensus needs to be fashioned. It concludes that this is not possible without political will on the part of a leadership that is credible and seen to be pursuing goals regarded as legitimate by the wider public.

1

# THE PAST AS PRESENT

*Ayesha Jalal*

A top columnist in a leading American newspaper recently described Pakistan as 'Paranoidistan'—'a state that suspects every U.S. move as designed to weaken Pakistan for the benefit of a secret U.S. alliance with India.'[1] Paranoia is a mental condition based on delusions of persecution, excessive jealousy and an exaggerated sense of self. Are Pakistanis paranoid and is Pakistan 'Paranoidistan'? A partial answer might seem to lie in the common perception of Pakistan as the world's largest assembly line of terrorists—a product of its compulsive uses of Islam as an instrument of domestic and foreign policy.[2] The botched-up bombing attempt of New York's Times Square by a Pakistani-born American has strengthened international opinion that, while all Pakistanis are not terrorists, most acts of terrorism in the contemporary world inexorably carry the Pakistani paw print.

Perceptions matter but devoid of historical grounding can fall short of providing a balanced perspective. Grasping the reasons for the Pakistani tendency for paranoia and violence requires assessing its troubling present in the light of a troubled past. Only then is it plausible to ask how, if at all, Pakistanis can be persuaded to change course, not only in a strategic sense but also in terms of recasting the rational and emotional framework through which they perceive the world and in turn are perceived by it.

*Ideological Fissures*

Billed as the epicentre of global terror, Pakistan has been in the grip of an unrelenting terrorist campaign by elements once supported by the state's own intelligence agencies to conduct 'jihad' in Afghanistan and Indian-controlled Kashmir. Over the past six years or so an estimated 22,110 people have died, including at least 2,637 security personnel, 7,004 civilians and 5,960 terrorists or insurgents.[3] While Pakistan has become a veritable killing field, its commitment to the American-led war against al Qaeda and Taliban in Afghanistan is under acute suspicion. Why does Pakistan elicit such scepticism and distrust?

With the spectre of Talibanization radiating out of the northwestern Federally Administered Tribal Areas (FATA), Pakistanis are split on the merits of their strategic alliance with the United States of America. A heated debate on how best to tackle the insurgency in FATA at the University of Peshawar ended in pandemonium when the former chief of Pakistan's Inter-Services Intelligence (ISI), Chief General (retd) Asad Durrani, blurted out, 'Leave all this discussion, let me ask the audience whether they want the Taliban to win or the US? Just raise your hand.'[4] The question underlines the deep ideological fissures inside Pakistan that has made it such a difficult ally for Washington.

Whether in private discussions, public fora, newspapers or back-to-back talk shows hosted on private television channels, a cross-section of Pakistanis are displaying a penchant for conspiracy theories over reasoned arguments supported by hard evidence. Instead of reporting bare facts and letting people draw their own conclusions, the media's opinion managers, assisted by a string of 'experts', are burnishing the old narrative of national insecurity with apocalyptic fear. Lending credence to the media's conspiratorial puffery are recurrent intelligence failures to prevent suicide bombings in urban centres in retaliation against military operations in Swat and South Waziristan and a spate of American drone attacks on militant hideouts in the northwestern tribal belt neighbouring Afghanistan. Terrorist attacks in key cities, even when claimed by the Pakistani Taliban, are ritually blamed on American private security agencies such as Blackwater and DynCorp as strategic revenge for Pakistan's refusal to break off ties with the Afghan Taliban and deliver the ever-elusive Osama bin Laden.

Besieged by enemies within and without, television's spin-doctors, impelled by the state's intelligence agencies, attribute Pakistan's multi-faceted problems to the machinations of invisible external hands, as opposed to historically verifiable causes of internal decline and decay. If India's hegemonic designs are not hindering Pakistan at every step, America and Israel are believed to be hatching plots to break up the world's only Muslim nuclear state. Call it paranoia, denial or intellectual paralysis, but Pakistan's deeply divided and traumatised people are groping for a magical formula to evade collective responsibility for their failure to gel as a nation. Individual voices of reason calling for sober analyses and pragmatic responses to an admittedly difficult situation are drowning in an upsurge of anti-American vitriolic. Seeing Pakistan's ills as gifts from abroad is not the bane of Islamic extremists alone. Liberal-minded Pakistanis are, for patriotic reasons, joining the national chorus condemning American-led conspiracies to destabilise Pakistan.

A psychologically introverted national mindset resistant to critical self-reflection tends to be suspicious and paranoid. This is not to say that there are no grounds for harbouring suspicions of friends and allies, not to mention enemies, but Pakistanis need to ponder why they have ended up as the world's favourite whipping boy. An informed, open-ended and sustained internal debate that can shed light on the root causes of their present predicament is impossible without some semblance of a shared historical consciousness. Yet the idea of history as a study of the past through rigorous investigative methods of critical enquiry has suffered from willful neglect in the interest of promoting new-fangled ideologies defined by regimes pursuing the politics of self-perpetuation. Instead of history, Pakistanis are given emotive lessons in ideology, along with a compendium of selective facts, which instead of opening up minds parrot the 'truths' of hastily constructed national myths. While myths are an important dimension of the historical imagination of a people, they are meaningful only when they bear a broad resemblance to actual history. Shorn of a history, people living in myths are just that—a mythical people whose thoughts and actions lack credibility and substance, a frustrated and depressed people.

Despite a well-orchestrated official nationalism, Pakistan ever since its creation has been searching for moorings somewhere in the twilight zone between myth and history. Not a novel occurrence in a newly independent state, it has—due to a dysfunctional educational system and a closed media (its recent commercialisation notwithstanding)—led to the dissemination of some remarkable distortions and mistruths. Curbs on freedom of speech during extended periods of military authoritarianism, declining educational standards, and an obsessive fear of Indian hegemonic designs, has stunted the development of a critical intellectual tradition. Intellectuals have been hounded and muzzled or bribed into subservience. History has been reduced to a jumble of clichés by official hacks expounding improbable versions of Pakistan's much-touted Islamic ideology. The achievements of essentially secular Muslim rule in Hindu India for millennia have been tweaked to assert Islamic superiority. Forced to imbibe official truths, the vast majority of literate Pakistanis take comfort in ignorance, scepticism and, most disconcertingly, in a contagion of belief in conspiracy theories. The self-glorification of an imagined past matched by habits of national denial have assumed crisis proportions today when Pakistan's existence is under far more serious threat from fellow Muslims than it was in 1947 from rival non-Muslim communities.

## Importance of History

Established as a homeland for Indian Muslims, Pakistan has fewer Muslims than in India and Bangladesh. Official Pakistani nationalism ascribes the country's creation to the 'two-nation' theory, according to which Indian Muslims were always a distinct community that had resisted assimilation into the subcontinent's predominantly Hindu culture. The claim is not corroborated by historical facts. Indian Muslims shared a common religious identity but were hardly united in their politics, which were more often defined by class, regional and ideological affiliations. An absence of unanimity in Muslim politics, not the commonalities of religion, allowed the Indian National Congress to cut the All-India Muslim League's demand for Pakistan down to size.

Mohammad Ali Jinnah had twice rejected the territorial contours of Pakistan as it emerged, describing them as 'mutilated, truncated and moth-eaten'. He had wanted a constitutional arrangement that gave Muslims something close to parity at a centre re-established on the basis of a partnership between two essentially sovereign states—Pakistan (representing Muslim-majority provinces) and Hindustan (representing Hindu-majority provinces).[5] Jinnah's hopes of a renegotiated Indian union based on confederal or treaty arrangements between Pakistan and Hindustan were dashed by Congress's refusal to share power and the British haste to draw the shutters on their Indian empire. If their claim to nationhood was conceded, Muslims as a 'nation' were divided into two hostile states. The contradiction between the claims of Muslim nationalism and the achievement of a territorial state was never resolved, confounding Pakistan's struggle to define an identity that is both Islamic and national.

The importance of history in building a cohesive nation was recognised, but the methods adopted proved inimical for national unity. Celebrating the rich diversity of Pakistan's regional cultures might have made for more judicious narrations of the nation. Portraying Pakistan as an Islamic entity distinct from Hindu India, the official scribes of nationalism saw regional identities as threats to the state. Using the Islamic bond to justify suppressing the distinctive linguistic and cultural mores of Pakistan's regional peoples, especially during prolonged bouts of military dictatorship, had politically divisive effects. Before and after Bangladesh's formation in 1971, official versions of Pakistani history elicited derision and resentment in some regions.

Without a credible history, a people cannot develop a historical consciousness, much less a national one. By devaluing history for political and ideological reasons, Pakistan has found it difficult to project a national identity that can strike a sympathetic chord with its heterogeneous people. Sixty-three years after independence, Pakistan is trying to define the inner and outer contours of its national identity. The dilemma flows from a stubborn refusal to accept the more awkward truths about the historical circumstances surrounding its birth. Pakistanis are conditioned to think that their country emerged from a religiously inspired separatist movement against Hindu domination in an independent India. This overlooks Congress's solution of India's Muslim problem. Not only were the two main Muslim majority provinces of Punjab and Bengal partitioned, but the Muslim League was also denied a share of power at the all-India level, an arrangement Jinnah had expected to negotiate in order to safeguard the interests of all Indian Muslims. Glossing over the historically weightier matter of the exclusion of Muslim-majority areas from India, the managers of Pakistan harped on fears of reabsorption into Hindu India. While relations between the two neighbours have been strained ever since 1947, particularly over Kashmir, it is arguable whether India wishes to reincorporate the Muslim majority areas and endanger its existing political balance between communities and regions. The desire to encircle and weaken Pakistan cannot be confused with the objective of undoing partition.

## The India Factor

The Indian bugbear helped turn Pakistan into a security state, but threats to its survival as a sovereign independent state invariably emanated from within. The Army and senior civil bureaucracy registered their dominance over parliament and elected bodies at the provincial and local levels within years of independence. The supremacy of the non-elected institutions survived the tentative experiment in parliamentary democracy during the first decade, controlled politics under military dispensation after 1958, and persisted after Pakistan's dismemberment in 1971. Against the backdrop of centre-province tensions, a gagged media, weak political parties and the organisational limitations of civil society, the emerging structural imbalance within the state was given constitutional legitimacy by a judiciary forced into submission by a presumptuous executive. The result was a centralised state structure, federal in form and unitary in substance, whose military authoritarian character was at odds with the tenor of politics in the regions. These structural asymmetries contributed to a lack of democratic institutions, inadequate mechanisms for public accountability, inequitable distribution of resources and chronic tensions between the centre and the provinces.

The uneasy symbiosis between a military authoritarian state and democratic political processes is often traced to the artificial nature of Pakistan and the lack of a neat fit between social identities at the base and the arbitrary frontiers drawn by the departing colonial masters. Yet India, with greater social diversities, laid the foundations of a constitutional democracy. This crucial difference between the two states that replaced the British Raj cannot be put down to a democracy deficit in the Muslim psyche. Nor can the complex and shifting political dynamics that thwarted Muslim dreams for peace and prosperity be blamed wholly on America's cynical exploitation of Pakistan's geostrategic location. A choice was made by the rulers of Pakistan in the face of Washington's efforts to charm New Delhi with generous amounts of economic assistance. The country's first finance minister, Ghulam Mohammad, summed up the feeling well when he told the Americans that Pakistanis felt like 'a prospective bride who observes her suitor spending very large sums on a mistress, i.e. India, while she herself can only look forward to not more than a token maintenance in the event of marriage'.[6]

Faced with the unenviable choice of accepting Indian hegemony or joining American-backed security alliances aimed at the containment of communism, the Pakistani leadership opted for the latter. By the mid 1950s, Pakistan had entered the South East Asian Treaty Organization (SEATO) and the Central Treaty Organization (CENTO) covering West Asia in return for American military and economic assistance. Hitching its wagons to the Anglo-American bloc dented Pakistan's efforts to project itself as a leader of the Muslim world. During the 1950s an Arab world rife with anti-imperialist and nationalist trends felt little affinity for a country flaunting its Islamic identity. Pakistan's alliance with the West bolstered Jawaharlal Nehru's bid to register India as a leader of the non-aligned movement. This served to heighten the Pakistani sense of inferiority vis-à-vis India, forcing an abject reliance on America whose capitalist-driven consumerism and military prowess was as much an object of resentment as of awe in the country.

*Manto's Letters*

The Urdu short story writer Saadat Hasan Manto conveyed the mood of ordinary Pakistanis reduced to silently watching the world's richest and most powerful country arming one of the poorest and weakest to counter the local bully on the block. 'My country is poor, but why is it ignorant?' Manto asked in the first of nine satirical letters to Uncle Sam. The percipient Uncle had to know the answer in his heart unless it had been removed by one of America's brilliant surgeons. Manto wondered where America got all its money from to be such a 'show off'. He loved his country, however poor and ignorant. Tired of wasting his considerable talents living a life of penury, Manto feared he might soon kill himself or die a natural death, 'because where flour sells at the price at which it sells here only a shame-faced person can complete his ordained time on earth.' The stark truth was that 'we neither know how to live nor how to die.' What Pakistanis needed most from the US were constitutional experts to help draft a constitution. A nation can do without a national anthem, but 'cannot do without a constitution.' This was why, unlike the United States, interesting things happened in Pakistan. Ministers changed every other day, would-be prophets made outlandish claims, countrywide disturbances brought no change and inquiry commissions worked under the direction of unnamed higher authorities. Manto liked the idea of an American military pact with Pakistan so long as he got a personal atom bomb to lob at *mullahs* whose habits of personal hygiene offended him. He was certain that American military aid was to arm the *mullahs*. Once the 'gang of mullahs is armed' and 'their pajamas stitched by American machines in strict conformity with the Sharia', the Soviets would have to shut down shop in Pakistan.[7]

As Manto anticipated, American influence marginalised the left and weakened an incipient democracy without substantially improving the lot of the toiling masses. Islam was regularly invoked but religion's role in state affairs was kept in check. Retrospectively constructed arguments about Islam being deployed as an instrument of foreign policy by successive governments ever since the emergence of Pakistan are in need of modification.[8] There was a vast difference between utilising religion for the state's internal homogenising logic or upstaging India at international fora and an ideologically driven policy of making Pakistan an ultra conservative Islamic state committed to waging 'jihad' against all and sundry. Campaigns by self-styled religious parties, looking to carve out a political niche in a state whose creation they had opposed, were fiercely contested and the 'tyranny of the *mullah*' resolutely condemned for the sake of more realistic foreign policy goals.[9]

*The Islamic Shift*

For all the lip service paid to Islam, Pakistan remained a relatively liberal and moderate Muslim state until the 1970s. The loss of the eastern wing in 1971 was a watershed with a transformative effect on the Pakistani psyche. Apart from subverting the 'two-nation' theory, a humiliating military defeat by India took a hefty toll on national pride. Unaccustomed to learning from history and more comfortable with myths of an imagined past, Pakistanis were susceptible to the Islamist charge that the ruling elite's lack of religiosity had caused the country's disintegration. Secular in his political convictions, Zulfikar Ali Bhutto instead tried reviving national morale by acquiring nuclear capability and rebuilding a shattered economy. He redoubled efforts to strengthen ties with Muslim oil-producing countries, especially Iran, Libya, and Saudi Arabia. In February 1974 Pakistan hosted the second summit of the Organization of the Islamic Conference in Lahore. The pomp and ceremony of the occasion provided the pretext for Pakistan formally recognising Bangladesh. Lines of credit were sought from friendly Arab states, softening the blows of the global oil shock for cash-starved Pakistan. The global reassertion of Islam on the back of Arab petrodollars won the admiration of Pakistan's rising middle classes, who sought to emulate the Saudi variant of Wahabi Islam.

This was grist to the mill of Islamist parties like Jamaat-e-Islami, who used the Saudi call to excommunicate the heterodox Ahmadi community from the Islamic fold to revive their own long-standing demand. Bhutto's cynical decision in 1974 to concede the exclusionary demand of the religious ideologues to declare Ahmadis a minority undermined the principle of equal citizenship rights in a modern nation-state. While the consequences of the decision have been far-reaching, the critical change in the role of religion in Pakistan came in the wake of the Iranian revolution and the Soviet invasion of Afghanistan. General Zia-ul-Haq (1977–1988) synchronised his so-called Islamisation policies with American-backed support for the Afghan resistance movement in the 1980s. Signalling a departure from earlier regimes that had restricted themselves to periodically appeasing the religious lobby with symbolic displays of Islamic rectitude, Zia upon becoming the Chief of Army Staff changed the Army's motto to 'Faith, Piety and Jihad' in lieu of 'Unity, Faith and Discipline' coined by Jinnah.

Handlers of the 'jihad' in the ISI developed a stake in the enterprise once billions of dollars flowed in from the US and Saudi Arabia to fight the Soviets in Afghanistan. Afghan rebels and local militants fighting the Soviets were regarded as assets that could help the Pakistan Army extend its influence in Afghanistan to achieve strategic depth against India. A sprawling state-sponsored 'jihad' industry was cultivated by funding *madrasahs* in the northwest that shared a common Pakhtun culture with over three million Afghan refugees who had poured into Pakistan. The blending of Saudi Wahabism with the neo-Deobandi ideology propagated by these seminaries made for a witch's brew of religious bigotry and sectarian hatred. State sponsorship of the Deobandis for strategic purposes upset the sectarian balance in predominantly Barelvi Pakistan. Long before the Taliban reared their heads in the tribal northwest of Pakistan, local rivalries dressed up as disagreements over Islam erupted in pitched battles between militant bands of Sunnis and Shi'as as well as Deobandis, Barelvis and the Ahl-i-Hadith.[10]

The surge in sectarian conflict occurred against the backdrop of administrative paralysis, mounting regional grievances and systemic corruption aggravated by a parallel arms and drugs economy. Despite elected PPP governments led by Benazir Bhutto, Zia's devoted legatees in the political fraternity stuck to the task of ideologically remapping Pakistan as the outpost of 'original' Islam in Saudi Arabia. An already compromised educational system with only a perfunctory commitment to research and critical analysis was gradually dismantled. A premium was placed on displays of piety without stemming the growing rot in social morality. The Soviet defeat in Afghanistan followed by the collapse of communism fanned illusions of Islamic grandeur that was harnessed by the ISI to project its preferred view of Pakistan's present and future security concerns. Relations with the US plummeted. In October 1990 Washington suspended military and economic aid to Pakistan for pursuing its nuclear ambitions. This felt like a betrayal after services rendered between 1979 and 1989. Suspicious of India and with Kashmir up in arms after 1989, the Pakistan Army's support of the Taliban in Afghanistan gave a fillip to religious militancy at home. India's nuclear tests in 1998 were duly matched by Pakistan, encouraging the Army's high command to check New Delhi's resolve by occupying the Kargil heights, making the Kashmir dispute more intractable than ever.

*Post-9/11 Challenge*

This is where matters stood when Pakistan was catapulted onto centre stage with the events of September 11 2001. While agreeing to support the US campaign against al Qaeda operatives, General Pervez Musharraf refused to abandon the time-honoured security paradigm of defense against India at all costs. The doctrine of strategic depth was predicated on denying India a foothold in Afghanistan, a prospect whose likelihood increased with the dismantling of the Taliban regime. Like most liberal Pakistanis, Musharraf understood that the world had zero tolerance for a country promoting extremism as an instrument of foreign policy. Yet elements in Pakistan's premier spy agency, the ISI, rejected the need for a paradigm shift in their strategic doctrine. They pointed to India's eager embrace of Hamid Karzai's government, warning that America would quit Afghanistan sooner rather than later. While delivering Arab members of al Qaeda to the Americans, the ISI continued supporting the Afghan Taliban through a clandestine network of retired officers from the Army and the Frontier Constabulary. In addition to helping resettle them in FATA, these 'rogue' ISI operatives built a command and control structure for the Taliban in Balochistan from where they launched attacks on American and NATO forces in southern Afghanistan.[11]

FATA's emergence as terrorism-central injected a new strain into the equation, threatening American and NATO forces in Afghanistan as well as Pakistan. After the crackdown on the Lal Masjid in Islamabad in the summer of 2007, a fulcrum of ISI-supported militants since the 80s, a spate of suicide bombings orchestrated by the Pakistani Tehrik-i-Talban targeted the Army and police personnel as well as politicians. As fighters from Central Asia, Western China, Turkey and various Arab countries combined with radicalised Pakhtun tribesmen to train a new generation of Pakistani and European Muslim militants, al Qaeda resurfaced in the tribal redoubts of northwestern Pakistan with a vengeance. The ongoing military operations in FATA have given cause for cautious optimism, but the Pakistani Army's reluctance to give up on the Afghan Taliban signifies its clash of interest with America in Afghanistan.

## Is a Turnabout Possible?

Pakistan cannot change course without neutralising or satisfying the security concerns of its all-powerful Army. So is there a realistic hope for a turnabout? The international community led by the USA, and including the European Union, NATO and the UN, has to urgently tackle the problems facing Pakistan and Afghanistan in a holistic fashion. This entails assisting Pakistan's civilian government to sort out its political and economic difficulties and weaning the Army away from its deadly gamble with religious extremism.

Peace will remain a forlorn hope so long as Pakistan and India continue to see their interests in Afghanistan as a zero sum game. The two nuclear states have to appreciate the threat a war-torn Afghanistan and unstable north western tribal areas in Pakistan pose to the future of the subcontinent as a whole. Washington too has to realise that the policy of de-hyphenating relations with India and Pakistan has its limitations and what is considered an opportunity in one may be the cause of the problem in the other.

The idea of the two archrivals sharing an interconnected future will raise the hackles of those used to viewing the past and the present through the refracting prism of ideology rather than history. Cooperating not subverting neighbours can be a more effective way for nation-states to re-establish control over rebellious regional *satraps*. An understanding between Rajeev Gandhi and Benazir Bhutto in the late 80s took the sting out of the Sikh uprising in the Indian Punjab that had been aided and abetted by the ISI. In marked contrast is the unresolved issue of Kashmir, which New Delhi imputes to Pakistan's backing for the popular insurgency in the valley and support for 'cross-border terrorism'. In the moral one-upmanship characteristic of their relations, Islamabad regularly accuses India of sponsoring acts of sabotage in Pakistani cities and, more recently, of fomenting dissent in Balochistan. The air of mutual distrust suffocating creative thinking in the Indian and Pakistani capitals has kept Kashmir on the boil. This has been detrimental not only for the Kashmiris but also for Indo–Pakistan trade relations that are widely believed to hold benefits for both countries at a time of crisis in the global economy. The Kashmir conflict has given Pakistan's military establishment an excuse for not abandoning its Afghan policy. Once America attacked Iraq and lowered its threat perception from Afghanistan, Pakistani intelligence hawks convinced Musharraf and his top generals that their self-interest demanded keeping lines open with the Taliban and reviving contacts with some of the ISI's former wards among the Afghan warlords. Accused by Americans of duplicity and not doing enough, the Army leadership has pointed to India's heightened presence in Afghanistan, which rejects the Durand line as its official border with Pakistan and claims the North West Frontier Province and parts of Balochistan.

From a military perspective, letting India use its influence over Kabul to squeeze Pakistan from both the eastern and the western fronts is suicidal and the reason why the Army top brass has resisted US dictation in Afghanistan. The contours of Pakistan's India centred strategic doctrine were etched soon after independence by a civilian leadership, which instead of addressing domestic political problems made the acquisition of Kashmir a national cause célèbre. With the Army's rise to dominance in the state, the legacy of inconclusive Indo-Pakistan wars over Kashmir and the psychologically bruising defeat of 1971, no elected civilian government has been permitted to alter the time-honoured security paradigm. Despite an ostensibly free press, out of the box discussions of strategic security are deemed anti-national. For the few who have questioned Pakistan's defence doctrine, many more take the path of least resistance by accepting the Army's claim that Indians, not the Taliban, are the main enemy.

Benazir Bhutto's assassination on 27 December 2007 removed the one politician publicly committed to fighting militancy as Pakistan's own war. After the 2008 elections, the PPP-led government took political ownership of military operations against insurgent hubs in FATA and settled areas in the northwest. Jamaat-e-Islami and other opposition parties accuse the government of waging war on its own people to satisfy its American paymasters. Mounting civilian casualties and the displacement of several hundreds of thousands of people has stirred popular anger, especially as the war is showing no signs of coming to an end anytime soon. The growing American presence in Afghanistan is a matter of great concern, as it is generally believed to be a prelude to a thrust into Pakistan and depriving it of its nuclear arsenal. The irony of needing to safeguard nuclear weapons instead of being protected by them is lost on Pakistanis. Pious hymns about national sovereignty run counter to the political and military leadership's eagerness for American financial and military assistance. In the absence of a well-developed critical tradition and an atmosphere for open dialogue and discourse, a testament to years of military dictatorship and the staggering infirmities of the educational system, the reality deficit in Pakistan is unlikely to take a self-corrective course in the foreseeable future.

The situation in FATA is grave enough to cause concern in all the neighbouring countries. India in particular needs to calculate the risks of Pakistan being overrun by unruly tribesmen or collapsing under the increasing weight of its own internal contradictions. In wanting to extract maximum advantages from their new partnership with India, the Americans too need to calibrate the dangers of treating Pakistan's strategic concerns with nonchalance and pretending they can win the Afghanistan War on their own terms. Ultimately Pakistanis have to take control of their own destiny by revising the premises of a national security paradigm that has eroded the basis of their state and derailed attempts at establishing a viable democratic system. Of the manifold challenges facing Pakistan, by far the most formidable is the need to educate the citizenry so that it can engage in an informed debate on how the country's foreign and defence policies can be squared with the requirements of internal political stability. Far from providing the proverbial glue, instrumentalist uses of Islam have created extreme divisiveness and widespread social corrosion. If the Tehrik-i-Taliban Pakistan is targeting Islamabad, radicalised elements in non-Punjabi provinces are talking secession or invoking the Muslim League's 1940 resolution with its confederal overtones to demand sovereignty.

## Conclusion

Insofar as nations are imagined communities that are limited and sovereign, the constructed myths of the Pakistani past cannot wish away the embedded divisions and tensions of the present. Instead of chasing mirages on a murky and receding horizon, Pakistanis will be better served if they are taught how to delve into the depths of their own history with the kind of open mindedness and spirit of freethinking enquiry that is the basis of mature understanding. It is only then that this troubled and troubling country of more than 170 million can begin shedding its curious penchant for myths, delusions and conspiracies, day in and day out of season. Critical awareness of Pakistan's present problems in the light of history can overcome the reality deficit and help create the political will that can allow Pakistan to navigate its way out of a daunting present and chart a future consistent with the aspirations of its rudderless and long-suffering people.

## 2

# WHY JINNAH MATTERS

## Dr Akbar Ahmed

The debate about the nature and character of the Pakistani state has never been more intense than it is today. Some still voice the demand for a theocratic state. The Pakistani Taliban is the most extreme expression of this, but a variety of more mainstream religious groups also call for the rule of the *Shari'a*. Others argue that Islam has little to do with the state. Most Pakistanis would perhaps reflect a balance between these two positions. In this debate, there is no voice more important than Mohammad Ali Jinnah's, the founder of Pakistan. Because of his seminal role in the country's creation and the high symbolism of his name, it is crucial for Pakistanis to know about his ideas on the role of religion in Pakistan.

### Pakistan, a Modern Muslim Nation

'There is no solution in sight; once there was mirth in the heart, now nothing makes me smile.' Ghalib's despondent verses, written in the mid-nineteenth century, reflected the nadir of Muslim politics; the depths of the collapse. Within a century of those lines being written, Jinnah had achieved the impossible: he had created an independent Muslim state. He had restored Muslim pride, given them a sense of destiny and secured them territory. It is no wonder they idolised him and called him the Quaid-i-Azam, the 'Great Leader'.

Jinnah's Muslim nation was not fully what he had wanted: it was 'truncated' and 'moth-eaten'. It appears Jinnah's willpower kept him going but in the last year of his life, after Pakistan had been created, he was seriously ill. He therefore focused his energies on the survival of the state, exhausting himself in the effort to keep Pakistan alive. The unending problems were of such magnitude that they demanded his immediate attention (which gave his critics the opportunity to accuse him of becoming autocratic): the influx of millions of refugees from India; the horror of the communal violence in which about two million people—Hindus, Muslims and Sikhs—died; a state of undeclared war in Kashmir; a tattered defence and administrative structure, torn in two, needing to be rebuilt; the near bankruptcy of the state; and the refusal of an increasingly hostile India to send Pakistan the agreed division of assets.

The awful reality of millions of Muslims stranded in India as 'hostages', not easily able to enter his Pakistan—a nightmare Jinnah tried so hard to avoid—soon dawned on him. The scale of the savage killing of refugees on both sides shook him to the core, hastening his end (this is precisely how Dina Wadia, Jinnah's daughter, saw her father's death; she believed that he had literally sacrificed himself for his nation).

Increasingly, Jinnah was opening his heart in an unprecedented manner to his people in official broadcasts, abandoning the formal posture of the skilful but aloof lawyer. Now he shared their hopes, their sorrow, their sense of personal tragedy and their feeling of frustration at the injustices of the world. One senses his anger and outrage, as he witnessed not only the machinations that would lose Pakistan the state of Kashmir but also the attempts to kill Pakistan at its birth.

In the first winter of Pakistan's existence, a group of officers, in welcoming him, assured him that they were prepared to follow him 'through sunshine and fire'. Jinnah replied, 'Are you prepared to undergo the fire? We are going through fire, the sunshine has yet to come.' He was aware of the dangers. The whole structure could rapidly unravel in spite of all the faith and commitment of the supporters of Pakistan. His question of whether Pakistanis were prepared to undergo the fire is as relevant today as when Jinnah raised it. Pakistanis are still going through fire. That is why they need to understand the vision of their founding father.

*Jinnah's Gettysburg Address*

What was Jinnah's vision of Pakistan? Would Pakistan be a modern democracy or a closed theocracy? Would non-Muslims be safe in it?

Since Jinnah did not write a book or monograph, the main clues to his thinking are to be found in his speeches. If we put together two of Jinnah's speeches in the crucial month of August 1947 when he had attained his Pakistan—indeed the first two speeches that he made to the new Constituent Assembly—we can glimpse his vision for the state he had created. The first was delivered on 11 August, when the Constituent Assembly of Pakistan elected him as their first President, and the second on 14 August, which is now celebrated as Independence Day. Together they comprise Jinnah's 'Gettysburg address' and would form the base for his subsequent speeches in the final year of his life.

Perhaps his most significant and most moving speech was the one given on 11 August. It was an outpouring of ideas on the state and the nature of society, almost a stream of consciousness and it was delivered without notes:

Now, if we want to make this great State of Pakistan happy and prosperous we should wholly and solely concentrate on the well-being of the people, and especially of the masses and the poor. If you will work in co-operation, forgetting the past, burying the hatchet, you are bound to succeed. If you change your past and work together in a spirit that every one of you, no matter to what community he belongs, no matter what relations he had with you in the past, no matter what is his colour, caste or creed, is first, second and last a citizen of this State with equal rights, privileges and obligations, there will be no end to the progress you will make.

I cannot emphasise it too much. We should begin to work in that spirit and in course of time all these angularities of the majority and minority communities, the Hindu community and the Muslim community—because even as regards Muslims you have Pathans, Punjabis, Shias, Sunnis and so on and among Hindus you have Brahmins, Vashnavas, Khatris, also Bengalees, Madrasis and so on—will vanish. Indeed if you ask me this has been the biggest hindrance in the way of India to attain the freedom and independence and but for this we would have been free peoples long long ago.[1]

From this powerful passage comes a vision of a brave new world, consciously an improvement in its spirit of tolerance to the old world he had just rejected:

You are free; you are free to go to your temples, you are free to go to your mosques or to any other place of worship in this State of Pakistan ... You may

23

belong to any religion or caste or creed—that has nothing to do with the business of the State ... We are starting in the days when there is no discrimination, no distinction between one community and another, no discrimination between one caste or creed and another. We are starting with this fundamental principle that we are all citizens and equal citizens of one State.[2]

If Pakistanis could follow these ideals, Jinnah would be confident of the future. Jinnah made a pledge: 'My guiding principle will be justice and complete impartiality, and I am sure that with your support and co-operation, I can look forward to Pakistan becoming one of the greatest nations of the world.'[3]

Two days later the Mountbattens flew to Karachi to help celebrate the formal transfer of power. In his formal speech to the Constituent Assembly on 14 August, Lord Mountbatten offered the example of Akbar the Great Mughal as the model of a tolerant Muslim ruler to Pakistan.

*Akbar the Great as a Model Muslim Ruler...*

Mountbatten had suggested Akbar advisedly. Akbar has always been a favourite of those who believe in cultural synthesis or what in our time passes for secular leadership. To most non-Muslims in South Asia, Akbar symbolised a tolerant, humane Muslim, one they could do business with. He avoided eating beef because the cow was sacred to the Hindus. The Rajputs provided Akbar's armies with soldiers and generals and gave his court influential wives.

But for many Muslims Akbar posed certain problems. Although he was a great king by many standards, he was a far from ideal Muslim ruler: there was too much of the willful Oriental despot in his behaviour. His harem was said to number a thousand wives. His drinking, his drugs and his blood lust were excessive even by Mughal standards.

Akbar also introduced a new religious philosophy, *din-e-ilahi*, an amalgamation of some of the established religions, with Akbar himself as a focal religious point. This was imperial capriciousness, little else; and it made the *ulema* unhappy.

Mountbatten would have been aware that six Mughal Emperors, beginning with Babar in 1526 and ending with Aurangzeb's death in 1707, had ruled India, giving it one of the most glorious periods of its history. The Mughal Empire did not end until the British finally killed it off in 1857, but its last great emperor was Aurangzeb.

These were six remarkable men, each one different and easily lending themselves to popular stereotypes. There was Babar the Warrior King, the founder; Humayun, good-natured but unlucky, who almost lost his father's kingdom; Akbar the Great, the man who joined together the various cultural and religious strands of India during his reign, thereby laying the foundations for a mighty state; Jahangir, artistic, drunken, troubled, who ruled mainly through his talented wife, the Empress Nur Jahan; Shah Jahan, who brought the empire to a pinnacle of artistic and architectural glory, the creator of the Taj Mahal; and finally Aurangzeb, whose long reign is seen as the watershed for Muslim rule in India and who himself evokes divided loyalties: orthodox Muslims regard him as an ideal ruler, while critics call him a fanatic and point out his harsh treatment of his father and brothers.

So Mountbatten's choice was neither random nor illogical. Yet he could also have selected Babar, who after all opened a new chapter of history in India, not unlike Jinnah.

The story of Babar—poet, autobiographer, loyal friend and devoted father—was perhaps too triumphalist for Mountbatten. But had Mountbatten and his staff done their homework they would have realised their blunder. In suggesting Akbar, Mountbatten was clearly unaware of the impression he was conveying. While his choice may have impressed some modernised Muslims, the majority would have thought it odd. Of the six great Mughal Emperors from Babar to Aurangzeb, Akbar is perhaps the one most self-avowedly neutral to Islam. To propose Akbar as an ideal ruler to a newly formed and self-consciously post-colonial Muslim nation was rather like suggesting to a convention of Muslim writers meeting in Iran or Pakistan in the 1990s that their literary model should be Salman Rushdie.

Akbar was the litmus test for Jinnah; perhaps a decade before he would have accepted Akbar as a model, but now he rejected the suggestion. In a rebuttal, which amounted to a public snub—Mountbatten was after all still the Viceroy of India—Jinnah presented an alternative model.

### …Or the Prophet of Islam

Jinnah in his reply pointed out that Muslims had a more permanent and more inspiring model to follow than that of Akbar—the holy Prophet of Islam:

The tolerance and goodwill that great Emperor Akbar showed to all the non-Muslims is not of recent origin. It dates back thirteen centuries ago when our Prophet not only by words but by deeds treated the Jews and Christians, after he had conquered them, with the utmost tolerance and regard and respect for their faith and beliefs. The whole history of Muslims, wherever they ruled, is replete with those humane and great principles which should be followed and practised.[4]

Jinnah reverted to the themes he had raised only three days earlier. The holy Prophet had not only created a new state but had also laid down the principles on which it could be organised and conducted. These principles were rooted in a compassionate understanding of society and the notions of justice and tolerance. Jinnah emphasised the special treatment the Prophet accorded to the minorities. Morality, piety, human tolerance—a society where colour and race did not matter: the Prophet had laid down a charter for social behaviour thirteen centuries before the United Nations.

It is interesting how even distinguished scholars have misread these speeches of Jinnah. Stanley Wolpert, an admirer of Jinnah, who analysed the first speech over several pages, concluded that what he termed the 'disjointed ramblings' suggested that Jinnah had lost his mind that he was wandering.[5] Was Jinnah aware, asked Wolpert, that he was abandoning his two-nation theory by talking of tolerance and so on?

In fact Jinnah's remarks must be seen in the context of Islamic culture and history. Jinnah, conscious that this was one of the last times he would be addressing his people because he was seriously ill, would find himself echoing the holy Prophet's own last message on Mount Arafat. For him too this was the summing up of his life and his achievement. Wolpert's dismissal of the speech is interesting; he was aware of the comparison with the Arafat address but he did not follow it through.

## The Last Testament

Jinnah often ended his speeches with a flourish. He reminded his audience that Pakistan was the largest Muslim nation in the world and the fifth largest in terms of population, that it had a special destiny and could become one of the most important states in the world. Jinnah did not want to create just another state; after all, even in his day there were many Muslim states. His dream was a grand one: what he wanted was nothing less than one of the greatest nations in the world, not just in the Muslim world. Even today the idea of Pakistan is greater than the reality of the country.

When he made these speeches he was an old man, and he knew he was dying; they were his last words. What makes a last testament valid is the fact that the speaker is about to die, about to meet his maker. A person's last words are therefore considered authentic; even the law accepts them as evidence. We can thus believe in the sincerity of Jinnah's speeches in the last months of his life, which establish that he was moving irrevocably towards his Muslim culture and religion.

Those who argue that Jinnah was cynical and exploited religion and custom need to understand the one-year he had in Pakistan before he died. Consider his position after the creation of Pakistan. He was by far the most popular and most powerful man in the country, the revered Quaid-i-Azam of Pakistan, respected by millions of people. If he had decided to defy tradition and custom, he would have gotten away with it. He could have dressed, spoken or eaten in any way he wanted and still been venerated. There was too much affection for him to be shaken by anything. The example of Kemal Atatürk who rejected Muslim culture and tradition in Turkey—another father of the nation—comes to mind. But Jinnah took the opposite route. He may have started life at one end of the spectrum in terms of culture and tradition, but by the finish he was at the other end of it.

A comparison of the two newly independent countries, India and Pakistan, reveals that by the time Mountbatten arrived in India Congress would be forming the government of an independent India, having worked towards this objective for almost half a century. Congress already had its leaders, a committed cadre, an all-India structure and networks that reached down to the village. It had struggled and sacrificed. Most important, it had a philosophy of how to run an independent India. The Pakistan movement, just a few years old in the 1940s, suffered in comparison.

Jinnah's ideas about Pakistan remained vague. Vagueness was both the strength and weakness of the Pakistan movement. It became all things to all men, drawing in a variety of people for different reasons; but it also meant that once Pakistan was achieved there would be no clear defining parameters. During the last year or two of his life, Jinnah had begun to sharpen his concept of Pakistan. He travelled extensively and spoke tirelessly on radio and in public.

*Vision of an Islamic Society*

These speeches, together with what I have called his Gettysburg address, reveal that several themes are repeated. The first is the unequivocal Islamic nature of Pakistan, drawing its inspiration from the Qur'an and the holy Prophet. This is the vision of an Islamic society which would be equitable, compassionate and tolerant, and from which the 'poison' of corruption, nepotism, mismanagement and inefficiency would be eradicated. Pakistan itself would be based on the high principles laid down by the Prophet in Arabia in the seventh century. Although Jinnah had pointed out the flaws in Western-style democracy, it was still the best system of government available to Muslims.

Jinnah specifically did not want a theocratic state run by *mullahs*. In a broadcast to the people of the United States of America recorded in February 1948, Jinnah made his position clear:

In any case, Pakistan is not going to be a theocratic State to be ruled by priests with a divine mission. We have many non-Muslims—Hindus, Christians and Parsees—but they are all Pakistanis. They will enjoy the same rights and privileges as any other citizens and will play their rightful part in the affairs of Pakistan.[6]

When his enthusiastic admirers addressed him as '*Maulana* Jinnah' (Our Master Jinnah) he put them down, saying: 'I am not a *maulana*, just plain Mr Jinnah.'

*Protection of Non-Muslims*

Acceptance of minorities is another theme in his speeches. Jinnah had regularly reminded his Muslim audience of what Islam maintains: 'our own history and our Prophet have given the clearest proof that non-Muslims have been treated not only justly and fairly but generously'.[7]

Jinnah's statements about minorities (whether Muslims in India or Hindus in Pakistan) are significant: 'I am going to constitute myself the Protector-General of the Hindu minority in Pakistan.'[8] He spent his first and only Christmas in December 1947 as a guest of the Christian community, joining in their celebrations. In that one act he incorporated the rituals of the minority community into Pakistani consciousness (a far cry from the somewhat pointed distancing of Pakistani leaders from the rituals and customs of the minorities in contemporary Pakistan.) Although pressed for time, in Dhaka he met a Hindu delegation and in Karachi and Quetta a Parsee one, assuring them of his intention to safeguard their interests.

Even after the creation of Pakistan he not only continued to have British personnel on his staff but also actively encouraged them to participate in the life of the new nation. Sir George Cunningham, to whom Jinnah sent a telegram in Scotland inviting him to return to his post as the Governor of the North West Frontier Province immediately after independence, is an example.

## Opposition to Provincialism

The other theme was the need to check provincialism, which was already rearing its head. In his speeches, for example in Peshawar and Dhaka, Jinnah stressed the evils of provincialism, which he warned would weaken the foundations of the state.[9]

In Pakistan people assume that the movement for ethnic assertion is recent, a product of Pakistan. On the contrary, such movements existed before the creation of Pakistan, as is clear in a letter to Jinnah of 14 May 1947, from G. H. Hidayatullah, a Sindhi leader based in Karachi:

Some enemies of my wife and myself have been making statements in the press that we two are advocating the principle that Sind is for the Sindhis only. This is entirely false and baseless. Both of us are ardent supporters of Pakistan, and we have given public expression to this. Islam teaches universal brotherhood, and we entirely subscribe to this... All this is nothing but false propaganda on the part of the enemies of the League.[10]

A week later Abdus-Sattar Pirzada issued a statement making clear that Pakistan would be the home for all Muslim immigrants from India: 'Sind has been the gateway of Islam in India and it shall be the gateway of Pakistan too.'[11]

Yet Jinnah sailed into an ethnic storm after the creation of Pakistan. In a momentous encounter in Dhaka, the capital of the province of East Pakistan (the future Bangladesh), he insisted that Urdu and Urdu alone would be the national language, although he conceded the use of the provincial language. Bengali students murmured in protest. The language movement would grow and in 1952 the first martyrs, protesting students, would be killed. In time a far wider expression of ethnic discontent would develop at the imagined and real humiliation coming from West Pakistan and in particular the Punjab. But that was in the future. Jinnah had for the time being clung to his idea of a united Pakistan; united in a political but also cultural sense.

*Diaspora: The Plight of the Refugees*

The plight of the refugees, their lives forever altered, moved Jinnah as nothing else in his life. Their killing, he repeated, was 'pre-planned genocide'.[12] He constantly referred to them:

A few days ago, I received harrowing accounts of the terrible happenings in the Punjab and the situation, from all accounts, appeared to be so grave that I decided to come to Lahore. On my arrival here, I immediately got in touch with various sources that were available to me and I was deeply grieved to realize that unfortunately there was a great deal of truth in what had been told to me. I am speaking to you under deep distress and with a heavy heart.[13]

Even the joyous occasion of Eid became a moment of reflection:

For us the last Eid-ul-Fitr which followed soon after the birth of Pakistan was marred by the tragic happenings in East Punjab. The bloodbath of last year and its aftermath—the mass migration of millions—presented a problem of unprecedented magnitude. To provide new moorings for this mass of drifting humanity strained our energies and resources to breaking point.[14]

Jinnah mobilised everything at hand for the poor, especially among the refugees:

Let every man and woman resolve from this day to live henceforth strictly on an austerity basis in respect of food, clothing and other amenities of life and let the money, foodstuffs and clothing thus saved be brought to this common pool for the relief of the stricken. The winter is approaching and in the Punjab and Delhi particularly, it is very severe and we must provide refugees protection against it.[15]

Jinnah acknowledges the generous response of the local, indigenous Pakistanis to the refugees:

But for the spirit of brotherhood shown by the people of Pakistan and the courage with which the people as well as the Government faced the almost overwhelming difficulties created by a catastrophe, unparalleled in the history of the world, the entire structure of the State might well have crumbled down.[16]

The support for the refugees was inspiring. Nadir Rahim, whose father was Commissioner of Lahore, told this author that locals and non-locals joined in, helping one another; the former became *ansaris*, helpers, the latter *muhajirs*, refugees. These were names revived from Islamic history when those who received the holy Prophet and his companions in Madinah came to be called *ansaris* and those who had fled Makkah *muhajirs*.

30

My own experiences in the early years of Pakistan confirm this. My father was a senior official in the new country, the first divisional Superintendent of the Pakistan Railways in Karachi, its capital. The movement of refugees, troops and goods all depended on the railways. He had a large official house where dozens of refugees were camped for months and where families lived with us for years.

People seemed to appear from nowhere in our house and then disappear for ever. They looked dazed, uncertain and withdrawn. I remember in particular two men: one old, respectable and orthodox, the other young, barely in his teens. The first seemed to have found strength in Islam and his punctilious observation of ritual. The young man was asleep most of the time wrapped in a white sheet as if he were a corpse. When he woke he had little to say. An expression of permanent sorrow was etched on his face. He wished to shut out the past. I do not know where he came from and what happened to him.

## Jinnah, Pakistan and India

To understand Jinnah's Pakistan, we need also to examine Jinnah's attitude towards Pakistan's relations with India, a crucial area that would determine the internal politics and foreign policy of the country. Jinnah wished for cordial relations with the state of India. He never changed his will, which left part of his estate to educational institutions in Aligarh, Bombay and Delhi. Hoping to visit his beloved Bombay, Jinnah also kept his property in India.

Jinnah's view of friendly relations between India and Pakistan after partition was recorded in an interview with General Ismay, Chief of Staff to the Viceroy:

Mr. Jinnah said with the greatest earnestness that once partition had been decided upon, everyone would know exactly where they were, all troubles would cease, and they would live happily ever after. He quoted me the case of two brothers who hated each other like poison as a result of the portions allotted to them under their father's will. Finally they could bear it no longer and took the case to court. Mr. Jinnah defended one of them and the case was fought with the utmost venom. Two years later Mr. Jinnah met his client and asked how he was getting on and how was his brother, and he said: 'oh, once the case was decided, we became the greatest friends'.[17]

Jinnah wished for a civilized discourse, maintaining standards of neighbourly courtesy, in his dealings with India. On his final flight from Delhi he conveyed this message to the new Indian government:

I bid farewell to the citizens of Delhi, amongst whom I have many friends of all communities and I earnestly appeal to everyone to live in this great and historic city with peace. The past must be buried and let us start afresh as two independent sovereign States of Hindustan [India] and Pakistan. I wish Hindustan prosperity and peace.[18]

Seervai, the Indian writer, comments on the Indian response to Jinnah's message:

Jinnah left India for Pakistan on 7 August 1947, with an appeal to both Hindus and Muslims to 'bury the past' and wished India success and prosperity. The next day, Vallabhbhai Patel said in Delhi, 'The poison had been removed from the body of India.'[19]

Patel went on:

As for the Muslims they have their roots, their sacred places and their centres here. I do not know what they can possibly do in Pakistan. It will not be long before they return to us.[20]

'Hardly the words,' concludes Seervai, 'to promote goodwill and neighbourliness either then or in the days to come.'

As for the Hindu citizens of Pakistan, there was never any doubt in Jinnah's mind that they would be protected as citizens and given full rights. Speech after speech confirmed this. When Pakistan was created, Jinnah had seven ministers in the Cabinet, one a Hindu.

In one of his first radio broadcasts as head of state Jinnah abandoned his normal reserve and opened his heart to the nation:

I am speaking to you under deep distress and with a heavy heart. We have undoubtedly achieved Pakistan and that too without bloody war and practically, peacefully, by moral and intellectual force and with the power of pen which is no less mighty than the sword and so our righteous cause has triumphed. Are we now going to besmear and tarnish this greatest achievement for which there is no parallel in the whole history of the world by resorting to frenzy, savagery and butchery?[21]

In early October 1947 Muslims in West Punjab began to react to the horror stories coming from India. Jinnah reminded the authorities in both countries:

The division of India was agreed upon with a solemn and sacred undertaking that minorities would be protected by the two Dominion Governments and that the minorities had nothing to fear so long as they remained loyal to the State.[22]

He urged the government of India to 'put a stop to the process of victimization of Muslims.'[23] To calm the situation Jinnah flew to

Lahore, which had borne the full brunt of the refugees arriving from India with their heart-rending tales, and in a public meeting urged restraint:

Despite the treatment which is being meted out to the Muslim minorities in India, we must make it a matter of our prestige and honour to safeguard the lives of the minority communities and to create a sense of security among them.[24]

On the death of Gandhi on 30 January 1948, Jinnah issued a statement that angered and disappointed many Indians because it spoke of Gandhi only as a great Hindu leader. This was unfair to Jinnah, who used the word 'great' three times in his brief message. Once again, we need to read Jinnah's full statement, especially in conjunction with the one made later in which he states that the Muslims of India had lost their main support. The official version is as follows:

I am shocked to learn of the most dastardly attack on the life of Mr. Gandhi, resulting in his death. There can be no controversy in the face of death. Whatever our political differences, he was one of the greatest men produced by the Hindu community, and a leader who commanded their universal confidence and respect. I wish to express my deep sorrow, and sincerely sympathize with the great Hindu community and his family in their bereavement at this momentous, historical and critical juncture so soon after the birth of freedom and freedom for Hindustan and Pakistan. The loss to the Dominion of India is irreparable, and it will be very difficult to fill the vacuum created by the passing away of such a great man at this moment.[25]

Just before his own death, Jinnah proposed a joint defence pact with India as the Cold War started to shape the world and the two power blocs began to form. Jinnah was still thinking as a South Asian nationalist. Since he had won the rights and security of his community through the creation of Pakistan, he thought the problem of national defence was over. Alas, it was not to be.

With relations souring so quickly at the creation of Pakistan, the relationship between the two countries—and therefore the two communities in the subcontinent as a whole—was set on a collision course and has unfortunately remained so ever since. As this conflict is rooted in history political parties who see an easy gain to be made readily exploit it.

Had Jinnah's vision prevailed—and found an echo in India—we would have seen a very different South Asia. There would have been two stable nations—India and Pakistan, both supplementing and supporting each other. Indeed Jinnah's idea of a joint defence system against the outside world would have ensured that there would have been no crippling defence expenditures. There would have been no reason to join one or other camp of the Cold War. There would have been open borders, free trade and regular visiting between the two countries.

The lack of tension would have ensured that the minorities were not under pressure and, as both Jinnah and Congress leaders like Gandhi and Nehru wanted, lived as secure and integrated citizens. The fabric of society would have been different, and a more humane subcontinent might have emerged: a land truer to the vision of its leaders and spirit of its ages.

In 1971, when Pakistan was broken in two, its critics jubilantly cried, 'Jinnah's Pakistan is dead.' They were wrong. Jinnah's Pakistan will be alive as long as there are Muslims who feel for the dignity, the identity and the destiny of other Muslims, and who care for the oppressed and the minorities in their midst. In that sense Jinnah's Pakistan will remain alive forever. Muslims must learn to say with pride: 'I am Muslim.' They must live up to the nobility and compassion of Islamic ideals; they must carry themselves with dignity in their identity as Muslims. Most important, they must stand up for their rights; this is their destiny and they cannot ignore it. This is the lesson that Jinnah taught them; that is why Jinnah remains relevant today.

3

# WHY PAKISTAN WILL SURVIVE

*Mohsin Hamid*

Ever since returning to live in Pakistan several months ago, I've been struck by the pervasive negativity of views here about our country. Whether in conversation, on television, or in the newspaper, what I hear and read often tends to boil down to the same message: our country is going down the drain.

But I'm not convinced that it is.

I don't dispute for a second that these are hard times. Thousands of us died last year in terrorist attacks. Hundreds of thousands were displaced by military operations. Most of us don't have access to decent schools. Inflation is squeezing our poor and middle class. Millions are, if not starving, hungry. Even those who can afford electricity don't have it half the day. Yet, despite this desperate suffering, Pakistan is also something of a miracle. It's worth pointing this out, because incessant pessimism robs us of an important resource: hope.

First, we are a vast nation. We are the sixth most populous country in the world. One in every forty human beings is Pakistani. There are more people aged fourteen and younger in Pakistan than there are in America. A nation is its people, and in our people we have a huge, and significantly untapped, sea of potential.

Second, we are spectacularly diverse. I have travelled to all six of the world's inhabited continents, and I have seen few countries whose diversity comes close to matching ours. Linguistically, we are home to many major languages. Punjabi is spoken in Pakistan by more people than the entire population of France; Pushto by more than the population of Saudi Arabia; Sindhi by more than Australia; Seraiki by more than the Netherlands; Urdu by more than Cuba, and Balochi by more than Singapore.

Pakistani diversity is not limited to language. Religiously we are overwhelmingly Muslim, but still we have more non-Muslims than there are people in either Toronto or Miami. We have more Shi'as than any country besides Iran. Even our majority Sunnis include followers of the Barelvi, Deobandi and numerous other schools, as well as, in all likelihood, many millions who have no idea what school they belong to and don't really care.

Culturally, too, we are incredibly diverse. We have transvestite talk-show hosts, advocates for 'eunuch rights', burqa-wearers, turbaned men with beards, outstanding fast bowlers, mediocre opening batsmen, tribal chieftains, bhang-drinking farmers, semi-nomadic shepherds, and at least one champion female sprinter. We have the Communist Mazdoor Kissan Party and we have Porsche dealerships. We are nobody's stereotype.

Diversity is an enormous advantage. Not only is there brilliance and potential in our differences, a wealth of experience and ideas, but also our lack of sameness forces us to accommodate each other, to find ways to coexist. This brings me to our third great asset. 'Tolerance' seems a strange word to apply to a country where women are still buried alive and teenagers have started detonating themselves in busy shopping districts. Yet these acts shock us because they are aberrations, not the norm. Pakistan is characterised not by the outliers among its citizens who are willing to kill those unlike themselves, but by the millions of us who reject every opportunity to do so. Our different linguistic, religious and cultural groups mostly live side by side in relative peace. It usually takes state intervention (whether by our own state, our allies or our enemies) to get us to kill one another, and even then, those who do so are a tiny minority.

The ability to hold our noses and put up with fellow citizens we don't much like is surely a modern Pakistani characteristic. It could be the result of geography and history, of millennia of invading, being invaded, and dealing with the aftermath. Europe learned the value of peace from World Wars One and Two. Maybe we learned our lesson from the violence of partition or 1971. Call it pragmatism or cosmopolitanism or whatever you want, but I think most Pakistanis have it. I will call it coexistence-ism, and it is a blessing.

Over the past sixty or so years, with many disastrous missteps along the way, our vastness, diversity and coexistence-ism have forced us to develop (or to begin to develop, for it is a work in progress) our fourth great asset: the many related components of our democracy. Between India and Europe, there is no country with a combination of diversity and democracy that comes close to ours. Other than Turkey, the rest are dictatorships, monarchies, apartheid states or under foreign occupation.

We, on the other hand, are evolving a system that allows our population to decide how they will be ruled. Many of our politicians may be corrupt and venal, but they are part of a lively and contested multiparty democracy. Many in our media may be immature or serving vested interests, but collectively they engage in a no-holds-barred debate that exposes, criticises, entertains and informs—and through television they have given our country, for the first time in its history, a genuine public space. Our judges may have a rather unusual understanding of the correct relationship between legislature and judiciary, but they are undoubtedly expanding the rule of law—and hence the power of the average citizen—in a land where it has been almost absent.

As I see it, the Pakistan project is a messy search for ways to improve the lives of 170 million very different citizens. False nationalism will not work: we are too diverse to believe it. That is why our dictatorships inevitably end. Theocracy will not work: we are too diverse to agree on the interpretation of religious laws. That is why the Taliban will not win.

Can democracy deliver? In some ways it already is. The NFC (National Finance Commission) award and, hopefully, the Eighteenth Amendment, are powerful moves towards devolution of power to the provinces. Too much centralisation has been stifling in a country as diverse as Pakistan. That is about to change. The pressure of democracy seems likely to go further, moving power below the provinces to regions and districts. Cities like Karachi and Lahore have shown that good local governance is possible in Pakistan. That lesson can now start to spread.

Similarly, democracy is pushing us to raise revenue. Our taxes amount to a mere 10 per cent of GDP. After spending on defence and interest on our debt, we are left with precious little for schools, hospitals, roads, electricity, water and social support. We, and especially our rich, must pay more. American economic aid amounts to less than $9 per Pakistani per year. That isn't much, and the secret is: we shouldn't need it; new taxes, whether as VAT or in some other form, could give us far more.

Our free assemblies, powerful media and independent judiciary collectively contain within them both pressures to raise taxes and mechanisms to see that taxes actually get paid. This is new for Pakistan. Our number one war shouldn't be a War on Terrorists or a cold war with India or a war against fishing for the ball outside off-stump (although all of those matter): it should be a war on free riders, on people taking advantage of what Pakistan offers without paying their fair share in taxes to our society. Luckily this war looks like it is ready to escalate, and not a moment too soon.

I have no idea if things will work out for the best. The pessimists may be right. But it seems mistaken to write Pakistan off. We have reasons for optimism too.

### Questions of Identity

Recently, I've heard it said that the insurmountable problem with Pakistan is that we don't have a national identity. America has a national identity. Even India has a national identity. So why don't we? My own view is that national identity is overrated.

I say this not just as a man who chose to move back to Pakistan after many years abroad, who wore a green wig to last year's T20 World Cup final at Lords, and who experienced undeniable pleasure at the fact that his first child was born on 14 August. I am a Pakistani, no doubt about it.

At least, I am a Pakistani to me. But if the test of being a Pakistani is that I am by definition anti-Indian, then I fail. I don't like Pakistan losing to the Indian team in cricket. I dislike the Indian government's position on Kashmir. And I deeply dislike Indian leaders' talk about launching air strikes against Pakistan. Am I fundamentally anti-Indian, though? No. If it were up to me, I would have both countries compromise on our disputes, end our dangerous military standoff, and institute visa-free travel.

Similarly, if the test of being a Pakistani is that I would like our country to look more like what Zia-ul-Haq had in mind—in other words, a country where you could happily live your life according to any interpretation of Islam so long as it was his interpretation of Islam—then I fail again. I don't want my government imposing its view of religion on me. There is a reason why differences between Sunnis and Shi'as exist, and why differences between Barelvis and Deobandis exist. The reason these differences exist is that Muslims disagree. So I support the idea that Pakistan should be a place where Muslims are free to practise their religion according to their own conscience, and where religious minorities are free to do the same.

But let's say I was different. Let's say I hated India to the core. In Canada there are aging Sikh supporters of Khalistan who probably hate India to the core. Does hating India make me somehow Canadian? Or let's say that I liked Zia's particular vision of Islam. Maybe there are people in Saudi Arabia who like it too. So am I really a Saudi? My point is that neither being virulently anti-Indian nor having a rigid, government-sponsored interpretation of religion necessarily makes someone Pakistani.

What does make someone Pakistani then? In its simplest terms: being from here. If you're from Pakistan, then you're a Pakistani. I recognise that this definition of national identity, which takes as its starting point people and geography rather than abstract ideology, may seem pretty useless. But I don't think it is useless at all, for three reasons.

First, being able to define Pakistanis simply as people from Pakistan should come as a relief. Before 1947, there was no Pakistan. For some decades after, it looked like we might be overrun by a hostile India. Yet we're still here. We're sixty-three years old. We've just about lived a human lifetime. We don't need to conjure ourselves into existence through struggle and bloodshed and political will because we already exist. We are not a dream, we are reality. We are not some weird idea for a country, we are a country. We're normal. At last. And part of being normal is we don't have to justify to anyone else why there should be a Pakistan. There is a Pakistan. Let's move on.

Second, if we think about our national identity in this way we can stop clinging to oppressive ideologies to hold our ethnically diverse country together. We really should not be at much risk of splitting apart. Take each of our provinces in turn. The Hazara minority issue aside, the Pathans of Khyber Pakhtunkhwa are unlikely to want to join up with their brethren in Afghanistan for the simple reason that life in Afghanistan is much worse than it is in Pakistan. Sindh and Balochistan, their names notwithstanding, are multi-ethnic provinces that would themselves face ethnic divisions should they attempt to build independent states on the basis of ethnicity. The same is true of Punjab, which is landlocked besides. Of course, oppressing ethnic groups could drive them out of our federation, but provided we treat each other fairly, our reasons to remain together are more powerful.

Third, if we can accept that we're real people in a real place (instead of an idea of an imagined utopia), and that we are one country because we actually choose to be (instead of a sand castle in desperate need of wave-resistant ideology), then we can focus on what really matters: understanding who our country is for. In a democracy, the answer is clear: our country is for us. It exists to allow as many of us as possible to live better lives. At the moment, a few of us are living like kings. But most of us are living on weekly wages worth not much more than a kilo of pine nuts. When you're paid pine nuts, so to speak, you have every right to demand that things improve.

The stories countries tell themselves about their national identities are always partly fictional. Among millions of people, in any country, there will be differences. National identities are ways of denying those differences. After its civil war between North and South, America re-forged its national identity in conflicts against Native Americans, Germany, Japan, and the Soviet Union. Now its conflict is with a few thousand terrorists.

But the latter is hardly an adversary powerful enough to unite a nation of 300 million people. Cracks in America's national identity are re-emerging, with more uncompromising partisanship and political groupings that appear in many ways to be descended from those of the old North and South of a century and a half ago, even if now the terms used are Red and Blue.

In India too, some sections of society seem determined to forge a national identity as an upcoming superpower. It is perhaps no accident that this has been accompanied by the rise of anti-Muslim political parties and a backlash of Maoist tribal rebellions. The official Indian national identity appears to be growing more distant from one that can encompass all of its people. Pakistan has been making the same mistake, but we can stop. The problem with Pakistan is not our national identity. The problem is that we have allowed ourselves to be distracted and bogged down in the name of national identity for too long.

I am Pakistani. Surely that should be enough.

*Pakistan's Secret*

And here's the great secret about Pakistan: we are not as poor as we like to think.

Over the years I've travelled a fair bit around our country. I've ridden on the back of a motorbike in Gwadar, walked down streets in Karachi, explored bazaars in Peshawar. I've hiked in Skardu, fished (unsuccessfully) in Naran, sat down to a meal in a village outside Multan. I'm no expert, but I believe what my eyes tell me and there's no doubt about it: times are incredibly tough.

For most Pakistanis, meat is a luxury. Drinking water is contaminated with urine, faeces or industrial chemicals. School is a building that exists only on paper or otherwise employs a teacher who is barely literate. Electricity is so intermittent as to be almost a force of nature, like rain or a breeze.

The budget reveals that the Pakistani government plans to generate Rs. 1.5tr in taxes this year. With an estimated population of 170 million people, this equals approximately Rs. 9,000 each per year; a little over Rs. 700 per month per person.

That is not enough. Yes, we get money from other sources. We borrow, and sell off state assets, and ask for aid from anyone willing to give it to us. But still, what we can raise ourselves in taxes accounts for most of what our government can spend. And when your goal is enough power plants and teacher training and low-income support and (since we seem intent on buying them) F-16s for the world's sixth most populous country, Rs. 700, the equivalent of a large Pizza Hut pizza in taxes for each of us every month doesn't go very far.

Why is Pakistan not delivering what we hope for? Because of dictatorships, or India, or the Americans? Perhaps, but these days a large part of the reason is this: we citizens aren't paying enough for Pakistan to flourish.

On my travels around our country I haven't just seen malnourished children and exhausted farmers and hardworking forty-year-old women who look like they're eighty. I've also seen huge ancestral landholdings and giant textile factories and Mobilink offices with lines of customers stretching out the door. I've seen shopkeepers turn up to buy Honda Civics with cash. I've seen armies of private security guards, fleets of private electricity generators. I've seen more handwritten non-official receipts than I can possibly count.

Many of our rich have tens of millions of dollars in assets. And our middle class numbers tens of millions of people. The resources of our country are enormous. We've just made a collective decision not to use them. We pay only about 10 per cent of our GDP in taxes. (Our GDP is our total economy, what all of us together earn in a year.) Meanwhile, Sri Lankans pay 15 per cent of their GDP in taxes, Indians pay 17 per cent, Turks pay 24 per cent, Americans pay 28 per cent and Swedes pay a fat 50 per cent. We Pakistanis pay a pittance in comparison.

That is fabulous news, because it can change. Raising taxes doesn't depend on foreign policy, getting a wink from Uncle Sam or a nod from King so-and-so. It doesn't require a breakthrough in technology or a year of good rain. It's under our control.

What would happen, for example, if we raised tax revenues by a fifth: from 10 per cent of GDP to 12 per cent? Well, that would give us Rs. 300 billion a year. We could use that to rent a million classrooms for Rs. 10,000 per month, give jobs as teachers to a million graduates for Rs. 15,000 per month, and ensure that every single child in our country received a decent education. By raising taxes to the level of Sri Lanka, 15 per cent of GDP, we would generate additional revenue equal to twice our official defence budget. Match India at 17 per cent of GDP and the additional money would equal a staggering twenty-five times our current education, health and housing budgets combined.

So if you are a progressive who wants the state to do more to help the poor, you should support more taxes. If you are an industrialist who wants to see that Taliban recruits are rehabilitated and retrained, you should support more taxes. If you are a professional who wants electricity and better police, you should support more taxes. If you are an anti-American who wants us to stop taking US aid, you should support more taxes. If you are a diehard militarist who wants us to buy lots of F-16s, you should support more taxes.

The only people who shouldn't support more taxes are those who think that the situation in Pakistan right now is already too good.

Taxes are the big hope for Pakistan. It isn't complicated. Anyone who says we can't solve our problems or afford to give our people a decent standard of living isn't telling the truth. We can afford it. We've just chosen not to.

This is where our democracy can make a difference. We have elected our representatives. Horribly imperfect as they are, they represent us. And because they represent us, they have the right to ask us to act in our shared self-interest, to contribute more to the collective pot that is Pakistan. It seems they are starting to do so. And perhaps rampant inflation and a dozen hours of load-shedding a day are making even many formerly comfortable and tax-averse citizens more amenable to change.

But what about corruption? Yes, there's no doubt that much of officialdom is corrupt. But so are we, the citizens. Every time we accept a fake receipt, or fail to declare any income, we are stealing from our country in precisely the same way our politicians and bureaucrats are. Our thefts as taxpayers might be comparatively small, but that is because taxes are so low in our country to begin with. At the moment, we feed off each other. As we citizens start to display more probity in tax, we're likely to demand more probity in how our money is spent, and our strengthening courts and media are likely to help us get it.

The tax revolution is not going to happen overnight. It will take time. But there is good reason to hope it is coming, and to slowly shift the weight of our votes, our accounts and our attitudes to support the right side.

A brighter future awaits us if we, as Pakistani citizens, are willing to pay for it.

4

# BEYOND THE CRISIS STATE

## Dr Maleeha Lodhi

Pakistan is at the crossroads of its political destiny. It can either remain trapped in a quagmire of weak governance, politics-as-usual, economic stagnation and crumbling public faith in state institutions; or it can take advantage of social changes underway to chart a new course.

How can this moment of opportunity be described? Is this a democratic moment? An opportunity to consolidate a process that has remained vulnerable to repeated disruption and derailment? Or is this a transformational opportunity when challenges to traditional politics hold out possibilities for change? Representational and electoral politics have remained stuck in an old mode and increasingly lagged behind the social and economic changes that have been altering the country's political landscape. The economic centre of gravity has been shifting but politics has yet to catch up with its implications.

Already members of a growing and politically assertive urban middle class are using the opportunities created by globalisation and technological change to demand better governance and a greater voice in the country's politics. Although estimates of the size of Pakistan's middle class vary depending on the criterion employed, if Purchasing Power Parity is used as the yardstick it can be put at around thirty million people.[1] This includes educated, professional groups as well as middle-income employees in state and business enterprises.

This raises the question: is a middle-class moment approaching? Can their rise in numbers and activism lead to a shift in the centres and instruments of power and influence? Can the increasing mismatch between a more empowered middle class and family- or clan-dominated politics unleash dynamics that can ultimately yield an accountable and functional system of governance? Or are recent changes too limited to pose any real threat to the entrenched position of a narrow and oligarchic power elite—drawn from the landowning and mercantile elites and the civilian and military bureaucracy?

Answers must necessarily be tentative. While Pakistan is in the throes of change, its nature and direction is still unfolding. It is also unclear how the traditional elite will respond to the rising pressures on their power and authority.

But governance challenges are multiplying. These include daunting problems of security, solvency, mounting energy and water shortages, and an increasing youth bulge—representing a mass of unfulfilled expectations—in an environment of economic weakness. Catastrophic floods that swept the country in the summer of 2010 compounded the country's woes. They sharpened questions of whether Pakistan's political and governance structures—and the quality of leadership—are capable of addressing and surmounting the gravest challenges ever faced. Can Pakistan acquire the means to govern itself better?

The historical record is not encouraging on two related counts. One, establishing a viable political order and a predictable environment to solve the country's problems; two, evolving a political consensus on priorities and how to address them in a context of stable civil-military relations.

Complicating the quest to resolve these problems is the impact of external developments on the country's fate and fortunes. The external and internal have been so intertwined in Pakistan's history—as they are today—as to compound political challenges. The country's ability to weather the storms of global geo-politics has been repeatedly tested. Struggling to deal with this from a position of domestic fragility has ended up emaciating and exhausting Pakistan. Its much-celebrated geo-strategic location has been more of a challenge than an asset. Successive governments believed geography translated into power whereas it actually drained the country's power.

The issues of security, economy and governance have intersected in mutually compounding ways, which makes it difficult to establish the source and direction of causation. Has the security preoccupation hobbled political development, preempted resources and been the main source of economic problems? Have dysfunctional politics been at the root of Pakistan's governance deficit and economic misfortunes? What is certain is that these issues have become so intermeshed that the systemic crisis can now only be resolved by tackling them together and not in isolation from one another.

## *The Burden of History*

The sweep of Pakistan's tangled history reveals an unedifying record of governance failures and missed opportunities. Political instability has been endemic, as the country has shuttled between ineffectual civilian government and military rule in an unbroken cycle punctuated by outbreaks of public protests demanding change and better governance.

Half of its existence has been spent under military rule and half under civilian or quasi-civilian governments. Pakistan's turbulent history has also been tragic. The early death of its founder so soon after partition meant that the mantle of a towering figure was inherited by a succession of squabbling political lightweights. As several members of this ruling elite came from the Muslim-majority areas of India they increasingly sought the support of the civil-military bureaucracy to prop them up against indigenous political groups. When politicians bickered over issues of identity, provincial autonomy and the role of religion in the state, constitution-making was hobbled. This created a political vacuum that encouraged the military's creeping entry and eventual control of the political system.

The dictates of the early chaotic years resulted in the postponement of crucial reforms that could have set Pakistan on a different course. Opportunities were missed to recast colonial instruments of control into those serving the needs of economic development and a participatory democracy. As order, not representative government, was seen as the overwhelming priority, the need for reforms was ignored. No significant land reforms were instituted that could have broken the political and economic stranglehold of the feudal or landed elite that dominated the country's politics for decades to come, and frustrated economic modernisation.

Elections were repeatedly postponed. Only in 1970 did Pakistan hold its first free and fair election—twenty-three years after its birth.

Postponed reforms also meant that the symbiotic nexus forged between the powerful civil-military bureaucracy and feudal clans thwarted the country's democratic evolution. Pakistan's revolving-door democracy neither yielded stability nor realised the country's economic potential.

The most traumatic failure came in 1971 when the stubborn resistance by the ruling political and military elite to accommodate Bengali aspirations led to the breakup of Pakistan after a humiliating military defeat inflicted by India which intervened militarily to mid-wife the creation of Bangladesh. This military debacle gave way to democracy. But Pakistan's first popularly elected and charismatic leader, Zulfiqar Ali Bhutto's ill-focussed attempt at 'socialist' reform entailed sweeping nationalisation as well as concentration and personalisation of power. This not only set back economic development but also descended into autocratic rule. While Bhutto made powerful enemies he managed to retain the loyalty of his populist base. But his failure to institutionalise his party meant that his vote-bank could not be mobilised to save either his government or his life.

The Army seized power to usher in Pakistan's longest spell of military dictatorship under General Zia-ul-Haq who was to leave the most toxic and enduring legacy. His use of Islam to legitimise his rule stoked sectarian tensions and encouraged extremist tendencies in Pakistani society.

Added to this volatile mix was Pakistan's long engagement in the last of the Cold War conflicts aimed at ejecting Soviet occupation forces from Afghanistan. This earned Zia enthusiastic Western support. But it brought the country a witches' brew of problems: induction of Islamic militancy, proliferation of weapons, spread of narcotics, exponential growth in *madrasahs*, growing violence and a large Afghan refugee population (over three million at the peak, close to two million today). Pakistan's intimate involvement in the war of unintended consequences came at an extraordinary cost: the country's own stability. This established a pattern of behaviour that was to resonate throughout its history. While its rulers played geo-political games that sought to enhance Pakistan's regional influence, the neglect of pressing domestic problems exacted a heavy price.

Eleven disastrous years under General Zia left the country reeling in economic, political and institutional chaos. They also marked a missed economic opportunity. Just when Western concessional assistance was forthcoming, inflows of remittances from overseas Pakistani workers also peaked. Between 1975 and 1985 Pakistan received over $25 billion in remittances. Failure to direct this into investment in productive sectors meant a unique set of fortuitous factors was squandered. Lack of investment in the physical infrastructure—a policy blunder later repeated in the Musharraf years—sowed the seeds of the crippling shortages in power and essential public services that challenge Pakistan today and blight its economic future.

It was during the lost decade of the 1980s that the prevailing budgetary resource crisis emerged as a chronic threat to Pakistan's financial stability. Fiscal indiscipline was not new but 1985 marked a sharp break in Pakistan's budgetary history, when revenue no longer matched even the government's current expenditure. Successive governments borrowed heavily to finance not only development but also consumption for the next decade. In the process the country accumulated unsustainable debt both by borrowing abroad and at home. This burden continues to cripple the economy today.

The air crash that killed General Zia and his top military colleagues yielded democracy. But the decade of the 1990s produced disappointingly feeble civilian rule and fractious politics. Governments changed in rapid succession with the country's two principal parties led by Benazir Bhutto and Nawaz Sharif alternating in power. Both took turns to undermine the other in bouts of confrontational politics that became fatal distractions from improving governance.

Civilian leaders gave little thought to the omnipresent danger that their endless feuds would open space for the military's return to the political stage. When neither of the two parties lived up to the test of effective governance it was only a matter of time before the Army was sucked in. Pakistan's fourth coup led by General Pervez Musharraf ushered in another decade of military rule.

Much of the Musharraf period was dominated by Pakistan's involvement in the US-led 'War on Terror' waged in the aftermath of the 9/11 terrorist attacks on America.[2] This placed Pakistan at the frontlines of international attention. It saw the war in Afghanistan spill over in to the country's borderlands to gravely jeopardise its stability. The repercussions for Pakistan of a confused and flawed US strategy in Afghanistan were far reaching: spread of radicalisation, intensification of violence and the further undermining of a febrile economy.

The twin and connected crises of security and solvency that Pakistan is struggling with today are in part the fallout of the protracted conflicts in Afghanistan. They were also a consequence of the lack of policy foresight and divisive politics pursued by the Musharraf government like its military predecessors.

In another important way the Musharraf years resembled the Ayub Khan era. Despite their flawed politics and lack of longer term economic policies both ushered in a period of accelerated economic growth that led to a significant rise in per capita incomes and a more urbanised society. This produced a dramatic expansion in Pakistan's middle class, generating a new political dynamic that ultimately contained the seeds of the military government's own demise.[3]

Unlike Ayub and Zia, President Musharraf allowed an unprecedented opening of the country's media. Powerful new fora of public expression combined with the dynamics of a newly empowered middle class to pose a challenge to a regime whose political vehicle (the ruling Muslim League) failed to represent public aspirations or erode the support base of its rival League faction led by Sharif and the Pakistan People's Party (PPP).

The general elections in February 2008 confirmed the hold on voters of the two major political parties, the PPP of Benazir Bhutto and Nawaz Sharif's Muslim League. But tragedy intervened to deprive the nation of a national leader at a pivotal moment in its democratic transition. Benazir Bhutto's assassination in an election rally in December 2007 left the country in shock and disarray.

The leadership of the PPP controversially passed to her spouse Asif Ali Zardari, who became known as the country's accidental leader. After Musharraf was forced from office in August 2008 Zardari became President of the Islamic Republic. But his corruption-tainted past denuded him of credibility or popular appeal, and raised questions about the political future of the PPP as both a government and party.

*Governance Challenges*

Chronic instability and an oligarchic-dominated political order impeded the evolution of modern governance. Patronage-based politics practiced by democratic and military governments alike relied on working networks of influential political families, clans or kinship groups (*biradaries*)[4] to maintain themselves in power but this mode of governance failed to meet the needs of an increasingly complex society.

Governance challenges intensified with a force and intensity that derived from a complex interplay between internal and external factors:

a) The first had to do with managing the blowback from the country's protracted Cold War engagements and the impact of great power rivalries and global geo-politics. Few countries have had to face the headwinds blowing from their location as Pakistan. If the tyranny of geography imposed heavy burdens the myopic policies pursued by successive governments exacerbated the situation. This is not to suggest that the multifaceted fallout of the two Afghan wars (in the 1980s and that following the US-led military intervention in 2001) was of Pakistan's making. But its destabilising consequences were poorly anticipated and ineptly managed by ruling elites interested more in short-term goals and self-preservation than in protecting their society from the adverse repercussions of great power interests and regional politics.

b) A second related factor that complicated the governance challenge has to do with Pakistan's troubled relations with India and the 'unfinished business' of partition epitomised by the dispute over Kashmir. Dealing with a hostile India pursuing hegemonic policies drove a perpetual fear of conflict and became an abiding preoccupation for Pakistan's policy-makers. This made the goal of security and deterring India (through conventional military means as well as by the acquisition of a nuclear capability) an overwhelming priority. But there was an inevitable tradeoff: the development needs of the country in education, health and other public services could not be adequately addressed. This meant that while the state's hard power increased, human security deteriorated. Every missile test Pakistan conducted offered a stunning contrast to the desperate state of its social and physical infrastructure with the literacy deficit and energy shortages representing perilous tips of this iceberg.

c) A third factor that contributed to governance problems emerged from the economic legacy of the Bhutto years. Extensive state intervention in the economy through sweeping nationalisation in the 1970s produced a phenomenon of too much government, too little governance for decades to come. Mismanagement of a vast network of state enterprises became a huge drain on the national exchequer, crowded out private investment and sucked scarce resources away from the social sector including education, the bedrock of economic progress. Privatisation of some enterprises in the 1990s and the Musharraf years helped to reduce but not end this burden. By 2010 public sector corporations still required huge government subsidies;

losses in these enterprises were estimated at $4 billion a year with the hemorrhage in the power sector alone accounting for Rs. 256 billion ($3 billion) in 2010.[5] The impact of this on an anemic economy cannot be underestimated. A weakened economy cast a huge shadow on the country's ability to come to grips with rising demographic pressures and the basic needs of its citizens.

The confluence of these foreign and domestic factors was to pose governance challenges of unprecedented magnitude, but in a setting in which commensurate responses were stymied by a number of fault lines in the country's polity to which I now turn.

## Fault Lines in Pakistan's Polity

Pakistan's political experience or predicament has been shaped by a number of mostly overlapping factors that seem to have become enduring faultlines.[6] The following five factors are central to understanding the Pakistan story:

1) The power asymmetry between political and non-political or un-elected institutions.
2) A feudal-dominated political order and culture that has fostered clientelist politics.
3) Reliance by an oligarchic elite on 'borrowed' growth and bailouts to address the country's chronic financial crises and its resistance to taxing itself and its network of supporters.
4) The intersection between efforts to 'leverage' geography in pursuit of national security goals and the role of outside powers.
5) The persistence of centrifugal forces and bitter ideological controversies over the role of Islam in the state and society.

## Asymmetry in Power between Political and Non-Political Institutions

The imbalance was rooted as much in the colonial heritage as impelled by the fraught circumstances of a newly established country. This meant that the 'steel frame' of civil-military state organs easily established their dominance over weak political institutions.[7] Pakistan's independence party, the Muslim League, unlike its Indian counterpart, the Congress Party, did not have the advantage of a leader's stewardship to steer the new nation because Jinnah died so soon after partition. Moreover as the leadership of the League came predominantly from India, it could not compete with the indigenous political elites without enlisting the support of the civil-military bureaucracy.[8]

The military's preeminence also owed itself to managing the political turmoil that followed partition and the early war with India over Kashmir. But it was also able to establish itself as the arbiter in a situation marked by political wrangling and fierce conflict between the indigenous and non-indigenous power elites.

The coup of 1958 marked a decisive institutional shift, with non-elected institutions becoming ascendant over the political system. This was accompanied by the phenomenon of state intervention in the political process, which was witnessed with even greater intensity under Zia and then in the Musharraf era.

This left political forces weak and divided. Long periods of military rule also thwarted the evolution of parties and other political institutions, accentuating this asymmetry. The military's dominance was also reinforced by the focus on security driven by unrelenting tensions with India.

The primacy of unelected institutions over representative organs left Parliament weak and subservient to the executive. Parliamentary subordination to a powerful executive had its roots in the weak credentials of the legislature in Pakistan's early years. With no popularly or directed-elected legislature until the 1970 polls, the assemblies that functioned between 1947 and 1970 were elected by a restricted franchise, which denuded Parliament of real legitimacy and authority. This also cast the state's evolving structure into a specific mould, retarding the development of party structures and organisation.

There is, however, an important subtext to this story often obscured by the binary focus on civil-military power asymmetries. That has to do with the personalised nature of parties and the fact that the major ones resembled not modern organisations but were built around traditional kinship groups and local influentials to effectively become family fiefdoms. Even today the dynastic character of parties illustrates the primacy of personalism over organisation. The PPP is led by Benazir Bhutto's widower and co-chaired by her young son, and the Muslim League is run by the Sharif brothers with the progeny of Shahbaz Sharif being prepared for future leadership. Even religious parties have not been immune to this. The Jamiat Ulema-e-Islam led by Maulana Fazl-ur-Rahman who inherited this position from his father Mufti

Mahmud, nominated his brother to the coalition cabinet of Prime Minister Yousuf Raza Gilani. The former Amir of the Jamaat-e-Islami, Qazi Hussain Ahmad ensured that his daughter was awarded a seat reserved for women in the 2002 parliament.

The personalised nature of parties has contributed to their organisational weakness and deprived them of the dynamism that modern organisations bring to politics including the expertise needed to run a government. Dynasties have constrained wider participation, as they are the antithesis of modern inclusionary politics. They have also impeded parties from acquiring institutional autonomy from the whims of the leader.

This has been reinforced by the telling absence of democracy within most parties. Leaders of major parties—the PPP, factions of the Muslim League and the regional Awami National Party—are not elected but assume their positions by 'acclamation'. Nor do regular elections determine which occupants hold office at different tiers. They are usually 'selected' by the leader on the basis of their loyalty and 'connections'. Party leaders' resistance to internal democracy was amply demonstrated in April 2010 when their lawmakers deleted the constitutional obligation to hold party elections from the Eighth Constitutional Amendment that Parliament adopted to do away with the changes Musharraf had made to rebalance powers between the President and the Prime Minister and the centre and the provinces.

The military, whose social composition has increasingly become middle or lower middle class, has often counterposed itself to these traditional political entities as an institution that offers social mobility and operates on the basis of merit and professionalism. But there is an irony to this: when the military has forged political alliances to rule it has turned to the very traditional political forces that it is so contemptuous of and depicts as retrogressive and incompetent. Expediency has defined its politics just like that of the political class.

*Clientelist Politics*

The personalised nature of politics is closely related to the dominant position enjoyed throughout Pakistan's history by a narrowly-based political elite that was feudal and tribal in origin and has remained so in outlook even as it gradually came to share power with well-to-do urban groups. The latter is epitomised by the rise of Mian Nawaz

Sharif who came from a mercantile background. While different in social origin and background, members of this power elite shared a similar 'feudal-tribal' style of conducting politics: personalised, based on 'primordial' social hierarchies, characterised by patronage-seeking activity and preoccupied with protecting and promoting their economic interests and privileged status.

Clientelism has been the principal hallmark of Pakistani politics, which is widely defined in the literature as one that relies on an exchange of material favours for political support among actors with asymmetric power.[9] Aspects of clientelism exist in even advanced democracies. But such politics are not defined or organised around exploitative patron-client relationships, which thrive in a context of hierarchical social relations based on lineage. It operates in the Pakistani case in a manner that is antithetical to the notion of citizenship.

'Feudal' here refers not so much to a 'mode of agricultural production' but to social structures that have given rise to networks of relationships of obligation and patronage. In this sense feudal attitudes reinforced by a social system of tribal and *biradari* alignments have long spilled into and influenced Pakistan's urban politics. This political culture has extended beyond rural landowners or tribal chiefs and their economic or geographical sphere of operation.[10] It has expressed itself in patron-client forms of political representation and behaviour.

This helps explain why urban-based parties such as the Nawaz League adopt an approach that is tradition-bound rather than one defined by their ostensibly 'modern' urban background. The urban rich function much like their rural counterparts with their efforts at political mobilisation resting more on working lineage and *biradari* connections and alliances than representing wider urban interests.

It is how they conduct politics that blurs the rural-urban distinction. Oriented more to patronage than to policy, their politics is essentially about recruiting and managing familial and clan networks. Access to power enhances their capacity to do so. Political competition is rarely about programmes or policy issues; it is about access to the spoils of office.

Parties are extensions of *biradaries* and influential families. Electoral competition is principally about gaining control of state patronage to cement patron-client relationships and reward supporters. Such clientelist politics is geared to the 'local' or parochial and is inimical to encouraging wider mobilisation and fostering attitudes or thinking about larger national issues. The criterion of allocation of 'public goods' is particularistic not universalistic. This tends to keep politics primordial and oriented to narrow issues. It also reduces any incentive for political leaders to ask the citizenry to contribute their share to the 'national good' by way of taxes or the full cost of public services.

Much of the politics of the so-called 1950s parliamentary period, the controlled politics of the 1960s and the 1990s decade of democracy displayed these features. The PPP has been more representative of landowning interests (with its strongholds in rural Sindh and southern Punjab) than the Nawaz League. The struggle for power between these parties has exhibited few of the attributes of modern political contests, in which there is a battle of ideas with clear-cut platforms and policy alternatives. Instead they have sought to represent the economic interests of their clientelist bases of support even as the PPP has retained some of its populist roots. In the classic style of clientelism, governance is embedded in the notion of rewarding their 'clients' rather than the electorate as citizens. Their preoccupation with 'rulership' rather than public 'service' is in keeping with the patrimonial structures of traditional society.

It is true that Sharif's party has inducted several urban politicians and professionals who are more oriented to providing services to constituents rather than catering to a select, clientelist base. But they are neither numerous nor politically influential enough to modify the overall character of the party.

Members of the political elite have frequently split off to join or serve as junior partners in military governments in return for the accretion of their power by entry into the spoils system. The Muslim League that served as the 'King's party' under Musharraf is a case in point. It consisted of former PPP or Nawaz supporters who broke to ally themselves with the military regime and find berths in various cabinets during 1999–2008.

The narrow social base of this political elite is evidenced by a number of factors. Influential families from a rural landowning and tribal background continue to dominate Pakistan's legislatures. This reflects remarkable continuity with the past. A familiar array of names representing landed families, tribal dynasties and extended clans have found their way into every assembly since independence. The tickets awarded by the three main parties vying for power in 2008 showed an overwhelming number went to influential rural and urban families.

One writer has estimated that a few hundred families have dominated virtually all of Pakistan's legislatures, including the present ones.[11] The political baton has been passed on to scions of these families in the current Parliament: Gilanis, Qureshis, Tamans, Mehars, Bijranis, Rinds, Raisanis, Jhakaranis, Makhdums of Hala, Shahs of Nawabpur, the Khan of Kalabagh's family and others.

This political class has resisted meaningful reform—whether reforms in land holdings, taxation, social welfare or in governance. The power elite has also acquired 'rentier' characteristics: using public office as a means of leveraging state resources (credit from state-owned banks, state land at nominal prices, and 'development spending') to transfer wealth and secure sources of unearned income. This has been a common feature of both the civilian and military elites. It also helps to explain why with few exceptions their economic management has been so similar. This brings up the next faultline.

## The Politics of 'Borrowed Growth'

This has been the inescapable consequence of rule by an oligarchic elite that has been unwilling to mobilise resources preferring 'pain-free' ways of managing public finances. The enigma of successive civilian and military governments living beyond their means can only be explained in terms of a privilegentsia that is averse to measures that would either erode its position or threaten its class or corporate interests.

This has contributed to miring Pakistan in perpetual financial crisis with virtually every government in the past two decades leaving the economy in much worse shape for its successor. Half-hearted efforts to raise revenue are laid bare by the dismal statistics. Tax as a percentage of GDP has remained static over decades even though the country's overall output has steadily increased. The tax-GDP ratio has hovered around 11 per cent in the 1990s, but fell to 9 per cent during the Musharraf era and continues to decline making it the lowest in the region and in the developing world.[12]

The number of income taxpayers rose from an abysmal quarter of a million in 1995 to a million in 2000. By 2010 this had gone up to 2.5 million. But almost 70 per cent of this is 'withholding' and presumptive taxes, many of which are a tax on transactions not income. Less than 1 per cent of the population pays direct tax, a lower proportion than in most countries at a similar stage of development.

These figures signify the absence of a tax culture. They point to a fiscally irresponsible governing elite that has consistently failed to make a serious or sustained effort to generate the resources to pay for the cost of running the government and providing essential public services. The most spectacular example of the elite's refusal to contribute its share to revenue is the absence of a tax on agricultural income. Agriculture accounts for 22 per cent of GDP but yields only 1 per cent of revenue. This has been mirrored to some extent in urban Pakistan by the exemption from general sales tax enjoyed (until changes announced in November 2010) by the textile industry among other sectors that contribute to exports and which also receive state subsidies in different guises.

A task force set up to reform the tax system in 2001 found that 50 per cent of taxes that are due never reach the treasury, an example of the power of the rich to thwart the law.[13] The IMF estimates that about $3 billion raised in taxes never make it to the exchequer because of the corrupt collusion between tax collectors and influential taxpayers. Even a flawed tax regime has been subverted by the politically powerful.

The ramshackle tax system is narrow and skewed, imposing a greater burden on those least able to bear it. Indirect taxes yield more than double the revenue raised from direct ones. General sales tax accounts for over 54 per cent of all indirect taxation. As currently executed this is a regressive measure as the rich and poor have to pay the same amount. The service sector, which has expanded dramatically in the last two decades and contributes the largest share of GDP at 54 per cent, is undertaxed and has a significantly higher rate of evasion. Noncompliance is widespread. Out of an estimated one million retail outlets only 160,000 are registered for the general sales tax—even as efforts to expand this were hesitantly announced in November 2010 under intense donor pressure.

Several new economic sectors, such as information technology, remain outside the tax net. Property tax collections are minimal. This lets the urban propertied off the hook. A modest Rs. 2.5 billion is collected in tax from real estate in the country's most populous province, Punjab. A provincial judge overturned the increase in property tax attempted in the 1990s. He was believed to be upset at the rise in his own property tax obligation that worked out at Rs. 30 a day for the provision of all municipal services including the maintenance of a road in front of his home.[14]

Efforts at tax reform were fitful and poorly enforced throughout the 1990s and much of the Musharraf years. These governments did not make any sustained effort to document the vast underground economy. If GDP in 2009 was \$170 billion, the real but undocumented economy was estimated to be twice that size. This places a large swath of the economy beyond the tax net—60 per cent according to some estimates.[15]

The inability to raise resources along with low levels of savings and investment, meant that successive governments since the 1980s ran up huge deficits in national expenditure and on the external account. These twin deficits—budget and balance of payments—were financed by printing more currency notes and by the inflow of funds from abroad including remittances from overseas workers.[16]

The reliance on external resources to finance both development and consumption was facilitated by the availability of assistance due to the country's foreign alignments. Cold War assistance accompanied Pakistan's close alliance with the US. In the 1980s Western aid flowed as a strategic pay off for Pakistan's pivotal role in resisting the Soviet occupation of Afghanistan. Pakistan's strategic value to the US was again enhanced after 9/11. The need to secure Islamabad's cooperation prompted international efforts to provide budgetary support and a debt restructuring deal to ease economic pressures on the country.

The availability of these external resources along with high levels of remittances enabled Pakistan to achieve impressive rates of economic growth—6–7 per cent annually during much of the Zia and Musharraf years. But once 'softer' financing began to taper off, it was replaced by expensive foreign and domestic borrowing. This 'borrowed growth' was unsustainable.

As rising defence needs were not matched by a growing revenue-base, high military expenditure combined with rising internal and external debt service obligations to mire Pakistan in a classic debt trap. This economic management in the 1990s and much of the 2000s not only had a destabilising impact on the economy but also exacerbated poverty and drained resources from health and education. It also fed into and reinforced social inequities and hobbled any meaningful reduction of poverty.

Economic management that relied on someone else's money permitted the country's rulers to avoid much needed structural reforms that could have placed the economy on a viable, self-reliant path. Instead, quick fixes, which momentarily created the illusion of good economic management, led to an exorbitant rise in debt as more was borrowed to service old debt. Bank borrowing served as a sharply regressive measure because it translated into a forced transfer of savings to the government from the people least able to bear the burden of inflation, the most pernicious tax on the poor.

'Borrowed growth' may not have had such deleterious consequences if the fiscal space it provided was used to launch reforms to address underlying structural problems: broadening the tax net, documenting the economy, diversifying the export base, and encouraging savings to finance a level of investment that could sustain a growth rate higher than the rise in population.

The early years of the Musharraf administration moved towards this direction but fell short of the needed effort. Its own task force on tax reform put it starkly:

Pakistan's fiscal crisis is deep...taxes are insufficient for debt service and defence. If the tax to GDP ratio does not increase significantly Pakistan cannot be governed effectively, essential public services cannot be delivered and high inflation is inevitable. Reform of the tax administration is the single most important economic task for the government.[17]

This urgent counsel was trumped by political expediency. Once Musharraf's military regime was obliged to find political allies for the 2002 elections, its commitment to reform waned precipitously.

Crisis management also meant that little investment or planning took place in power generation and water resources. As a result shortages reached crisis proportions. The social and physical infrastructure was similarly neglected. The failure to make investments in human development saddled Pakistan with a rising pool of uneducated youth and prevented the country from deriving a demographic dividend from the youthful structure of its growing population. Instead a fast growing population, with 60 per cent under thirty years old, held out the danger of future social unrest given the widening gap between state resources and the rising needs of a multiplying population.

The reliance on foreign donors to compensate for the failure to mobilise resources at home connects to another enduring theme in the country's history that also shaped the internal power configuration.

## Enduring Quest for Security

Pakistan's internal political evolution and foreign alignments have been greatly influenced by its enduring quest for security. The shadow of an overbearing and hostile eastern neighbour and contested borders bequeathed by colonialism were the two key factors that accentuated the country's insecurity. The unresolved dispute over Kashmir—the cause of two of the three wars with India and many crises (1990, 1998, 2001 and 2009)—was among the principal sources of tensions between Pakistan and India for over half a century. On the western frontier, the border with Afghanistan demarcated as the Durand Line by the British became the basis of irredentist claims by successive governments in Kabul.

Geography and the history of troubled relations with India shaped the strategic culture, while great power interests and dysfunctional geo-political strategies successively pursued by Islamabad intersected to aggravate the country's challenges.

The problem of insecure borders was compounded by another set of issues spawned by its lack of geographical depth. Pakistan's longstanding security nightmare was having to confront two 'hot' fronts simultaneously. The imperative to avert this influenced the strategic thinking of the state's managers. Pakistan's fears were reinforced by Delhi's conduct in the country's formative years. Whether it was the transfer of Pakistan's share of assets inherited from British India, the coercive absorption of several princely states into the Indian union, including Kashmir or the sharing of river waters, Pakistan saw India seeking to impose its will in disregard of agreements that governed partition. These early experiences contributed to a 'siege mentality'.

The security preoccupation skewed the civil-military balance and had ramifications for the internal configuration of power. They included fostering a highly centralised state structure counterposed between weak political institutions in a society wracked by provincial and ethnic tensions.

Other consequences followed. The strategy that was crafted to deal with India was to seek extra-regional alignments to counter-balance its power, apart from occasional adventurist forays such as provoking the Kargil conflict. It was this external balancing paradigm that drove Pakistan to forge Cold War alliances with the US-led Western coalition, which was then looking for allies in the struggle against communism.

Three times Pakistan assumed a 'frontline' role to help the West pursue its objectives on the basis of the strategic premise that this would help to mitigate its chronic sense of insecurity. But superpower intrusion into the region injected its own dynamics plunging Pakistan into the vortex of regional conflict and rivalries. The unanticipated consequences of Pakistan's Cold War engagements and especially its role in the anti-Soviet Afghan war were sweeping and devastating. These blowback effects became enduring aspects of the domestic landscape to exacerbate governance challenges.

The most toxic fallout was the growth of religious extremism and the advent of militancy in the country. Some 20,000 to 30,000 foreign nationals from the Muslim world were imported to the region by the US-led international coalition that helped arm and train them for the jihad against the Russians. Once the Soviets were expelled, some left, but most didn't. Many were to morph into al Qaeda and other militant groups that came to threaten Pakistan as well as global security.

There was another consequence. The economic and military assistance received through various phases of these alignments created an official mindset of dependence. As discussed earlier this set up perverse incentives for internal reform.

It also found reflection in an approach that looked outside to deal with mounting problems and address the sources of internal weakness. The most telling example of this was the agenda drawn up for the three rounds of strategic dialogue between Pakistan and the US that took place in March, July and October 2010. Thirteen sectors were identified for engagement, which included energy, water management, agriculture, health and education—areas where Islamabad either sought American financial or policy help. This showed the extent to which the ruling elite had come to see outsiders as catalytic agents to solve their problems.

## National Unity Tested by Regional and Religious Pressures

The issues of religion and regionalism have persistently tested both the nature and purpose of the state. The salience of these issues have fluctuated in a terrain of shifting politics and state priorities as well as in public traction.

Religion and regionalism would perhaps not have been such enduring sources of discord had efforts to establish a functional state been successful—one that met the economic and social needs of its people. Poor governance created the breeding ground for religious schisms and for provincial/ethnic sentiment to acquire political potency.

Often public discontent was cast in ethnic terms and held out as evidence of the lack of distributive justice between provinces. The meteoric rise of the Muttahida Qaumi Movement (MQM) as a party representing Sindh's Urdu-speaking migrants from India is rooted in the perceived discrimination felt by *muhajirs* (refugees) in the distribution of state resources and jobs. Similarly religion has been used as the language of protest, as for example in the 1977 opposition-led mass demonstrations against Bhutto's autocratic rule.

The confluence between Pakistan's ethnic diversity and the provincial configuration—with Punjab more populous than the other three provinces put together—underscored the need to make federalism a reality not just a constitutional percept. The failure to work a federal arrangement was writ large in the rise of the Bengali nationalist movement that culminated in the break up of Pakistan.

The 1973 Constitution, a consensus document, assured provincial autonomy and enjoined reciprocal obligations between the federal units. But this was observed more in its breach than in its adherence. This resulted in an insurgency in Balochistan in the 1970s and 2000s. It also fanned the flames of Pashtun nationalism until more recently when the people of what was once called the North West Frontier Province became more economically and politically integrated with the rest of the country and better represented in the civil-military bureaucracy. In April 2010 the province was renamed Khyber Pakhtunkhwa (KP) in deference to popular wishes.

Unquestioningly long periods of unrepresentative rule magnified resentment among the smaller provinces by centralising power, and also because the Army was predominantly drawn from the Punjab. If Sindhi nationalism was fanned in the Zia era by the execution of the country's first elected Prime Minister from Sindh, Musharraf's rule accentuated Baloch disaffection. The killing of Baloch leader Akbar Bugti during a military operation in 2006 further inflamed the situation.

Provincial tensions have not just been an expression of the diversity of language and culture and the limitations of nation-building efforts. They have also reflected disputes over the distribution of financial and natural resources, water and gas, in an environment of scarcity. Widening social disparities have produced a resurgence in ethnic and provincial identities. For eighteen years squabbles over resources prevented any accord in the National Finance Commission, the federal body changed with determining financial allocations between the provinces. When agreement was reached in March 2010 it was justifiably hailed as a 'victory' for the revived democratic process in the country.

Competition for scarce resources also continues to be an impetus for intra-provincial tensions—between indigenous Sindhis and Muhajirs in Sindh, and between Pashtuns and Baloch in Balochistan. The demand voiced during 2010 for a new Hazara province in KP and for a separate Seraiki province in Punjab illustrates that issues of distributive justice have fused with the continuing difficulties of building a larger national identity. The clientelist nature of politics delays this by its focus on the particular rather than the whole. This serves as another example of Pakistan's interlocked faultlines.

The influence of religion in national politics has also ebbed and flowed. Questions about the role of Islam in the state and society were rooted in the very origin of Pakistan, intended by its secular founders as a Muslim-majority state. But this vision was contested by the religious parties—notably the Jamaat-e-Islami and a section of the clergy. They pressed for an Islamic state but without specifying what this meant. Some of their demands that were accommodated by various governments found expression in the Hudood Ordinance, blasphemy laws, and the establishment of the Islamic Ideology Council charged with ascertaining if laws adopted were contrary to Islam.

Nevertheless the poor showing of religious parties in successive elections helped the overall secular operation of the state through much of its history. Their combined vote never exceeded 11 per cent. This is what the Muttahida Majlis-i-Amal (MMA), an alliance of five religious parties, polled in 2002, a controversial election because of Musharraf's backing for this grouping. Even then the MMA could win only 20 per cent of seats in Parliament's Lower House. It won control of the NWFP and Balochistan governments but its uninspiring performance in office ensured its rout in the 2008 polls.

Religious parties wielded disproportionate political influence only when they were allied to the state or enjoyed the patronage of military governments. But as various governments used religion or its symbols to mobilise the country behind certain goals, the role of Islam was elevated in national life, which unleashed unplanned dynamics that became a source of division rather than unity. But as Ayesha Jalal points out in this volume, for the first three decades or more of its existence Pakistan functioned as a moderate, liberal state with Islam 'kept in check' in state affairs.

This was to change under General Zia as he embarked upon a self-assigned mission to Islamise the country including its legal and educational system. Zia fused politics and religion in using Islam to legitimate his rule. These policies set off a host of deleterious effects that polarised society along religious and sectarian lines. Combined with the effects of the Afghan war, this spawned extremism and saw the birth of militant groups.

The use of some of these groups to advance foreign policy goals was to haunt Pakistan for years to come. Zia's patronisation of countervailing political, ethnic and sectarian groups to undercut support for opposition parties further fragmented society.

Political Islam was to see its influence decline due to electoral politics in the 1990s and also in the post-Musharraf democratic era. But it gave way to a more dangerous phenomenon—militant Islam. Militancy was born in the complex and heady environment of jihad against the Russians. Later, the forces of militancy were emboldened by the rise of the Taliban in Afghanistan. But it was after the 2001 US-led attack on Afghanistan that they became more potent.

The consequences of this intervention was to push the war into Pakistan's border regions, fuel and then unify militant forces behind the common goal to help the Afghan Taliban resist foreign occupation. The rise of the Pakistani Taliban—and the Tehrik-i-Taliban Pakistan alliance announced in December 2007—was closely associated with the Taliban insurgency against US-NATO forces in Afghanistan. Linked to the Afghan Taliban by bonds of tribal affiliation, Pashtun identity, a broadly shared ideology and a common nexus with al Qaeda, the Pakistani Taliban also began to pursue local goals to impose *Shari'a* in areas under their influence. This brought them into direct confrontation with Pakistan's security institutions on which they declared war for being 'agents' of the Americans.

In 2008 and 2009 the TTP created mayhem in the country, launching suicide attacks in the cities, taking over Swat and establishing an infrastructure of terrorism across the tribal areas especially in South Waziristan. To counter this and halt the Taliban's advance the military finally acted in 2009. Fierce offensives in Swat and South Waziristan drove out the Taliban, dismantled their sanctuaries and re-established the government's writ. While it was apparent that defeating the forces of militancy would be a long haul, the people, many of the *ulema* and most religious parties rejected the militant notion that the *Shari'a* could be imposed at gunpoint. This helped to explode the myth that militancy could not be rolled back.

While militant Islam did not pose an existential threat to the country its ability to exploit local grievances and play off governance failures underlined the tough task that lay ahead to neutralise its influence.

## Transformational Trends

The discussion above demonstrates how the interplay between domestic and external factors produced governance failures. And how squandered opportunities and unresolved economic and political problems left the country facing unprecedented challenges at the start of the second decade of the twenty-first century.

But as the country struggled with the linked issues of security and solvency a key question was raised: could changes that had also been set in motion help the country escape its past and enable it to move towards better governance and a more inclusive political system?

Several developments of the past decade open up possibilities to make progress in this direction. This does not mean that entrenched structures of politics have been transformed or that faultlines have faded away. But prospects for a departure from politics-as-usual are better now than ever in the past. This is due to a number of factors to which I now turn.

In crystallising some of these changes 2007–2009 proved to be the watershed years—setting off transformative dynamics that can eventually open the way for a reconfiguration in power relations, and eventually the redistribution of power in a more widely enfranchised and empowered polity.[18]

What set the stage for the chain of dramatic political events during 2007–2009 were the economic and social changes of the preceding seven years. These involved accelerated economic growth, a wave of urbanisation, an exponential expansion in the independent broadcast media and a telecom boom. All of these strengthened modernising trends in society just when, paradoxically militancy and terrorist violence were posing greater threats.

These socio-economic transformations obscured—at the time—the lopsided planning that was to produce crippling shortages and problems that plague the country today and may even have been attained at the cost of longer-term social stability. But they provided the basis for the tumultuous events that were to culminate in General Musharraf's forced resignation and the end of military rule.

During 2000–2007, Pakistan's economy grew at an average of 6–7 per cent a year, which made it one of the fastest growing Asian economies. The size of the economy doubled while per capita incomes increased from $527 in 2000 to $925 in 2007 (over $1,250 in 2009). In Purchasing Power Parity terms Pakistan's per capita GDP reached $3,000 per head of the population. Exports doubled in dollar terms. Foreign direct investment went up to a record $7 billion in 2006, and remittances hit an all time high at $7 billion in 2007.

The economic surge was also visible in urbanisation that rose to 35 per cent by 2007. The urban population's contribution to GDP reached three quarters of the total and accounted for almost all of government revenue. A natural consequence of this was the increase in the numbers of the middle class. By 2008 economists were calculating that the size of the middle class had risen to around thirty million earning an estimated $10,000—$15,000 (in PPP terms)—bigger than the population of 185 countries. Ishrat Husain, the former governor of the State Bank endorsed this number, as did the former World Bank Vice President Shahid Javed Burki.

If the yardstick of consumption is used to determine the growth of the middle class, this further substantiates the phenomenon. Consumer-led growth between 2002 and 2007 saw a surge in car and television sales, which grew at 20 per cent and 29 per cent respectively. By 2005 well over half of all households owned a TV. Economic liberalisation yielded dramatic dividends. The telecommunications sector saw record foreign investment and growth. Mobile phone subscribers rose from one million in 1999 to seventy million by 2007 (in 2010 the number reached 120 million). By 2006–07 close to 90 per cent of the population had access to telecom services giving the country the highest teledensity in the region. Internet subscribers went up fourfold in this period. By 2006–07, 11 per cent of the population were internet users, higher than that in India.[19]

Similarly, opening up the broadcast media to the private sector saw rapid expansion in the number of independent television networks. 2008–2009 recorded a 118 per cent annual growth in privately-owned cable TV networks. In 1999 there was only one state-owned TV network. By 2007 the number had gone up to over fifty (around 100 in 2010) including two dozen news channels.[20] Together these developments pointed not just to a more numerous middle class but to a more 'connected' and empowered urban society benefiting from globalisation. A 'stronger' society was emerging just when state capacity in many areas was eroding and the pressure intensifying from a surging population, growing at over 2 per cent a year.

While the social and economic ground was shifting, the political system was stagnant as General Musharraf sought to consolidate rather than loosen his grip on power. With his presidential term due to expire in November 2007 he sought to secure a second term ahead of the parliamentary elections scheduled for 2008. This was to pit him in a protracted and fatal confrontation with Pakistan's hitherto quiescent higher judiciary and set the stage for a number of landmark developments that changed the power equation and opened up space for the emergence of newer forms of politics.

The rocky road to Musharraf's bid for another presidential term saw dramatic but vain interventions by the US and UK to help him retain power. Their officials played an active role in negotiations to forge a deal between the General and Benazir Bhutto to enable her to return to the country.[21] Thereafter a series of events shook the country starting with her tragic assassination and followed by elections that returned her party to power and revived the political fortunes of Nawaz Sharif. These events were to culminate in Musharraf's ouster, but not before other developments altered the political landscape and balance of power.

External intrusion in Pakistan's domestic affairs—a familiar theme in the country's life—loomed large in the high drama of the politically charged year of 2007. Washington and London saw political continuity in Pakistan to be pivotal for successfully prosecuting their 'War on Terror' and pacifying Afghanistan. Musharraf's continued leadership was deemed necessary for these goals. But by himself he could neither assure stability nor mobilise public support for the fight against terror. Enter Benazir Bhutto, whose party's popularity and lobbying efforts in Washington had convinced many that she deserved another chance to steer her country towards a moderate course.

The genesis of an eventual Musharraf–Bhutto deal lay in a secret public opinion survey conducted in 2005 by the British High Commission.[22] This found that Musharraf's 'king's party' would lose in the coming elections and the PPP would win a plurality of seats even though the President received the highest approval ratings.

Armed with this survey, Britain's then High Commissioner Mark Lyall Grant and his American counterpart Ryan Crocker held a series of meetings with Musharraf and his political confidante, Tariq Aziz to convince them of a deal with Benazir. She would be persuaded to support another Presidential term for him. In return he would drop long-standing corruption cases and allow her to contest elections. Long discussions at Army House between Musharraf, the American and British envoys, Aziz and the President's chief of staff General Hamid Javed shaped the contours of this deal. They also paved the way for two secret though testy meetings between Musharraf and Bhutto in Dubai.[23]

Although Musharraf had insisted Benazir return after the elections, her calculations changed as she saw his position weaken. When Sharif announced plans to return to the country Benazir decided to do the same. This all but shattered her 'deal' with Musharraf.

Three decisions Musharraf took completely changed the political dynamic and spelt the beginning of the end for him. The first was the bloody assault on Islamabad's Lal Masjid that had been taken over by a motley crew of religious fanatics and militants suspected by the authorities of close ties with al Qaeda. Musharraf's vacillation had allowed the situation to deteriorate to such a point that when Special Forces were ordered—under much international pressure—to storm the mosque, the botched operation left over a hundred people dead. This became the lightning rod for a deadly wave of militant violence that swept the country in 2007. It also unified different militant factions into violent opposition to Musharraf's rule.

Moreover, his increasing dependence on Washington in an environment of growing anti-Americanism further contributed to his unpopularity.

The second decision Musharraf took was in March 2007 to force the resignation of Chief Justice Iftikhar Mohammed Choudhry. A series of public-interest judicial interventions sent Choudhry's popularity soaring and he emerged from this process as a potential obstacle to Musharraf's re-election.

Musharraf tried and failed to force Chaudhry's resignation. He then suspended him and confined him to house detention. This caused a national outrage, with lawyers leading street protests across the country, joined by opposition parties, civil society organisations and other professional groups including women in large numbers. This protest received 24/7 coverage by an energetic broadcast media, which supported the burgeoning anti-Musharraf movement. It coalesced with other groups into an urban coalition united by the desire to see the

General relinquish power. The pro-democracy spirit that animated this constellation of groups was reinforced by popular aspirations for the rule of law epitomised by an independent judiciary. Four months of protests led the Supreme Court to rule that the sacked Chief Justice should be reinstated.

The implications of the judicial triumph by the democratic movement were however ignored by the Musharraf. Flying in the face of public sentiment he went ahead to have himself re-elected on 6 October 2007. While he won the vote from a parliament controlled by the 'king's party' the endorsement from an outgoing legislature rather than a freshly mandated one deprived his election of legitimacy. It also exposed him to challenge by the country's apex court.

In this changed political scenario Bhutto returned to the country on 19 October to a rapturous welcome from her supporters. Sensing how vulnerable Musharraf had become she made increasingly strident political demands in support of Iftikhar Chaudhry and called on Musharraf to give up his army post. The rising pressure—including 'quiet counsel' from Washington—eventually forced Musharraf to relinquish the position of Chief of Army Staff (COAS) and hand over charge to General Ashfaq Parvez Kayani on 28 November 2007.

An increasingly beleaguered and isolated Musharraf then made the biggest political blunder: fearful that the Supreme Court would strike down his re-election, he declared a state of emergency on 3 November, citing a deteriorating law and order situation, and placed thousands of lawyers, opposition leaders including Bhutto in house detention or jail. This action split the establishment (even his own Chief of Staff opposed the emergency) and led to the draining of support from the Army for an increasingly unpopular leader.

This, and the fallout of Bhutto's assassination, sealed Musharraf's fate. He lifted the state of emergency but his political standing had been irrevocably damaged. The general election in February 2008 struck the decisive blow. The official party was routed. The PPP emerged as a single largest party. Sharif's Muslim League came second and triumphed in the Punjab to seize political control of the province. It was now just a matter of time for Musharraf to be forced out. The threat of impeachment by the two victorious parties and their allies and the Army's withdrawal of support left him no option but to quit on 18 August 2008.

Pakistan's fourth period of military rule came to an unceremonious end. Another phase of democratic governance began but under the unlikely stewardship of a man with no experience in government. Bereft of a popular national leader and led instead by a man dogged by his past, the PPP's ascent to power was accompanied by doubts about its capacity to govern at a pivotal moment for the country.

Musharraf was gone but the changes he had helped to initiate outlasted him and transformed many aspects of the country's political terrain. The most significant of those was the emergence of a more politically confident middle class—fostered by the economic growth and consumer boom of his era and empowered by the information revolution that his initially liberal media policies made possible. Indeed Musharraf ultimately became a casualty of his own policies of economic, cultural and media liberalisation—which expanded the space for political activity and provided new avenues for political engagement for better educated and more self-confident urban citizens.

Within months of the February 2008 polls the same political coalition that forced Musharraf from power reactivated itself. This owed itself to the Zardari-led administration's resistance to restoring Chaudhry and sixty other judges who had been removed earlier to their positions. The resistance was born of the fear that corruption cases might be re-opened against top PPP leaders including Zardari. President Zardari held an office that ostensibly provided him immunity from judicial proceedings but he appeared unsure whether Chaudhry and his team of judges would accept this legal position.

Once again a nationwide campaign led by lawyers and members of civil society got underway with thousands pouring into the streets in a virtual replay of what had happened against Musharraf. The movement was joined by Nawaz Sharif and other opposition leaders and reinforced by a groundswell of public support. Widely characterised at the time as the 'black coat revolt' (named after the lawyers' attire) and a 'middle-class uprising' this campaign had a single-point agenda to restore the judges. But it came to reflect wider liberal-democratic aspirations. This was spearheaded by middle-class professionals, with politicians following them rather than leading this extraordinary urban upsurge.

In March 2008 the movement reached a climax. When Sharif threatened a 'Long March' on Islamabad the spectre of confrontation and chaos loomed. In this fraught situation, the Army Chief, General Kayani, and American officials separately intervened to persuade both Zardari and Sharif to step back from the brink. The crisis was defused when

Zardari agreed to reinstate Choudhry and the other judges. In what came to be seen as a spectacular victory for a two-year movement for constitutional rule, this also foreshadowed other political trends. A re-empowered judiciary aided by a more influential media had changed the country's power balance.

Not only did the campaign energise Pakistan's urban society, but it also reflected widespread support for a secular principle in the midst of the country's struggle with militancy. Those who had long argued that the quintessence of Pakistan was its silent but moderate majority could point to this movement and its goals as the latest testimony. This coalition also signified another new phenomenon: professional associations and civil society organisations being able to offer different paths to political engagement and activism outside the framework of traditional political parties and electoral politics.

### Continuity—and Change in the Post-Musharraf Democratic Era

What does this portend for the future? Can the dynamics set off by the extraordinary developments of 2007–08 begin to break the rigid traditional mould of politics that has often hindered rather than helped governance? Can the more active role played by the urban middle class in an environment transformed by the effects of globalisation lead to a significant change in the country's politics and professionalise governance?

If the post-2008 scenario is seen through the lens of electoral politics it would appear that continuity continues to trump change. The 2008 polls returned the PPP to power heading a coalition at the centre and the PML-N in the Punjab. Familiar regional and ethnic parties secured provincial dominance: ANP in KP and the MQM in Sindh.

Members or scions of prominent political dynasties won seats to the national and provincial assemblies. This lineup testified to the continuing electoral ascendancy of the traditional political elite of landowners, urban businessmen, *biradari* chiefs and other local influentials. Parties—with the notable exception of the MQM, which describes itself as Pakistan's only middle class political organisation—still preferred to award tickets to members of this elite rather than from the rising middle class.

The most striking aspect of continuity was the fact that the top two elected positions in government—Prime Minister and Foreign Minister—were filled by scions of the Gilanis and Qureshis, two of southern Punjab's leading landowning families who are also the *Sajjada Nashins* (keepers of the Sufi shrines) of their region, a spiritual role that they use to buttress their feudal power. In one sense Yusuf Raza Gilani and Shah Mahmud Qureshi's ascent to these offices was a reminder of how little election politics had changed since 1947.

By-elections in 2009 and 2010 also showed similar trends: reaffirming the dominance of the country's two major parties and the economic and social constituencies they represented. But this has to be tempered by the fact that a significant chunk of the electorate did not vote for these parties. It did not in fact vote at all.

Nonvoters accounted for as much as 56 per cent of the electorate in 2008. And although fewer ballots are usually cast in by-elections the turnout of 20 per cent (in a Lahore seat in March 2010) and marginally more elsewhere denotes a phenomenon that merits more attention than it has received. This low and declining voter turnout is explained as much by voter disinterest in the political process as their rejection of a narrow choice that reflects neither their interests nor their aspirations.

This gives rise to a central paradox of Pakistani politics today: while traditional politics continue to hold sway in the electoral arena, the political ground is shifting in ways parties have not yet come to grips with. The gap between electoral politics and the rise of new and vocal groups will need to be addressed to align politics with a changing society. If the trend of a falling voter turnout continues this will call into question parties' representative credentials.

A key reason why the rural elite has continued to dominate electorally in spite of greater urbanisation is because constituencies are delimited on the basis of old data and boundary demarcations reflect the distribution of kinship or *biradari* groups especially in the Punjab. As the latter suits the major parties it has rarely been questioned. The 2008 election was conducted on the basis of the 1998 census.[24] There has been no census since. A fresh census and elections predicated on new numbers would shift the balance towards the urban areas challenging the power of politically influential rural families. Until there is a comprehensive delimitation of parliamentary seats (rather than tweaking before elections) to reflect new economic and social realities, electoral politics will continue to lag behind changing national dynamics.

Can closing the gap between representational politics and a changing society invest the polity with the means to tackle and surmount the fault lines that have been identified? Pakistan's checkered history shows that clientelist-based politics have failed to provide the governance that meets the needs of the broad populace. Politics embedded in narrow transactional forms of mobilisation and which reinforce patrimonial structures lack the capacity to address Pakistan's complex challenges.

This is because political clientelism, as emphasised before, has a patronage not policy focus, encourages rentier behaviour as well as corrupt practices. This form of politics places the accent on the local and hobbles thinking about larger, national issues. It is not geared to resolving issues of modern governance or structural economic problems that warrant urgent policy attention. Clientelist politics are in fact dysfunctional to the needs of a modernising society, however uneven that process.

Moreover clientelism operating in an environment of scarcity—in resources and opportunity—makes for uncompromising politics and bitter conflict that serves to reinforce instability and contributes to making the country more ungovernable. But if politics remains trapped in these structures and partisan feuds that are increasingly out of touch with the people how can Pakistan be better governed? Is there a way out of this? While it is important not to overstate ongoing changes—including rising middle-class clout—or suggest that entrenched political patterns can easily be transcended they do open up opportunities.

Pakistan's middle class may well in the years ahead become a significant political force and be able to impact more on national life. Greater 'connectivity' in society is already changing the way people relate to and think about politics and governance. Television viewership for example is estimated to have risen to over 80 per cent of households and this is making people better informed and more aware of their rights.

Some analysts have correctly portrayed these developments as having produced a stronger nation and society in the context of a weaker state.[25] Others including perceptive foreign observers have seen the expansion of the lower middle class to have increasingly redefined Pakistan's national identity. The 'Mehran man', wrote a foreign journalist who identified the growth of a more prosperous lower middle class with ownership of cars like the Mehran (local name for the Suzuki Alto), has a satellite television and is more politically conscious. Their rise signifies 'the shift away from the rural elites once co-opted by colonialism.'[26]

These developments have been driven by the shift in the economic centre of power in the past decade. An important indicator of this is the declining share of agriculture in national output. This has fallen from 40 per cent in the 1970s to almost half that at the end of the 2000s. The urban sector now accounts for much of GDP; rising from 52 per cent in the 1960s to 78 per cent in 2010. These economic realities together with technology-induced changes and the information revolution have made the political centre of gravity more diffuse.

The changing patterns of political engagement are also evident in the growth of a more diverse and vibrant civil society. As space has opened up for newer civil society organisations to emerge these have come to reflect the interests and concerns of a more politically aware urban society and enabled the middle class to press their views and interests with greater vigour.

The fast-expanding broadcast media has offered a new and more potent platform to citizens to raise issues and mobilise opinion. A more effective 'opposition' or 'watchdog' has emerged from within civil society working in tandem with the media. This informal coalition has held the government to account, subjected executive action to rigorous oversight, helped to set priorities and suggested policy courses for national problems that parties have singularly failed to do either out of lethargy or lack of political will.

The national consensus that emerged against militancy in 2009 was forged and sustained in this manner. Government missteps in the energy sector exemplified by the controversial rental power projects as well as instances of corruption were also exposed this way.

While the democratic dividends of these newer forms of political activism are evident, the key question is whether these can go beyond informal, sporadic checks on executive conduct or single-issue political campaigns? Can they morph into a critical mass to transform traditional party structures and politics to find more organised, institutional expression? This will depend on a number of variables. They include a modicum of economic stability and at the very least a halt to the downward economic spiral. This will also depend on the continuity of the political and democratic process, because all too often military rule has simply frozen the status quo and put brakes on its natural evolution, closing potential avenues for political reform.

The role of external actors and their regional policies will be no less important. An inability to find an early political end to the Afghan war along with a prolonged Western military presence in the neighbour-hood can, apart from their other destabilising effects, distort political dynamics in Pakistan in different ways. For example, by reinforcing the ruling elite's dependence mindset that acts as a disincentive for reform and by propping up status quo forces in the name of stability. Another consequence could be to provoke a nationalist backlash that might make for xenophobic tendencies among the middle class and weaken its modernist impulses.

Looking ahead, five possible scenarios can be envisioned. The first one is muddling through, which means more of the same with politics stuck in a traditional, moribund groove, unable to reflect changing political dynamics or shifts in the distribution of economic power in Pakistani society. This would mean little change in both the substance and style of governance, which will translate into a diminished capac-ity to address the country's problems and faultlines. Instead a fire-fighting crisis-management approach will continue but with a declining capacity to reverse the downward trajectory in multiple areas with adverse consequences for the country's stability.

The muddling-through scenario however is untenable for at least two reasons. One, governance challenges have come to a head and are no longer amenable to tinkering or marginal half steps. The more urgent reform is delayed the greater the risk that problems will become intractable. Two, a more urbanised society will continue to press for change, not only because it is unlikely to settle for the continuance of the status quo but also because it has now discovered that organised action provides it with the means to demand greater accountability and responsiveness to their economic and political interests.

The second scenario is another experiment in military-backed civil-ian technocratic rule. But the past record of such an arrangement has already exposed its sharp limits in terms of both legitimacy and perform-ance, so this is unlikely to yield outcomes different from previous ones. The historical experience also suggests that while such an arrangement is temporarily able to halt the national slide, it is unable to resolve the country's deep-seated problems because that requires political consen-sus. The political alignments in this scenario will so closely mirror that in the muddling through model that it will be unable to overcome tra-ditional clientele politics and therefore impede rather than foster the modernisation of governance.

A third scenario frequently peddled by outsiders is social break-down under the weight of a systemic crisis. This is seen as leading to state collapse followed by a takeover by Islamic extremists. This alarmist scenario is based more on fear or ignorance than empirical reality. It ignores that effective counter forces exist in a strong military and resilient society to prevent such a descent into chaos. This scenario can also be ruled out because it rests on an exaggerated view of the strength and cohesiveness of extremist forces. As the military operations in Swat and the tribal areas in 2009 showed—which enjoyed wide political backing—the forces of militancy can be beaten back and dislodged. They have no capacity to take over the state even if they can cause large-scale disruption. The state's ability to reassert its authority has been demonstrated by these actions.

The fourth scenario is one in which one or more of the established parties begin to adapt and adjust to socio-economic changes by making a paradigm shift from patronage to issue-based politics and evolve into modern political organisations. Although Sharif's urban-based Muslim League is perhaps better positioned to do this, it is uncertain whether such a move would be impeded by other characteristics: the party's dynastic or personality-dominated nature, mainly mercantile base of urban support built around clientelist networks of local influentials, and clan or business dynasties.

Nevertheless, Pakistan's existing political parties can, in theory reinvent themselves by tapping the new aspirations of people empowered by social and economic changes. At the very least this means changing their ticketing policies to induct members of the middle class including professionals and giving them a role at the highest levels of party leadership. It also means adopting platforms aligned with the demands of citizens for efficient and purposeful governance.

The fifth scenario is the most exciting for its potential for Pakistan to break from past practices that have been roadblocks in its economic and political progress. This is of a middle class-led coalition spearheading an agenda of reform that aims to make governance more effective and also more accountable and responsive to the aspirations of its people.

The elements of such a coalition for change were to some extent foreshadowed in the lawyers-led movement of 2007–09. That women also powered this middle-class assertion is also significant. Not only were women present in significant numbers in the protests but also the role of female TV anchors in shaping the political agenda underlined the multiple platforms they have been using to make their voice heard.

But while that agitation was a single-issue campaign, in this scenario such a coalition would have to be built on a more durable basis to pursue a broader agenda. It would also have to reach out to and fashion a larger constituency including among the underprivileged. It would need to engage the rural middle class not least because of the large population that still resides in the countryside. It would also have to either ally with a party to induce it to move in the direction of social and political reform, or find a new vehicle that becomes the standard bearer of this agenda.

The prospects of such an outcome may not appear strong in the short term but it would be a mistake to minimise the stirring for change that continues to manifest itself in many different ways and whose expression can be heard daily in the media. This urge for change may yet crystallise into a new politics that connects governance to public purpose. It holds the promise of tapping the resilience of the Pakistani nation and establishing a political foundation for good governance that the country has long deserved but found so elusive.

5

# ARMY AND POLITICS

## Shuja Nawaz

Pakistan is a prisoner of its geography and history. Its strategic location at the cusp of the Middle East, the Persian Gulf, and South Asia
and at the door of Central Asia and China gives it significance on the
regional and global scene. Its proximity to a large and dominating
neighbour, India, shapes Pakistan's foreign and defence policies on the
one hand and informs its domestic debates on the other. The presence
of nuclear weapons and missile delivery systems in both Indian and
Pakistani hands makes this an even more volatile region than in the
past. At the same time, Pakistan's historical wars with India constantly
revive memories of the past and have thrust the Pakistani military into
the centre of decision-making on issues related to its foreign policy,
especially policy toward India (Kashmir, specifically) and Afghanistan,
as well as nuclear matters.

Pakistan's political reins have been effectively in the hands of the
Army for more than thirty-eight years since its independence. The
country is wracked by internal divisions between provinces and
between the forces of modernism and militant and radical Islam. These
continuing wars have created political uncertainty and tumult, leading
to the assassination of former Prime Minister Benazir Bhutto in December 2007. The 2008 elections gave some hope, allowing the leading
political parties, Bhutto's Pakistan Peoples Party and former Prime

Minister Nawaz Sharif's Pakistan Muslim League (N group) to return to power. And the Islamist alliance in the North West Frontier Province was trounced by the Pashtun secular, though quite feudal, Awami National Party.

At the heart of the political maelstrom is the Pakistan Army, probably the best organised group and a veritable political force unto itself, whose every action and hint creates reverberations in Pakistan's polity. Under its present Army Chief, General Ashfaq Parvez Kayani, who has sworn to take the Army back into the barracks, there are many doubters who see the politicians facing a huge challenge in running the country effectively after nine years of autocratic rule by President Pervez Musharraf. They point to the gradual destruction or diminution of institutions: the judiciary, the constitution, the bureaucracy, and the legislature, and to the transmogrification of a parliamentary system of government into a presidential system by Musharraf.

Against this background, cynics point to past promises by other Army chiefs who promised to keep the Army out of politics but ultimately assumed power to fill what they considered to be a political vacuum. The weight of history leans towards a continuing role of the Army in Pakistan's polity, whether overt or behind the scenes. Whatever path it takes, the Army too faces daunting challenges, as it begins the fight against homegrown insurgencies. For it too has changed dramatically over the years.

Pakistan came into being in 1947 as the most populous Muslim nation on the planet but the debate over its national identity has not been conducted democratically nor concluded. It has also yet to craft a stable political system that establishes the supremacy of the civil over the military, as envisioned by its founder Mohammad Ali Jinnah, the *Quaid-i-Azam*. Its political parties too have yet to root their thinking and actions in well-crafted mandates and manifestos or to allow democratic selection of their own leaders: most are run on familial or dynastic lines. Without a powerful base of support in the country as a whole, they have not been able to provide the counterweight to the highly trained and disciplined Pakistan Army that is all too ready to step in when the politicians falter.

Although the Muslim way of life was a motive behind the call for Pakistan, its early political leadership did not give an Islamic blueprint for its political development or goals. The reason for this was that the movement for Pakistan was not an Islamic movement as much as it was a movement by Indian Muslims to seek greater social and economic opportunity for themselves.

## Early Nod to Islam

The Pakistan Army, the largely Muslim rump of the British Indian Army, was also saddled at birth with this paradoxical identity: the symbols of Islam but the substance of a colonial force, quite distant from the body politic of the fledgling state. It adopted, for instance, the numbers 786 for the identification of its General Headquarters in Rawalpindi. In Islamic numerology, 786 represents the Arabic *Bismillah ir-Rahman ir-Rahim:* the invocation that Muslims intone at the start of any action or venture of note. This numerical code was emblazoned on all gateposts and vehicles, as a reminder that this was the Army of a Muslim country. For its badge, it chose two crossed swords holding up an Islamic rising crescent and five-pointed star against a green background.

But the Islamic identity was in name only at that stage. The senior echelons of the Pakistan Army at its birth were still British officers who had opted to stay on and they were succeeded by their native clones: men who saw the Army as a unique institution, separate and apart from the rest of civil society and authority. This was the dominant cultural ethos of the Army at the time. With time, this schism between the cantonment and the city pervaded the Army's thought processes and seemed to guide, as well as bedevil, the military's relationship with the civilian sector. The Army initially retained its largely moderate and secular nature.

Pakistan's history is one of conflict between the underdeveloped political system and a well-organised army that grew in strength as a counterweight to a hostile India next door and in relation to the political system. In the words of former Army Chief, General Jehangir Karamat: 'Whenever there is a breakdown in ...stability, as has happened frequently in Pakistan, the military translates its potential into the will to dominate, and we have military intervention followed by military rule.' But, he adds, 'as far as the track record of the military as rulers in the past is concerned, I am afraid it is not much better than the civilians'.[1] The most recent direct rule of General Pervez Musharraf supports this assessment. While it ushered in a period of false stability and ostensibly opened public discourse, it stunted political growth and badly damaged the ability of civil society to participate freely in the political process. In many ways, Musharraf was a 'liberal autocrat' who lost his liberal bearings.

Over time the Army gained the respect of Pakistan's population for its spirited defence of the country's borders against a powerful India, and continued to attract large numbers of youth to its ranks, but its dominance of the polity of Pakistan eventually produced public questioning of its role. Through coups and largely unfettered access to state resources, the Army won the battle between authority, represented by the state's various instruments of government, and coercive power, reflected in the Army's military prowess, leaving the instruments of state weakened and unable to function even when the military returned to its barracks.

*Power Brokers*

The paradox of power that hobbled Pakistan's slow political development was that as the Army grew in strength and size, it stunted the growth of the political system whose leaders either made no attempt to rebalance the relationship between the state and the centre of power, the Army, or worse, invited the Army to settle political differences amongst themselves. Successive political leaders suborned and eviscerated the vaunted bureaucracy and managed to weaken the educational system, thus depriving the country of alternative governance mechanisms and an informed electorate. The Army meanwhile learned over time to establish patron-client relationships with the bureaucracy and with Islamist parties, whom it used in its efforts to fight internal populist leaders in both East and West Pakistan and fuel the Kashmiri insurgency against Indian rule. The result: a persistent Praetorian state with military or quasi-military rule for over half its life after independence from the British.

Pakistan's existence has been marked by attempts to build a nation but without first building the institutional foundations that are needed to allow a stable federal entity to evolve in a democratic and pluralistic setting. Ethnic and regional strife, sectarian violence, and the persistent intrusion of foreign powers into the region in the pursuit of their global agendas, all have created the setting for uneven political and economic development.

The 1999 coup that brought General Pervez Musharraf to power resorted to legal legerdemain to avoid being classified as a martial law regime but effectively operated under a temporary legal dispensation that allowed it to operate beyond the ambit of the constitution of the country. The 'second coup', in November 2007, by Musharraf effectively allowed him to replace the judiciary wholesale, muzzle the media, and 'win' re-election to the Presidency but in the process he had to shed his uniform, opening the door to a return to civilian rule of sorts.

*Today's Insurgency*

Today, Pakistan is at another crossroads, as a partner of the West in the global war against militancy and terror. And its Army is operating in a changed and highly charged domestic political environment. Its two leading mainstream parties (the Pakistan Muslim League of Sharif and the PPP of Benazir Bhutto) were largely excluded from the political process under Musharraf. Only in late 2007 were their leaders allowed back from exile and re-enter Pakistani politics. The assassination of Bhutto deprived the country of a political counterweight to Musharraf. After decades of conflicts with India, today for the first time, Pakistan's Army is waging a largely futile war against an unseen enemy: Islamist terrorists within its own border.

The eastern front against India is relatively calmer and there is promise of some progress in normalising ties, though that may be illusionary, given the mood swings of governments on both sides. But the western front bordering Afghanistan is awash with insurgent activity spilling over from Afghanistan and also homegrown, involving radical Islamists the Taliban, who are intent on fighting the United States in Afghanistan and putting their stamp on the tribal areas of the Federally Administered Tribal Areas (FATA) of Pakistan.

For the first time in decades, the Pakistan Army is today operating in force inside its own borders. The 'enemy' this time is a growing Islamist militant movement known as 'Talibanization', after the radical right-wing and fundamentalist former regime of Afghanistan. 'Foreign' elements aligned with al Qaeda, the amorphous network of well-trained terrorists begun by Osama bin Laden and operating in the FATA, which form that ambiguous region between Pakistan's North West Frontier Province (now re-named Khyber Pakhtunkhwa or KP) and Afghanistan's eastern border, the Durand Line.

Although the Army has now taken control of the Nuclear Command and Control System through the Strategic Plans Division of the Army

Headquarters, and oversight by the National Security Council and appears to have met the approval of strict Western referees, the fear persists abroad that radical elements in the country or within the military may one day decide to use Pakistan's arsenal of nuclear weapons regionally or resort to proliferation, especially to other Muslim nations. The fuse for a constantly brewing conflict with neighbouring India is the Muslim-majority state of Kashmir, representing the unfinished part of the 1947 partition of British India that has been the cause of at least three wars between the two countries. Whether that fuse will be lit or be snuffed out lies in the hands of the Army.

## The Corporate Army

Increasingly, the Pakistan Army is seen by many as a corporate entity that functions as the most effective political party in the country, protecting its interests, sometimes even at the expense of national interests. A recent study of 'Milbus', or military business interests, by Ayesha Siddiqa in her book *Military Inc.* focuses on Pakistan to characterise the role of the military as 'predatory'. While this study does not ascribe acquisition of assets through legalised means solely to the military (recognising the prevalence of these actions among the civil sector too), it assigns personal aggrandisement as the motive force behind the actions of senior serving and retired military officers. In a country where a culture of entitlement has taken hold since the late 1970s, this criticism is valid against all actors on the political stage, who use state resources for personal gain. Over time, the Army has benefited from this culture and there does not appear to be any move to roll back the system of privileges that higher ranks bring with them.

## Nature of the Army

Pakistanis proudly point to the fact that theirs is a volunteer army with a long historical tradition. In many ways, it is often talked about in the same terms as the Army of its political ally and brother country, Turkey. As author Stephen Kinzer states in his study of contemporary Turkey:

Turks ... feel deep gratitude and a genuine connection to their army. They believe it exists and works for them. But Turks want to escape from its political power, which has become intrusive and suffocating. They have learned the lessons of democracy and now want to live by them.

While many may debate whether Pakistan has truly learned the lessons of democracy, the sentiments in Pakistan today are similar to those in Turkey, whose army is often cited as a model for Pakistan's Army.

Yet there are those who see a closer resemblance to the Army of Indonesia under Presidents Sukarno and Suharto where the *dwi fungsi* or dual functions of the Army became entrenched. Army officers saw themselves as 'saviours of the country' and also developed a role in ruling the country via a revolving door policy under which military officers were given civilian jobs and then moved out to make room for new officers.

Ayesha Siddiqa attempts to quantify the extent of the military's business interests in Pakistan and comes up with a figure of $10 billion. While her calculations are open to dispute and indeed have been challenged by the military, the gist of her arguments raises relevant questions: to what extent is the military's access to state resources crowding out the private sector and preventing expenditure on other more productive sectors, such as health and education? More important, is this model sustainable?

General Kayani early in his tenure realised the need for the Army to revert to its professional roots and began to distance himself from the former Chief, Musharraf. But disengaging the Army from the economy and from commercial enterprises will take time. After he won a second full term, Kayani may have the time to be able to tackle some of the issues that previous chiefs could not, about removing fat from the system and fighting corruption within the burgeoning ranks of the civil-military bureaucracy that the Army has spawned.

## The Wide Footprint

Both the size and nature of the Pakistan Army have a huge impact on the country's economy and society. Rising from a relatively small force at independence, Pakistan today has an army of over 800,000, including over 550,000 regular army and the rest as paramilitary forces or reserves. It is larger than the regular army of the United States. It increased its force size even after losing half the country in 1971 with the independence of Bangladesh (formerly East Pakistan). In the process, Pakistan's security threat from India grew, forcing it to meet India's rapid growth of military might on the one hand and the appearance of the Soviet Armed Forces in Afghanistan to its west in the 1980s.

In 2005, according to World Bank data, defence spending as a percentage of Gross Domestic Product in Pakistan was around 3.4 per cent compared with India's 2.3 per cent, among the highest burdens of military spending in the world. As Pakistan develops and its economy grows, the opportunity cost of its defence-spending will rise dramatically. This is a huge challenge for the regime, as it ponders its political future on the one hand and the nature of the Army that Pakistan needs to ensure its security on the other.

How can one increase development expenditure or have a thorough discussion of the overall budget? The military share of the budget has ranged from 30–40 per cent but it is still kept as a one-line item that is not subjected to any detailed examination or debate in the national assembly. Expenditures on education account for no more than 1.6 per cent of GDP and on health for 0.5 per cent (compared with defence-spending at 3.4 per cent, mentioned above).

The issue facing Pakistan and its military today is one that confronts many other developing countries. Apart from crowding out other more useful investments, the relatively large size of the defence sector and its gradual expansion into other economic activities, as has been the case in Pakistan, Turkey, and Indonesia, for example, creates a host of ills associated with such enterprises: featherbedding or over-employment, heavy and often hidden subsidies, privileged access to scarce resources, and the creation of a powerful and new vested interest group in economic activities: the serving military and ex-servicemen. There is no hard financial scrutiny or supervision of these enterprises or, more importantly, overall defence-spending. This distorts the allocation of scarce domestic resources and retards economic development. Accompanying this economic domination of the political landscape, the Army has also strengthened its political status within the rubric of the state's system of assigning seniority to different representatives of government.

*Army vs. Civil Hierarchy*

Even two-time former Prime Minister Nawaz Sharif shook his head when asked by me if he knew about the application of the Warrant of Precedence during his terms in office. Yet this list that Pakistan inherited from the British and that established the relative ranking of civil and military officials for protocol purposes has been a major path to the rise of the military in Pakistani society and polity. Beyond simple protocol, this list symbolises the relative roles of officials from the civil and the military in the nation's polity and provided a map of their relationships. The Warrant of Precedence issued by the Ministry of Interior from Karachi in February 1950 ranked the top officials of the then Dominion of Pakistan, with the Governor General at the head, followed by the Prime Minister. Notably, the Commander in Chief of the Pakistan Army came in at number fifteen, below, among others, the Judges of the Federal Court, the chief justices of the high courts of the provinces, and deputy ministers of the Dominion. The Chief of Staff of the Pakistan Army came in at number twenty while Lieutenant Generals came in at number twenty-one, followed by General Officers Commanding divisions at number twenty-two, both below federal secretaries and the Governor of the State Bank of Pakistan.

Pakistan changed this warrant de facto when General Ayub Khan, the C-in-C of the Army, was made Defence Minister and afterwards when he took over as Chief Martial Law Administrator and then President. Today the Chairman, JCSC, and Chiefs of Army, Air, and Naval Staff are ranked at number six, while Lieutenant Generals remain at par with federal secretaries at number sixteen. None of the civilian prime ministers in recent decades has made any attempt to change this order. Indeed, all of them have elevated military officers to levels beyond those envisaged by the founders of Pakistan and then complained publicly about the military asserting itself in the polity of Pakistan.

## Protecting its Own

A frequent complaint about the Army in today's Pakistan stems from its overwhelming power and ubiquity in all spheres of civil endeavour, and its ability to operate outside the bounds of normal legal systems. As a result, when its members choose to ignore the law or take it into their own hands, the first instinct of the higher command is to keep the matter out of the public's eye. Concomitant with this tendency has been the growing power and involvement of the Inter-Services Intelligence agency and the Military Intelligence in domestic political and civil issues, as policy advisors and implementers rather than providing policy-neutral intelligence for military purposes or conducting counter-intelligence against the external enemies of Pakistan.

The ISI, a highly effective counter-intelligence entity, came in to its own during the Afghan Jihad but in recent years has often been called a 'rogue' agency or a 'state within a state'. In fact, it often operates at the behest of the government, civil and military, aligning with whatever centre of power is deemed more powerful or supportive of its functions. Because its role has been confused by its masters, who want it to serve not only an intelligence function but also as the crafter and implementer of policy, it takes the heat for some of its actions on their behalf. The civilian Intelligence Bureau, which used to be tasked with internal security matters, is now an appendage of the military agencies. Under the Musharraf regime, it was headed by a retired Brigadier, a personal friend of the Chief of Army Staff and President. Under the previous civilian regime of Prime Minister Sharif, the IB was used for political purposes and even then was headed by a former military officer. Even the Army's own Military Intelligence Directorate was brought in to the political sphere by Musharraf and a number of his predecessors. To make these agencies effective and to remove from them the opprobrium associated with their extra-legal actions, they need to be subjected to public scrutiny and controls not only within the Army's structure but also by parliament.

*Today and Tomorrow*

Over the years the Pakistan Army has been regarded, with some merit, as a highly disciplined and trained force, relying on volunteer recruitment. The Pakistani population traditionally has shown great respect, even adulation, for its soldiers and officers. Many youth sign up voluntarily for service in the Army as officers or soldiers following family or tribal traditions and recently as a means of upward social and economic mobility. Its soldiers and junior officers have time and again shown their abilities on the battlefield. But the leadership of the Army has let down the forces and the country repeatedly. Gradually, instead of respect, feelings of fear and loathing have pervaded the political discourse on the Army and its role in the country's polity.

The Pakistan Army of today, though large and ubiquitous, is ill equipped for low-intensity conflict and has suffered heavily at the hands of well-trained guerrillas that melt into the population. Increasingly, its association with the American superpower that is driving the war against the Taliban in Afghanistan pits the Army against its own tribes. Even the United States is now putting pressure on Pakistan to do more to plug the gaps in the porous and rugged 1,350-mile border with Afghanistan, something that the relatively small US and coalition forces have failed to do from their side of the divide. The terror network has struck back not just in FATA but also against the Army inside Pakistan proper, with a new weapon: suicide bombers. The Army faces a long war on this front.

## Undergoing Change

The conditions that led to the weaknesses of the military system are not just societal but also arise from the recruitment patterns of the Pakistan Army that define the nature of its officer class and other ranks (soldiers). Traditionally, the Army was a predominantly Punjabi force. In British India, three districts: Campbellpur (now Attock), Rawalpindi, and Jhelum dominated the recruitment flows that helped India send some 2.5 million soldiers to fight in World War II on behalf of the British Empire. The North West Frontier Province (NWFP) gradually began supplying troops and officers, as settled areas Pushtun tribesmen joined the military.

Over time, with the provision of waivers for both physical and educational qualifications, recruitment has been increased from the formerly less well-represented areas. Based on separate GHQ data for soldiers and officers, Punjab shows an overall decline in recruitment of soldiers from 63.86 per cent in 1991 to 43.33 in 2005, with Central Punjab outpacing Northern Punjab, the traditional recruitment ground, by 7,500 to 5,000 recruits in 2005. Southern Punjab had 1,800 recruits. The NWFP and FATA increased from 20.91 per cent to 22.43 per cent, Sindh rose from 8.85 per cent to 23.02 per cent, with rural Sindh accounting for the majority of the recruits (5,095 to 2,500 in 2005), Balochistan rose from 0.49 per cent to 1.52 per cent in 2005 with 200 Urban to 300 rural recruits in 2005, and Azad Kashmir and the Northern Areas rising from 5.86 per cent to 9.70 per cent. The induction of 4,000 Baluch soldiers into the Army on October 28, 2010 with the goal of increasing this number to 10,000 is a good sign of national integration.

Comparing the officers commissioned into service during the period 1970–89 to those commissioned between 1990–2006 reveals a change in the relative share of different parts of the country. The Punjab rose marginally from 66.46 per cent to 66.93 per cent, but within the Punjab there are notable changes in the home districts of the officers shifting to the more populous and emerging urban centres of Central and even Southern Punjab. This is in line with rapid urbanisation trends nationwide. These bigger cities and towns are also the traditional strongholds of Islamist parties and growing conservatism associated with the petit bourgeoisie. The Zia period (reflected in the statistics for 1980–89) shows a sharp bulge in all cases, as the Army became a visibly more lucrative and attractive profession for urban youth and a means for upward social mobility.

The importance of the bulge in the Zia period is also underscored by the fact that the officers who joined in that decade are now poised to rise into the General Officer category. When the current group of senior Lieutenant Generals retires, most of whom were commissioned in the late 1960s and early 1970s, the Zia *Bharti* (recruits) will take over the running of the Pakistan Army. Apart from being inducted into the Army during the middle of Zia's Islamist ethos and official fostering of religious ideology and dogma, this group suffered at the hands of the US and Western European embargo of aid to Pakistan and was largely deprived of training opportunities in the West. Not only was it deprived of advanced overseas training during its formative years, but this officer cohort was also denied exposure to the world outside till late in their careers, by which time their worldview had formed and in many cases become entrenched.

The current cohort of senior Army leaders in Pakistan, including the Army Chief, General Kayani, represent the last group of officers who were able to take advantage of overseas training in their early years and were exposed to wider external influences. The effects of such training and exposure are reflected in some of its thinking on national issues.

## Penetration of Civil Society

Another visible manifestation of military domination of the civil sector during the Musharraf period was the re-employment of retired or even serving officers in civil institutions and in the host of military-owned enterprises that provides a longer term of employment for army officers. Even today, military officers head education and training institutions in the civil sector. All the major civil service training establishments, for example, are now under retired army officers. Under Musharrraf, they also headed universities and state-owned corporations. Some 1200 army officers were inducted into key civil slots during the Musharraf period. While military rule or military-dominated rule has something to do with this, the role of the civilian rulers cannot be downplayed, for they have allowed the military free ingress into their domain over the years and indeed have elevated the military presence to the detriment of the civil sector. The earliest moves by General Kayani to withdraw some 300 serving army officers from civilian positions was a good sign of changes in thinking on this front. But many still remain in the civil administration, especially dominating the Ministry of Defence.

### Defending the Homeland

Pakistan's lack of national cohesion on the one hand and its location in a tough neighbourhood dictates that it should maintain a strong defence establishment. However, as assessments by the Army itself have shown, there are different ways of achieving security without making the Army so large and burdensome that it dwarfs and stifles economic development. There are sound military reasons for re-evaluating the nature, size, and organisation of the Army too.

Today, Pakistan has a large conventional army, tasked with defending every inch of its borders: a hostile one on the east against India and in the west against Afghanistan, with a potential for unrest on the Iranian frontier, if the internal insurgency situation in that neighbour's Balochistan province becomes a cross border issue. Internally, the Army needs to reorient its training and force structure not only to cope with external threats but also to combat internal insurgencies, starting with the current situation in FATA. It needs specialised units and training in low-intensity Fourth Generation warfare and to indoctrinate officers and soldiers both in the principles of such warfare, where ideas not weapons alone matter.

### Looking Ahead

It is important for the Army to help create a stable national polity by subjecting itself in practice to civilian oversight and control. It needs to ensure that it does not become the instrument of civilian dictatorship by subjecting itself to wider parliamentary controls and oversights of its operations. This should extend to ratification of senior appointments of the service chiefs, the proposed regional commanders, and the Chairman of the JCSC. It must also be prepared to expose more of its expenditure details to scrutiny by government and parliament.

On its side, civilian government needs to ensure that it follows the constitution fully and does not involve the military in political disputes. As past experience shows, when politicians run to the Army Chief for help, it upsets the balance of the civilian system of government and eventually brings the Army into power.

While the military has an advantage over the civil in employing force, it has a comparative disadvantage in building political loyalty from a civilian base. The reason is their lack of ability to foster and sustain open debate and discussion on key issues. The culture is still largely top-down. Few military regimes have succeeded in constructing mass political; when they tried, they had difficulty in adjusting to open participation by the masses. The military system of orders and obedience does not easily adjust to the noise of democracy and dissent. The Pakistani experience certainly supports these views, although successive military leaders, including Musharraf, have felt that they can buck this trend.

In the face of hostility, Pakistan's defence lies in a smaller, highly mobile, and powerful military, relying on a nuclear and conventional weapons system, and the capability of delivering a damaging riposte. But an even better defence lies in creating a powerful, pluralistic polity residing in a strong economy, built on a society that values education and the welfare of its population.

*The Immediate Challenges*

In the near term, the Army Chief, General Kayani, and his commanders will face a number of challenges, not least of which is the constant tussle for power at the centre between the coalition government headed by President Asif Ali Zardari and the main opposition of Mr Sharif.

His main focus will remain the counterinsurgency campaign and its follow-up in the frontier badlands bordering Afghanistan and in Swat. By all accounts he has pressed his colleagues to move quickly to prepare the logistical ground for anti-terror operations in those areas. But it will be important for him to allow the civilian government to make the political decisions on the use of the Army in that mode and to

define the collaboration with the Afghan and United States governments. This will be a hard transition for an army that has been used to
independently working with its foreign partners under Musharraf.
Equally important will be the need for Kayani to recognise what the
US under the thinking General David Petraeus has come to learn the
hard way in Iraq that counterinsurgency operations are 90 per cent
political and economic and only 10 per cent military.

Ultimately, counterinsurgency campaigns are won by strong policing
and the isolation of militants from the population by good governance
and protection from within communities by strong and dedicated
police forces. The military can only address the symptoms not the
causes of insurgency. Nor is it equipped for counter-terrorism. The
civilian government failed in its first few years to set up an adequate
National Counter Terrorism Authority. It will need to make up for lost
time. Moreover, a strong civil-military partnership will be needed for
post-military operations in FATA and Swat and Malakand. None is
evident as yet.

Without the Army's support, given the current power balance in
Pakistan, the civilian government will not be able to move quickly on
resolving issues with a dominant and potentially hegemonic India to
the east. Kayani recognises the need for peace and open borders but he
is also aware that he cannot move too far ahead of the general public
sentiment. India too will need to show an open-mindedness that has
been absent in its public discourse on Kashmir or open borders. For
many in Pakistan, there is deep-seated fear of India swamping Pakistan
economically and culturally. However, Kayani appears to be a man of
inner confidence, hence the quiet that marks his demeanour. Unlike
Musharraf's one-step forward, two-steps back approach on key issues
relating to India, he could well leapfrog history by taking those bold
steps forward that matter most and stick to them. This would help the
civilian government gain confidence in dealing with India and opening
borders in due course.

With a civilian government in charge again, the role of the ISI will
need to be tempered. The Army High Command will want to favour
greater oversight of the ISI by the civil authority and even parliament,
with the involvement of the military. If Kayani's studied silence in the
episode involving the browbeating in Army House in March 2007 and
subsequent arbitrary removal of the former Chief Justice by Musharraf
is any indication, he could end up favouring a reduced political role of

the ISI, allowing it to concentrate on important counter-intelligence operations. His main focus though will be returning the Army to its professional roots and keeping it out of politics.

As stated earlier, the composition of the Pakistan Army today better represents the society in which it operates than the Army at independence. It is also more professional and better trained than ever before. As it expands its membership into other less represented areas and provinces, it can become a true national army and regain its position of trust and devotion. If it does not, and if the civilian politicians also fail to pay heed to the changes around them, then the rising tide of conservatism may be transformed into a radical Islamist wave that will sweep both civil society and the Pakistan Army, with results that are entirely predictable and not what Pakistan nor its neighbours and friends desire. The longer the country remains under military domination, the greater the chance of state failure.

The latest recruitment statistics indicate that Pakistan's Army today is no longer the same homogeneous force of the past with its limited recruitment base. It now reflects a broader range of the country's rapidly urbanising population. The emergence of new media and public discourse has also challenged the military's ability to control life in the country with an iron hand.

While the Army remains a conservative institution at heart, it is not yet a breeding ground for large numbers of radical Islamists that many fear. Islam though remains a visible force in Pakistani society and in the Army today. Keeping the Islamists at bay remains a daunting task but it need not be used only as a scary scenario to gain Western support. A progressive Pakistan needs to provide opportunities for its citizens to lead their lives without fear of the radical forces of Islam that are vying for power today.

More important, given the dominant role of the Army in Pakistan's polity, if Pakistan is to mature, thrive, and survive as a successful state and a nation, the Army needs to take a back seat and allow the politicians and civil society to make their mistakes and allow the other critically important elements of society: media, businesses, professionals, lawyers, etc., to function unfettered. These are the challenges that both the Army and civil society in Pakistan must surmount through a return to democratic norms so that they can fulfill their promises to the country and win the long war against insurgents and terrorists.

6

# PRAETORIANS AND THE PEOPLE

*Saeed Shafqat*

In Pakistan's post-February 2008 election era two contradictory trends are evident. The first is political continuity in that the third and fourth generations of the traditional feudal, tribal, religious and business families are entering the political arena. Second, the social class origins of the dominant institutions, namely, the military and civil bureaucracy are undergoing change—the recruitment pattern is shifting from the upper middle class to the lower middle class.

This means that the social composition of Pakistani elites is undergoing change. The emerging elite have humbler origins, hold conservative social and political views and reflect authoritarian tendencies in society rather than democratic values. Some elite circulation appears to be taking place but the implications for strengthening democracy and a party system remain uncertain.

For making a transition from a military-hegemonic system to a party-based representative system, elections are an important procedural element to measure democratic aspirations in a society. In Pakistan's case this is severely conscribed by the military-hegemonic system. While holding elections and transitioning to democracy are important, attention also needs to be paid to strengthening the substantive components of democracy: the rule of law, respect and tolerance of dissent and minority rights, religious freedom, cultural pluralism, and freedom of association.[1]

At sixty-three Pakistan is deeply troubled. Its people are despondent as they watch a ruling class concerned more with its own privileges than with serving the public, which has driven the debate in the media that demands a reordering of the state and society. This discourse has also projected competing visions of transforming Pakistan and also urges the restoration of the dignity and self respect of ordinary citizens. This should be putting pressure on the Pakistani elites to mend their behaviour but are they listening?

Three sets of arguments are presented in this chapter. First, the argument that the transformations in elite structures are changing the dynamics of elite interactions, which in turn are shaping the direction of civil-military relations. Second, it makes the case that despite serious limitations the political leadership is striving to sustain a multi-party system and redefining government-opposition relations. Third, that the War on Terror is affecting the prospects of democratic development and contributing to reordering civil-military relations in Pakistan.

## Elites and Democracy

The theoretical literature concerning why democracy flourishes in a society can be summarised into four basic approaches. One, that democracy is a function of the level of economic development; the higher the level of economic development, the better the prospects for democracy. Economic development leads to a vibrant middle class whose interest is in sustaining a free market economy, protecting rights and freedoms and building democracy. Two, that democracy is a function of the level of education; the higher the education levels of a society, the greater the chances of a successful democracy. Third, that democracy is a function of cultural pluralism and work ethics; that a correlation exists between the culture of a society and its chances to create a representative government. This represents the Weberian hypothesis arguing that the rise of democracy in Western Europe was directly linked to the Protestant ethic. Four, that democracy is a function of the elites' ability to bargain, compromise and build consensus on the normative aspects of democracy—rule of law, respect for dissent, protection of minority and women's rights.

It is this author's contention that in the Pakistani case a focus on elites and elite interactions is more instructive in explaining the functioning or absence of democracy as compared to the other three approaches. It is pertinent to ask: do the elites have faith in democracy and representative government? How are decisions made and policies adopted that subvert constitutional norms and resurrect the hegemonic position of the military?

To answer these questions, the chapter begins with the premise that the people and the general public might help in sustaining democracy but constructing democracy is a function of the elites. It is thus important to study the evolution and transformation of Pakistani elites to review the prospects of political stability and change in Pakistan.

In the last thirty-nine years the structure of the Pakistani elites has undergone social and political transformation. At least five complex and contradictory trends are evident. The Pakistani elites consist of the military and civil bureaucracy, leaders of political parties, the religious clergy and members of the emerging electronic media. Among these elite structures, the role of the military is distinctive because it has been involved in the 'construction' of other elites. As Pakistan's history attests, each military regime has patronised a new set of individuals to construct political elites who would adopt the political system that the military favoured. The following section provides an analytic framework and dynamics of emerging trends in each elite category.

## The Military Elite

During the 1970s and particularly since 1979, the social origins of the military elite have undergone change. Generals Jehangir Karamat and Pervez Musharraf and their cohorts were the last of the pre-independence generation. The year 2007 marked the ascendancy of an indigenous post-independence generation at the helm of military decision-making. Until 1971 the base of military elites (Brigadiers to General) was relatively small, totalling approximately 120 officers. Today there is a five-fold increase—the base of military elites has considerably expanded to over 600 officers. However, strategic decision-making is confined to the ten Corps Commanders and another thirty to forty top staff officers. Their ethnic, social class and educational composition have also become noticeably diffuse.

There is considerable debate about the ideological orientation of military elites. During the 1960s and until the mid 1970s, the generals from a rural background and the Potohar—the so-called 'martial' races'—were dominant. But the new breed is more urban and comes from more modest social backgrounds. There is a noticeable shift from the 'Huntingtonian model of military professionalism' to the 'Janowitzian model'—moving beyond a soldierly profession and assuming constabulary functions.[2]

In the post-1979 period, with the exception of the Kargil conflict (1999), the military has increasingly been involved in combating internal disorder, fighting insurgency, designing counterinsurgency plans and, since 2002, increasingly fighting global terrorism; extensively performing UN peacekeeping and policing functions. During this decade more military officers have interacted and been trained at American military institutions compared to the previous three decades. It would be worth watching how these interactions and trainings impact the ideological orientation and professional skills of the emerging elites. What is significant, though, is that the military has already entrenched itself in managing industrial, business, commercial and real estate ventures. To understand the dynamics of this change it is important to recognise the transformation in officers' professional skills, levels of competence and ideological orientation at the rank of Brigadier and not just at the rank of Lieutenant Colonel. The first noticeable trend is that the military has become a corporate entity, its role and relationship in Pakistani society has undergone transformation—it has acquired a new sense of confidence and is tentative and cautious in showing 'deference' to the political leadership. Second, the military elites have been vigorous and aggressive in consolidating control on security, defence and the foreign policy arena.

Is there any noticeable shift in this trend in the post-February 2008 period? The indications are that the military has made a tactical withdrawal because under General Musharraf (1999–2007), particularly after 2001, its policies had become too closely identified with the US-led global War on Terror. The operations that the military launched in 2005–06 in the tribal areas and the North West Frontier Province did not secure adequate political or public support, which had a demoralising effect on the troops.[3] As political and professional costs mounted the military leadership sought to regain the trust and confidence of the people. In the post-Musharraf era the military elites re-assessed and re-strategised their role and relationship with the civilian leadership. They have shown 'deference' to the political leadership, galvanised public support for the military operations against the Taliban in Khyber Pakhtunkhwa and the tribal areas and refurbished its professional image. Occasionally the military high command has also shown measured resistance to American policy. Examples include the opposition to the Kerry-Lugar Bill (which sets out conditions for US assistance) and pursuing nuclear cooperation with China.[4]

Has the Army been able to restore its public image and rebuild trust? Indications are that the return to normalcy in Swat where the military operation in 2009 drove out the Pakistani Taliban has considerably restored public trust. The July–August 2010 floods—which claimed 1600 lives, displaced millions of people in the country and caused extensive infrastructure and crop damage—saw the military take a lead role in relief and rescue operations[5] and in reconstruction. This contrasted with the weak response from political leaders and political parties in managing the catastrophe. All of this means that it is too soon to tell whether the 'deference' the military has shown for the political leadership is a tactical shift or more deeply-rooted.

## The Bureaucratic Elite

The second visible trend is the changing composition, orientation and educational background of the bureaucracy. The Pakistan civil service—the pivotal pillar of governance and until the 1980s the backbone of administration—is now plagued by institutional decline and a crisis of moral authority. Unlike the first three decades after Pakistan's independence it no longer attracts the best and the brightest that instead prefer to go in to business and other private sector professions. Since the mid 1990s recruitment has shifted from the upper middle class to the lower middle class who, for status enhancement and limited choices of personal advancement, still find the competitive examination for the civil service as the only vehicle for social mobility. At the same time, in public perception and in reality, the integrity of the Federal Public Services Commission (FPSC) has been considerably eroded. Since 2001 the Police is the most preferred occupation group for new entrants. The yearly reports of the FPSC show that the choice of service suggests that the change in composition is not conducive to promoting representative government but appears more supportive of authoritarian and clientelist type of political system. At the mid-career level the retention of civil servants remains a major policy challenge.

The past two decades have witnessed the emergence of a new breed of civil servants, 'the Laptop *Wallas*', who are well-versed in information technology and governance issues, have acquired a foreign degree, and are professionally competent and increasingly attuned to the language of the international donor community. Their number is small but growing. This is a genre that has put in ten to fifteen years of service and is under forty years of age. These are the new 'project managers' who are either part of the federal or provincial government or working on a project run by the government but funded by a donor agency. These 'Laptop *Wallas*' get an enhanced salary package and invariably demonstrate professional competence and effective managerial skills. While this is a phenomenon that exhibits individual competence it doesn't necessarily translate in to better delivery of services and implementation of policies for a host of other reasons.

The transition to party-led government has not only accelerated the politicisation of bureaucracy but also widened the gap between the small number of professionally competent and the larger number of inadequately trained bureaucrats. Civil bureaucracy remains the lifeline of governance in the country. But its growing ineffectiveness raises concerns about capacity-building and the prospects for reform.

*The Political Elite*

The third trend is that the elites leading the political parties are becoming more dynastic and their leaders unabashed in giving key party positions to family members. The landowners, tribal leaders, business families, religious leaders, a few professionals and a sprinkling of the middle classes continue to comprise the dominant political elite. But political parties are in decay, organisationally weak, lacking vision and programme and with no leadership succession plan. The current ruling coalition led by the PPP has banded together not on the basis of any principle but on the basis of expediency and desire for power.

Thus the outcome has been progress only in the procedural dimension of democracy because they have acquired power through election. But the normative dimension of democracy—respect for rule of law and core values of tolerance, accommodation and consensus remains weak. Analysts remain sceptical that the political parties, who have done little to promote a democratic culture internally, who pursue power with little regard to the public good, whose leaders are unable to communicate with each other without an 'international broker', can provide an alternative to the military. Yet, despite political uncertainty, the restoration of party-based representative government is a positive development as it aids nation-building and helps in consensus building on issues of national significance. After the 2008 elections, the leaders of the PPP, Pakistan Muslim League–Nawaz (PML-N) and the Awami National Party (ANP) have conducted politics by consultation and consensus building which has created an expectation that they will be able to sustain a coalition government and stable government-opposition relations. This transition towards a multi-party system is still heavily dependent on the role and behaviour of the two larger parties, namely the PPP and PML-N. But Asif Zardari, Nawaz Sharif and Asfandyar Wali are neither visionary nor transformational leaders but pragmatic and deft politicians. Yet this fragile consensus could rupture if the 'international brokers' (mainly the United States) withdraw support, change direction or lose interest in 'managing' Pakistan's internal politics.

*The Religious Elite*

A significant change has been underway among religious institutions and the religious leadership, which represents the fourth trend. The past thirty years have seen the rise of *madrasahs* as a source of social status and political power. It is significant that these *madrasahs* have produced a new breed of religious leaders that claim legitimacy on the basis of scholarship as well as by assuming political roles. These religious leaders are relatively young, mostly in their late thirties or early forties. This religious elite is not necessarily well-versed in religious scholarship but is enthusiastic in instrumentalising Islam; they have increasingly become assertive and uncompromising in projecting their own form of *Shari'a*. In the late 1970s and 1980s state patronage, the Afghan jihad (supported by the US and Saudi Arabia) and trading communities were instrumental in supporting these new religious elites.[6]

This has greatly influenced the Pakistani political discourse as religiosity rather than religious principles and ethics has acquired primacy leading to constraints on social, cultural, political and economic activities. For example, if one were to tabulate the religious congregations that took place during the decade (between mid October and November each year) in Lahore and its surroundings—the Tablighi Jamaat, Ahle-Hadith Conference, Dawat-e-Islami (Maulana Ilyas Qadri) and Jamaat-e-Islami etc., the number would be a significant trend indicator.

These congregations perform symbolic, substantive and ideological messaging functions.[7] The critical question is: to what extent has this religiosity fanned a jihadi culture? There is considerable evidence to support the view that without state connivance and support from the religious elites a jihadi culture could not have flourished in the country. Nor would militancy have become the monster it has. In any case, the main casualty has been the liberal political space which has shrunk as a consequence. The emerging religious elites are self-confident and have emerged as a potent political force.

*The US Factor*

The fifth transformation, which has greatest significance, is the structural presence of the US in Pakistan's policy and strategic decision-making. Because of the close collaboration of the Pakistani ruling elites—military, bureaucratic, political—it has become hard to differentiate between the interests of US policy-makers and these domestic elites. In recent years the US presence has become more pervasive and reveals a strategic shift in US thinking on Pakistan. According to media reports, of the 240 plus members of the 2002 national assembly, thirty-five members had US nationality.[8]

During the 1950s the military elites set the ball rolling with the provision of air space. This later extended to logistical support and then intelligence gathering after 2001. Now almost all aspects of internal law and order, regional relations, counter-terrorism, anti-money laundering and nuclear non-proliferation policies are influenced one way or another by the relationship with Washington. Most ministries (including Interior, Defence, Commerce and Finance) have bilateral arrangements with the US.[9] The commander of CENTCOM (US Central Command) makes regular trips to Pakistan. Invariably, the new CENTCOM chief's first destination is Pakistan.[10]

What all of this means is that the Pakistani state is hard put to make a case for sovereignty so deeply penetrated that its ally is in its affairs. Pakistan's governance issues are no longer internal, as outside help—especially economic support—has become essential to governing the country. Here is the paradox: while power elites collaborate, connive and compromise to consolidate this structural presence it leads to occasional official outbursts against outside interference which deepens the existing resentment against the US on the street. There is in fact a growing disconnect between the elites and civil society which opposes the US role and presence. If this disconnect deepens and spins out of control it could rupture the carefully crafted Western encouraged transition to democracy in Pakistan.

## State Under Siege

As a consequence of these transformations the very structure or institutional landscape of the Pakistani state has undergone change. While one of the key functions of the state is to have a legitimate monopoly over the means of coercion there are various parts of Pakistan where the writ of the state is either weak or being challenged. The Pakistani state is under pressure and struggling with the question of how to accommodate competing interests while expanding its room to manoeuvre and restoring its writ. The critical challenge is whether it will be able to acquire a more legitimate basis of authority through institutions or a credible political leader. The answer to this question lies in understanding the dynamics of changing relationships among the elites and particularly the shifting dynamics of civil and military relations. This complex but contradictory change among Pakistani elite structures is transforming civil-military relations and a new pattern is emerging. The following section will focus on these transformations.

## From Military Hegemony to Coalition Politics

For over sixty years, Pakistan has oscillated between military-hegemonic and dominant party political systems. Persistent and prolonged military rule has entrenched the military in politics, business and even the social sphere in the militarisation of Pakistani society. Despite this, military rule has never gained legitimacy among citizens. In a military-hegemonic system, the military has a monopoly over strategic policy issues and decision-making institutions. It can manipulate and direct the behaviour of political leaders and interest groups in a chosen direction.

The military-hegemonic system functions via three identifiable processes: first, political control through executive orders/ordinances; second, political exclusion through restrictions on parties and other political groups or urban professional groups; and third, the building of a strategic partnership with the United States. Pakistan's history shows that military-hegemony evokes resistance. The longer the period

103

of military rule the stronger resistance movements become in their push for free and fair elections. Upsurges of opposition and demands for the restoration of democracy by civil society groups and political parties have accompanied each period of military rule (General Ayub Khan, 1958–69; General Yahya Khan, 1969–71; General Zia-ul-Haq, 1977–88; and General Pervez Musharraf, 1999–2008). The recurring pattern has been that the collapse or more often a weakening of the military regime paves the way for elections which then facilitate a transition to civilian-led party governments.

It is distressing, however, that with each election opportunities for consolidating civilian-led party governments have mostly been squandered by Pakistan's parties. Political leaders have not been successful in constructing a party system nor promoting democratic values. Construction of democratic values and ingraining a democratic culture in society is a time-consuming and long term project. A culture of respect for dissent, necessary for a representative form of government, has yet to be developed. The tendency has been for parties, when in power, to establish their dominance. In particular, the Pakistan Peoples Party led by Zulfikar Ali Bhutto from 1971 to 1977; the Pakistan Muslim League led by Muhammad Khan Junejo from 1985 to 1988; and both the Benazir Bhutto-led PPP and Nawaz Sharif-led Muslim League (PML-N) from 1988 to 1999, all attempted to establish political dominance by weakening the opposition.[11]

In the post-2008 period there is a significant change. The issue is no longer projecting 'dominance of a political party' but maintaining a balance among multiple political parties. This is the consequence of coalition politics as no party got an overall majority in the 2008 polls. While this balance is evolving the dynamics of governance remain the same—who gets what and how much.

The lack of development of civilian-led party rule does not inspire confidence that the rule of law, good governance and the values of constitutional liberalism will be strengthened. Since the first general elections of 1970, the winning political party has adopted a post-election policy of establishing dominance rather than creating the political space necessary for opposition parties. Each time the military withdrew, political leaders neither paid any attention to reform nor democratising their political parties. Personalities drove the parties instead of organisation or programmes. Both the party in power and opposition parties pursued confrontational politics and failed to build consensus on how to restrict the role of the military in politics. The military, in turn, took advantage of the discord among parties and implicitly encouraged confrontation rather than cooperation. The party in power focused on establishing dominance and excluding political opponents instead of devising ways to restrain the military.

The party system and representative government could not be institutionalised. Thus both the military and the political parties have failed in creating pluralist norms and values necessary for a democratic society. Given this history, why should one expect political parties to behave differently now? Before addressing this question, Pakistan's history in the past decade must be examined.

General Pervez Musharraf assumed power in October 1999, overthrowing the civilian government of Prime Minister Nawaz Sharif. From 2002–2007, Musharraf enhanced presidential power via constitutional amendments and ordinances and ruled by decree, confining the role of the legislature to that of a decree-stamping institution.[12] Until 2006 he maintained a political order that created a semblance of stability, but 2007 was perhaps the worst year in Pakistan's legal and political history. In that year the president misused his powers through a series of unlawful acts: on 9 March 2007 he dismissed the Chief Justice of Pakistan, and on 9 November 2007 he issued a decree firing over sixty judges of the superior judiciary.[13] Musharraf then managed to get re-elected as President in his capacity as both the Chief of the Army and serving general. Lawyers' protests were ruthlessly suppressed.[14]

Under domestic and international pressure, Musharraf announced that elections would be held on 7 January 2008. Political parties responded by demanding the return of exiled leaders Benazir Bhutto and Nawaz Sharif. They also initiated a consultative process which led to the signing of the Charter of Democracy. Through this charter, they agreed to work together to restore democracy, seek independence of the judiciary and curb the political role of the military. On 5 October 2007, Musharraf issued the National Reconciliation Ordinance (NRO), which exonerated political leaders from charges in cases of corruption. This paved the way for the return of these leaders especially Bhutto, which came to be known as the Musharraf-Bhutto deal.

As the election campaign progressed, key electoral issues included restoration of judges, the curtailment of presidential powers, disengagement of the military from politics, recognition of terrorism as a national issue, the use of political engagement rather than force to deal with religious extremists, the transfer of power to elected representatives and the supremacy of the legislature.

On 18 October 2007, Bhutto returned to Karachi to a rousing reception. Although she narrowly survived a suicide bomb at her welcome procession, the bomb killed over 100 participants.[15] Bhutto continued to campaign despite threats to her life. On 27 December 2007, Bhutto met a tragic death in a bombing of her election rally in Rawalpindi. This became a defining moment in Pakistan's history. It sparked anger and a wave of sympathy not only for her party, the PPP, but also other political leaders. Bhutto's death intensified the revolt of urban professionals, which had been simmering since the removal of the Chief Justice in March 2007. The lawyers' protests gave new meaning to the electoral process. Bhutto's death jolted Pakistan and precipitated an expectation among the people that political party leaders would seize this opportunity to construct a civilian-led democratic order.

For almost two decades, Bhutto was centre stage, regardless of whether she was in or out of power, within or outside the country. She showed courage and imagination in confronting military rule and in the process facilitated a democratic transition. By winning two elections in 1988 and in 1993 she assumed the office of Prime Minister, a distinction in Pakistani politics. In the eyes of many, she was poised to win the 2008 elections. Despite her disappointing performance as Prime Minister, the promise and mystique of her leadership persisted. Her ten weeks of electoral campaigning from 18 October 2007 to 27 December 2007 demonstrated how, despite threats to her life, she galvanised the PPP base across the country. In her speeches and interviews, she courageously attacked religious extremists and terrorists. She forcefully argued that democracy was the only alternative to an authoritarian military dictatorship. At the time of her death, she had re-emerged as the most popular political leader in recent history.

Her death was followed by massive protests and violence, creating much uncertainty. Elections were delayed by a full month, yet that did not diminish the PPP support base. The party secured victory even if it did not gain an overall parliamentary majority. Bhutto's husband, Asif Ali Zardari emerged as the strongman of the party. Despite a past tainted by corruption allegations he showed considerable political acumen in the period following Bhutto's death.[16] He has also been adept in consolidating control over the party and has sought reconciliation with the other major parties, particularly the Awami National Party

(ANP), the PML-N, the Jamiat Ulema-e-Islam (JUI) and even the Muttahida Qaumi Movement (MQM). In June 2008, the MQM joined the provincial government in Sindh.

The outcome of the 2008 elections raised expectations that Pakistan would move away from a dominant-party system to a multi-party system where the PPP, PML-N, ANP, JUI and MQM would work as coalition partners. Each has a different agenda and support base yet they seem to agree on the idea of a minimal consensus. The politics of coalition building are not new to Pakistan and alliance-forming coalitions have emerged as effective oppositional groups. In the 1960s, 70s and 80s, politicians built alliances that became formidable opposition movements. This gave rise to both military-hegemonic and party-dominant regimes.

The 1990s saw Pakistan's political parties and their leaders pursue the politics of regime confrontation, elite manipulation and even street agitation, but not reconciliation and consensus. Thus sustaining coalitions that would lead to politics of accommodation, consensus building and national reconciliation remained weak. Today, the multi-party coalition led by the PPP remains tenuous but holds the promise of setting a new direction for coalition politics.

Leaders of the PPP, PML-N, MQM and ANP seem to be learning that politics is about compromise, bargain and consensus. But increasingly coalition parties have begun to reveal three disturbing trends. First, leadership is increasingly dynastic. Second, these parties are a coalition of landed elites, business groups, tribal elders and religious groups. Third, these leaders are driven by considerations of personal gain and power rather than public good and institution building. The leaders are reluctant to change the status quo despite their apparent recognition that their supporters expect them to work together to improve security and governance, provide justice and reduce poverty.

In spite of these worrying trends, there are at least six reasons why coalition politics may lead to the development of a multi-party system. First, even though the three major political parties, the PPP, PML-N and ANP, were quick to build a consensus against President Musharraf, the parties differed in their approach to his removal from office. The PML-N was vocal in demanding Musharraf's removal (and are currently demanding his trial) and the reinstatement of the judges, while the PPP was less confrontational and searched for ways to define a basis for a workable relationship with Musharraf. The PPP also wished to dilute the issue of the restoration of the judges, which strained the coalition, as the PML-N's expectation was that the judges would be promptly restored. When that did not happen, the PML-N's ministers resigned from the coalition and the party withdrew from the government. This jolted the coalition, and the PML-N chose to become the opposition party in the National Assembly.[16] The transition has been bumpy and is likely to remain so.

Second, there are indications of an emerging consensus on the political role of the military. The political parties remained focused on ensuring the removal of Musharraf, who resigned in August 2008. His departure helped define power-sharing with the military rather than establish the supremacy of the civilian leaders. The Chief of Army Staff (COAS), General Ashfaq Parvez Kayani, took a number of steps, such as withdrawing serving military officer from civilian positions.[17]

Third, there appears to be a realisation among the leaders of the political parties that they must refrain from repeating the mistakes of the 1990s when confrontation between the PPP and PML-N paved the way for military intervention. Therefore, despite the confrontational politics and brinksmanship at the height of the lawyers' protest in 2008, the PPP and PML-N leaders kept the channel of communication open. The leadership of the parliamentary parties seemed eager to sustain the dialogue in order to dispel any mistrust. This spirit was best reflected in the adoption of the Eighteenth Amendment which swept away Musharraf's constitutional changes.[18]

Fourth, there is a strong desire among leaders who were either jailed (for example, Asif Ali Zardari) or compelled to go abroad (such as Nawaz and Shahbaz Sharif) to ensure that no one will be forced into exile or put in prison. This has helped improve the levels of trust among political leaders, with the bonds of prison and past exile giving new meaning to the politics of coalition building. Nawaz Sharif conveys the image of a confident but confrontational and somewhat defiant leader who remained focused on the restoration of judges and Musharraf's removal. Zardari appears calm, calculating and somewhat tentative but tenacious and leaning toward reconciliation. Both seem to understand that the politics of mass mobilisation could unleash social forces that can quickly become uncontrollable. For public posturing time and again Nawaz Sharif has engaged in a war of words but shown restraint in taking to the streets in protest.

Fifth, party leaders, despite the serious differences in their approaches, have evolved a consensus in recognising terrorism as Pakistan's own problem, and the need to curb militants, particularly the Tehrik-i-Taliban Pakistan (TTP) and others who provide sanctuary to al Qaeda.[19] This implies that the various leaders are, through consultation, repositioning themselves on how to handle extremism. While still evolving, the retention of a balance between engagement with the militants and the application of force is of critical importance. It is this balance between engagement and force that has improved levels of trust or necessitated teamwork between the civilian and military leadership.

Finally, since the middle of 2006, the US and Pakistan have been reviewing and reassessing their anti-terrorism policies in the tribal areas of Pakistan. In addition to pressing Pakistan to intensify military operations in these areas Washington also initiated dialogue with ANP leader Asfandyar Wali, who was invited to meet with the State Department and CENTCOM.[20] During 2007, US Deputy Secretary of State John Negroponte visited Pakistan three times; these visits were supplemented by those of congressional leaders. Besides conducting regular meetings with Pakistani government officials, the Deputy Secretary and congressional leaders also met the heads of almost all the major political parties. In 2008, the United States embarked on a three-pronged approach to reset its policy toward Pakistan. The Pentagon, Department of State and House and Senate leadership acted in concert to engage the Pakistani civil and military leadership on wide-ranging domestic and bilateral concerns.[21] This has deepened and expanded the scale and interactions of Pakistani and US officials.

In July 2008, President Bush invited Prime Minister Gilani to Washington, and in November President Zardari attended a UN forum on the 'Culture of Peace'. Gilani and Zardari both made efforts to assure US policy-makers and the global community that the civilian leadership of Pakistan was determined to combat terrorism and needed sympathy along with financial support.[22] Relations have continued to grow in 2009 with an official visit to the US by President Zardari to negotiate issues ranging from supporting democracy to socio-economic reform to combating terrorism, a promising sign for the transition to democracy and evolution of a multi-party system.

The PPP-led coalition government is now in the third year of its rule. But corruption, violence and sectarian strife continue to deepen the crisis of governance. Despite significant political achievements including the passage of the Eighteenth Amendment, the seventh National Finance Commission Award (which governs the distribution of resources between the four provinces) and a Balochistan package (economic and other measures to address provincial sentiment after Musharraf's use of force there) the regime's public stock has been low on account of its weak governance and its inability to solve the deepening energy crisis, rising inflation and unemployment levels. All of this has eroded public confidence in party government and democracy.[23] Furthermore its poor and insensitive handling of the worst floods in Pakistan's history in the summer of 2010 could turn out to be a watershed for the resurgence of the military and even the demise of party rule.

Given these changing dynamics of civil-military relations, what are the prospects of democratic consolidation? There are many indications that despite serious crises civil-military relations are undergoing an important transformation. This is borne out by several developments. In July 2010 Prime Minister Gilani ended rising speculation about General Kayani by granting him a three-year extension. This suggests an improved level of trust between the civil and military leadership that is helping to define the parameters of their evolving relationship.[24] In theory and constitutionally this establishes the norm of the supremacy of civilian leadership. The past had seen a tussle between the president and the prime minister over who has the right to appoint the Chiefs of the Armed Forces and the Chairman of the Joint Chief of Staff. Although the constitutional position on the issue has always been clear both Benazir Bhutto and Nawaz Sharif as prime ministers found limits to their authority in this regard. The prime minister and the president should through mutual consultation develop a consensus on the selection of service chiefs.[25] In reality, they have quarrelled over this matter. This reflects the weakness of the civilian leaders and the power of the military.

However, once the Chief of Army Staff is selected he assumes the role of an arbiter, sometimes broker, and of course a potential intervener in the country's political process. What role the Chief of Army Staff (COAS) chooses to play depends on three factors: his personal orientation, political circumstances and the corporate interests of the military. Seen from this perspective General Kayani has been careful and discreet so as to reveal little about his political or ideological beliefs except on national security issues. He went public in stating that the Pakistan military is 'India-centric' in its orientation and approach.[26] Nationally and internationally he is recognised as a 'professional soldier'. In 2009 *Time* magazine declared General Kayani as the 'most influential General in the world'.[27] Officials who have worked with General Kayani convey that he is calm, calculating, and prudent and keeps his cards close to his chest.

General Kayani earned Musharraf's trust and confidence after he successfully investigated the assassination attempts on the former President in 2003 with professional competence and utmost discretion. Consequently, he was appointed as the head of the Inter-Services Intelligence (ISI) in 2004 and held that position till 2007. Earlier in his career he had briefly served in the office of the military secretary to Prime Minister Benazir Bhutto. This position provided him an opportunity to witness first hand political elite interactions and decision-making. Given his association with Musharraf and Bhutto he was ideally positioned to play a pivotal role in their 'reconciliation' in 2007. He also demonstrated the courage of his conviction on 9 March 2007 when Musharraf and his close aides read out a charge sheet to Chief Justice (CJ) Iftikhar Mohammed Chaudhry, asking him to step down. Kayani was part of that team but remained silent throughout the meeting and refused to present an affidavit to the Supreme Court in the reference Musharraf had filed against the CJ and others.[28]

Kayani has shown vigour and determination in conducting effective counter-terrorist operations in FATA and Khyber Pakhtunkhwa. In the post-Musharraf phase General Kayani had also carefully rebuilt the image of the military and strived to win the trust of his troops and the people. For example, as COAS, one of his first acts was to raise the salaries of Junior Commissioned Officers (JCOs). Furthermore he announced that the Army will not interfere in politics and political decisions. He has cultivated an image of staying aloof from politics but on issues of security and foreign policy—particularly the strategic dialogue with the US—he has taken charge. In this regard he took the unprecedented step of calling and presiding over a meeting of the federal secretaries at General Headquarters (GHQ). This earned him the distinction of being the first and the only COAS who summoned a meeting of the country's top civil servants in the presence of a civilian democratic government.[29]

Simultaneously, Kayani has played a key role in moving the US-Pakistan strategic dialogue forward, while gradually gaining American trust and confidence. He has become the person who most important officials in the Pentagon, the White House and NATO want to communicate with when deciding matters relating to Afghanistan and other regional security issues. A different kind of example of his power is provided in the immediate aftermath of the terrorist attack on Mumbai. President Zardari wanted to send the ISI head to India to calm down New Delhi but Kayani swiftly vetoed that. The person calling the shots on policy towards India is Kayani.[30]

It is evident from this that on defence and foreign policy the military retains hegemony. But this is also a reflection of the lack of competence and ability on the part of the civilian leaders in this sphere. A different kind of interpretation would argue that by allowing this space on external policy to the COAS the civilian leadership is delineating policy arenas where it accepts a legitimate military voice.

## Conclusion

Against this backdrop the future of civil-military relations holds both the promise of change and the peril of business-as-usual. Continuity is indicated on strategic policy issues on which military hegemony will likely persist. This means that the military can be expected to play the decisive role in navigating defence and foreign policy and determining strategic decisions, while the civilian government will handle the economy and issues of 'low' politics at home. An optimistic interpretation could be that civil-military relations are improving because an improvement in the trust level between the civilian and military elites reduces the possibility of a military coup. So while the military's primacy in decision-making on strategic issues is conceded by the civilian regime, in return it would expect the military to support the political government and enable it to complete its parliamentary term.

In the short term a system of power sharing seems to be evolving rather than military subordination to civilian supremacy. At this stage the political leaders may concede that power sharing is a short term but unavoidable goal. The hope is that as the electoral process becomes a regular one and political parties pursue internal reform to democratise their internal structures they may over time be able to provide a viable alternative to military hegemony. This would happen, if the political elites and political parties demonstrate the will to strengthen the party system; improve governance and rule of law; prioritise citizen welfare policies and the media and judiciary band together in promoting accountability and dispensing social justice. However, until then civil-military relations in terms of power and authority will remain skewed even if there is greater mutual trust between them.

# 7

# IDEOLOGICALLY ADRIFT*

## Ziad Haider

What role has Islam played in Pakistan's evolution? Has the issue of religion that has been used for multiple objectives—from nation build-ing to strategic security—produced a deadly blowback that is now confronting Pakistan with unprecedented challenges? This chapter addresses these vital questions by providing a political and cultural understanding of the role of ideology in Pakistan to argue that its via-bility as a state depends in large part on its ability to develop a new and progressive Islamic narrative. The question is not whether religion has a role but how it can be channelled as a force for progressive change.

### Contested Idea

Pakistan was a contested idea at its birth in 1947. Having lost their privileged status when the British supplanted India's Mughal rulers, Indian Muslims divided in responding to their deepening cultural and political insecurity under colonial rule. Culturally, a schism emerged

* Based on the author's *The Ideological Struggle for Pakistan*, from the essay series by the Herbert and Jane Dwight Working Group on Islamism and the International Order, with the permission of the publisher, Hoover Institution Press. © 2010 by the Board of Trustees of the Leland Stanford Junior University.

between the Aligarh tradition, which balanced selectively embracing Western notions of modernity and learning with retaining an Islamic identity, and the Deoband tradition, which rejected Western mores as a deviation from religious orthodoxy. Politically, as the independence struggle gathered pace, Muslims divided into three main groups. The first, affiliated with the Indian Congress Party, advocated territorial nationalism. The second was affiliated with the All-India Muslim League led by Mohammad Ali Jinnah, which contended that Muslims had a special identity that would be erased in a Hindu-majority India—an argument that evolved from calls for political safeguards and a federation to an eventual demand for a separate Muslim homeland. The third included the religious parties that shared the Muslim League's concerns but opposed a separate Muslim homeland on the grounds that the *ummah* should not be divided by the dubious concept of a nation-state. Ultimately, the Muslim League prevailed and Pakistan was carved out of the subcontinent.

The irony of the dedicated struggle for Pakistan was the ambiguity over the end goal. As Ayesha Jalal has argued, the lack of consensus over Pakistan's ideological and territorial contours was vital to its establishment:

Jinnah's resort to religion was not an ideology to which he was ever committed or even a device to use against rival communities; it was simply a way of giving a semblance of unity and solidity to his divided Muslim constituents. Jinnah needed a demand that was specifically ambiguous and imprecise to command general support, something specifically Muslim though unspecific in every other respect. The intentionally obscure cry for a 'Pakistan' was contrived to meet this requirement.[1]

This ambiguity played out in the pivotal 1945–46 elections in which the Muslim League was able to demonstrate that it was the sole representative of India's Muslims and Jinnah the sole spokesman. Jinnah and many of the Muslim League's leaders, though secular in their personal orientation, invoked Islam to make their case for an undefined Pakistan to Muslim voters.[2]

Proponents of Jinnah's secular vision for Pakistan often point to his eloquent speech delivered before the Constituent Assembly three days before independence on 11 August 1947:

You are free, free to go to your temples; you are free to go to your mosques or to any other places of worship in this state of Pakistan. You may belong to any religion or caste or creed that has nothing to do with the business of the state.... In the course of time Hindus would cease to be Hindus and Muslims would cease to be Muslims, not in the religious sense, because that is the personal faith of each individual, but in the political sense as citizens of the State.[3]

The speech's inclusive message, however, has been diluted with time.[4]

The climax of this ideological debate in Pakistan's early days was the adoption of the Objectives Resolution in 1949. The Resolution laid out the principles for Pakistan's future constitution, notably calling for a state wherein 'the principles of democracy, freedom, equality, and tolerance as enunciated by Islam shall be fully observed' and 'the Muslims shall be enabled to order their lives in the individual and collective spheres in accordance with the teachings and requirements of Islam as set out in the Holy Quran and Sunnah'.[5] The Resolution injected religion into the core of Pakistan. Such a formal association between Islam and Pakistan was in many ways natural but it was the subsequent manipulation of religion for political and strategic ends that sadly emerges as a central theme in Pakistan's Islamic narrative.

In reflecting on the rampant religious extremism and sectarianism wracking Pakistan today, many liberal Pakistani commentators wistfully point to how far Pakistan has deviated from Jinnah's original vision. But Jinnah was ultimately part of a movement that was shaped by circumstances and alliances—one that evolved from fashioning an equitable postcolonial constitutional arrangement for India's Muslims to securing an independent nation. Indeed, throughout the movement, there never was a uniform vision of Pakistan or the role of Islam. This means that Pakistan was and remains a product of contesting visions.

*Fortifying a Nation*

After independence, Pakistan's leadership was faced with the daunting task of defending and consolidating a fragmented state against real and perceived external and internal threats. The Pakistan that emerged from the ravages of Partition consisted of an ethnically fractured West and East Pakistan divided by a thousand miles of Indian territory. Many Muslims had remained in India, undercutting the two-nation theory of Muslims needing a separate homeland. Looming over this ideological and territorial vulnerability was the conviction that an irrevocably hostile India was bent on unraveling Pakistan, as it continued to stonewall on the delivery of Pakistan's vital and due share of resources inherited from the British. It was in this atmosphere of insecurity that Pakistan's rulers embarked on the process of using Islam to fortify a nation.

An early manifestation of this was to leverage the notion of *jihad* in shoring up the country's borders. Squaring off against India over the disputed territory of Kashmir in the hour of their separation, officers in the Pakistan Army involved in the Kashmir operation of 1947–48 invoked jihad to mobilise tribesmen from the frontier and send them to raid and seize Kashmir; the government in turn called on religious scholars to issue supportive *fatwas* or religious decrees. This was to be the beginning of a longstanding state policy of using religiously motivated proxies to asymmetrically secure political and territorial gains vis-à-vis a seemingly hegemonic India.

The notion of jihad has historic roots in Pakistan's frontier in particular. In *Partisans of Allah: Jihad in South Asia*, Ayesha Jalal describes the Deoband-inspired Sayyid Ahmad's jihad against the Sikh empire in his quest for an Islamic state in the northern areas as a landmark event.[7] In the early days of Pakistan, the Army—though defined by a secular British military tradition—tapped these jihadi sentiments as part of its campaigns. Unsuccessful in wresting away Kashmir in 1948, the Army again sent irregular forces into Kashmir in 1965 only to fight an all-out war resulting in a stalemate.

Just as Islam was leveraged in response to the external threat of India, it was also used to tackle internal challenges, from discrediting political adversaries to unifying a divided nation. As early as 1953, Jinnah's vision of a pluralistic Pakistan was challenged by street protests calling for a declaration that Ahmadis—followers of an alleged nineteenth-century messiah called Mirza Ghulam Ahmed—were non-Muslims. The protests were orchestrated in part to destabilise the federal government by calling for the resignation of Pakistan's first foreign minister, Sir Zafarullah Khan, an Ahmadi.

It was in this explosive environment that the 1954 Munir Report, authored by two justices of the Federal Court, was issued, sounding perhaps the most far-sighted warning about ideological dangers. Calling on the government to refrain from declaring Ahmadis as non-Muslims, the report cautioned against the notion that Pakistan was an Islamic state and that the state should define who is a Muslim; this would only foment charges of apostasy, divide the nation, and be inconsistent with Jinnah's vision of an inclusive polity:

The result of this part of inquiry, however, has been anything but satisfactory and if considerable confusion exists in the minds of our *ulama* [religious scholars] on such a simple matter, one can easily imagine what the differences on more complicated matters will be.... Keeping in view the several different definitions given by the *ulama*, need we make any comment except that no two learned divines are agreed on this fundamental.

These words were to fall on deaf ears. In 1974, Ahmadis were officially declared non-Muslims through a constitutional amendment.

In a similar strain, during the first indirect presidential elections held under Ayub Khan in 1965, Khan's allies sought to discredit his adversary, Fatimah Jinnah—the Quaid's sister—by having a *fatwa* issued that Islam did not allow a female head of state—a refrain that would echo decades later about Benazir Bhutto—Pakistan's first female prime minister. Such attempts to Islamically delegitimise political players and segments of civil society—be it Ahmadis or later the Shi'a—has assumed an increasingly lethal undercurrent in Pakistan as many militants pave the way for killing their fellow Muslim citizens through *takfir* or declaring them as non-Muslims.

A more legitimate challenge facing Pakistan's political and military elite was how to unify a fractured state. For many, despite their secular orientation, the answer lay in the systematic promotion of an Islamic ideology as part of a top-down nationalist project.[10] Upon assuming power, Ayub Khan in a 1960 *Foreign Affairs* article spoke of his intention of 'liberating the basic concept of our ideology from the dust of vagueness.'[11] Elaborating in his autobiography on a people's need for an ideology, he stated, 'they will have tremendous power of cohesion and resistance. Such an ideology with us is obviously Islam. It was on that basis that we fought for and got Pakistan, but having got it, we failed to define the ideology in a simple and understandable form....'[13]

The execution of this thinking was parochial as illustrated in the education sector. As taught in schools, the history of Pakistan was no longer a product of a postcolonial constitutional power-sharing struggle or the subcontinent's syncretic and shared Hindu-Muslim heritage, but an almost inexorable culmination of the arrival of Islam on the subcontinent. Notions of implacable Hindu and Indian hostility were reinforced.

But Ayub Khan's vision of Islamic ideology did not go unchallenged. In the spirit of the Munir Report, Huseyn Shaheed Suhrawardy, who briefly served as Pakistan's prime minister from 1956 to 1957, argued

117

that an emphasis on ideology, 'would keep alive within Pakistan the divisive communal emotions by which the subcontinent was riven before the achievement of independence.'[14] Instead, he argued for a Pakistan with 'a durable identity between government and people derived through the operation of consent'—a vision that has yet to prevail.

## Ideology and Integrity

Under Ayub Khan's military successor, General Yahya Khan, developing an Islamic identity for Pakistan's unity and defence remained paramount. Brigadier A. R. Siddiqui, head of military Inter-Services Public Relations, described the ideology and rhetoric espoused as follows:

Expressions like the 'ideology of Pakistan' and the 'glory of Islam' used by the military high command were becoming stock phrases.... They sounded more like high priests than soldiers when they urged men to rededicate themselves to the sacred cause of ensuring the 'security, solidarity, integrity of the country and its ideology.'[15]

Seeking to retain power, Yahya Khan utilised the intelligence agencies to orchestrate attacks by Islamic parties against the two major political parties—the Awami League and the Pakistan People's Party. Both were accused of being un-Islamic for their secular and socialist beliefs. Suspicious of its own Islamic political allies such as the Jamaat-e-Islami, the regime even encouraged the emergence of other countervailing Islamic groups. As political and ethnic tensions boiled over in East Pakistan, the military launched a campaign that descended into a full-blown civil war leading to Indian intervention.

The war in 1971 was framed as a struggle for Pakistan's Islamic identity, threatened now by the Bengalis of East Pakistan, who though Muslims, were periodically depicted as corrupted Muslims and in collusion with Hindu India. As in previous wars, religious zeal was systematically employed to motivate soldiers and frame the cause. General A. A. K. Niazi, who led the forces in East Pakistan, invoked the 'spirit of jihad and dedication to Islam' that would enable the defeat of an enemy 'whose goal and ambition is the disintegration of Pakistan.'[16] The Jamaat-e-Islami was enlisted in East Pakistan in helping launch two paramilitary counterinsurgency wings. The enemies of Pakistan, according to Yahya Khan, were doing 'their level best to undo our dear country[,] ... a people whose life is pulsating with love of the Holy Prophet.... [E]veryone of us is a *mujahid* [holy warrior].'[17]

The 1971 war ended in catastrophe for Pakistan. East Pakistan separated, becoming Bangladesh, while nearly eighty thousand Pakistani soldiers became prisoners of war. Pakistani fears of India's hegemonic designs deepened; Ayub Khan and Yahya Khan's use of Islam to promote Pakistan's ideology and integrity failed; the rhetoric masked military interventions that weakened civilian rule, papered over legitimate ethnic grievances, and resulted in the loss of over half the nation. As in the wake of previous crises, an invaluable opportunity arose in the ashes of defeat to create a new national narrative.

## Bhutto's Islamic Socialism

The task of defining this new narrative fell to Zulfikar Ali Bhutto—the first civilian politician to rule Pakistan after nearly fifteen years of army rule. Having formed the Pakistan People's Party (PPP) only four years earlier, Bhutto ascended to power on a populist platform embodied in the slogan 'roti [bread], kapra [cloth], makan [house]'. Like his predecessors Bhutto had to wrestle with questions of Islam and ideology. Some contemporary commentators pointed out that the separation of East Pakistan had resulted in a more compact entity where Islam was presumably no longer needed to bind the state. Unity could have derived from a robust democratic process accommodating political and ethnic differences and looking toward 'geological, geographic, ethnic, and historic grounds for regarding the Indus Valley and its western and northern mountain marches as a distinct national unit separate from the rest of South Asia.'[18] The Islamic parties, however, vociferously attacked Bhutto and his socialist ideology as a threat to Islam. Bhutto settled on the concept of 'Islamic socialism' as his defining manifesto to stave off his critics on the religious right and to create a new national narrative that promisingly leveraged core Islamic principles of justice, equity, and poverty alleviation to tackle a developing nation's fundamental socio-economic challenges.

Yet with the passage of time Bhutto's regime adopted a more conservative bent—a posture fuelled by his insecurity vis-à-vis the military and his authoritarian tendencies. Bhutto introduced a ban on alcohol and gambling and made Friday a non-work day. In 1974, unwilling to stand up to street protests by the Islamic parties against Ahmadis he supported a constitutional amendment that declared Ahmadis non-Muslims. For the first time in the country's history, a minister for religious affairs was appointed to the central cabinet. Eager to burnish his Islamic credentials, in 1976, Bhutto invited the Imams of the Prophet's mosque in Medina and the mosque at the Ka'ba—two of Islam's holiest sites—to visit Pakistan.

Bhutto's Islamic orientation was also reflected in his foreign policy. In 1974, Bhutto hosted a major Organisation of Islamic Conference meeting in Lahore, reorienting Pakistan away from South Asia and toward the Middle East. Following India's allegedly 'peaceful nuclear explosion' in 1974, Bhutto launched Pakistan's nuclear weapons program, rhetorically declaring, 'There's a Hindu bomb, a Jewish bomb and a Christian bomb. There must be an Islamic bomb.'[19] In light of Pakistan's unsettled border with Afghanistan that divided a restive ethnic Pashtun population between both countries, the Bhutto government also began to support two Afghan Islamist militias to gain leverage over Kabul on the border issue: Burhanuddin Rabbani's Jamiat-e-Islami and Gulbuddin Hekmatyar's Hizb-e-Islami. The decision was to have far-reaching consequences. Both militias played a key role in the uprising against the Soviets.

Ultimately, Bhutto's promise of Islamic socialism was compromised by narrower political and foreign policy objectives as he failed to fully realise a new and progressive national ideology. In the wake of rampant street agitation led by the Islamic parties in conjunction with elements in the military, General Zia-ul-Haq deposed him. It was Zia who would initiate the wholesale process of converting Pakistan to an Islamic state.

## Islamisation of Pakistan

General Zia's decade in power was a setback for a faltering democratic process and ushered in an era of religious obscurantism that affected every facet of domestic life and foreign policy. In his very first speech as Chief Martial Law Administrator after removing Bhutto from power, Zia, who was sincerely devout, described himself as a 'soldier of Islam' and spelled out his vision: 'Pakistan, which was created in the name of Islam, will continue to survive only if it sticks to Islam. That is why I consider the introduction of Islamic system as an essential prerequisite for the country.'[20] As such, in contrast to Ayub Khan and Yahya Khan, who saw Islam as part of an ongoing and overarching nationalist project, Zia saw Islam as part of a revolutionary process to overhaul Pakistan.

The domestic impact was manifold. Beginning with the Army, Zia, upon being appointed Army Chief by Bhutto, changed the slogan of the Pakistan Army to '*Iman* [faith], *Taqwa* [piety], and *Jihad fi Sabil Allah* [jihad for the sake of God]'. Officer evaluation forms included a box of comments on an officer's religious sincerity. Proselytising groups such as the Tablighi Jamat linked to the Deobandi tradition enjoyed greater access to military officers and civil servants. Like his military predecessors, Zia cynically used the Islamic parties as a counter to his civilian political foes but also extended them unprecedented political patronage, initially appointing a number of Jamaat-e-Islami members to head key ministries. In the process, Zia also politicised other Islamic parties that had largely remained apolitical and empowered them. Along with separate electorates being introduced for non-Muslims, registration criteria that excluded most secular parties were introduced during elections.

Zia's Islamisation also encompassed Pakistan's judicial system. The government constituted provincial Shariat benches at the High Court level and an appellate Shariat Bench at the Supreme Court level tasked with deciding if any parliamentary law was Islamic or not and whether the government should change them. Particularly troubling was the introduction of the Hudood Ordinance based on a distorted under-standing of Quranic injunctions and introducing punishments such as flogging, stoning and amputation (albeit punishments that the state never applied). The ordinance's most controversial application was and remains the imprisonment of female rape victims on the grounds of adultery. An effort was also launched to Islamise the education sector. In 1981, the University Grants Commission issued the following direc-tive to prospective textbook authors:

...to demonstrate that the basis of Pakistan is not to be founded in racial, lin-guistic, or geographical factors, but rather in the shared experience of a com-mon religion. To get students to know and appreciate the Ideology of Pakistan, and to popularize it with slogans. To guide students towards the ultimate goal of Pakistan—the creation of a completely Islamicized State.[21]

The underlying motive behind these various genuine and cosmetic 'reforms' was a moral zeal that animated Zia. Islam was no longer just an overarching ideology to harness to unify and to defend the state; it was the road to salvation. Decrying endemic corruption and economic ills in Pakistan in a 1979 interview, Zia stated: 'In the last thirty years in general but more so in the last seven years there has been a complete erosion of the moral values of our society.... Islam from that point of view is the fundamental factor.'[22]

Under Zia a similar moral zeal characterised Pakistan's central foreign policy preoccupation in the 1980s: the Soviet invasion of Afghanistan. During Zia's rule, Pakistan became a staging ground for the war against the Soviet Union, which was characterised as jihad. In this effort, the Pakistani military leveraged the proxy Islamic groups it had backed since the 1970s, providing them with arms and financing in coordination with the US and Saudi Arabia, among other states. Hekmatyar's Hizb-i-Islami, in particular, was a favourite of the Inter-Services Intelligence (ISI), which spearheaded the covert operation in Afghanistan.

Ultimately, Zia's goal in transforming a limited Islamist rebellion into a full-scale jihad was to extend Pakistani influence into Afghanistan in light of its historic territorial concerns, secure significant assistance by helping the US bleed its Cold War adversary, and allegedly 'to make Pakistan the source of a natural Islamic revolutionary movement, replacing artificial alliances such as the Baghdad Pact.' 'This would be the means,' continued one of Zia's confidants in describing his vision, 'of starting a new era of greatness for the Muslim nations of Asia and Africa.'[23]

In pursuing these strategic goals, the Zia regime with international aid systematically cultivated a virulent strain of Islamist ideology in Pakistan. The ISI made right-wing Islamic parties such as the Jamaat-e-Islami and Jamiat Ulema-e-Islam key partners in recruiting among the millions of Afghan refugees in Pakistan and students at religious schools or *madrasahs*—lionising those who volunteered as *mujahideen* fighting in the name of God. In the process, these parties developed extensive networks throughout Pakistan and deepened their influence. Students from impoverished backgrounds at the *madrasahs* were taught an obscurantist understanding of Islam with no modern subjects, making them easy prey for their handlers. Meanwhile, Saudi and United States funding directly facilitated this indoctrination. From 1984 to 1994, for example, the United States Agency for International Development gave a $51 million grant to the University of Nebraska-Omaha to develop textbooks filled with violent images and militant Islamic teachings as part of a covert effort to inspire anti-Soviet resistance.[24] Zia further opened Pakistan's doors to volunteers from all over the world who participated in the jihad in Afghanistan and who estab-

IDEOLOGICALLY ADRIFT

lished offices, raised funds, and issued statements on Pakistani soil. Pakistan became the epicentre of a global jihad movement.

Alongside this jihadi culture, Pakistan under Zia witnessed an unprecedented rise in sectarianism—once again triggered by both external and internal factors—which has claimed tens of thousands of lives in Pakistan. Externally, in the wake of the 1979 Islamic revolution in Iran, the Khomeini regime began exporting its revolutionary message across the Muslim world. Neighbouring Pakistan became a battleground in a 'transplanted war' between Iran and Saudi Arabia that sought to limit Shi'a influence—a struggle that violently played out among a hydra of sectarian groups.[25] On one side was the Iranian-backed Tehrik-i-Nifaz-i-Fiqh-i-Jafria (Movement for the Implementation of Shiite Religious Law); on the other were Sunni extremist groups such as the Sipah-e-Sahaba, ideologically equipped with *fatwas* issued by Deobandi seminaries in Pakistan and India declaring the Shi'a as apostates. Sipah-e-Sahaba's political demand was that the state should declare the Shi'a—15–20 per cent of Pakistan's population—non-Muslims through a constitutional amendment, as done with the Ahmadis.

The cumulative effect of the Zia years in Pakistan was not just a wholesale Islamisation of the Pakistani state to varying degrees but also the explosion of a jihadi and sectarian culture in response to external forces that were nurtured for political and ideological reasons. It was in the throes of this period that Pakistan's drift into extremism began.

*Decade of Instability*

Upon the demise of General Zia in 1988, Pakistan entered a tumultuous decade of political instability, near bankruptcy, international isolation, and a hardening jihadi culture—a period during which it remained dangerously adrift.

The decade saw four consecutive democratic governments—alternating twice under Benazir Bhutto and Nawaz Sharif—come crashing down before any could finish a full term. The jostling among Pakistan's power troika—the Army Chief, the president, and the prime minister—kept Pakistan at the brink of a political precipice. Although Bhutto and Sharif's governments were discredited in large part by their own corruption and malfeasance, as in the past, the intelligence services in collaboration with a range of Islamic parties and other elements undermined them and the democratic process. The prime example was during the 1988 election that brought Bhutto to power. During this election, the ISI-backed Islami Jamhoori Ittehad (IJI) bitterly attacked Bhutto on the grounds that Islam did not permit a woman to serve as a head of state and that she would be unable to safeguard the country's ideological and national security interests.

Yet Pakistan's mainstream politicians were not immune to such manipulation either. In 1999, Sharif as prime minister tried to make Shar'ia (Islamic law) part of Pakistan's constitution. The bill passed the lower house and was slated to pass the upper house in 2000 when Sharif's party was expected to gain control of the Senate. But Sharif was deposed in a coup by his handpicked Army Chief, Pervez Musharraf, which marked the end of Pakistan's decade of democracy. During this period, no attempt was made to chart a new course for Pakistan as it swirled in a political maelstrom with stunted development, providing fertile ground for unemployment, illiteracy, and extremism.

Yet, in contrast to its internal political vicissitudes, Pakistan externally pursued a consistent policy of leveraging Islamic proxies against its neighbours to advance perceived national security goals. With the Soviet withdrawal from Afghanistan and the imposition of sanctions on Pakistan in light of its nuclear program, Pakistan entered the 1990s isolated, economically crippled, and, in its view, abandoned by the United States with a jihadi corps in its midst. Many of these elements were redirected to Kashmir to wage a proxy war against India, hijacking the nationalist movement that had emerged in Indian-held Kashmir. Although Pakistan claimed to provide political and moral support to the Kashmiri struggle, the strategic rationale was to tie down Indian troops in Kashmir and bleed it by a thousand cuts in order to bring it to the table to negotiate on Kashmir.

On the western front, keen to avoid at best a continuing descent into chaos in Afghanistan and at worst a hostile regime that might play the Pashtun card in Pakistan, the Army, with the civilian leadership fully on board, began to back the military campaign of a new class of warriors that had emerged from Pakistan's madrasahs—the Taliban. Both in Kashmir and Afghanistan, the goal was to leverage Islamic groups to offset Pakistan's seemingly hostile neighbours—a policy with clear historical antecedents. Although the goals were rational the means resulted in lethal blowback.

*Enlightened Moderation*

With Musharraf's coup and alignment with the US-led 'War on Terror' after 9/11, Pakistan once again arrived at a critical crossroads. Forced to confront the spectre of Islamic extremism in the international lime-light, the country faced an age-old question: What was its Islamic ethos? Musharraf's answer was, 'enlightened moderation'.

Beginning with his landmark address to the nation in January 2002 where he called for rejecting terrorism in Kashmir and combating extremism and intolerance, Musharraf throughout his time in power made his plea for enlightened moderation.[26] Enlightened moderation, as outlined by him, was a two-pronged strategy:

The first part is for the Muslim world to shun militancy and extremism and adopt the path of socioeconomic uplift. The second is for the West and the United States in particular to seek to resolve all political disputes with justice and to aid in the socioeconomic betterment of the deprived Muslim world.[27]

Although Musharraf's formulation was an important attempt to provide an overarching vision for Pakistan and to nationally delegiti-mise extremism, its execution was deficient and resulted in anything but moderation.

While taking some tentative steps in the spirit of enlightened mod-eration, Musharraf eventually faltered. Measures such as banning a number of key militant groups and beginning the process of registering *madrasahs* and reforming their curricula proved tentative: militant groups sprung up under other names, the registration process came to a grinding halt, and longstanding deficiencies in the public education curriculum remained largely unaddressed. Meanwhile, Musharraf's alliance of political expediency with the Islamic parties and ban of the heads of the two mainstream political parties—Bhutto and Sharif—resulted in a political vacuum that was filled by the Islamic parties and enabled the further flourishing of obscurantism in the country.

Moreover, while decisive in tackling al Qaeda, the Army did not fully sever links with the Taliban or with a number of militant groups oper-ating in Afghanistan and Kashmir, again in the interests of retaining strategic proxies. Compounding the challenge was that some groups such as Lashkar-e-Taiba, operating in Kashmir, had over time become part of the social fabric of Pakistan in terms of their perceived heroism in allegedly championing the Kashmiri cause and also in delivering critical social services, for example in the wake of the Kashmir earthquake. Moving against them at the seeming behest of the United States or India could trigger a public backlash.

In sum, Musharraf failed to successfully anchor enlightened moderation, largely due to policies that empowered the Islamic parties and tolerated militant groups. Militant groups that had once trained their guns across the border turned them inward and expanded their control in the frontier region through government-initiated peace deals; fiery clerics and vigilante youth squads who tasked themselves with enforcing Islamic morality proliferated in parts of the country, culminating in the taking over of the Red Mosque in Islamabad in 2007 and its storming by the Army. As enlightened moderation dimmed, it gave way to a darker phenomenon: Talibanization.

## Talibanization

Today, Pakistan faces an existential militant Islamist threat that its elected government is trying to combat in collaboration with the Army. Suicide attacks against army headquarters, academic institutions and other public places reflect the critical threat the Pakistani state faces as these extremists strike at both the hardest and softest of targets and instill pervasive fear and insecurity. Whereas once Islam underpinned the state's flawed narrative of nation building and strategic security non-state actors have hijacked that narrative with an extremist interpretation of Islam for a variety of motives, including the pursuit of a new Islamic order. It is this hijacking of the national Islamic narrative that is a defining feature of Pakistan's current troubles.

On one hand, there are groups that regard the Pakistani state as an enemy of Islam for having sided with the United States in the invasion of Afghanistan and applying force against them. The Army remains locked in a struggle with the Tehrik-i-Taliban Pakistan (TTP), commonly referred to as the Pakistani Taliban, in the Federally Administered Tribal Areas (FATA)—once a staging ground for the Soviet jihad. The reach of extremism in Pakistan today, however, can only be fully understood by examining the presence of a multitude of establishment-spawned jihadi groups in the Punjabi heartland of Pakistan that are turning on the state. These include the Sipah-e-Sahaba Pakistan (SSP), Lashkar-e-Jhangvi (LeJ), Jaish-e-Mohammad (JeM), and Lashkar-e-Taiba (LeT), who thrive in southern Punjab amidst poverty and unemployment. Their recruits come from the more than 3,000 *madrasahs* in

Punjab, many of which have provided foot soldiers for the Soviet jihad, the Kashmir struggle, sectarian conflict, and now al Qaeda's terrorist operations in Pakistan and Afghanistan.[28]

Alongside these groups are ones waving the banner of an Islamic state and a return to religious purity as the antidote to the Pakistani state's inability to provide basic services, tackle economic inequities, and deliver justice. Their narrative is a direct function of state failure; their goal is a new if entirely undefined Islamic state. The conflict in Swat is a prime example where a longstanding movement for the implementation of *Shari'a* law, fuelled by anger at a broken system of justice and an exploitative landed class, violently boiled over with TTP support. Through a series of agreements with the government to cease fire in exchange for the implementation of Islamic law, militants steadily moved within one hundred miles of Islamabad, with one of the leaders claiming that democracy was not an appropriate system of governance in Pakistan. Although the military eventually rebuffed these groups, for the first time their territorial and ideological aspiration vis-à-vis the Pakistani state became clear.

Although the military response to combat these groups is well known and documented, the ideological response is equally important. Here the role of the Islamic parties and clerics is of particular interest. There has always been some tension among Pakistan's Islamic parties about whether to pursue their avowed goal of an Islamic state through democracy or armed struggle. Although they have never gotten more than 12 per cent of the national vote, and during the Musharraf era, riding a wave of anti-United States sentiment following the invasion of Afghanistan, the Islamic parties continue to project influence well beyond their numbers. They have, however, largely bought into the democratic process and have periodically spoken out against the violent tactics of insurgents. Alongside the role of the Islamic parties in disavowing such violent means is the question of mounting an ideological defence and reclaiming, if not the narrative, at least a less radical understanding of Islam. The current government has attempted to do this by setting up a seven-member Sufi Advisory Council (SAC) with the aim of combating extremism and fanaticism by spreading Sufism—a more peaceful and less rigid form of Islam anchored in the subcontinent's history—throughout the country.[29]

Currently, as the state finds itself on the defensive against an array of groups claiming to wave the banner of Islam, it must decisively counter their ideology. In doing so, it must recognise that the core issue is not always a quest for Islamic purity but a reliance on Islamic rhetoric to mask more earthy concerns related to power, poverty, and justice that circle back to the need for better governance in Pakistan. At the same time, jihad—long sanctioned by the state for its strategic security reasons—to achieve these ends must be delegitimised. According to Khalid Aziz, a former chief secretary of the North West Frontier Province, 'The national narrative in support of jihad has confused the Pakistani mind.... All along we've been saying these people are trying to fight a war of Islam, but there is a need for transforming the national narrative.'[30]

## Yeh Hum Naheen (This is Not Us)

To stave off the ideological inroads of extremism and generate a progressive narrative in Pakistan, the most important constituency is the people of Pakistan. In the Western media, Pakistan is often portrayed as a radicalising society, caught between the mosque and military and teetering on the brink of fundamentalism. The reality is more complex. Pakistan has a robust civil society as seen in the 2007–2009 lawyers' movement; its media is among the most prolific in the Muslim world. A moderate majority exists that rejects extremism and suicide bombing yet believes in the concept of a Muslim *ummah* and is anti-US on a host of issues; that condemns the actions of the Taliban as a distortion of Islam yet is uncertain about the means to counter them, particularly the use of force against fellow citizens and Muslims.

Deep schisms exist among 'moderate' Pakistani Muslims, tracing back to the divide between the Aligarh and Deoband schools pre-Partition—those who embrace religions and notions of modernity and those who seek salvation in Islam's perceived fundamentals. To understand Pakistan's Islamic ideology, it is vital to examine this not just at the state level but also at a societal level.

The pervasive strand of Islam among the subcontinent's Muslims has historically been Sufi or Barelvi Islam. Sufi Islam is viewed as more inclusive and flexible, paying no heed to caste, creed, ethnicity, or race. Its physical manifestation in the subcontinent has long been the plethora of shrines across Pakistan frequented by the masses seeking relief from living saints or *pirs* for their ills, though this insertion of a conduit between man and God has been ripe for manipulation. Since independence, Pakistan's Sufi culture has come under great strain due to internal and external reasons. Internally, successive regimes have co-opted influential *pirs*, who, in becoming increasingly politicised and prosperous, came to be viewed by many as part of the hegemonic socio-economic order in Pakistan.

Meanwhile, beginning in the 1970s, more conservative Deobandi and Wahabi views gained greater currency based on four factors: the importation of this ideology by Pakistani workers who went to Saudi Arabia and the Gulf to capitalise on the oil boom; the embrace of these views by many in the middle class as Sufism came to be identified with a particular hegemonic order and the state's failings came to be viewed as only remediable by returning to a purer if amorphous form of Islam; the pan-Islamic revivalism following the Iranian revolution and Saudi attempts to ideologically counter Iranian influence, including in Pakistan; and the aggressive promotion of Wahabi and Deobandi thought in Pakistan during the Soviet jihad through a burst of Saudi financing, *madrasahs*, and state policy. As such, Pakistani society's complex Islamic texture has emerged from the top down and bottom up as a more conservative form of Islam and gained currency in a changing socio-economic context.[31]

Over the decades, there has been an increase in conservatism ranging from more women taking to wearing the veil or headscarf; music and dancing being viewed by many as un-Islamic; increased censorship in the name of Islam; and in light of a defunct public education system, *madrasahs* churning out thousands of students who project a parochial moral zeal and fear far beyond their numbers. A pervasive austerity has hardened across Pakistani society, yet many Pakistanis are cognizant of the distinction between conservatism and fanaticism. One example of this was the strong public support for a military response in the Swat Valley under Taliban sway in the spring and summer of 2009. This was catalysed by the release of a video showing a woman being brutally flogged by the Taliban—a video that provoked widespread public anger, highlighting the increasing power of Pakistan's media in shaping perceptions. An expression of the public rejection of extremism is the *Yeh Hum Naheen* (This Is Not Us) movement in Pakistan, with billboards in major cities urging Pakistanis to reject violent extremism and claiming that Islam is a religion of peace. These expressions of civil society even when emanating from specific strata are important to consider in understanding the way ordinary people perceive the role of religion in their lives as well as its distortion. Indeed, a coherent consolidation and injection of such expressions into the national discourse is a vital antidote to the extremism coursing through the veins of Pakistani society.

## A New Narrative

From the very creation of Pakistan, Islam has been and will remain a central social and political force. This chapter sought to paint a broad picture of how Islam has been harnessed through Pakistan's history for everything from nation building to security—an enterprise that was radically escalated during the Zia era. The blowback of this is clear today. The Islamic narrative in Pakistan has been hijacked by an array of groups who use religion as a means to diverse ends: to secure political and territorial power, exorcise corrosive Western influence, engage in class warfare, and redress perceived injustices.

The use and understanding of Islam in Pakistan has always been in flux, evolving in response to time and internal and external events. The question that arises, then, is not whether religion has a role in Pakistan but how it can be channelled as a force for progressive change. What form should an enabling narrative of Islam in Pakistan assume? Part of the answer lies in focusing on building an inclusive and robust Pakistani state invoking progressive Islamic values. The onus lies with the Pakistani leadership and people, but the international community can help in the promotion of good governance, education reform, and economic opportunity, as well as in the resolution of deep-seated regional insecurities and grievances that have led to the cultivation of extremist entities as a matter of state policy.

# 8

# BATTLING MILITANCY

## Zahid Hussain

Pakistan today faces a growing threat from violent extremists and Islamic militants. This is the result of a combination of factors. It reflects the fallout of the continuing war in Afghanistan and the limited gains achieved both by the US and Pakistan against al Qaeda, with the organisation showing a remarkable ability to adapt to mounting pressure and find local partners. It also reflects the increasingly violent activism of longer established organisations that have been spawned over the past twenty years but which have been making common cause with militants of more recent vintage.

As militant violence in Pakistan has escalated, it has grown not only in numbers but also in sophistication. A host of violent extremist groups, which were once only loosely associated or were previously at odds with one another, have formed an increasingly interconnected web. Close collaboration is emerging between Pakistani militant groups including the Pakistani Taliban and al Qaeda and the Afghan Taliban.

In the first several years after the US-led attack on Afghanistan, mainly Pashtun militants based in Pakistan conducted attacks almost exclusively in Afghanistan, seeking to drive the US-dominated coalition forces from the country and overthrow the Hamid Karzai government. Since 2007 they have also turned their guns on the Pakistani military and security agencies, launching attacks of increasing sophistication and intensity, as well as perpetrating an escalating and more violent wave of suicide bombings against civilians in major urban centres across Pakistan. A distinctive Pakistani Taliban movement has evolved with an agenda to establish its retrogressive rule not only in the tribal areas but also in the adjoining Khyber Pakhtunkhwa province.

Al Qaeda has grown in strength due to the new alliances it has made with Pakistani militants. Though recent assessments have asserted that al Qaeda has been crippled, and the number of foreign militants operating out of Pakistan's tribal territories has been estimated at a few hundred, the reality is that there is a new generation of al Qaeda in Pakistan. Comprised primarily of Pakistanis, it includes a flood of new recruits from youth and the educated middle class. This new generation of al Qaeda is strongly committed to the cause of global jihad and has acted as a magnet for radicalised Muslims, including a number of Western Muslim citizens who have travelled to Pakistan to receive training in camps in the tribal regions.

The emergence of the local Taliban movement occurred simultaneously with Pakistan's battle to flush out al Qaeda fighters from the borderlands. This did not happen overnight. It was a consequence of war in Afghanistan and military operations carried out by Pakistan that severely undermined the age-old administrative structure in the tribal areas. The members of the tribal council or maliks through whom the federal government established its authority were either killed or driven out by the militants. A new crop of Pakistani militants or Taliban emerged to fill the vacuum created by the collapse of the administrative system in the Federally Administered Tribal Areas (FATA) over which the Pakistani government had at best tenuous control.

The situation worsened in 2006 as Taliban groups sprang up in the adjoining areas of Khyber Pakhtunkhwa province. These militants forcibly closed down video and audio shops, as well as Internet cafes, declaring them un-Islamic. The Taliban also ordered barbers not to shave beards. People were prohibited to play music, even at weddings and traditional fairs, which provided some form of entertainment to the public.

The emerging Taliban mostly came from the ranks of the mainstream Islamic political parties, which had ruled northwestern Pakistan from 2002 to 2007. The six-party Islamic alliance known as Muttahida Majlis-i-Amal (MMA) (The United Council for Action)—comprising Jamaat-e-Islami and Jamiat Ulema-e-Islam, the two most powerful religious political parties—was swept into power in what was then called the North West Frontier Province after winning pluralities in the 2002 parliamentary elections during the administration of President Pervez Musharraf. The alliance was also a part of a coalition government in Balochistan, making it a formidable political force in the country. It was the first time in Pakistan's history that squabbling religious groups representing different Islamic sects had united in an alliance.

The MMA grew from an informal grouping of religious and jihadi groups that took shape following the events of September 11 and the subsequent US military campaign in Afghanistan. Initially, approximately thirty-six Islamic groups united under the banner of the Defence of Afghanistan Council in a show of solidarity with the Taliban regime and Osama bin Laden. It was later renamed Defence of Afghanistan and Pakistan Council with the aim of opposing US military action in Afghanistan. In the weeks and months following October 2001 the council organised demonstrations across the country in support of the Taliban regime.

The MMA itself was hurriedly cobbled together just before the 2002 polls with the blessings of the military leadership. For the Musharraf regime this alliance represented a counterbalance to its liberal opponents. Their new-found unity was predicated on a shared perception of the post-September 11 world and an anti-US position. Its electoral success came on a wave of strong anti-American sentiments among Pakistan's Pashtun population.

Despite being mainstream political parties, both Jamaat-e-Islami and Jamiat Ulema-e-Islam—the two major components of the alliance—had a long history of active association with jihadist politics. Their members overlapped with those of militant and sectarian organisations. Several militant commanders who had fought in Afghanistan and Kashmir were elected to the National and NWFP state assemblies. Outlawed militant and sectarian groups played a significant role in the MMA's election campaign. They saw the electoral success of the alliance as a triumph for their cause of jihad. The Islamists used their new-found political power to enforce rigid Islamic rule in the province. Besides pushing for the adoption of *Shari'a* laws, their administration pledged to end co-education and close down movie cinemas, which it considered as a mark of ungodly Western values.

These policies created an enabling environment for extremists within the ruling alliance to press their agenda, which also opposed female education. In July 2005 the NWFP provincial assembly passed the controversial Hisba (accountability) law which envisaged the setting up of a watchdog body to ensure people respected calls to prayer, did not engage in commerce at the time of Friday prayers and that single men and women did not appear in public places together. The law also prohibited singing and dancing. Reminiscent of the infamous Department of Vice and Virtue in the Taliban's Afghanistan the law proposed the appointment of a 'Mohtasib' (one who holds others accountable) to monitor the populace and ensure conduct consistent with Islamic tenets. This marked a dangerous step towards Talibanization and establishment of the kind of religious fascism Pakistan had never experienced before. But the law was never to be implemented as the Supreme Court of Pakistan, encouraged by the Musharraf government, struck it down as contrary to the country's constitution.

But other measures taken by the MMA government during its five-year rule provided a favourable environment for extremists who advocated use of force to achieve their objectives. Many activists, particularly from the JUI, broke away from the party and joined the ranks of those militants who were later to form the Tehrik-i-Taliban Pakistan (TTP) in 2007.

JUI had its origin in the Jamiat Ulema-e-Hind which was founded by a group of clerics of the Deobandi Muslim movement in pre-partition India. This movement for Islamic revival had first emerged after the 1857 rebellion against British rule. A branch of Sunni Hanafi Islam, their creed is named after a religious seminary established in 1867 in Deoband near Delhi. The founders of the seminary drew their spiritual guidance from Shah Wali Ullah, an eighteenth-century Islamic scholar who endeavoured to bind different Islamic schools of thought. Primarily an anti-British movement, the Deobandis argued that Muslims could coexist with other religions in a society where they were not the majority. That was also the basis of their opposition to the division of India and creation of Pakistan as a separate homeland for Muslims. Deobandis initially stressed on how to revive Islamic life while living under a colonial regime, eschewing politics and focusing on Islamic practices and personal belief, as opposed to the overtly political goals promoted by Islamist thinkers such as Maulana Maudoodi and Hassan al Banna, the founder of Egypt's Muslim Brotherhood.

These ideas inspired the formation of the JUI as a separate organisation after independence in 1947. The party had a significant support base in the rural areas of southern NWFP. In the initial years, the organisation functioned strictly as a religious movement, which concentrated on setting up mosques and preaching. But gradually it developed into a politico-religious party, taking part in the political process and elections. The JUI leadership had traditionally been closer to nationalist and progressive parties than to the proponents of political Islam like the JI. In 1971 the party became a coalition partner of the Pashtun nationalist National Awami Party in the NWFP and Balochistan provincial governments.

With the invasion of Afghanistan by Soviet forces in the 1980s, the party's political orientation transformed. With the help of funding from Saudi Arabia and other Middle Eastern countries, the Deobandi clerics established thousands of *madrasahs* in NWFP and Balochistan along the border with Afghanistan which provided volunteers to fight against communist forces. This brought about a series of transformations of the party, first from a religious movement to a political party and then to a party involved in jihadi politics.

The decade long conflict in Afghanistan gave the Islamists a rallying point and training field. Young Muslims around the world flocked to Afghanistan to fight against a foreign invader. The Afghan resistance was projected by the US-led Western coalition as part of the global jihad against communism. The training of guerrillas was integrated in to the teaching of Islam. The prominent theme was that Islam was a complete socio-political ideology under threat from communist atheists. The Afghan war produced a new radical Islamic movement. Besides the holy warriors from Islamic countries, thousands more were recruited from the expanding *madrasah* network.

General Zia-ul-Haq not only ushered Pakistan into its longest period of military rule but also tried to turn the country into an ideological state. Zia argued that as Pakistan was created on the basis of the two-nation theory and Islamic ideology, it was the duty of the 'soldiers of Islam to safeguard its security, integrity and sovereignty at all costs, both from internal turmoil and external aggression'. He claimed the state was created exclusively to provide its people with the opportunity to follow, 'the Islamic way of life.'[1] Preservation of the country's Islamic character was seen to be as important as the security of the country's geographical frontiers.

Zia's beliefs and politics empowered the clergy. His efforts to Islamise the state and society found ready allies among the religious parties, many of which already had close ties with the military. The Jamaat-e-Islami and other Islamic groups were co-opted by his government with leading figures serving in his martial law cabinet. For the first time in Pakistan's history the Islamists occupied important government positions. Being in power helped the JI penetrate state institutions. Thousands of party activists and sympathisers were given jobs in the judiciary, civil service and educational institutions. These appointments strengthened the hold of the Islamists on crucial parts of the state apparatus for years to come.

The regional and international climate of the 1980s favoured Zia's orthodox Islamisation, and the alliance with the West served the military's institutional interests. As a front-line ally of the US in the Soviet-Afghan War, the military benefited from billions of dollars in military and economic aid, while Zia promoted a militant version of Islam to fight the jihad and crush his democratic foes at home. Consequently, the Islamic movements and parties also thrived in this new-found jihadi culture. Jihad became the main pillar of Zia's vision of an Islamic state and society. Religious parties came to use militancy to further their cause.

Afghanistan provided inspiration to an entire generation of Pakistani Islamic radicals who considered it their religious duty to fight the oppression of Muslims anywhere in the world. It gave a new dimension to the idea of jihad, which till then had only been employed by the Pakistani state in the context of mobilising the population against the archrival—India. The Afghan War saw the privatisation of the concept of jihad. Militant groups emerged from the ranks of traditional religious movements, which took the path of an armed struggle for the cause of Islam.

While the first Pakistani jihadi groups emerged in the 1980s, by 2002 the country had become home to twenty-four militant groups.[2] Within a decade and a half highly disciplined paramilitary organisations were operating across the country pursuing their own internal and external agendas. The largest among them were the Lashkar-e-Taiba (LeT), Jaish-e-Mohammed (JeM), Harakat-ul-Mujahideen (HuM) and Harkat-al-Jihad-al Islami (HJI). All these paramilitary groups had similar motivations and goals, and recruited from the same kind of people (often unemployed youth from the Punjab and KP Provinces). The only difference was in patronage: HuM and HJI were both strongly linked with the Taliban, whilst LeT had strong links with Wahabi groups in Saudi Arabia.

These militant organisations were not clandestine and had not sprouted surreptitiously. Their growth, even when not sponsored by state functionaries was viewed with favour by them. Their activities were no secret and found expression in graffiti, wallposters and pamphlets all over the country, inviting Muslims to join forces with them. They also carried addresses and telephone numbers to contact for training. 'Jihad is the shortest route to paradise',[3] declares one of the many exhortations in such literature. 'A martyr ensures salvation for the entire family.' Every jihadi organisation had funds to help the families of 'martyrs'. Although money was not the motivation of these jihadis, funding was essential to sustain the culture of jihad.[4] The state's patronage helped the jihadis raise funds at public places. The militant groups developed powerful propaganda machinery. Their publications gained a large readership and their messages also became available on video and audiotapes.

During the 1980s and 1990s, the objective of the jihadi movements in Pakistan was not like that of Arab Salafists such as Osama bin Laden: to establish a global Islamic caliphate. Their objectives were more in line with the regional strategy of the Pakistani military establishment: the liberation of Kashmir from India and promoting a Pashtun government in Afghanistan. Most of these militant groups served as instruments of Pakistan's regional policy.

In the mid-1990s the JUI was deeply involved with the Taliban regime in Afghanistan. Thousands of Afghan and Pakistani students from the *madrasahs* run by the JUI formed the nucleus of the Taliban militia, which swept Afghanistan in 1996 to install a conservative Islamic regime in Kabul. The rise of the Taliban in Afghanistan encouraged Pakistani militant groups like Harkat-ul-Mujahideen, Jaish-e-Mohammed and Lashkar-e-Jhangvi. Afghanistan became a base for their operations. Their leaders shared common origins, personnel and often patrons. Many of the Pakistani militants came from the same seminaries in the Pakistani border region from where the Afghan Taliban movement had emerged. Some of these groups were patronised by Pakistan's intelligence agencies which also supported the Afghan Taliban. Both were important in furthering Pakistan's strategic interests—to extend its influence in Afghanistan.

Almost all the top militant leaders in the tribal region who later formed the nucleus of the Pakistani Taliban movement were initially associated with the JUI. Baitullah Mehsud, Hafiz Gul Bahadur and

Mullah Nazir all emerged from the ranks of the JUI which was the only political party allowed by the authorities to operate openly in the tribal areas (where formally political parties remained banned till a 2008 reform announcement that is yet to be implemented). As a result of al Qaeda's influence, the leaders rejected the political and democratic path pursued by the JUI, which lead to a falling out between the JUI and the Pakistani Taliban.

The new generation of Pakistani Taliban became more brutal than their Afghan comrades. Beheading and public executions of opponents and government officials became common practice. The videos of those brutal actions were then distributed to create fear. These sadistic actions were unknown in traditional Pushtun culture. This behaviour was greatly influenced by Arab and Uzbek militants. The Pakistani Taliban's creed probably stemmed from Salafi-Jihadism ideology espoused by al Qaeda. It was also the result of Wahabism found in the Saudi-funded *madrasahs*, which created a new kind of radical Deobandism specific to the Taliban.

On 14 December 2007 some forty militant leaders commanding some 40,000 fighters gathered in South Waziristan to form a united front under the banner of Tehrik-e-Taliban Pakistan. They unanimously elected Baitullah Mehsud, already the most powerful commander, as 'Emir' or supreme leader of the new organisation.

The meeting was attended by almost all the top militant leaders operating in the tribal regions and NWFP or their representatives who managed to set aside their differences. Prominent among them were Hafiz Gul Bahadur from North Waziristan, Mullah Nazir from South Waziristan, Faqir Mohammed from Bajaur and Maulana Fazalullah from Swat. The presence of Gul Bahadur and Mullah Nazir, both belonging to Wazir tribe was curious because of their historic rivalry with Baitullah, from the Mehsud tribe. What had likely brought them together was the military assault ordered by Musharraf on Islamabad's Red Mosque in July 2007.

The Shura or central council not only had representation from all the seven tribal agencies but also from the parts of KP including Swat, Malakand, Buner and Dera Ismail Khan where the Taliban movement was active. The eight-point charter called for the enforcement of *Shari'a* rule and vowed to continue fighting against foreign forces in Afghanistan. The TTP also declared what it described as 'defensive' jihad against the Pakistani military. The newly formed TTP was in fact little more than an extension of al Qaeda. Its formation followed Osama's declaration of war against the Pakistani state in the aftermath of the siege of the Red Mosque. Its charter clearly reflected al Qaeda's new strategy to extend its war to Pakistan. Almost all the top leaders of the new organisation, particularly its supreme leader Baitullah had a long association with al Qaeda. Afghan Taliban leaders were also closely involved in the formation of the organisation which implicitly declared its allegiance to Osama and Mullah Omar.

The period after the formation of the TTP saw a marked rise in militant activity. Just ten days after its creation former Prime Minister Benazir Bhutto was assassinated a few weeks after her return to the country after a protracted time in exile. A suicide bomber blew himself up after firing gunshots at her as she came out of an election rally in Rawalpindi. The militants who missed her in the previous attack on her election rally in Karachi attack appeared to have finally succeeded in removing the leader who dared to confront them. Baitullah was blamed for a murder which was to completely change Pakistan's political landscape.

The Taliban insurgency spread rapidly with the formation of the TTP and came to engulf all the seven tribal regions as well as parts of the NWFP. The movement was most violent in the Swat valley where the followers of Mullah Fazlullah established a brutal regime until they were driven out by Pakistani military in June 2009.

The rise of a distinctive Pakistani Taliban movement represented a new and more violent phase of Islamic militancy in the country. Suicide terrorism, which targeted both the military and civilians, saw a massive rise after the Red Mosque assault when al Qaeda and its Pakistani allies declared jihad against the Pakistani state. This marked a shift in jihadi strategy making the government and military the primary targets. In time security forces accounted for more than 60 per cent of the targets as human bombers became the most potent weapons in the militant war.

More than 3,000 people, including senior army and intelligence officials, became victims of those attacks between 2007 and 2009. On average ninety people were killed a month in suicide bombings during 2009 with an attack occurring almost every five to six days across the country. Jihadi groups also expanded their attacks to Islamabad. They launched spectacular suicide raids in high security zones, including the Danish Embassy compound and the Marriot Hotel in June and September 2007, which killed more than sixty people. Both these attacks showed the growing power of the militants' intelligence network. Both attacks were directly linked to al Qaeda backed militants.

Despite the rise in suicide bombings the number of casualties in these attacks remained low compared to other violent assaults. But they had much greater impact. Suicide bombing as a weapon had seldom been used by Pakistani militant groups before, though some jihadi groups had used *fidayeen* raids against Indian security forces in Kashmir. The term '*fidayeen* attack' was used by the militants for target operations.

The concept of *fidayeen* (self-sacrifice) was different from that of a suicide bomber who blew himself up to kill others. Until then most militant groups considered suicide to be un-Islamic. A *fidayee*, on the other hand, was one who had to achieve his mission even in the worst of circumstances and come back alive. Suicide attacks were rarely used by the Afghan *mujahideen* in the War against the Soviet forces in the 1980s, though there were a few incidents involving Arab jihadists.

The use of suicide bombings by Pakistani militants was largely a post-9/11 phenomenon. Some clerics had hailed the nineteen hijackers involved in the attack as 'great heroes of Islam'. The more radical among them had even issued a *fatwa* giving religious sanction to suicide attacks against American forces in Afghanistan and Pakistani soldiers fighting in South Waziristan. This sanction was also used by Muslim sectarian groups to justify actions targeting religious congregations of rival denominations.

For militants the Western presence in both Afghanistan and Pakistan was a threat to Islam itself. This view became the ultimate rationale for jihadist militancy in Pakistan. Anybody allied with the enemy or those who seemed to be complicit in the war on the side of Western forces such as soldiers charged with safe passage for NATO convoys, civilians, moderate clerics and more recently, the government officials were regarded as fair game.

Over the past few years several militant leaders have been killed in operations conducted by Pakistani military and CIA drone strikes, but they have been quickly replaced by new and more aggressive successors. The drone strikes have been a part of the CIA's 'secret war' against al Qaeda in the tribal areas since 2004. But after 2009 there was a marked increase in these attacks. Shortly after his inauguration President Barack Obama ordered an escalation of the strikes as a part of his overall review of Afghan war strategy. In August 2009 Hellfire missiles fired by a pilotless Predator killed Baitullah and his young wife while the Taliban leader was being treated for his kidney ailment in his house in Makin in South Waziristan. His killing was perhaps the most successful strike in the eight-year history of the CIA's drone operations in Pakistan.

The drone strikes have been effective in eliminating leading al Qaeda and other militant commanders. But they have also had serious blowback effects. The escalation and increasing number of civilian deaths have stirred intense anger among the Pakistani public. This so-called secret war has become a focus of both militant rage and public protest. The United States has never officially acknowledged that it is launching the strikes and Islamabad has denied any collaboration. But the drone operations have been carried out with the tacit cooperation of the Pakistani government. With the reported deaths of women and children public anger has surged. The strikes have also spurred a significant rise in the number of recruits joining militant groups.

Baitullah Mehsud's killing, hailed as such a pivotal victory in Pakistan's war against militants, resulted in only a brief lull in attacks by the Pakistani Taliban. He was quickly succeeded by a fierce commander, Hakimullah Mehsud. Just months after Baitullah's death, the Pakistani Taliban took its wave of violence to a new level, launching a series of highly coordinated suicide bombings and attacks in the major Pakistani cities targeting even higher-security military installations. The closely synchronised attacks exposed weaknesses in Pakistan's security apparatus and demonstrated that the militants had become more daring and sophisticated in planning and tactics.

The TTP also developed a close nexus with other Pakistani militant factions, which had over time mutated into small cells after being proscribed by the Musharraf government in 2002. A new generation of young educated militants from urban areas, most of them splinters of mainstream Islamic political parties including the JI joined the new jihadist movement making it a formidable challenge to the Pakistani state. The movement began to draw young, middle-class professionals who were products of universities rather than of Islamic seminaries. Children of opportunity rather than deprivation, they became the planners of many terrorist attacks that heralded a new phase of militancy sweeping the country after 2007.

Meanwhile al Qaeda, operating from the borderland, managed to transform and replenish itself with new recruits from among the Pakistani militant groups. This enabled it to also survive the capture and killing of many of its senior operatives. Founder members mostly from Saudi Arabia, Egypt and Libya, known as 'Sheikhs', continued to provide ideological leadership, but the rank and file of the network increasingly comprised the new militants from Pakistan and other countries including Somalia, Turkey, Indonesia, and Bangladesh who managed to slip into the border region.

Pakistani intelligence agencies got the first clear idea of how al Qaeda had expanded its network into Pakistan's urban centres from the arrest of Naeem Noor Khan in Lahore in July 2004. The twenty-eight year old computer wizard from an educated middle-class family had for years worked as al Qaeda's communication chief. An engineer by training, Naeem had left a promising career to join the jihad. Information acquired from his computer revealed that Naeem was a key link between bin Laden's inner circle hiding in the mountainous tribal region and al Qaeda's operatives around the world. It also provided unprecedented insight into its inner workings and international operations. Naeem was lured into jihad when he was still a student at a top engineering university in Karachi. Although he grew up in a liberal atmosphere he was greatly influenced by radical Muslim causes from Palestine to Bosnia.

There were many other Pakistanis from the ranks of JI who were also involved with al Qaeda operating, thus giving the group a new depth in the country. The cadre al Qaeda attracted was ideologically and politically motivated. Thousands of well-trained militants who were battle-hardened in Kashmir and Afghanistan provided ready recruits. Pakistani militant groups like JeM, HuM, LeJ and HUJI that had disintegrated into small cells became an extension.

The more Islamabad aligned itself with the United States the more young members of militant organisations turned inwards to target the military. The Karachi-based Jundullah (Army of God) was a prime example of the changing face of al Qaeda in Pakistan. The group was founded by Ata-ur-Rehman, a university graduate who was arrested in June 2004 on the charge of masterminding a series of terrorist attacks targeting security forces and government installations. The son of a prosperous businessman, Ata-ur-Rehman grew up in a middle class neighbourhood in Karachi. Many of his close relatives were settled in the United States. He turned to militancy after completing his Master's degree in Statistics in 1991. Rehman was initially associated with Islami Jamiat-e-Talba, the student wing of JI.

Like thousands of Pakistani militants he went to Afghanistan in the mid 1990s to receive military training. Rehman formed the group in 2003 after Pakistani security forces captured many top al Qaeda leaders including Khalid Shaikh Mohammed. A well-knit cell comprising twenty militants, most of them in their twenties and thirties, Jundullah was the most ruthless of al Qaeda linked groups involved in a spate of violent attacks in Karachi. The group hit the headlines after an audacious attack in June 2004 on the cavalcade of a top army commander in the city. More than eleven soldiers and officers were killed in the raid in a busy street.

The emergence of groups like Jundullah showed how new jihadi cells quickly formed after others were wound up. The rise of small terrorist cells made the task of countering them harder. These terrorist groups multiplied with the escalation in the Pakistani military offensives in the northwest and tribal regions. Some of these groups had just four or five members making them hard to detect.

Among others who were arrested for association with Jundullah were Arshad Waheed and his brother Akmal Waheed, a neurosurgeon. Both men, in their mid thirties, were also JI members. Doctor Arshad Waheed was a well-known orthopaedic surgeon running his own hospital in Karachi and actively involved with the Jamaat. He moved to Kandahar after the 2001 US invasion of Afghanistan apparently to provide medical help to the Taliban. The experience radicalised him further. Back in Pakistan he started mobilising people for jihad in Afghanistan. He criticised Pakistani religious political parties for seeking to gain power through elections. Disillusioned with the Jamaat's politics he became associated with a little known militant group, Jundullah.

Official Pakistani investigations showed that the two doctors had close links with al Qaeda. Besides sheltering terrorists they provided financial and medical help to the militants. JI ran an intense campaign for the release of the two doctors. The two brothers disappeared after being released on bail a few months later. They were later spotted in South Waziristan where Dr Arshad Waheed got actively involved with al Qaeda and took the war name, Sheikh Moaz. There he became a trained fighter and also provided medical training. Dr Arshad Waheed was killed in March 2008 when a CIA-operated drone struck his hideout in Dhok Pir Bagh near Wana. An al Qaeda video tape released after his death hailed him as a martyr who was 'unparalleled in faith, love for his religion, and belief in Allah.'

The Waheed brothers' role in al Qaeda raised questions about the JI's connection with the organisation. This was not an isolated case. In 2003 Khalid Shaikh Mohammed was captured from the house of a leader of the party's women's wing in the Rawalpindi cantonment area. The raid produced another important catch: Mustafa Ahmed al Hawsawi, a Saudi Arabian national accused of bankrolling the September 11 attacks. There were several other incidents where JI members were found to have provided refuge to al Qaeda fugitives. In January 2003 two al Qaeda operatives were arrested after a shootout in the house of another leader of the party's women's wing in Karachi.

In 2003 the security agencies arrested Khawja Javed, a leading physician, and his brother for harbouring senior al Qaeda operatives and their families on their sprawling residential compound outside Lahore. Both were associated with JI. In 2005, security agencies arrested Ahsan Aziz, from Mirpur a town in Pakistani controlled Kashmir. He was another JI member with al Qaeda links. This underscored the support network that al Qaeda enjoyed among mainstream Islamic parties.

The association of al Qaeda operatives with JI was not accidental. The country's most powerful Islamic political party was after all the original face of jihad in Pakistan. In terms of its organisational capability, media skills, political experience and influence within the state institutions, JI emerged as the most powerful religious lobby in the country. In many respects JI was the main architect of official Islam in Pakistan. Abul Ala Maududi, founder of the Jamaat-e-Islami, was a leading proponent of political Islam along with Hasan al Banna and Sayyid Qutb, founder of the Muslim Brotherhood. Maududi's influence went beyond the sub-continent and his writings gained a wide audience in the Islamic world.

Maududi formed the JI in 1941 as an Islamic revivalist movement to promote Islamic values and practices. The basic objective of the party was to seize state power and establish Islamic rule. It pledged not to adopt any illegal or underground means to come to power. 'It will educate people in the first course about real Islamic values and participate in elections', the foundation manifesto declared. Maududi was a prolific writer. In hundreds of books and pamphlets he laid out an elaborate ideological vision. He argued that Islam is as much a political ideology as it is a religion and that the basic division in the world was between 'Islam and un-Islam'. He described the political system of Islam as 'theo-democracy' a system in which officials would be elected, but would be subject to divine laws interpreted by the theologically learned.

Over the years JI increasingly used force to assert its politics. The party's first venture into military jihad came in 1971 when its cadres sided with the Pakistan Army in opposing independence for Bangladesh. The party members were organised into two militant groups, Al-Badr and Al-Shams, and were trained by the Pakistan Army to carry out operations against Bengali nationalists seeking separation from Pakistan. JI was the only political party that actively supported the military operation which killed thousands of Bengalis and ultimately resulted in the dismemberment of the country less than twenty-five years after its creation.

Since the 1970s militancy became an integral part of JI politics. By 1976 the Jamaat's street power had multiplied and the number of its members and supporters jumped to two million. The party also organised armed groups to intimidate the opposition. As pointed out earlier General Zia's regime gave the Jamaat unprecedented influence.

Following the Soviet invasion of Afghanistan in 1979, JI found the opportunity to establish itself as the main exponent of Jihad. Maududi died in an American hospital just a few months before Soviet President Brezhnev ordered his troops to march into Afghanistan in 1979. JI, which by then had become completely intertwined with the military, played a major role in the Afghan jihad sponsored by the CIA and the ISI. Thousands of its members joined the *mujahideen* fighting the Soviet forces. It was also the period when the party developed close contacts with Arab jihadists, many of whom were associated with the Muslim Brotherhood. There was a very close ideological bond between the two parties striving for international Islamic revolution. Many of these Brotherhood fighters, including al Zawahiri, would form the main nucleus of al Qaeda in later years.

During the Afghan Jihad JI was able to build a significant infrastructure, including *madrasahs*, businesses and charities with the help of generous financial contributions from governments and private individuals in the Gulf States. Thousands of JI cadres received training alongside foreign and Afghan fighters, developing a close affinity with them.

By the time of the Soviet withdrawal from Afghanistan the party had developed close ties with Islamist groups throughout the world. Islamist liberation movements seeking redress of perceived and real grievances in places remote from Pakistan, such as Chechnya, Bosnia and Southern Philippines congregated in Pakistan. JI raised funds for these groups and provided military training for their members in addition to allowing its own younger members to participate in jihad around the world. Once an ally of the United States, JI now became part of global jihad. Hundreds of its cadres were killed fighting in Kashmir, Chechnya, Bosnia and Afghanistan.

The arrests of al Qaeda leaders from residences belonging to JI members brought the party under national and international scrutiny, but there was little evidence that the party itself collaborated in any terrorist actions. Although JI sympathised with various jihadi movements, it took care not to cross the line from being primarily an ideological-political movement, or in Maududi's words 'the vanguard of Islamic revolution.'

The rise in the number of cadres from mainstream Islamic political parties joining the militant war against Pakistani forces has made the threat to the country much more serious. Over the years the Pakistani government and the military underestimated and ignored this rising threat. A policy of appeasement from 2001 to 2009 allowed the Taliban to establish control not only in all the seven tribal agencies of FATA but also sweep parts of the KP.

Taking advantage of a peace deal with the government in 2009, the Taliban led by an instigating cleric, Mullah Fazlullah, not only established retrogressive rule in the Swat Valley but also expanded his influence in the neighbouring districts of Dir and Buner. The advance of the Taliban to areas just 70 miles from the capital raised a nightmare scenario of militants raging out of control. At the same time Baitullah's supporters stepped up terrorist attacks in mainland Pakistan. The alarming development raised serious concern in Washington and other Western capitals.

The Taliban advance finally forced the military to move against them. In the first week of May 2009 the Army launched a three-pronged offensive involving approximately 30,000 troops, backed by air force jets and helicopter gunships, turning a large area of the Swat Valley into a battle zone. It was the bloodiest battle yet in Pakistan's struggle against militancy. The fighting forced some two million people to leave their homes creating the worst humanitarian crisis in the country's history.

After fierce fighting government forces were able to seize control of the region, but the war was far from over. The military success in Swat dealt a serious blow to the Taliban, and won the praise of the United States and other Western allies, but it also prompted the insurgents to expand the guerrilla war into the country's heartland. There was a marked increase in suicide attacks on security forces and installations around the country in the months that followed.

In a daring attack in mid October militants attacked the high security Army General Headquarters in Rawalpindi and held some thirty-nine officers and civilians hostage for twenty-two hours. The attackers had pulled off a security breach at one of the most sensitive national defence establishments in the country and had threatened the safety of the Army's top commanders. The GHQ attack was carried out with the objective of sending the message that despite the setback in Swat, the militants still had the capacity to hit wherever they wanted.

It was a joint operation by the Taliban and elements of a number of outlawed groups, which are dominated by militants from the Punjab.[4] Such collaboration had been revealed in a number of other terrorist attacks in major Pakistani cities. These signalled the existence of strong bases of support for militant terrorism in the heartland and the emergence of an ever more intertwined nexus between educated professionals and tribal militants. The GHQ attack left the military with no other option but to move against the bastion of Taliban power in South Waziristan. The long-awaited offensive began on 17 October 2009, with the deployment of more than forty-five thousand troops, backed by the air force. The massive use of force was considered critical to quickly wind up the operation. With these troops added to those still deployed in the Swat, the size of the total force engaged in the battle reached a record 100,000.

Security forces were able to drive out the Taliban fighters from most of their stronghold in South Waziristan by the end of 2009. But the military's hold remained tentative with most of the insurgent leaders escaping to neighbouring North Waziristan and other tribal regions. The Army extended the operation to the Orakzai tribal agency which had also become the centre for Taliban activities. Despite the military success in Swat, South Waziristan and other tribal agencies, there has been little abatement in the militant violence.

Pakistan's major problem in dealing with rising militancy is lack of a comprehensive and integrated counter-terrorism strategy. In the areas that have been cleared of militants there is still no effective civil administration that has been put in place making it more difficult to consolidate military gains. The use of military force alone cannot win the war against rising militancy, which poses the biggest internal security threat to the country. To reverse the tide of militancy there is a need to take a holistic approach which also includes the political mobilisation of the people to combat terrorism.

Although public opinion seems to have turned against militancy, the absence of a concerted government effort to leverage this as part of evolving a coherent strategy means that the most important aspect of reversing the tide of militancy remains to be addressed. Important gains have been made in the past two years, but unless these are reinforced by non-military measures to neutralise the militants and their toxic creed and buttressed by effective governance these gains may turn out to be ephemeral.

# 9

# RETOOLING INSTITUTIONS

*Dr Ishrat Husain*

In the last two decades theoretical and empirical evidence have offered a new insight: that broader socio-economic development including the distribution of the benefits of growth is determined by the quality of governance and institutions. Economic policies, however sound or benign they may be, cannot disperse the gains widely unless the institutions intermediating these policies are strong, efficient and effective.

Although it is hard to precisely define governance there is wide consensus that good governance enables the state, the civil society and the private sector to enhance the well-being of a large segment of the population. According to the World Bank,[1] governance refers to the manner in which public officials and institutions acquire and exercise the authority to shape public policy and provide public goods and services. The key dimensions of governance are: public sector management, accountability, the legal framework for development and information and transparency.

Research by the Overseas Development Institute[2] has shown that the historical context, previous regime, socio-cultural context, economic system and international environment are the main determinants of governance and development.

The six core principles identified by Hyden et al.[3] that are related to good governance are: (a) Participation, (b) Fairness, (c) Decency, (d) Accountability, (e) Transparency and (f) Efficiency.

Each nation's path to good governance will be different depending on culture, geography, political and administrative traditions, economic conditions and many other factors. The scope of activities allocated to the public and private sector diverges markedly and so does variation in scale. Yet governments share many features. They face similar responsibilities in that they need to establish a basic policy framework, provide critical goods and services, protect and administer the rule of law and advance social equity.

What has been the experience of Pakistan with respect to governance and how has the tension between the goal of collective good of society and the self-interests of state actors been managed? What can be done to improve governance and strengthen institutions to promote the welfare of the majority?

Most observers and analysts within and outside Pakistan firmly believe that the quality of economic governance and decision-making and the capacity of the key institutions have gradually deteriorated over time.[4] Pakistan's main problem in holding on to macro-economic stability, sustaining economic growth and delivering stability, sustaining economic growth and delivering public services to the poor is due to weak governance and a gradual but perceptible decline in institutional capacity. The elitist nature of the state[5] and the society, and both the conflict and collusion among the various power structures of the country can explain this phenomenon. It is not the content of public policies that has been wanting but the implementation of those policies that has proved to be the major culprit. The implementation capacity itself is a function of the vision and objectives of the political leadership, the competence of civil service and the capabilities of public institutions.

Improvement of economic governance has not been consistently pursued in Pakistan as implementation requires several decades while elected and military governments have short-term horizons. Elected governments, in their pursuit of winning the next election, and military governments, in their attempts to gain legitimacy, get bogged down in ad-hoc and occasionally populist measures without addressing the root cause: that is, building institutional capacity to deliver improved living standards for the majority of the population and setting up a viable governance structure. Personalised decision-making according to the whims and caprices of individuals at the helm has therefore displaced and informed well thought out institutionalised processes.

150

Chronic political instability and frequent changes in political regimes have also caused disastrous consequences for economic governance. During the 1990s the changes were too many and too chaotic. Invariably, the incoming governments abruptly abandoned, discontinued or slowed down the implementation of the policies, projects and programs inherited from their predecessors. As institutions take a long time to nurture, the implementation of projects is spread over a multi year period and the impact of policies is felt with considerable time-lag, premature abandonment caused more damage than good. Starting all over again and before the benefits started accruing, the government was either overthrown or had to step down before completing its tenure. The incoming government began the cycle again with a fresh set. The majority of the populace never witnessed any benefits while unending costs were incurred by every successive regime.

The situation is quite the opposite in India as aptly summed up by Arun Shourie:

In India, there is a consensus in practice so that whenever a group is in office, wherever it is in office, it attempts to do the same sorts of things. But when it is in opposition, where it is in opposition, it strains to block the same measures. We have the Communists in West Bengal garnering credit for implementing reforms in the State that they are blocking at the Centre.[6]

What is the effect of this unending cycle of politically motivated economic governance on the majority of the population? A sense of deprivation and denial of basic economic rights creates feelings of cynicism, negativism and frustration. The credibility of governments in power—any government—is completely eroded. Distrust of 'government' becomes so widespread and credibility of 'government' so low that unfounded and unsubstantiated rumours, mudslinging and suspicion about their motives assume a momentum of their own. In the last six to seven years the media, taking advantage of this widespread lack of government credibility have taken over the role of an opposition party and thus accentuated feelings of negativism.

Markets, on the other hand, function on sentiments. If market participants have confidence in the government and its institutions the overall result is stability in the markets. But if there is lack of credibility, an air of uncertainty, and crisis of confidence, the markets become nervous and jittery and high volatility is witnessed. However good and sound the policies may be, under these circumstances, private investment is hobbled and the economy suffers.

A society with positive attitude will give enterprises far greater freedom to compete than a society that perceives businesses to be unethical or in partnership with the government for personal aggrandisement. Patronage and cronyism in the form of licenses, tariff concessions, tax exemptions to only a selected few or sale of public assets to the favourites of the rulers or appointments to key public offices not on merit but on the basis of loyalty, affiliation and friendship sharpen the negative sentiment. Therefore the program of privatisation of public enterprises, economically desirable and so badly needed, has almost been abandoned ever since the perception, right or wrong, gained currency that the Pakistan Steel Mills was being sold for too low a price to the cronies of the government.

Alesina's survey of literature[7] suggests that when the values of political-institutional variables are compared for the ten slowest and ten fastest growing economies in the sample, the slowest countries tend to be more ethnically fractionalised and more politically unstable. They also tend to have much poorer indicators of the rule of law and institutional quality, much higher black market premium and greater income inequality. Alesina et al.[8] found that political instability, government fragility (frequency of government changes and coup d'états) and socio-political instability (Political assassinations, riots and revolutions) have a negative effect on growth. Pakistan fits this model quite well as the frequency of government changes and socio-economic instability have been associated with low growth and macro-economic turbulence.

What are the essential ingredients of good economic governance? Participation, transparency, credibility, rule of Law, efficiency and accountability are now accepted as essential and are measured through indicators[9] such as (a) voice and accountability, (b) political stability, (c) government effectiveness, (d) regulatory burden, (e) rule of law and (f) corruption.

How does Pakistan fare against these indicators? The common view about participation is that the Centre has assumed too much power and authority and this excessive concentration of power has led to inefficiency, social fragmentation, and ethnic divisiveness. Political leaders with the help of a small coterie of loyalists exercise absolute power and take all important decisions. Dissent within the political parties is hardly tolerated and Parliaments usually rubber stamp decisions taken by the leader of the party. Party cadres and National and Provincial assembly members are usually excluded from decision-making.

Devolution of powers to Local governments introduced in 2001 was a step in the right direction to promote broader participation but has not been fully implemented either in letter or in spirit. The incoming governments, instead of removing the deficiencies revealed during implementation have decided to dismantle the system simply because it was the handiwork of the previous government. There is no consensus as yet on the contours of the new system. Meanwhile whatever access the common citizens at grass-roots level had begun to experience is being hampered because the power and authority are gradually reverting to the provincial capitals. It is quite ironic that while the Provincial legislators and ministers are quite vociferous in demanding autonomy from the Federal Government they are the most fierce opponents of devolution of powers to the local governments. This lack of consistency and absence of continuity in our governance structure have more hazards than is generally recognised.

Transparency in the actions of the government can be achieved by several means, i.e. hearings of Parliamentary Committees, question hours in the National and Provincial Assemblies, Freedom of Information Act, removal of several clauses of the Official Secrets Act, introduction of e-government and investigative reporting by competent and responsible journalists. Most of these measures exist but more in form rather than substance. In India, however, the Right of Information Act is bringing about a silent revolution and civil society is using access to information to expose corruption in public places and secure the rights of the poor. The bureaucrats have become more cautious as their actions are open to public scrutiny. In Pakistan, excessive misuse of newly acquired power by some media representatives in assassinating the character of political leaders or public servants without substantiation or evidence may prove to be more detrimental to the cause of disclosure and transparency.

The rule of law has been a subject of debate in Pakistan since March 2007. The lawyers' movement demonstrated that if a particular community gets rallied around a legitimate cause it could make a difference. The judiciary at the highest level is indeed trying to assert its independence, enforce the rule of law and expedite disposal of cases. But it is not clear if a common citizen is any better off today in terms of access to justice, speedy redressal of grievances, enforcement of contracts or property rights. The reality is quite sobering.

Efficiency, as measured by government effectiveness either in maintenance of security of life or property, law and order or delivery of basic services, has rapidly declined over time. Most institutions entrusted with these responsibilities at the time of independence were relatively well run. But the opposite is true after sixty-three years. It is only a rarity that a public institution is found to be functioning smoothly and effectively. The differential treatment meted out to the well-to-do and influential segments on one hand and the rest of the population on the other violates the principle of fairness and equality for all citizens irrespective of caste, creed or social status. But this deference to the rich and connected has become the norm of bureaucratic behaviour in Pakistan. With each change of government a new cast of political elites and well-connected influentials occupy the space vacated by their predecessors.

A number of laws and institutions exist in the name of accountability in Pakistan. Starting from the Public Accounts Committees at the Federal and the Provincial Assembly level there is a plethora of committees, bureaus and task forces, charged with this responsibility. The National Accountability Bureau made a very promising start and instilled some fear and induced a deterrence effect but this was only for a short period of the initial three years of the Musharraf government. Soon after, political compulsions gave way to a pragmatic approach whereby the impartiality and neutrality of the NAB came under serious questioning. Thus despite a very strong legal instrument and a well organised infrastructure of investigation, prosecution and courts, the practice of true accountability was once again set aside. Accountability has therefore lost its true sense and meaning in the vocabulary of governance and instead become associated with retribution, settling political scores and a tool for winning over opponents and witch hunting the recalcitrant.

The strategy for bringing about improved governance in the context of Pakistan would involve the breakup of the monopoly of economic and political power that has been amassed by a small class of politicians, large businessmen, military and civil service officers, professionals and *zamindars* over the last five decades. The locus of power has become too much tilted in favour of entrenched interest groups and only a reduction in their power will be able to improve the quality and standards of living of the majority of the population. A more difficult question that remains unanswered is: How can this be done? This is an arduous task and there should be no illusions about it. All that can be done at this juncture is to spell out a long term agenda for system-wide reform based on diagnosis, field observations, evidence and consultations with stakeholders.

As the agenda for governance reforms spans over the tenures of several elected governments it is difficult to find ownership for these reforms. An enlightened leadership that has a sense of history and is not totally driven by the politics of electoral cycles can implement this agenda. The main ingredients of the agenda for governance and institutional reform[10] would consist of:

a) Improving the quality and performance of Civil Services.
b) Restructuring the organisation of the Federal, Provincial and District governments.
c) Revamping the mechanism for delivery of basic public goods and services.
d) Strengthening key institutions engaged in economic governance.
e) Introducing checks and balances in the system by building up the capacity and authority of certain institutions of restraint.

*Civil Service Reforms*

In a recent study on Pakistan's Civil Service,[11] the International Crisis Group (ICG) concluded that:

Decades of mismanagement, political manipulation and corruption have rendered Pakistan's Civil Service incapable of providing effective governance and basic public services. In public perception, the country's 2.4 million civil servants are widely seen as unresponsive and corrupt, and bureaucratic procedures cumbersome and exploitative.

To remedy this situation the best talent available in the country has to be attracted to the civil services, and a holistic approach that affects the entire human resource policy value chain has to be implemented.

The main elements of this value chain are:

a) Recruitment at all levels and grades of public services should be open, transparent, merit based with regional representation as laid down in the Constitution. These principles have been successfully practiced for decades, e.g. Pakistan Atomic Energy Commission, National Highway police, State Bank of Pakistan.
b) The artificial distinction between superior and non-superior services has to be replaced by the equality of all services at all Pakistan, Federal and Provincial levels. Terms and conditions of all the serv-

ices in matters of recruitment, promotion, career progression, compensation, would be similar. The specialists and professionals would have to be brought at par with the cadre services.

c) To provide equality of opportunity to all deserving civil servants, National Executive Service (NES) and Provincial Executive Services (PES) ought to be constituted to man all the Federal and Provincial Secretariat and senior management positions. The selection should be made on merit by the Public Service Commission with due regard for provincial quota and reservation for women. The NES ought to have three streams—General, Social Sector and Economic Sector, thus promoting some limited specialisation among our civil servants.

d) Training of all civil servants should be mandatory at post-induction, mid-career and senior management levels. Promotions to the next grade ought to be linked with completion of training at various stages in the career.

e) Promotions and career progression for all public sector employees should be determined by their on-the-job performance, responsiveness to public and training outcomes.

f) The present outdated system of Annual Confidential Reports (ACRs) should be replaced by the modern Performance Management System (PMS), which evaluates performance objectively and identifies and provides development opportunities to individual employees.

g) Compensation packages should be revamped to reflect market conditions and a decent living wage and retirement benefits should be made available to all public sector employees. Corruption among the majority of civil servants cannot be curbed by moral persuasion but by providing them with an adequate compensation package. To keep the wage bill of the government within the limits of the fiscal deficit, a freeze should be imposed on fresh recruitment to lower grades except for teachers, health workers and police.

h) As most of the interaction between an ordinary citizen takes place at the district level and the present level of functionaries consists of ill-trained, poorly paid, unhelpful, discourteous individuals enjoying arbitrary powers, District Service should be constituted for each District Government. This will minimise the political pressures for transfers and postings as 1.2 million out of 1.8 million employees working in the provinces will remain in their respective District

Governments. Training in technical and soft skills will be made mandatory for all members of the District services.

i) Education, health, police and judiciary which are critical for delivery of basic services should be excluded from the uniform Basic Pay Scales at it has created serious distortions. The backward districts and regions are lagging behind as the teachers, health workers, etc. have no incentive to serve these areas. Local labour market conditions of demand and supply should determine the salary structure of teachers, health workers and other professionals.

j) Security of tenure of office for a specified period of time should be guaranteed and implemented. The current practice of frequent transfer at the discretion of the political leaders has weakened the moral fabric of the civil servants who cannot withstand the social and financial costs of dislocation and at-times ostracisation. Pleasing the boss, whether or not his orders are legal, has become the norm, making fair and impartial dispensation of services difficult.

*Restructuring Federal, Provincial and District Governments*

Two significant structural changes of a historical nature have taken place under the PPP-led coalition government that came to power in 2008. First, powers and functions on the concurrent list under the constitution have been transferred to the Provinces making provincial autonomy a more meaningful and operational concept. Second, the 2009 award of the National Finance Commission has tilted the balance of resource distribution in favour of the provincial governments. Henceforth, the provinces rightfully would receive a larger share of the divisible pool. The next logical step is to form Provincial Finance Commissions and divide the resources among the Provincial and district governments. This requires demarcation of responsibilities between the two tiers, which is currently in a state of flux. The devolution of twelve departments from the Provincial Government to the districts has improved access to basic services by the common citizens compared to the previous system. Local elected representatives are more responsive to the needs of their constituents in contrast to the Provincial and National Assembly members, who after getting elected, become quite inaccessible. They spend most of their time in Islamabad or provincial capitals and visit their constituencies for a day or two in the week. The local representatives, on the other hand, are available and accessible 24/7.

The 2001 Local Government suffers from many weaknesses including excessive strengthening of the office of District Nazim—an indirectly elected leader. Law and order, maintenance of revenue records and crisis and disaster management are the functions that require impartial and neutral administrators. The Local Government System should eliminate these weaknesses but the present efforts of the provincial governments and legislators to restore the 1979 Local Government System and completely dismantle the 2001 system would be a retrogressive step—a step away from good governance.

Several studies[12] have produced evidence that the choices of development projects made by local councils had superior outcomes and more efficient resource allocation and utilisation compared to the centralised approvals made at the provincial capitals. Twelve devolved departments should remain the responsibilities of the District Governments with further devolution to the Tehsil and Union Councils. Provincial Governments should formulate policies, set up standards of performance, monitor the finances, performance and outcomes and take punitive actions against those indulging in malpractices and corruption. Well-functioning Local Governments can, in fact, bring political dividends as the population is better served and feels satisfied with the services rendered by the government. In an ethnically diverse society a sense of direct participation in local governance is essential.

The main reforms that are required to implement the Eighteenth Constitutional amendment as well as the NFC award are:

a) The Federal Government should immediately shed powers and functions from the concurrent list to the provincial. Given the ethnic and regional composition of the country and the growing needs of an expanding population, the provinces and districts have to be empowered. A National Council of Ministers, consisting of the Federal and Provincial Ministers working under the Council for Common Interest (CCI) should formulate the national policies for these transferred subjects. Consequently, the number of Federal Ministers can be cut to one half and the number of Divisions reduced by one third. In view of the new challenges that are facing the country, some new ministries, for example, for energy, human resource development, social protection etc., should be established.

b) The existing large number of autonomous bodies and attached departments and corporations at the Federal and Provincial levels, should be regrouped and rationalised through merger, privatisation and liquidation, which will save enormous financial resources that can be diverted towards basic service delivery.

c) The District Government has to be strengthened by establishing administrative linkages between the Union Councils, Town Committees/Tehsil Councils and District Governments. Executive magistrates have to be revived and Law and Order, Disaster Management and Land Record Management taken away from the purview of the District Nazim.

d) E-government tools and development in digital technology should be utilised for improving the efficiency of government, reducing the costs of transactions, conveniencing ordinary citizens, introducing transparency and reducing discretionary powers and corruption and tracking the performance and output. Training of those already working in the government should make a smooth transition from a paper-based environment to electronic filing, messaging, sharing and exchanging of documents, retrieving, reporting and archiving.

e) Uneven and discriminatory application of government rules, regulations and instructions are also a source of grief to citizens. A number of junior functionaries exploit their knowledge of the rules for their personal benefits. Multiple rules exist on the same subject as there has been no systematic weeding out exercise undertaken. All government manuals ought to be revised, updated and then uploaded on the websites of the government so that they are accessible to the public at large.

*Reforms in Delivery of Basic Services*

a) Education is badly needed to increase literacy in the country. Clear boundaries in the delivery of education have to be demarcated. The Federal Government should focus on higher education financing, regulations and standards and curriculum, the Provincial Governments on college, technical and vocational education and the District Governments on primary and secondary education up to matric. Examination reforms have to be carried out to bring the standards of various boards at par. Management and teaching cadres should be separated and the career paths for the two cadres should not discriminate against the teachers.

To bring about coordination and ensure uniformity in standards of public, private and not for profit schools, a district education board consisting of eminent citizens of integrity and competence should be established in each district. The Board should be assisted by the school management committees empowered to oversee the school's functioning. Head teachers will enjoy more administrative authority in running the schools and disciplining the teachers with the Board arranging inspection of schools periodically. Endowment funds should be established to provide scholarships and financial assistance to the poorer talented students. Student vouchers or stipends should be given to meritorious children from the poor families to attend private schools of their choice. Private-public partnerships should be encouraged and offered incentives. Only female teachers should be employed where possible.

b) Most of the problems in health care delivery arise not from financial constraints but poor management practices. A health management cadre should therefore be separated from teaching, and service providers and those selected as health managers trained at the health academies. The district, teaching and specialised hospital should have their own autonomous board of directors with full powers for administrative, financial, legal and human resource matters and accountability. Health manpower development, the nursing and paramedical professions, should be given priority. Health regulatory framework should be made more effective and decentralised to the Provincial Governments.

c) There is almost a consensus that law enforcement and security problems that have worsened in the recent years have in large part reflected the inefficiency, corruption and politicisation of the police force. The original Police Order 2002 has been compromised by amendments that have weakened the functioning as well as the accountability of the police. Legislative amendments and revised disciplinary rules are needed to allow police officers to perform their duties in accordance with the Police Order. Disciplinary rules of police forces should be like other uniformed forces and not fall under the purview of the Civil Servants Act. Investigation and prosecution are the weakest functions that are resulting in low rates of conviction by the courts. Judicial reforms at the lower level are also badly needed both for expeditious disposal of cases and honest adjudication of disputes. Police stations should be merged, upgraded, their records computerised and headed by a directly recruited Grade 17 officer with full responsibility for watch and ward, investigation and operations. Training, allowances, mobility, logistics support, lodging and boarding, medical facilities and welfare of the police force should be reviewed and strengthened. Traffic Police in all large cities should be organised and operated on the lines of Motorway Police.

d) Land records as maintained by the Patwari are the single largest source of disputes and litigation in the country. The attempts to create a digital database of land records have remained half hearted. Land revenue assessment and collection, adjudication and dispute resolution should remain under the District Government but the maintenance and update of land records should be taken away from the District Government and placed directly under the Board of Revenue. Patwari should be replaced by a Revenue Assistant recruited through Provincial Public Service Commission. Priority should be given to complete the computerisation of land records. Colonisation of Government Lands (Punjab) Act 1912 should be revised for better and transparent allocation and use of state land.

## Strengthening Key Institutions of Governance

About a hundred key public sector institutions in the country such as PIA, WAPDA, OGDC, PEPCO, Pakistan Railways and Pakistan Steel, suffer from multiple problems—political interference, nepotism in appointments, over-manning, subsidised pricing, leakages, waste, and corruption. As a result, the budget has to allocate almost 20 per cent of all tax revenue to meet recurring losses or subsidies to those corporations. There have been serious questions about the appointments of chief executives and the boards of these organisations. Professionalisation of these institutions is the only way out to make them financially viable and operationally efficient. The process of appointments has to be made transparent and merit-based so that the Chief Executive or the Board member is chosen through a well laid out procedure. This process should minimise discretionary powers in appointments and attract capable candidates for these key jobs, which will make an enormous difference in the quality and efficiency of these organisations.

Several of these institutions are included in the government's agenda for privatisation. It is imperative that these institutions are privatised sooner rather than later. For others that are retained in the public sector, and particularly public utilities and other monopolies, strong regulatory agencies should be put in place.

The selection process starts by identifying a broad pool of eligible candidates through open advertising. Only those who meet the job requirements are selected through a competitive process. They are provided with operational autonomy, paid competitive remuneration packages and held accountable for results. Special Selection Board (SSB) should be constituted for the recruitment of the Chief Executive Officers (CEOs) and the Board of Directors in all of these 100 institutions. The SSB, after interviewing the shortlisted candidates, would submit a panel of three candidates to the Prime Minister for selection as chief executive and recommend a panel of names for the membership of the BoD.

*Institutions of Restraint*[13]

A few institutions can play a restraining influence on mis-governance and excessive discretionary powers by the government. These institutions fall into two categories: formal and informal. Under the former there are two distinct classes: state-centred and civil society-centred. Historically, the emphasis has been on state-centred institutions and it is only recently that the civil society-centred institutions such as the media and NGOs have begun to assert themselves.

Trust, social capital, and civic norms—the pillars of informal institutions have also eroded gradually in Pakistan during the last few decades. Mistrust, suspicion and divisiveness have instead taken hold. So in effect both the formal and informal institutions of restraint have decayed and need to be resuscitated.

A schematic representation of the institutions is provided in Table 1.

Among the state-centred institutions the judiciary is at a much higher plane than any other institution and underpins the whole system of accountability. In addition to the judiciary, there are at least eight institutions that can make a difference. The first are the Parliamentary committees particularly the Public Accounts Committee. Bipartisan committees chaired by respected and qualified MNAs or Senators and staffed by full time professional and technical personnel should hold regular hearings, confirm the appointments of those heading these institutions, receive annual reports of performance, question reported irregularities and recommend action against those found responsible for wrongdoings. All procurement contracts above a certain financial limit, all fiscal exemptions and concessions and modifications to the

Table 1: Institutions of Restraint in Pakistan

| Spheres of Influence/Restraint | |
|---|---|
| **FORMAL** | |
| *A. State-Centred* | |
| Judiciary | Protection of Basic Human Rights, Security of Life and Property, Contract Enforcement |
| Parliamentary Committees/ Accounts Committee | Avoiding misuse and abuse of discretion powers of the Executive branch |
| Auditor General | Detecting and reporting of financial irregularities in public accounts |
| Ombudsman | Redressal of grievances of citizens against the excesses of public sector agencies |
| Public Service Commission | Transparency in appointments and promotions to Civil services |
| State Bank of Pakistan | Probity, supervision and regulation of the financial institutions |
| Federal Election Commission | Screening of candidates for the elected public offices on the basis of integrity |
| Securities and Exchange Commission | Ensuring high standards of Corporate governance in publicly listed companies |
| National Accountability Bureau | Curbing corruption and misuse of public office for private gains |
| *B. Civil Society-Centred* | |
| Media | Investigating and reporting of instances of corrupt practices in the country |
| Non-governmental Organisations | Monitoring and advocacy of Governance issues and participation in delivery of social services |
| Academic Institutions/Think Tanks | Research and analysis of the performance of the state organs, media and NGOs |
| Professional Organisations | Providing inputs into a participatory decision-making process |
| Private Sector Organisations | Regulating code of ethics among the private sector |
| Religious Bodies | Building trust and harmony among various groups of society |
| **INFORMAL** | |
| Trust | |
| Social Capital | |
| Civic Norms | |

tax provisions should be placed before the PAC. The proceedings of these Committees should be open to the public and the media.

Second is the State Bank of Pakistan. An independent and autonomous State Bank provides a guarantee against the excessive and irresponsible actions of politicians and bureaucrats in economic management. At the same time its regulatory and supervision functions act as a safeguard against possible malpractices in the award of credit and recovery of loans. It must be recognised that there has already been significant improvement in the working of the State Bank since it was granted autonomy in the 1990s. The banking sector in Pakistan, after the reforms of the last decade, has emerged quite strong and was able to withstand domestic and external shocks.

Third is the Auditor General of Pakistan. The constitutional protection given to the office of the AG has not been fully utilised in Pakistan to unearth and detect financial bungling rampant in public sector agencies. The extended time lapse between the occurrence of the financial irregularity and actual detection and reporting by the Auditors has improved in recent years. But the lack of professional expertise and lack of prioritisation among core and peripheral cases still mute the efficacy of this office. AG organisation should be converted into a supreme audit institution with autonomy, resources and accountability to Parliament. The AG should commission third party audits by professional firms of repute, use the broader 'value for money' concept and enlarge its scope of activities to cover all major public sector commercial and industrial enterprises particularly WAPDA/KESC, Sui Northern/Southern, Railways, Steel Mill, OGDC, PIA, etc.

Fourth is the Securities and Exchange Commission. Capital markets in Pakistan are very shallow and have not played an effective role in intermediation required in an emerging market. Corporate governance of the publicly listed companies is weak and dominated by major family shareholders with due regard to the right of minority shareholders. Insider trading is perceived to be widely rampant and disclosure of information standards is loosely enforced. The SEC needs operational autonomy, resources and skills to carry out its mandate.

Fifth is the Federal/Provincial Public Service Commission. Most of the current difficulties in governance have arisen due to the politicisation of the higher services in the post-1973 period. There is general recognition that the merit-based system of recruitment, appointments and promotions, served the nation better and the present sifarish based and buy-the-post system is causing havoc. The responsibilities for all recruitment and promotions should be reverted to the Commissions without exception. Only men and women of proven integrity and impeccable credentials should be appointed as Chairman and members of the Commission.

Sixth is the Federal/Provincial Ombudsman. The fanfare with which these offices were established under the Zia-ul-Haq Government died down fairly quickly. They are now perceived to be grinding the same millstone as the rest of the bureaucracy. In fact, they can become an effective instrument for quick, fair and judicious redress of grievances of ordinary citizens against the arbitrary harassment of the overzealous or corrupt officials. There are very few people who are aware of the scope and mandate of this office and who have trust in the organisation. A proactive educational role, a demonstrative effect of its reach accompanied by selection of the right persons to the job can make it work.

Seventh is the Federal Election Commission. A powerful, independent and assertive FEC can play a preventive role by careful screening, scrutiny and investigation of the candidates for all tiers of elected offices and disqualifying those who are ill reputed and of dubious character. They should forcefully enforce the criteria prescribed under the Constitution augmented by appropriate rules and regulations. This fundamental shift in the quality of our elected public officials would bring about a significant change in the overall structure of governance in the country.

Eighth is the National Accountability Bureau (NAB). The law establishing the Bureau was quite a significant measure in holding to account the corrupt and those who derive personal gains from public office. But the implementation of the law was selective and the Bureau soon lost its credibility and moral authority. The recent move to place the Bureau under the Ministry of Law is a step in the wrong direction. The Bureau or its successor organisation should be given complete operational and financial autonomy and protected from political interference. It is the fear of the Bureau that should act as a deterrent.

*How can these Institutions of Restraint be Strengthened?*

There are certain pre-conditions under which these institutions of restraint can be strengthened. First, a system of checks and balances can flourish only if various countervailing forces such as the parliament, judiciary, media and the civil society organisations are allowed to play an independent role. There should be no presumption that any one entity whether it is the executive or the judiciary or the media or civil society will enjoy monopoly power or act as a self-righteous body of vigilance. It is the interaction of these various entities and balance between them which will generate the optimal results. Second, no new institutions are being proposed but only the revitalisation, revamping and re-engineering of those already in existence under the constitution is being suggested. There is a common tendency and an easy way out for both national government and international donors to abandon the existing institutions and create new agencies which start out with a big bang but soon fall prey to the same whirlpool of inaction and ineptitude. The reasons for failure are the same as those which explain the non-performance of existing institutions. Unless the underlying dynamics is set right the institutional morass will grow. The history of Pakistan is laden with the creation of a plethora of new institutions which have been given blurred mandates, inadequate resources, little operational autonomy and are never held accountable for results.

Finally, this proposal does not favour the periodic, swift, abrupt, highly visible and publicised, extra-institutional measures against recalcitrant officials which have been the norm in Pakistan since the 1958 screening of senior civil servants under Ayub Khan. The subsequent actions by successive governments resorting to the purge of 303 or 1500 civil servants paradoxically created greater insecurity, uncertainty and unpredictability which are the breeding grounds for increased corruption.

The approach advocated here is to create an environment whereby the acts of misdemeanour and malfeasance are exposed routinely, increased vigilance and scrutiny is exercised continuously, early detection, investigation and fixing of responsibility are carried out resolutely and disciplinary actions against those found guilty are taken promptly. Such an environment would act as a more effective deterrent in curbing corrupt practices than creating many laws and anti-corruption agencies with enormous powers which are misused. This approach will not work if the federal and provincial investigation agencies are not organised on modern and professional lines. It will also be difficult to implement it if the government does not do away with the widespread and mindless application of the Official Secrets Act which has encouraged opacity of decision-making by politicians and civil servants. Outside the matters of national defence and internal security, all decisions—particularly in matters of public finance, foreign trade, contract awards and allocation of other public resources—should be wholly transparent and made public liberally under the Freedom of Information Act.

These eight pillars of good governance can together make the difference, provided (a) they are headed by widely respected, strong and competent managers of known integrity (we have many of them in the country); (b) the terms of reference, responsibilities, functions and powers of these institutions are clearly defined; (c) there is no political interference in their working but at the same time they are held publicly accountable for their actions and the results; (d) they are providing adequate financial resources and professional staff of calibre; (e) they follow open and transparent procedures and processes. To ensure non-partisan political support for these institutions their heads should be confirmed by the Parliamentary Committees. In this way, the changes in the government will not disrupt their smooth functioning.

Together, these eight pillars, if allowed to work effectively, will be able to plug in some of the conduits that lead to corrupt practices. The most difficult question to answer is: Who will bell the cat? Who has the courage to put these changes in place? Of course, an enlightened government that has a sense of history rather than sights fixed on the next election. Pakistan has not been fortunate in having such a government so far.

*Conclusion*

The story of Pakistan provides ample confirmation of the validity of theoretical literature and empirical evidence about governance in developing countries. The distinctive characteristics that dominate the Pakistani scene, are the elitist capture of the state, excessive centralisation of power by both the elected and military rulers, chronic political instability and until recently collusion between the power structures— the politicians, the Army and the judiciary. The conflicts that took place at times between these power structures were not rooted in benign balancing acts for the larger collective good of the society but assertion of the authority by different actors to advance their narrow interests. Unlike other societies, the cost Pakistan had to pay for poor governance and institutional decay has been very high.

The path ahead is clearly defined. The agenda for reforms has to be carved out in the light of historical experience, internationally established best practices and the various characteristics peculiar to the Pakistani situation. This can form a logical sequence to the Eighteenth Constitutional Amendment and the National Finance Commission Award of 2010. There is an urgent need to realise that only taking this reform agenda to its culmination point over the next five years can complete the value chain.

10

# AN ECONOMIC CRISIS STATE?

*Dr Meekal Ahmed**

A trend-setter in Asia up to the sixties, economic management in Pakistan has steadily deteriorated to the point where the economy has, for the past few decades, lurched from one financial crisis to the next. At the heart of the problem has been the poor management of public finances and deep-seated unresolved structural issues in the economy that bad management and poor governance has exacerbated. The consequences of this secular decline in economic governance are plain to see: macroeconomic instability, high inflation, poor public services, criminal neglect of the social sectors, widespread corruption, crippling power outages, growing unemployment, deepening poverty and a deteriorating debt profile.

*The Early Years*

Pakistan has experienced many crises in recent years. Each one of them has been a caricature of the previous one with an economic boom, typically fuelled by official aid inflows, followed by bust which ends in

* The author is grateful for comments, refinements and corrections made by Muhammad Yaqub, Zubair Iqbal, Javed Talat, Azizali Mohammad, Faizullah Khilji, Atiq Rehman and Syed Iqbal Zaidi. The usual caveats apply.

a severe balance of payments crisis. In the early years, the economic scene was marked by relative stability, strong growth and low inflation. In Ayub Khan's era, Pakistan was considered to be a 'model of development' and 'aid-effectiveness'. Ayub Khan was deeply interested in economic development. He placed the Planning Commission under the President's Secretariat and himself became the Chairman. The Planning Commission was staffed with some of Pakistan's best and brightest economic minds. It was ably supported by a number of fine economists from the former East Pakistan who worked in the Pakistan Institute of Development Economics, as well as economists and policy analysts from the Harvard Advisory Group. Ayub Khan listened to their advice and often deferred to their judgment over the views of the mighty ICS/CSP. Pakistan's Second Five-Year Plan came to be widely regarded as the best produced in Pakistan and the developing world. It was not only well-crafted and technically sound but embodied targets and objectives that were realistically ambitious. The report on the Evaluation of the Second Five-Year Plan showed that most plan targets had been met or exceeded both in the macroeconomic field and with respect to projects and programs bearing testimony to the fundamental soundness and realism of the plan.

Pakistan was also blessed with other fine institutions led by persons of great integrity and competence: PIA, WAPDA, the Railways, PICIC, IDBP, the State Bank, the ICS/CSP, and so on. All these institutions operated at high levels of efficiency and in the case of commercial entities were profitable. The economy grew at a steady pace with some sectors such as manufacturing racing ahead at double-digits. Inflation remained tame with agricultural productivity boosted by the fruits of the Green Revolution. The domestic and external deficits were kept in check. Of course, at the time, the economy was closed and tightly controlled and rationing of some food items and especially foreign exchange was commonplace. Yet there was no evidence of price pressures suggesting that the underlying balance between demand and supply was being maintained. Even exports performed well despite the clumsy and opaque 'Bonus Voucher Scheme' with its multiple exchange rates.

It is true that foreign aid, at that time mostly in the form of outright grants and PL-480 grain shipments paid for in rupee counterpart funds and thus non-external debt-creating, fuelled much of the growth. By supplementing domestic savings, aid allowed Pakistan to invest more than might have otherwise been possible with domestic resources alone. Importantly, the aid was well spent in building social and physical infrastructure, in particular large hydro-power dams in the context of the Indus Basin Treaty which was brokered by the World Bank. The investment to incremental capital-output ratio, a good summary measure of capital efficiency, was low and produced high real growth rates per unit of capital invested. Plan projects and programs were well-prepared using the 'best-practice' techniques of project appraisal and analysis of the time. Monitoring of projects was rigorous and conducted on-site; project cost over-runs and delays were minimal; project benefits were delivered as promised; corruption was not spoken of and Plan guidelines were respected and Plan discipline enforced.

The external environment was exceptionally benign. The global economy was in the midst of an unprecedented period of expansion which started at the end of World War II with world trade growing at a healthy pace, markets relatively open, and little global inflation. Thus the economy experienced few of the shocks that could derail its steady upward trajectory and challenge policy-makers.

Ayub Khan was a victim of economic success. The revelation by none other than the Chief Economist of the Planning Commission—his most beloved institution which he headed—that twenty-two families controlled 70 per cent of manufacturing and 90 per cent of banking and insurance business in the country jolted his regime to its foundations. It was a supreme irony that Ayub Khan was following the growth philosophy as espoused by the Chief Economist of the Planning Commission in his Cambridge PhD thesis turned book, 'The Strategy of Economic Planning'. Growth philosophy argued that in the initial stages of economic development some concentration of income and wealth in a few hands was necessary and appropriate to stimulate 'animal spirits' and foster the conditions for rapid growth. Considerations of equity and income distribution could be tackled at a later stage of development. The reaction to the revelation of concentration of wealth in a few hands was hostile and swift. Pakistan's industrialists came to be called 'Robber Barons' who had earned monopolistic profits behind high walls of protection, subsidies and government patronage. An empirical study by Professor Lawrence White of New York University lent credence to this proposition. Furthermore, some of the industries that had been set-up behind high protective tariff barriers were generating 'negative value-added' when their inputs and outputs were valued at 'world' prices (rather than being valued at distorted domestic prices).

Factor price distortions, including an over-valued exchange rate had led to the choice of highly capital-intensive techniques of production, generating little employment per unit of capital and output. One study by an East Pakistan economist of repute calculated that factor intensity in Pakistan as measured by the capital-labour ratio was higher than in an advanced country like Japan. There had been economic growth to be sure; but it had been distorted in terms of factor proportions and allocative inefficiencies. Most importantly, it had exacted a high price in terms of inter-personal and, more ominously, inter-wing disparities in income and wealth. In West Pakistan the revelation of concentration of income and wealth provided the springboard for the rise of Mr Z.A. Bhutto's People's Party and its socialist agenda. In East Pakistan Mujibur Rahman used the finding of concentration of wealth in a few hands, mostly belonging to families in the West, to argue that East Pakistan had been exploited and robbed of its resources and wealth through policy-induced distortions in the inter-wing terms-of-trade.

Yahya Khan took over without much economic dislocation. There were a few tough words about the concentration of wealth but the government did not do much except set up a toothless Monopoly Control Authority with an ostensible mandate to look at and punish anti-competitive behaviour. It never did amount to much. The 1971 war placed pressure on government spending and imports and the dismemberment of the country gave pragmatic argument for the nationalisation of the financial sector.

Bhutto had little patience with economic matters. His nationalisation program was a shock to the system and a grievous blow to private sector confidence that would take years to rebuild. New private sector investment came to a virtual halt. There was much (concealed) capital flight as businessmen took their money out of the economy either before or after nationalisation and it would be many years for this capital flight to reverse itself. The economic effects of the break-up of Pakistan were profound. It caused vast disruptions to the financial and corporate sectors that had operated on the basis of a single country. The State Bank of Pakistan had been pushing the Pakistani commercial banks into increasing lending in East Pakistan while their deposit base was almost entirely in the western wing where most, if not all of them, were headquartered. The dissolution of the country created an imbalance between assets and liabilities that left most of the banks (with the solitary exception of the National Bank) in virtual bankruptcy; the same applied to the insurance sector where the largest private insurance company—Eastern Federal—was headquartered in Dhaka and lost access to its assets while most of its liabilities to life policy-holders were resident in the western wing. Nationalisation was the only way that a total bankruptcy of the financial system was avoided, especially as this postponed any question of compensating the shareholders, depositors and policy-holders. Many observers remain convinced that nationalisations of the financial system was a negative turning-point for the economy but this was only a proximate cause: the real cause lay in the country's break-up.

The corporate sector suffered similar fracturing of balance-sheets since some of the more adventurous business firms (like the Adamjees) were operating in both wings and lost their investments in the eastern wing at one stroke. To add insult to injury—and given the time lags involved in the income tax administration, many of these firms continued to be pressed for taxes on earlier years' profits earned in the eastern wing! That the private sector survived at all in the wake of this calamity and with the additional ideological nationalisations imposed by Mr Bhutto is, some feel, nothing short of a miracle. That said, nationalisation was by and large well-received by the people who saw it as an election promise fulfilled and a means of redressing the evils of concentration of wealth and wide disparities in income. Bhutto's boldest move on the economic front was to sharply devalue the Pakistan rupee and bring it closer to its 'equilibrium' value. The years of clinging to an artificially appreciated rate of Rs. 4.76 per US dollar, which was propped up by tight controls on foreign exchange and which created many distortions in the economy were finally over. His government faced the challenge of the first oil-price shock and turned to the IMF for short-term financing but there was not much conditionality attached and no reforms were implemented. To be fair to Mr Bhutto, the gods were not kind to him. Each year brought a drought or a flood—negative domestic exogenous shocks—which hurt growth and caused a pick-up in inflation. Yet the economy was kept afloat and on a reasonably even keel thanks to Bhutto's diplomatic success in securing financing from friendly Islamic countries (including $500 million from the Shah of Iran) and the Gulf, as well as an emerging new phenomenon: rising workers' remittances which were becoming an important source of financing the external accounts.

*From Aid-Fuelled Growth to Volatility*

Zia's regime represented the second episode of aid-fuelled growth after Pakistan became a 'front-line' state with the Soviet invasion of Afghanistan in 1979. His economic policies were otherwise unremarkable and devoid of any bold initiatives. The economy was kept on a stable path thanks to the ultra-conservative approach of the inimitable Ghulam Ishaq Khan who, as the country's financial kingpin, had an aversion to changing the economic status quo and little time or patience to hear about IMF/World Bank recommendations of freer markets, privatisation, exchange rate flexibility and a bigger role for the private sector. In a World Bank document outlining the conditionality of a Structural Adjustment Loan for Pakistan he wrote succinctly by hand, 'I am not prepared to hand over the management of the Pakistan economy to the World Bank for $250 million'. That was the end of that discussion.

While foreign aid once again was the main driver of growth, it cannot be said that the aid Pakistan received during these years was well spent. Indeed, as we know now, much of the aid was diverted to the military. Zia had other things on his mind and left much of the economic management to his Finance Minister who was content to keep a steady hand on the levers of economic policy. It must have been a blow to a hugely stubborn and proud man when Pakistan was forced to enter into a three-year arrangement with the IMF (an Extended Fund Facility) because of balance of payments difficulties. The program was treated as a secret document with only one copy of the program conditionality kept under lock and key. Even secretaries of ministries and divisions were not called to the meetings with the IMF so they could not present their views, had no idea of what had been agreed to or what they had to implement. In any event, the IMF program was abandoned without completing it or undertaking any economic reforms of substance (apart from minor tinkering with the trade and import tariff regime and some cosmetic steps towards restructuring the public enterprise sector), one of the many IMF programs that would meet the same fate.

The first signs of macroeconomic volatility seem to have started with the Benazir government. Her first tenure was labelled a 'comedy of errors'. There was some truth to that unflattering label despite the steadying hand of her experienced and able Advisor of Finance whom she, sadly, did not listen to often enough. Once again in economic distress, Pakistan entered into a major IMF program at the inception of her government. On a visit to Washington DC, the Managing Director of the IMF was so taken by her that he added $100 million with his own pen to the $1.2 billion the IMF staff had recommended for Pakistan. This was done on the understanding of cutting trade protection by 30 per cent while meeting a fiscal deficit target of 5 per cent of GDP. In the budget that followed, she did neither, bringing the IMF program to an ignominious halt.

Following much discussion and new commitments, the IMF program was re-started. Even then, economic growth was lackluster and volatile, fiscal slippages were routine and inflation picked up. Despite IMF resources there was constant pressure on the external accounts as manifest by the (growing) disparity between the parallel market for foreign exchange (or the 'hundi' rate) and the official market rate. This was because the budget was subject to extreme spending pressures since her weak mandate meant she had to please everyone. Budget supplmentaries (approvals for more spending not provided for in the original budget) became commonplace. The disparity between the official and 'hundi' rate was also widening, as the Prime Minister would give instructions to the State Bank not to move the exchange rate because it gave her a bad press and suggested economic failure. She was always concerned about 'my forex position' as she called it. But to her credit must go two accomplishments. She granted the State Bank of Pakistan a degree of autonomy (even if it was under IMF pressure and was part of a 'prior action' in the IMF program meaning an action to be taken before the program was approved) taking it out of the grip of the Ministry of Finance. Pakistan's tax-to-GDP ratio hit a short-lived peak during her twenty months in power in her first tenure in office. Once convinced, and that was never easy because she was opinionated and liked to argue, she showed a capacity to take bold measures and accept the political backlash. This was sustained and well-orchestrated with Nawaz Sharif and his 'bazaar-power' snapping at her heels from the Punjab asking his supporters not to pay taxes. Clandestine efforts were also made to spread panic in the foreign exchange market by planted rumours of massive capital flight. Pakistan's foreign exchange reserves took a frightening dip as the contrived rumours turned into a self-fulfilling prophecy. However, the situation stabilised quickly thereafter.

## Sharif's 'Far-Reaching' Reforms

Nawaz Sharif is widely regarded as bringing about an economic revolution in Pakistan with his 'far-reaching' economic reforms. His 'no-questions-asked' foreign currency deposits (FCDs) were a haven for tax evaders and under-filers—the scourge of Pakistan's economy—that could now 'whiten' their ill-gotten income with no taxation and no fear of detection. With no foreign exchange reserve cover to back them up, these deposits quickly swelled to close to $12 billion, of which 80 per cent belonged to resident Pakistanis who had converted their ill-gotten wealth into dollar accounts with no fear of questions as to the source of this income. To add insult to injury to those who did pay taxes, these FCDs were handsomely remunerated at above-market rates, guaranteed against exchange risk and allowed unrestricted withdrawal facilities. These features and capital gains from exchange rate depreciation made the scheme a highly attractive instrument. Since this was an age before concerns about 'money laundering' were openly talked about the IMF gave muted approval to this 'far-reaching' reform. However, as the IMF cautioned, an 'open capital account' (which incidentally inverted the sequence of external liberalisation since the current account should have been opened first) meant that economic policies would have to be especially disciplined so as not to shake the confidence of these holders of foreign exchange. The IMF also warned that the overhang of such foreign exchange demand liabilities, unmatched by parallel reserve accumulation, heightened the economy's vulnerability to downside risks and that bad policies or an adverse exogenous shock would quickly manifest itself in capital flight and bring the economy to its knees.

But many feel the Fund was not forceful enough. As the Fund's Independent Evaluation Office report on Pakistan noted, 'at the authorities request, the FCDs owned by residents were reported in the balance of payments "above the line" as part of private transfers (like workers' remittances) and even FCDs held by non-residents were not included in the stock of external debt'. Furthermore, FCDs held by residents, even though they represented a liquid claim on the central bank's foreign exchange holdings and generated a large 'open' position for the central bank, were not netted out for the purpose of program monitoring of net international reserves, or NIR (where changes in NIR are an important part of program conditionality).

The benefit to government of these resident FCDs was that it had access to foreign exchange that could be used to finance the external current account deficit. It also allowed the Sharif government (including, to be sure, successive governments) to postpone taking the necessary but difficult policy measures to address the fundamental disequilibrium in the balance of payments. However, by encouraging rapid 'dollarisation' of the economy it eroded confidence in the rupee, reduced the tax base, caused huge losses to the State Bank because of the exchange risk guarantee and immunity from enquiry, legalised capital flight and promoted the growth of the underground economy. Finally, at a policy level, the rising proportion of resident FCDs in total money supply constrained monetary policy management. Controlling domestic liquidity became more difficult and behavioural relationships between reserve money (operational target) broad money (intermediate target) and inflation (ultimate objective) became more complex.

Despite the economy's new vulnerability and the need to foster an environment of macroeconomic stability and low inflation, the government embarked on a number of grandiose schemes, the most notable of which were motorways and airports (all financed by non-concessional external borrowing) with the *pièce de résistance* being the yellow cab scheme. In short order, as rows of yellow cabs filled the parking lots at the Karachi Port, Pakistan's foreign exchange reserves started to dwindle with alarming speed until there was only $150 million left in the kitty (equivalent to about a day's worth of imports) against foreign exchange demand liabilities of $12 billion. Once again Pakistan turned to the IMF to bail it out.

*Shifting Sands*

General Musharraf acknowledged that he did not know economics. But he was a good listener, loved long-winded, coloured power-point presentations and he learnt well. As usual, given the precarious state of the economy with low foreign exchange reserves, Pakistan entered into an IMF program, which took the shape of a three-year highly concessional Poverty Reduction and Growth Facility (PRGF) with high access. Despite the arrangement, foreign exchange reserves initially continued to hover at the very low level of $1–1.7 billion. This changed dramatically after 9/11 reflecting the reverse flow of capital and re-flow of workers' remittances into the official market, both of

which occurred in response to fears of possible investigation of transactions in the money-changer market. Debt relief from the Paris Club,
increased disbursements of foreign assistance by the US after Pakistan's
cooperation in Afghanistan, also contributed to the reserve build-up.
In one year alone, foreign exchange reserves surged by more than $4
billion, boosting confidence, stabilising the exchange rate and reducing
the disparity between the official and parallel market rate for foreign
exchange. Indeed at one point the parallel market rate was less depreciated than the official exchange rate.

In a remarkable first, the government actually completed the three-
year PRGF. Whether this was done with a sleight of hand or not
remains a mystery. Pakistan had earlier confessed to cooking the fiscal
books and showing a lower fiscal deficit than the true one. Without
taking the Office of Executive Director in the IMF into confidence
beforehand, which may have allowed the matter of misreporting to be
handled quietly, the new Finance Minister stunned the IMF with a
letter of admission of misreporting of the fiscal deficit. An IMF mission was sent to Pakistan to investigate the matter and submitted a
report to the IMF Executive Board. Pakistan was fined millions of
SDRs (the IMF's synthetic unit of account) for this indiscretion and
had to return money to the IMF since it had been accessed (drawn on)
in the context of an IMF program and therefore under false pretences
(IMF News Brief No. 00/23). Whether this practice of massaging the
data to meet targets continued under the PRGF remains unknown.
With a few exceptions, Pakistan's national accounts are poor and bear
only a passing resemblance to the reality on the ground. This is especially so with regards to the fiscal accounts where an unknown but
certainly large amount of spending, particularly US-funded military
spending, is undertaken off-budget. The fiscal accounts, typically the
cornerstone of an IMF program are a tempting target for discreet and
deft manipulation.

With the IMF program completed, there was much rejoicing and
backslapping over having broken the 'begging bowl' and regaining our
'economic sovereignty'. To more sober and thoughtful minds, and
especially in the light of our past experience, many hearts sank since
such boastful declarations usually signal the beginning of another end.
And so it was this time as well. Now unconstrained in its decision-
making, the government embarked on a hasty and ill-conceived dash
for growth taking comfort from a significant level of foreign exchange

reserves, sharply rising workers' remittances, up-grades by rating agencies, large inflows of foreign private direct and portfolio investment, new bond flotation, and plentiful aid. The principal instrument to further the government's growth objective was to use monetary policy to finance consumption, a bizarre strategy in a savings-constrained economy with a large savings–investment gap (which was mirrored on the external side by the large disparity between imports and exports). To 'kick-start' the economy, interest rates were cut sharply to below inflation which meant that they were negative in inflation-adjusted terms flooding the economy with cheap money and excess liquidity. In the initial period, with some 'slack' in the economy (as reflected in underutilised labour and capital and a negative output-gap) growth did pick up and inflation stayed low. However, this slack was quickly taken up and the economy moved to above its 'potential growth' limit, defined as the maximum speed at which an economy can grow—given labour and capital resources and the shape of the technical progress function—without igniting inflationary pressures or straining macroeconomic imbalances.

The underlying trend of inflation is always a good indicator of resources pressure in an economy. Inflation was unusually low in the aftermath of September 11 at around 2 per cent per annum but started to pick-up. By the time inflation had reached 5–6 per cent per annum there was no cause for undue alarm since that is Pakistan's long-term 'steady-state' rate of inflation and one could argue that inflation had reverted to its long-term trend. There would have been even less cause for concern on the inflation front if the growth upswing had been accompanied by improvements in economy-wide Total Factor Productivity (TFP) that would augment the economy's potential non-inflationary growth limit. While a pick-up in TFP typically occurs in the initial phase of an economic upturn (as output grows faster than the existing stock of inputs of labour, capital and technology), the growth of TFP should reflect a permanent structural shift in the production function that is sustained and can therefore support the higher non-inflationary growth potential of the economy. There is no evidence to suggest that TFP growth following an initial pick-up was either permanent, structural or was sustained.

To a discerning economic observer it should have been clear that the economy had started to 'overheat' as aggregate demand raced ahead of the economy's aggregate supply potential largely fuelled by consumption. In addition to the loose and highly accommodative monetary policy stance of negative real interest rates, the fiscal deficit instead of serving as a counter-cyclical tool and attenuating demand pressures on the up-swing (as it normally should) was becoming dangerously pro-cyclical. Thus, both fiscal and monetary policy was imparting a strong expansionary impulse, pushing up inflation and spilling over into the external sector leading to surging imports while 'crowding out' exports when economic policy should have been aiming to do the reverse. The fact that the exchange rate was appreciating in real effective terms (a 'stable' nominal exchange rate set against a background of rising domestic inflation) made matters worse as export profitability was squeezed and the export-to-GDP ratio fell. As the external deficit widened there was sustained downward pressure on the country's foreign exchange reserves. This is always an unambiguous sign of an economy under stress.

A paper prepared by the Social Policy and Development Center as early as 2005 presented some striking numbers all pointing towards economic overheating. Economic growth was a solid 8.4 per cent, the highest in the world. But growth was not being driven by investment and net exports. It was being led by consumption and imports rather than the more sustainable route of investment and exports. In 2005 real private consumption rose by 17 per cent (double the rate of the previous year), imports by 44 per cent, exports by only 8 per cent (the large difference between imports and exports or net exports shaved off as much as 5 per cent from growth), private fixed investment rose by a modest 4.8 per cent, public investment fell 5 per cent and inflation accelerated into double-digits. Despite these numbers, which denoted an economy under stress, the 2005–06 budget took on an ominously expansionary and pro-cyclical stance.

Apologists for General Musharraf's regime argue that once it had become clear that the economy was overheating, the State Bank of Pakistan moved into a tightening phase and raised its policy interest rate to cool the economy. If that was the case the State Bank was hopelessly behind the policy-making curve. This is because it takes twelve to fifteen months for a change in the policy interest rate to start to affect outcomes. In view of these long lags, the State Bank should have acted preemptively at the first unmistakable signs of economic overheating (of which there were many) to dampen demand pressures and subdue inflation, which had now developed a worryingly unstoppable dimension.

With speculative bubbles developing in consumption, the real estate sector, the stock market and commodities such as gold, and accelerating inflation, all that was needed to tip an overheated economy with heightened vulnerability over the edge was a small unanticipated exogenous domestic or external shock. This came in the form of the large 'twin global shocks', the first of which was the surge in the global price of oil and other commodities; and the second the worst global financial crisis since the Great Depression. The former pushed Pakistan's fiscal deficit to beyond 8 per cent of GDP as the higher price of oil was absorbed into the budget as subsidies and was not passed through; correspondingly the higher imported cost of oil and commodities swelled the external current account deficit to in excess of 8 per cent of GDP. The 'Great Global Recession' also hurt the demand for Pakistan's exports at a time when import volume and unit values were rising strongly.

The new government inherited an economy in growing disarray as the lags from the deeply flawed policies of the previous government worked themselves out. Instead of quickly taking stock of the rapidly deteriorating economic situation and implementing strong corrective measures, the government seemed stupefied. A new concoction named 'Friends of Democratic Pakistan' (FoDP) pledged fresh assistance to Pakistan at a conference held in Tokyo, Japan but it was clear—or should have been clear—that translating these pledges into actual inflows that would help the budget and/or the balance of payments would take time. The Finance Minister informed the people that he had a 'Plan A', a 'Plan B' and a 'Plan C' in mind when it should have been clear to him that the only game in town was Plan F—the IMF.

It is true that countries that are in economic distress are reluctant to turn to the IMF for assistance, since doing so is an admission of economic failure and of a loss of control. Articles in the Pakistan press about 'fiscal servitude' and the 'social holocaust' an IMF program will bring in its wake, whether contrived or spontaneous, did not help the government make up its mind. However, delaying, prevaricating and hoping that someone would come to Pakistan's rescue only made the task of economic adjustment more painful. It is self-evident that the wrenching pain of adjustment and the strength of the corrective measures that would be needed to put the economy back on track would have been smaller and the costs in terms of lost output, employment and poverty less if Pakistan had turned to the IMF earlier rather than later.

As domestic and external deficits widened and inflation continued to climb, confidence was lost and there ensued unprecedented capital flight amid a rupee/dollar exchange rate in virtual free-fall. The stock market collapsed as private portfolio investment fled to safer heavens, bubbles popped and our foreign exchange reserves, in a painful repeat of the past, started to disappear with astonishing speed, at one time declining $700 million in a single week. In the end, Pakistan had no recourse except to turn once again to the IMF for 'exceptional financing'. It is highly likely that the FoDP made their support conditional on Pakistan engaging with the IMF.

In hindsight it is true that the twin external exogenous shocks served as the tipping point for the economy. But these shocks were neither the precipitating nor the initiating force behind Pakistan's latest economic crisis; they exacerbated it but did not cause it. The root cause of the crisis was the short-sighted and heedless pursuit of unsustainable policies, both fiscal and monetary, that produced an illusion of consumption-led growth and prosperity for a while but was bound to self-destruct.

With a little bit of foresight, attention to the build-up of pressures and carefully-calibrated preemptive steps to cool the economy, the economy would have made a 'soft landing' and Pakistan could have been as well-placed to cope with the twin exogenous shocks as other developing countries were. The economy could have continued on a less spectacular but more sustainable growth path with macroeconomic imbalances tending towards correction and inflationary pressure easing. Other developing countries had room to use their fiscal position as a counter-cyclical tool and ease monetary policy to cushion the turbulent downburst arising from 'The Great Global Recession' since their starting position was stronger.

Pakistan had to do the reverse. It had to tighten its macroeconomic policy stance, curb the fiscal deficit and push up interest rates in an effort to dampen demand pressures and inflation and forestall a full-blown balance of payments crisis and debt-default. The people of Pakistan were once again put through a painful exercise of economic readjustment. As economic growth slowed amid soaring inflation which hit an unprecedented headline rate of 26 per cent (core inflation which strips out the volatile components of inflation such as food and oil and is an unambiguous reflection of the underlying stance of macro-economic policies also hit an unprecedented high of 18 per cent), the economy was trapped in the grips of stagflation. Unemployment rose and millions of households were pushed back into poverty as high inflation cruelly eroded their living standards.

## Was the IMF Culpable?

It has been argued that the genesis of the crisis as described here is exaggerated because the IMF—the ever-watchful guardian of fiscal and monetary rectitude—would have said something. However, the truth of the matter is that with the IMF program having been completed, it had no leverage over the conduct and direction of Pakistan's economic policies. The annual obligatory Article IV Consultation discussion which the IMF holds with all member-counties (advanced and developing) is, compared to program negotiations, a relaxed affair and is taken lightly. This is unfortunate because IMF 'surveillance' over member's policies (whether they have an IMF program or not) goes to the heart of the IMF's mandate. The IMF is duty-bound to point out emerging risks and unsustainable policies and make recommendations for timely corrective action. How it should convey the message and what kind of language it should use has been the subject of much debate amongst IMF staff, management and the Executive Board. There is always the risk that strong words may rattle markets and precipitate a crisis when there was not one to begin with. On the other hand, the IMF can be too nuanced and subtle in its language (sometimes dubbed as 'Fund-speak') in glossing over fault lines. It has happened in South America and most infamously in the Asian Crisis of the 90s as well as in Mexico and Russia. Critical turning points can be missed, the language in staff reports to the Executive Board is insufficiently forthright and the IMF is caught off-guard when the crisis erupts.

Were the Pakistani authorities warned of the unsustainable nature of their policies or the economy's heightened vulnerability to shocks, and impending disaster? There is reason to believe they were, but only in private. These warnings were rebuffed with the Bushism that, 'You are either with us or against us'. In one case a critical report on the performance of the Pakistan economy was re-written, toning down the language and the Mission Chief's name was removed from the document. Obviously, neither the Pakistani authorities nor the IMF's Executive Board read the original unexpurgated report. That report presented in stark hard-hitting terms the escalating risks of an impending crisis and urged urgent corrective action in the fiscal, monetary, structural and exchange rate areas.

Is the IMF therefore culpable in Pakistan's most recent crisis? To an extent it was. The IMF is a professional organisation with some of the best macroeconomists under one roof but it is neither clairvoyant nor omnipotent. The IMF has also made mistakes and some very grievous ones. In Pakistan's case, the IMF has not been the overbearing, rigid and inflexible detractor that it is made out to be. It has not had a profound and deep impact on policy-making in Pakistan. Its influence has been intermittent, if not marginal. Those in Pakistan deeply committed to reforms lament the fact that the IMF has been insufficiently tough on Pakistan laying itself open to the charge that its policies serve to perpetuate Pakistan's corrupt ruling elites. Time and again Pakistan has been left off the proverbial hook when economic adversity and a need for exceptional financing from the IMF to stave off a financial crisis would have been the best time to push through deep-seated and lasting reform. These remarks apply to other multilateral lending agencies as well—the World Bank (WB) and Asian Development Bank (ADB).

*Ownership of Reforms*

The list of reforms Pakistan needs on the macroeconomic and structural side is a long one. It is also an agenda that remains largely unfulfilled even after sixty-three years and many failed IMF programs. Pakistan's record of taking reform steps and then rolling them back had earned it the sobriquet of 'stop-start adjustment'. An IMF program gets some reforms implemented as part of its conditionality but as soon as the program is over or ended by the authorities themselves mid-way, all the reforms are rolled back. Tax exemptions and concessions are a case in point. The IMF will insist that these exemptions and concessions be removed since they fragment the tax base and reduce revenue, are wasteful and ineffective. They are removed only to be put back once the IMF program is over. At the next program—and there always is another IMF program lurking down the road—the charade is repeated. Selective tax concessions and/or exemptions are doled out again to the politically powerful, the budget is burdened with ill-targeted subsidies which accrue largely to the rich and crowd-out much needed investment in social and physical infrastructure, and import protection is raised for specific products and sectors. Tax revenues fail to keep up with even the nominal growth of the economy because of poor compliance, corruption and insufficiently vigorous audits of tax under-filers.

The phenomenon of reforms being rolled-back and vitiating any good that may have been done is a striking manifestation of a lack of 'program ownership'. Pakistan needs to 'own' reforms not only undertake them, haltingly and grudgingly, or with a sleight of hand, under IMF duress. Program conditionality cannot substitute for ownership. The Fund has erred in this respect hoping that tighter conditionality can make up for a lack of ownership. The view so often heard that there can be no reforms because of powerful 'vested interests' has some weight but is not entirely persuasive. There are vested interests in other countries as well, whether in Brazil or India or Indonesia. Yet these countries have implemented reforms, they manage to keep their macro economy on a stable low inflation track, they anticipate and implement corrective measures promptly when risks emerge, they take bold decisions, and they do not turn to the IMF to bail them out every few years because they have mismanaged their economy and run out of foreign exchange reserves.

At the technical level, Pakistan has the talent of bright economic minds even if the best and the brightest had fled from the country to greener pastures in the Bank and the IMF around 1970. The talent of those who are still in Pakistan needs to be harnessed and their voices heard so they can convince the political leadership that reforms, which make for a more efficient and egalitarian economy and make inroads into poverty, are in their interest. These people have the skill to develop an economic and financial strategy of growth and poverty alleviation, which is underpinned by well-articulated policy measures and structural reforms. Even if the IMF needs to be called in, it should be Pakistan's program, and not what the IMF gives us, to which we react. Other countries do this. They present their own program to the IMF and treat the associated financial assistance as a reward of their belated display of virtue. This is the only way to ensure 'ownership', the most critical ingredient in successful and lasting reform implementation.

This is not to suggest that only economists can solve our economic problems and save the day. Pakistan has had the good fortune to produce some of the finest civil servants, who have served with distinction in key economic ministries and the central bank. Many of them have a deep and abiding commitment to reforms, listen to advice, understand the issues and know the art of the possible. Even economists know, or should know, that the ideal textbook solution to an economic problem is not always possible or doable. They must then work with second-best alternatives keeping in mind 'ground realities' and administrative and technical absorptive capacity.

The 2008 twenty-two-month IMF SBA has produced some positive results although the economic situation remains—to use a much-loved IMF word—'fragile'. Pakistan's external deficit is sharply down with most of it due to lower international prices for our imports but also due to macroeconomic adjustment taking root. Foreign exchange reserves have reached more comfortable levels; growth is picking up despite the strong headwinds associated with power shortages and a difficult security situation; asset markets have stabilised and the announcement of fresh inflows of US assistance following the 'Strategic' talks led to an appreciation of the rupee versus the US dollar. Market confidence is returning, interest rate spreads denoting country risk are narrowing and the international rating agencies appear to be close to up-grading our debt. Yet, despite these positive developments, risks abound. Fiscal slippages, especially on the spending side related to defence and security cloud the economic picture. Government borrowing from the central bank, which injects 'high-powered' money into the economic system and is therefore highly inflationary, has been in excess of prudent limits and inconsistent with the need to control inflation. The phenomenal, but not well-understood, rise in workers' remittances despite the turmoil in the Gulf countries, notably Dubai, shows signs of slowing down. This could portend the unwinding of a prolonged 'stock adjustment' process which when completed may see workers' remittances fall off sharply and weaken the external current account. Inflation appears to be making an unwelcome comeback suggesting that the process of monetary easing may have to be halted, or reversed, which will hurt growth.

Given these extant and emerging risks, it is well that the budget for 2010–11 attempts at another year of macroeconomic stabilisation. This would be good for inflation, which needs to come down further even if the end-of-period inflation target of 9.5 per cent per annum is disappointingly unambitious. The relatively tight stance of macro-policies should also ensure that the external deficit, a key source of vulnerability in the Pakistan economy and always a binding constraint, is kept in check and gross foreign exchange reserves stay at comfortable levels despite an anticipated pick-up in import volumes and prices as the domestic and global economic recovery gathers strength. Much of the debate on the fiscal measures in the budget has been overshadowed by a vigorous—if ill-informed—debate on Pakistan's commitment to the IMF to transition from the present GST (which operates in VAT-like-mode) to a full-fledged VAT. Some of the concerns and criticism are self-serving like that which comes from the wealthy with business interests in the National Assembly (dubbed as the centre of conflict of interest) who probably fear that the VAT will trap them in a seamless chain of value-addition, force them to document and pay some taxes for a change. Having successfully corrupted the GST through 'fake and flying invoices', or fake refund claims, they would have to start afresh to corrupt the VAT regime which would take time and effort and where success is not guaranteed. Some concerns are valid, especially the lack of education of all stakeholders on what VAT means and entails. In most other countries which moved to a VAT regime, the process of education is started eighteen months or more in advance.

There is concern about the impact of VAT on inflation. This seems to be over-stated since the present GST rate can vary from 17–27 per cent. Moving to a single 15 per cent standard rate should actually reduce taxes and hence prices across a broad range of commodities, an outcome which the Competition Commission of Pakistan needs to ensure and enforce. A high VAT threshold means that economic activity which is valued at below the threshold (Rs. 7.5 million) is exempt from VAT altogether. Neither the IMF nor the Government of Pakistan should be taxing or want to tax every '*khoka*' or '*ghara*' (small one-man retail shops and hand-driven cart retailer respectively) down the street. There are a limited list of exemptions, such as food, health services, education and medicines that are VAT-exempt, which impart some progressivity in the VAT regime. One would have hoped that private health and education institutions would not be exempted from VAT. Yet the VAT is an indirect tax and the budget regrettably took no measures to bring back progressive taxes such as the wealth tax, gift tax or inheritance tax which should never have been removed in the first place.

Most importantly, with the VAT not in place by 1 July 2010, Pakistan would have missed a 'performance criterion' under the on-going

GoP-IMF SBA program. This would, technically-speaking, bring the program to a halt and no further drawings can be made on IMF resources until Pakistan requests and receives a 'waiver' for non-compliance from the IMF's Executive Board. In the meantime, there is much discussion about a 'reformed' GST (instead of the VAT) although it is not clear what that means and, if feasible, raises the question: why was the GST not reformed a decade ago?

Whatever the final outcome, the question remains whether the Executive Board will grant the request for a waiver and whether Executive Directors will 'buy into' the 'reformed' GST as an equivalent, if not superior, substitute for the pure VAT. The US as the largest shareholder in the IMF is being lobbied intensely to soften its own stand and soften up other Executive Directors (especially those representing other G-7 countries) on the IMF Executive Board. It is amusing to see Pakistan play politics with the IMF (neither for the first time nor the last) while also complaining that the IMF is a political—and not a professional—institution dominated by, and serving, the interests of the same G-7.

If the waiver is granted (and there could be more than one request for waivers as there appears to be a breach of another 'performance criterion', namely, zero net borrowing from the central bank at end-quarter), the SBA program can be restarted. It would be in Pakistan's interest to do so and not allow the momentum of the adjustment program to stall. The task of stabilisation is unfinished and the critical transition to a higher growth path is on hand. Provided infrastructure constraints can be eased (such as in the energy sector) and the security situation improves for the better, there is no reason why the economy cannot post a growth rate of GDP of around 5–5.5 per cent in 2010–11 and move closer to potential of 6.0–6.5 per cent GDP growth the following year.

Once the SBA is over at end-2010, it would be surprising if the US and the other G-7 countries do not ask that Pakistan stay engaged with the IMF, since a stable macroeconomic environment strengthens the odds that aid inflows will be used wisely and well. Indeed, the grant of waivers for non-compliance of performance criteria mentioned earlier could well be given subject to Pakistan's commitment to a follow-on IMF program. The major donors know our undistinguished record of economic mismanagement and 'stop-start-rollback' record of adjustment. Whether we like it or not, an IMF arrangement serves as a disciplining force on the conduct of our economic policies. Pakistan should use the IMF as a political flack-jacket to push through deep-seated reforms. The IMF is used to playing that role and can take the flack. Many countries, both developing and advanced, use that ploy as well to good effect, the latest example being Greece where deep public-sector pay and pension cuts and fiscal austerity have been fiercely resisted but will go through as a condition for IMF and Euro-loans. Greece has no choice and the Euro-countries led by Germany and France would not want to see the Euro currency fail. Removing the IMF's disciplining force, no matter how much it is disliked and criticized could cause us to revert to the all-too-familiar paradigm of unconstrained decision-making which time and again has got us into trouble.

There are several possibilities of further IMF engagement. One possibility would be to ask the IMF for a 'precautionary' follow-on SBA (and not draw on relatively expensive SBA resources and exacerbate our external debt). One could also think of a looser arrangement, a sort of 'shadow' program that mimics an actual IMF arrangement but does not entail request for IMF resources. However, given the size of Pakistan's outstanding debt to the IMF, which exceeds 100 per cent of its quota, Pakistan may have no choice anyway but to submit to 'Post-Program Monitoring' with six monthly reviews that are published, implying a close watch over the conduct of our macroeconomic policies.

Whatever Pakistan's relations with the IMF in the immediate term, Pakistan needs to abjure the temptation to resort to overly-expansionary macroeconomic policies that only create the all-too-familiar cycle of boom, bubbles and bust. Pakistan's political leadership and policymakers need to recognise that there is an asymmetry between good and bad policies and their outcomes. Bad policies will quickly lead to bad outcomes from which there may be no turning back as negative dynamics take hold in a cumulative and circular self-fulfilling downturn. The rewards of implementing good policies takes a frustratingly long time to be felt because confidence of economic agents once lost is difficult to regain; moreover those who suffer from reform recognise their losses quickly and want to offset them rapidly while the beneficiaries either fail to appreciate their 'gains' or take a much longer time to do so. All governments are impatient to show results and want to be seen as responsive to the expectations of the people. But experience should teach that there is little to be gained by policy-induced distortions of macroeconomic policy instruments, such as interest rates that are close to zero or negative after adjusting for inflation encouraging excessive consumption and imports, imprudent borrowing, building up debt and discouraging savings. This creates a mirage of prosperity and a short-term burst in growth but eventually self-destructs. Nor is there anything to be gained by hastily conceived unviable spending initiatives that crowd-out more essential spending on education, health and other physical and social infrastructure which are critical to boosting the economy's medium-term growth potential.

There are many who argue, and rightly so, that talk about ensuring macroeconomic stability and low inflation is a non-starter unless governance issues are addressed first. There is no doubt that good governance is inextricably linked with good economic policies and vice-versa. The subject of good governance encompasses a daunting and vast field but by any calculus Pakistan ranks poorly when compared to other developing countries. No doubt, bad governance as manifest in mismanagement, deep-seated corruption and a flaunting of the rule of law, extracts a heavy toll in all sections of Pakistan society and creates the kind of economic instability and wrenching crisis that Pakistan has witnessed so many times before.

## Macroeconomic Reform Agenda

With a new economic team in Islamabad, Pakistan can either move forward or relapse to its old ways of destructive macroeconomic populism and face another balance of payments crisis in a very few years. Yet, despite the unhappy burden of economic history and heavy odds, a program of reform is neither dauntingly difficult nor impossible to implement. First, Pakistan needs to realise that macroeconomic stability and an environment of low inflation is pro-growth and pro-poor. No country has grown at a strong and steady pace while it is being buffeted with macroeconomic instability and high and variable inflation. The Asian Tigers succeeded in bringing poverty levels to the low teens by the determined implementation of pro-growth policies that simultaneously kept inflationary pressures in check. Bringing inflation down and keeping it down should be the government's highest priority since it will foster growth, reduce inter-personal tensions and alleviate poverty. Inflation is often called the 'cruellest tax of all' because it

190

hurts disproportionately those who can least afford to bear it or to offset it as the rich are most enabled to do.

At the very minimum, controlling inflation will require keeping the fiscal deficit—the root cause of recurring macro-instability, high inflation and balance of payments crises—under control. Time and again Pakistan has lost control of its fiscal situation because of tax revenue shortfalls and current spending over-runs. Keeping a control on the fiscal deficit should be spearheaded by spending restraint and where possible spending cuts since experience elsewhere has shown that spending cuts tend to be lasting and are associated with successful adjustment. Introducing the practice of zero budgeting and/or pay as you go might be a fruitful way to proceed. The Fiscal Deficit and Debt Limitation Act needs to be taken seriously and the Finance Minister called to account in the National Assembly to explain why deviations have occurred from the desirable path of fiscal adjustment and what the authorities plan to do to get it back on track and contain debt levels consistent with the stipulations of the Act.

On the monetary side, the State Bank needs to move to a system of inflation targeting and target an inflation 'band' rather than the present practice of targeting a single-point estimate which is unrealistic, gives a spurious impression of exactitude and is based on what looks good and acceptable from a political perspective. While the technical prerequisites for inflation targeting are onerous, they can be met. However, inflation targeting is not a magic bullet. It cannot work under a regime of 'fiscal dominance' where monetary policy is hostage to the vicissitudes of and slippages in the budget. In such an unbalanced policy regime, monetary policy will have to be tighter than it needs to be since it will be constantly seeking to off-set the demand pressures coming from the fiscal side in an effort to keep inflation down. The resulting high interest rates will stifle growth. Only a reasonably tight fiscal stance can give monetary policy the room and flexibility to guide policy interest rates and hence influence economic activity and market expectations of inflation.

The State Bank can start to target an inflation band of around 5–7 per cent per year and then gradually lower it and tighten the band as experience is gained and the transmission mechanisms between monetary policy action and output-price outcomes is better understood. The State Bank Governor should have a clause inserted in his contract that failure to meet the target band will call for an explanation in an open letter to government. Repeated failure to miss the band should result in the dismissal of the Governor as in other countries. The present IMF conditionality that there should be zero net borrowing from the State Bank of Pakistan at each end-quarter should become a law, not because it is an IMF requirement but because it is good for Pakistan and it will foster financial stability by putting a hard ceiling on net government borrowing. Similar ceilings should be placed on overdrafts and borrowing by provincial governments. Exceeding these ceilings should invite punitive fines. The Governor of the State Bank should not desist from bouncing a few checks as a signal that financial indiscipline and fiscal recklessness will not be tolerated. This was done in regards to provinces exceeding their 'ways and means' advances when for the first time in Pakistan's history the State Bank refused to honour payment orders issued by provinces in excess of their limits. This practice needs to continue.

Second, while the control of spending is important, Pakistan needs to learn to tax and do so equitably and effectively. Income earned in any economic venture should be subject to taxation. There should be no sector of the economy that is un-taxed, whether it is agriculture, the stock market, real estate or the services sector because there is no economic or moral justification not to tax income-earning activity in those sectors. A country which collects a stagnant 8–9 per cent of GDP in tax revenues (a ratio which risks falling further unless the VAT or the 'reformed' GST produces positive and sustainable results that can push our tax-to-GDP ratio to at least 15 per cent over the medium-term) does not have much of a future because it will never have the resources to finance essential social and physical infrastructure by the public sector, the key to boosting the economy's medium-term growth potential and complementing investment by the private sector. With a broader tax base with only a few selective concessions and exemptions, there should be room to cut tax rates (where rates are perceived to be high) while stepping up tax compliance through a sustained and vigorous program of random forensic and on-site tax audits.

Third, Pakistan needs to introduce social safety nets for the poor and vulnerable to protect them in times of high inflation and/or sharply slowing growth when wage earners are put on short-time on reduced pay or lose their jobs entirely with no unemployment compensation. The Benazir Income Support Program (BISP) is the first social safety net that Pakistan has developed and its implementation should be stepped-up to reach the poorest households. It will not be perfect and there will be leakages, corruption and misallocation. The scheme also risks being politicised. The BISP can be refined and better-targeted over time with experience and the process of 'learning-by-doing'. Cash transfers to poor households should be conditional on skill development so that the transferee can become economically independent.

Fourth, Pakistan needs to move away from reliance on politically-driven and volatile 'foreign savings' or more specifically official bilateral aid inflows. In addition to other debilitating effects, aid sets up perverse incentives by alleviating the pressure to implement urgently needed domestic reform. Indeed, there is evidence that foreign aid has over the years tended to supplant rather than supplement domestic savings. In place of aid, Pakistan should foster the conditions for raising domestic savings (and reducing government dissavings via the budget) by ensuring that banking deposits are remunerated in positive real terms and government savings instruments are linked to and fluctuate with nominal GDP growth rather than set through government fiat by committee. Issuing inflation index-linked bonds may also be a good idea since that would put pressure on the authorities to keep inflation in check.

In additional to raising domestic savings, official aid inflows should be substituted over time with a concerted effort to attract Foreign Direct Investment (FDI) inflows which embody the best managerial and marketing skills and 'best-practice' technology, especially to the lagging and undiversified export sector as other successful developing countries have done. While FDI will remain tentative under the present difficult security situation, Pakistan's growing domestic market and the untapped potential for developing new exports and finding new export markets makes the country an attractive destination for such investment. To be sure, this will mean addressing, *inter alia*, the country's acute power shortages and implementing a true fast-track 'one-window' operation for FDI approvals.

Fifth, and following from the above, Pakistan needs to implement a well-designed and coherent export-led development strategy. Despite the persistence of a large trade deficit, which has not been brought down over time, Pakistan has never articulated an explicit export-led development strategy. For sixty-three years the 'commodity concentration' and market destination of our exports has remained broadly unchanged. In other words, we export the same mix of commodities to the same markets. Exports as a ratio of GDP have stagnated and at times fallen suggesting, *inter alia*, that economic policies are 'crowding-out' or penalising exports. The unit price we receive for our exports is roughly half of what our competitors obtain in the world market for the same product, a dismaying fact which points to the unutilised scope for boosting export revenues from even the existing export base. While the large-scale manufacturing sector gets most of the policy attention not least because of its powerful lobbies, it represents the tip of the manufacturing sector iceberg. Some 80 per cent of output, 87 per cent of employment and 70 per cent of Pakistan's exports emanate from the Small and Medium Enterprise (SME) sector. Boosting the growth of the SME sector through targeted incentives that are per-formance based and technical assistance would pay large dividends as the scope for exports from this sector is exploited. Since these exports are labour-intensive, growth in the SME sector has important implica-tions for employment, wages, income distribution and poverty allevia-tion. Pakistan also needs to address the issue of export quality, meet the highest standards of packaging and hygiene and adhere to tight delivery dates, the so-called 'non-price' determinants of exports. Mar-kets once lost because of deficiencies in these areas are difficult if not impossible to regain.

Sixth, while maintaining macroeconomic stability is the prerequisite for achieving sustained growth with low inflation, Pakistan needs to implement efficiency-enhancing structural reforms that boost Total Factor Productivity (TFP). There exists a National Productivity Organ-ization in Pakistan but it is not clear how effective it has been in rais-ing TFP. Studies on 'Growth Accounting' round the world have shown that economic growth is not fully explained by factor accumulation (more labour and capital inputs of unchanging quality) but by perma-nent upward shifts in the production function brought about through technological progress. Technological progress in other countries typi-cally accounts for 70 per cent of growth and factor inputs for only 30 per cent. In Pakistan the situation is reversed. Technological progress makes a small (about 24 per cent) contribution to growth. This sug-gests that growth in Pakistan has been resource-intensive and factor-deepening and thus inefficient and wasteful. This has to change. Technological improvements and closing the 'technological gaps' between Pakistan and more advanced developing and industrial coun-tries needs to be given the highest priority in policy-making, whether in agriculture, manufacturing, energy, transport, exports or services. No country has progressed without sustained and rapid improvements in TFP over time.

Seventh, reforms of the macro economy will prove to be unavailing unless Pakistan addresses the challenge of restructuring Public Sector Enterprises (PSEs) which incur staggering losses that exceed the size of the development program. Adding their losses as 'quasi-fiscal deficits' to the narrower concept of the fiscal (budgetary) deficit would raise the Public Sector Borrowing Requirement (PSBR) by 2–3 per cent of GDP and provide a more honest—and more daunting picture—of the pre-emption of the public sector on the economy's resource envelope. To be successful and lasting PSE restructuring needs to start with the acceptance of the fact that it will have to be accompanied by draconian job and wage cuts across all levels of management and staff. Pakistan's recent experience with the restructuring of the banking system which was financed by a soft World Bank loan is instructive. All persons asked to leave employment were given a severance package or 'golden-handshake'. This experience needs to be replicated. Concurrently, management should commit to an up-front meaningful cut in salary and perks that are then held constant in nominal terms for, say, three years with no bonuses. No PSE restructuring anywhere in the world has been unaccompanied by a labour shake-out and a freeze on wages, salaries and bonuses of the retained workforce. Raising TFP and cutting costs with an unchanged workforce is impossible to achieve.

Finally, Pakistan needs to keep a careful watch on the evolution of the 'real' exchange rate, namely, the nominal exchange rate adjusted for inflation since the exporter is interested in the 'real' value of the rupees he earns per dollar of exports after allowing for inflation and not the nominal value before adjusting for inflation. Too often in the past, because of political pressure and the mistaken belief that a 'stable' nominal exchange rate is a reflection of good policies, the exchange rate has been allowed to appreciate in real terms, giving the exporter fewer real rupees per unit of exports. Price competitiveness, as reflected in the real exchange rate is an important—albeit not the only or exclusive—determinant of export success. Only by bringing our domestic inflation rate down in line with (or below) our competitors and trading partners can a stable nominal exchange rate be consistent with constant (or rising) real export profitability. Higher domestic relative inflation means that we need to push the nominal exchange rate downwards as we do now just to compensate for our higher relative inflation differential vis-à-vis our trading partners and competitors. This is a self-defeating policy since it makes the task of inflation control doubly-difficult as a depreciating currency pushes up import costs which percolate into the cost and price structure of other goods and service in the economy.

This is a broad brush listing of some of the key macroeconomic reforms that Pakistan urgently needs to implement. However, reforms of the macro economy need to be underpinned by sectoral and micro policy action. Much can be said about these sectoral reforms but that should be left to the sectoral experts in agriculture, energy, education and skill development, and health services. Suffice it to say, the true potential of Pakistan's agriculture sector remains largely untapped and new sources of growth can and must be found. Pakistan needs to move away from being a single-cash-crop economy and diversify into higher value-added commodities for domestic consumption but especially for export. It is self-evident that we must solve the problem of crippling power outages if the economy is to resume steady growth and create new employment opportunities. The unfortunate saga of the rental power projects is an evil that the economy will have to live with as a short-term solution until more cost-efficient sources of power can be brought on stream, including hydropower and nuclear power. In the social sectors such as health and education, the government should use hard rising floors to protect development allocations for these sectors and keep them in line with or ahead of inflation. A system of floors will also help safeguard allocations in times of fiscal stringency. The practice of cutting development spending or withholding releases of funds for ongoing projects and programs to meet fiscal targets needs to stop. Since across-the-board cuts in development are non-discriminatory, they play havoc with the economic viability of good projects by pushing up costs and lowering promised benefits. By lowering investment efficiency, and the rate of return on the public sector capital stock, such unpredictable cuts undermine the medium-term growth potential of the economy and reduce TFP.

*Postscript: The Great Flood of 2010*

The Great Flood in the summer of 2010 caused widespread damage to the economy, especially to major and minor crops and the livestock sector. Irrigation, transport and power sectors were also badly hurt.

Manufacturing was for the most part spared by the ferocity of the flood. The World Bank and Asian Development Bank's estimate of the flood damage was around $10 billion. What all this means for the economy going forward is difficult to tell but a plausible scenario can be sketched out.

In the very short-term (perhaps the first two quarters of 2010–11), real GDP is likely to contract by about 1.5 per cent amidst a spike in inflation, especially food inflation trapping the economy in stagflation from which it emerged only recently. Both the domestic and external deficits will come under strain. In the former case this would be because of the need to spend vast sums on rehabilitation and rebuilding damaged/destroyed physical and social infrastructure as well as pay one-time compensation to those affected or displaced by the flood. Externally, exports could falter—especially of traditional items such as textiles and leather. Import demand will be strong-led by food, raw cotton and the import content of replacement capital investment. Nevertheless, the external side need not come under undue pressure. Workers' remittances could see a significant further rise as families ask for larger transfers to cope with their needs for food, clothing, shelter, medicines and buying of livestock and other agricultural inputs lost in the floods.

Foreign aid inflows (including reimbursement from the US Coalition Support Funds), additional IMF financing under their low-conditionality natural disasters facility ($451 million), as well as further drawings under the ongoing SBA arrangement should help keep foreign exchange reserves at a comfortable level with a 'cover' of five to seven months of projected imports.

The government announced new 'measures' in a revised budget for 2010–11 to reflect post-flood realities. On the revenue side, it tabled before Parliament the Reformed GST (RGST) with a single rate of tax of 15 per cent along with a sweeping elimination of exemptions as well as bringing the hitherto untaxed services sector under the RGST net.

Since the old GST tax rates varied from 17 per cent to 25 per cent, a single 15 per cent rate of tax under the RGST could imply price reductions across a broad range of items. In Autumn 2010 the authorities announced a temporary flood surcharge on incomes above a certain exemption threshold in addition to a doubling of the Special Excise Tax on selected non-essential imports to 2 per cent. Fears of a renewed bout of inflation resulting from these measures appeared to be overblown.

Nevertheless, the Competition Commission of Pakistan (CCP) will have to be vigilant to ensure that price reductions do take place where taxes have been cut while being watchful about cases of price-gouging or other anti-competitive abuse in the new tax environment. The CCP's excellent track record of enforcement gives confidence that they will help to protect the interest of the Pakistani consumer.

On the spending side, non-interest non-defence expenditures at the federal level have been frozen in nominal terms, whilst the public sector development program has undergone a drastic cut in size with new projects put on hold and implementation of ongoing, externally-financed projects and programs being accelerated. Along with the cut, there was significant reprioritising of the development program, shifting resources to sectors directly helpful to and related to post-flood reconstruction. The provinces have also been asked to pare down their overly ambitious development program to bring them more in line with their technical and administrative capacity to implement them. This would reduce their presently large deficit budgets. Taken together, these revenue and expenditure-saving measures at the federal and provincial levels are expected to yield a consolidated (federal plus provincial) overall fiscal deficit of around 4.7 per cent of GDP in 2010–11, which by all accounts has the begrudging blessings of the IMF who would have wanted the pre-flood end-year deficit target to remain unchanged at 4 per cent of GDP. However, even with this upward revision in the deficit target, Pakistan should be in a position to secure the next tranche under the continuing SBA, provided the Executive Board of the IMF approves requests for waivers for non-compliance of performance criterion, since the measures taken now have been delayed and the performance criterion set earlier were breached.

It is unfortunate that the government did not take advantage of the crisis to push through more radical—and highly desirable—measures, such as imposing a 10 per cent tax on the market value of all immoveable properties (residential and commercial) in the major cities, along with insisting that the provinces tax agricultural income above a certain threshold from land not affected by the floods. To many, a deep flaw in the recent National Finance Commission (NFC) award—which saw a significant shift of resources devolve to the provinces—is the lack of any conditionality. Fiscal devolution should have been accompanied by a clear understanding that, should the provinces fail to raise their own revenues, releases from the NFC award would be withheld by the amount of the tax revenues foregone. There has not been any hint of bringing back more progressive forms of taxation, such as the wealth tax or gift tax, which would not only be revenue-enhancing but would also impart greater progressivity to the tax system. However that may be, if the authorities are able to achieve a consolidated fiscal out-turn of 4.7 per cent of GDP in 2010–11, aggregate demand pressures in the economy would be reduced, government borrowing and hence interest rates would decrease, the private sector would be 'crowded-in' and inflation could start to subside quickly, thus enabling the central bank to cut its policy rate of interest and boost growth.

The Great Flood has caused widespread hardship and misery—displacing some twenty million people who were already poor and vulnerable—and significant capital destruction. However, the task of rebuilding the capital stock presents a unique opportunity for Pakistan to build anew and invest in new-vintage technologies that would raise productive efficiency and boost Total Factor Productivity. Once the relief phase is complete, the task of rebuilding could result in a sustained surge in domestic demand led by new investment. Provided this phase is handled in the context of an overall macroeconomic framework that is prudent and fully-financed by non-inflationary methods, real GDP growth could rebound in a V-shaped recovery accompanied by significant gains in employment, wages and poverty reduction with the demand stimulus lasting for three or four years. After contracting in the first two quarters, real year-on-year GDP growth in 2010–11 could be in the region of 2–3 per cent—an estimated outcome that is in line with the central bank's most recently published report on the economy. Such an outcome could be said to be satisfactory, given the dire starting circumstances. Once economic recovery takes hold, Pakistan's policy-makers should take the opportunity to start the process of implementing the macroeconomic and structural reform agenda sketched out in the main body of this chapter with far-reaching structural reforms making the economy resilient, more efficient and self-sustaining.

11

# BOOSTING COMPETITIVENESS

*Muddassar Mazhar Malik*

Over the last two decades Pakistan has had the resilience to survive against all odds. How can it succeed is the main topic of this chapter.

Despite its many challenges, during this period, Pakistan has grown at an average rate of over five per cent. As a country with a population of 175 million people today, it is important to understand that 99 per cent of the fabric of a diverse and rich culture and people can and do make a difference. Pakistan remains open for business despite the enormous challenges it confronts. Whilst international media and policy think tanks focus on how to tackle militancy and extremism, the vast majority of the people who live and work in Pakistan today say openly that this minority does not represent them as a people and ask why the international media cannot recognise the simple fact that every Pakistani is not a militant or extremist.

During 2010 Aisam ul Haq Qureshi became the first Pakistani to reach the US Open doubles final. After losing the final, he addressed a 15,000 strong gathering at the Arthur Ashe Stadium with millions of people watching across the world. He said, 'I want to say something on behalf of all Pakistanis. Every time I come here, there's a wrong perception about the people of Pakistan. They are very friendly, very loving people. We want peace in this world as much as you.' The crowd cheered and the hearts of Pakistani citizens around the world warmed to his remarks of respect for its people. In many ways, this thirty-year-old was able to capture for a moment what the Pakistani diplomatic community has failed to achieve—to project Pakistan in its true light. The point is that stimulating economic growth in a country requires investment, which in turn requires market access to capital investment. Pakistan's market access is severely compromised by its negative perception. Addressing this problem head on has to remain a priority for all stakeholders.

That said, Pakistan's future outlook and its strong underlying fundamentals mean that it is difficult for investors to ignore the opportunities it has to offer. What is even more important as the process of institutional re-building gains momentum, is the gradual yet distinct realisation by all stakeholders that having a clear Pakistan game plan for success is essential and sticking to the script has to be part of the game plan. If the goal is to realise Pakistan's full potential, then putting the house in order is a fundamental pre-requisite for the success story to unfold at a time when most critics argue otherwise.

One example of such an adversity is the catastrophic floods in Pakistan in the summer of 2010—the worst natural disaster in the country's history. These have resulted in a colossal setback to its economy. The extensive damage to infrastructure will mean years of rebuilding, and the mass displacement of people will require the rehabilitation of millions across the country. All of this will need an extraordinary amount of resources, thus compounding Pakistan's economic woes and exacerbating long-standing challenges. Among these challenges are macroeconomic instability, an inadequate infrastructure to support business activity, poor social indicators, a deep governance deficit and limited integration into the global economy at a time when competition from China, India and other regional countries grows in key export sectors including textiles.

With the world still dealing with global recession and the country struggling with the aftermath of floods, sceptics suggest that Pakistan is today less able to handle such shocks than it was ten or twenty years ago. They argue that Pakistan's economic future is at best perilous given decades of political instability and economic mismanagement and that it is far down on the list of global capital-seeking-investment.[1] Against this backdrop, addressing structural challenges acquires a sense of urgency and priority at all levels of government, industry and businesses. To achieve a sustainable rebound, policy priorities must be set clearly to meet the needs of reconstruction and deal with critical economic, social and political issues in the face of fierce competition, shrinking global demand and increasing geo-political risk. Now more than ever, it is imperative to identify what Pakistan needs to do to become more competitive and be among the winners in the coming decades.

This chapter is an attempt to challenge the view of the sceptics. By focusing on the most critical policy measures needed to achieve competitiveness, Pakistan has the ability to capture the energy and dynamism of its natural advantages, accelerate growth and 'catch up' on the global economic stage.

*Pakistan's Potential*

In 2005 Goldman Sachs formulated the notion of the Next-11 (N-11) as a group of countries that have the economic potential to become important players in the global system after the so-called BRIC, an acronym for Brazil, Russia, India and China.[2] The N-11 though diverse in many ways was identified as rapidly developing economies with the ability to match, if not eventually overtake, the Group of Seven (G-7) countries. The main criterion was demographic—with the result that the N-11 is a group of large population countries beyond BRIC. Pakistan was identified as one among these countries owing to its size, its growing population, and its industrial base. All these factors give Pakistan an ability to produce consumer goods and have a substantial domestic market with the capacity to consume them.

The following are some of Pakistan's main advantages, fundamental to its long-term growth. Not surprisingly, some of these are similar to those that are propelling growth and attracting global investment flows to the rapidly developing Asian economies in the region including China and India.

*A resilient economy.* First, despite seven changes in government in the past twenty years, Pakistan has maintained an average growth rate of 5 per cent per annum.[3] Until recently, Pakistan was being touted as one of the most dramatic turnaround stories of the last decade. Driven by domestic demand and population growth, GDP growth averaged over 6 per cent a year from 2003–2008. This translated into an investment and infrastructure-led growth cycle fuelling expansion in the housing, health care, education, food, infrastructure, energy, telecommunications, IT and financial services sectors. This has meant that Pakistan's economy has progressively moved from its traditional agricultural base to manufacturing and increasingly to services. In that sense, Pakistan's economic structure is much closer to that of India and China, and is unlike many smaller Asian countries, which are more dependent on export growth.

Official IMF estimates of the country's per capita income are US$1,200, which, on a Purchasing Power Parity basis, is US$2,500[4]. Additional estimates suggest about twenty-five to thirty million people, or one sixth of Pakistan's population, have a per capita income on a PPP basis of between US$8,000 to US$10,000. Part of the growth is accounted for by a large and vibrant informal economy which is estimated to be at least 30 to 50 per cent of the size of the formal economy and which is growing as much as 13 per cent per annum. Pakistan's thriving informal economy is not documented and consists of a vast network of smugglers, traders and agriculturalists. The energy and dynamism of the informal economy has, in part, been responsible for continued growth. With better documentation, this has the prospects of being channelled into formal sectors. This can help to raise tax collection and attract investment capital to roll out much needed capacity in healthcare, education, law and order and energy sectors. This will not only have a direct impact on alleviating poverty but also allow the productive economic base to expand in a sustained manner.

Over the last two decades, Pakistan has undergone meaningful banking sector, tax and corporate governance reforms and has a solid financial system. Its economy is more open to trade and investment compared to countries at a similar stage of development. Pakistan's English-speaking professional elite, a well-developed legal system based on English common law and a significant pool of overseas Pakistanis have allowed a reasonable degree of integration with the global economy. Pakistan's business community has historically been westward looking and has also developed strong links to the Middle East and Asian economies and China. Today, over 300 foreign multinationals have well established business operations in Pakistan. The US, European Union and Japan remain the three largest foreign direct investors with new inflows emanating from the Middle East and China. Other key indicators suggest a positive growth trend—foreign remittances hit around $9 billion in 2010 up from $984 million in 2000, foreign exchange reserves were around $16 billion in June 2010 up from $1.7

billion in 2000 and exports were $20 billion in 2010 up from $8 billion in 2000.[5]

This resilience has also been demonstrated in key capital market indicators. In 2009, Pakistan's KSE100 index surged over 60 per cent in a year. Pakistan was wracked by increased violence and many of its state institutions were overwhelmed by security challenges. From 1998–2010, there has been an enormous increase of over 700 per cent in the KSE100 after accounting for rupee depreciation.[6] This makes Pakistan the best performing market in a twelve-year period and significantly better than the BRIC economies.

Pakistan's stock market capitalisation to GDP (PPP basis) ratio is approximately 7 per cent. This is very low compared to the BRIC economies, where market capitalisation to GDP ratio ranges from 25 per cent in Russia to 60 per cent in Brazil. This ratio is a measure of the extent of development of a country's capital market and of the valuation of its listed assets relative to the overall size of the economy. More developed economies like Hong Kong tend to have ratios in excess of 100 per cent. This highlights the comparatively low valuations for Pakistan relative to the BRIC economies. These low valuations in turn reflect the extent of investor pessimism as well as potential upside for investors if Pakistan's growth begins to surge.

*Withstanding geo-political risk.* Second, Pakistan has been the victim of two major international events in the last three decades. The Russian invasion of Afghanistan resulted in a war that saw the influx of 3.5 million refugees and led to the rise of militancy in the region. The US-led invasion of Afghanistan after 9/11 compounded Pakistan's security challenges which dealt heavy blows to its economy. In the current security situation, it has been difficult to attract foreign and mobilise domestic investment. Pakistan has not been given a preferred status for exports to the United States or the European Union, which are Pakistan's main export markets. As a consequence of geo-political risks, Pakistan is not seen as a friendly investment destination. Despite this, Pakistan's investment to GDP ratio has averaged 17 per cent for the last decade and is 17 per cent today after reaching a peak of 23 per cent in 2007. In many ways, Pakistan's corporate leaders and professionals as amongst the most 'battle hardened' pool of managerial talent in the world with the ability to manage risk and still show growth under the most challenging business conditions.

*Demographic asset.* Third, with a population of 175 million people, almost a quarter the size of Europe's population, Pakistan is the sixth most populous country in the world. This has resulted in rapid growth in urbanisation, which presents opportunities as well as challenges. With a large and expanding workforce and relatively few people in the dependent age bracket of under fifteen and over sixty-four, Pakistan is ideally positioned to reap the demographic dividend.

While Pakistan's young population of around a hundred million is already becoming an engine of growth, its youth can become the backbone of its middle class that can, in turn, drive economic growth. This offers Pakistani businesses an opportunity to grow and produce goods and services the population needs. At a time when the Western world is facing the crisis of ageing populations, Pakistan has the potential for economic expansion created by a young population provided, of course, that it can be educated and empowered with the right skills.

*Natural resources.* Fourth, Pakistan's landmass, equal to that of Brazil's, is rich in natural resources, including mineral wealth and arable land. It is the world's fourth largest cotton producer and its coal reserves—the fourth largest in the world—are estimated around 186 billion tons, which in terms of energy output is at least equal to if not more than the oil reserves of Saudi Arabia. Balochistan has one of the largest copper reserves in the world estimated at eighteen million tons of copper and thirty-five million ounces of residual gold. Pakistan is the world's fifth largest dairy producer and increasing its exports of both milk and beef to the Middle East in addition to meeting domestic needs.

*Strategic location.* Fifth, Pakistan's location gives it a unique advantage. Although location is currently responsible for much of its negative image, this can be turned around. As the economic centre of gravity shifts to Asia it is situated at the crossroads of opportunity: large energy resources and one of the largest pools of liquidity in the world. For large parts of western China, Afghanistan and the Central Asian Republics, the shortest and cheapest trade route is through Pakistan. The government has been capitalising on this by creating a strategic trade and energy corridor. A major new port in Gawadar has been completed and the Singapore Port Authority has the mandate to manage it. There is a network of highways linking China and Central Asia to the port city of Gawadar. This is an important long term growth opportunity offered by Pakistan and has recently been reinforced by the Pakistan Afghan Transit Trade Agreement (PATTA) signed in 2010 allowing the opening up of trade through Pakistan to Afghanistan and beyond.

To summarise, Pakistan's resilience in the face of problems and its strong fundamentals give it the potential to turn into an economic success story. But it will have to surmount formidable challenges in order to do so. To capitalise on its advantages Pakistan needs to grow by 7–8 per cent per annum for the next ten years; 1 per cent growth in GDP requires a 2.5 to 3 per cent growth in the investment rate. Therefore GDP growth rate of 7 per cent will require annual investment rates of over 21 per cent as a percentage of GDP. Given Pakistan's weak social, political and economic infrastructure, can Pakistan achieve the required investment to turn the economic corner, grow and compete globally? So the question is—what needs to be done for Pakistan to attain competitiveness and create national wealth?

## Where Does Pakistan Stand Globally?

Any country that wants to succeed in the global economy needs to closely study competition, not to mimic but to understand how other countries have identified what works for them and how to benchmark themselves with what others do globally. The table below is from the Global Competitiveness Report, a survey conducted annually by the World Economic Forum.[7] It is a useful tool summarising the factors on which the competitiveness of 133 countries are assessed on a relative scale. Based on the twelve pillars of assessment, Pakistan ranks 101 out of 113 countries in the 2009–2010 survey. This shines a light on the areas where Pakistan has to work to achieve greater competitiveness.

## What Does Pakistan Need to do to Become Competitive?

Improving the competitiveness of any country is not easy and Pakistan is no exception. But its potential can be achieved if a clear roadmap is developed. This will require not just fresh ideas, public-private partnerships and foreign investment but also improving the infrastructure, developing its human capital and funding critical new technologies. A plan to achieve this will need the following:

*Clear vision.* First, Pakistan needs a coherent vision and strategy. Attaining competitiveness is synonymous with creating national

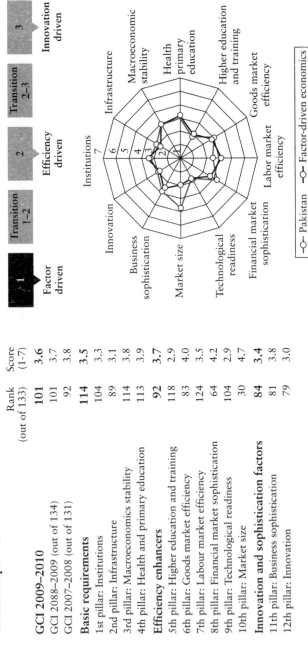

Global competitiveness index

|  | Rank (out of 133) | Score (1–7) |
|---|---|---|
| **GCI 2009–2010** | **101** | **3.6** |
| GCI 2088–2009 (out of 134) | 101 | 3.7 |
| GCI 2007–2008 (out of 131) | 92 | 3.8 |
| **Basic requirements** | **114** | **3.5** |
| 1st pillar: Institutions | 104 | 3.3 |
| 2nd pillar: Infrastructure | 89 | 3.1 |
| 3rd pillar: Macroeconomics stability | 114 | 3.8 |
| 4th pillar: Health and primary education | 113 | 3.9 |
| **Efficiency enhancers** | **92** | **3.7** |
| 5th pillar: Higher education and training | 118 | 2.9 |
| 6th pillar: Goods market efficiency | 83 | 4.0 |
| 7th pillar: Labour market efficiency | 124 | 3.5 |
| 8th pillar: Financial market sophistication | 64 | 4.2 |
| 9th pillar: Technological readiness | 104 | 2.9 |
| 10th pillar: Market size | 30 | 4.7 |
| **Innovation and sophistication factors** | **84** | **3.4** |
| 11th pillar: Business sophistication | 81 | 3.8 |
| 12th pillar: Innovation | 79 | 3.0 |

The most problematic factors for doing business

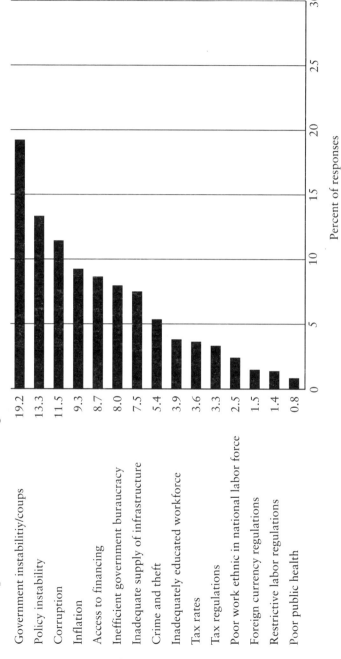

| Government instability/coups | 19.2 |
| Policy instability | 13.3 |
| Corruption | 11.5 |
| Inflation | 9.3 |
| Access to financing | 8.7 |
| Inefficient government buraucracy | 8.0 |
| Inadequate supply of infrastructure | 7.5 |
| Crime and theft | 5.4 |
| Inadequately educated workforce | 3.9 |
| Tax rates | 3.6 |
| Tax regulations | 3.3 |
| Poor work ethnic in national labor force | 2.5 |
| Foreign currency regulations | 1.5 |
| Restrictive labor regulations | 1.4 |
| Poor public health | 0.8 |

Percent of responses

Source: Global Competitiveness Report (2009–10), World Economic Forum.

wealth. Owing to its geography and demography, Pakistani industry and business have the ability to become more competitive for its own domestic market and compete regionally and globally, if they act in a structured and collective manner. Experts in the field have increasingly started citing South Asia as the fastest growing region in the world. While this conclusion is driven by India's nascent economic strength, which in turn is premised on India's fast growing middle class, educated population base and stable politics, it is important to recognise that Pakistan possesses similar characteristics and potential.

There are some key problems in evolving a clear vision. There is lack of consensus about what this vision should be. This stems from a psychological barrier in the minds of Pakistan's public and private sector players that Pakistan cannot be globally competitive. Overwhelmed by current challenges, there is little appreciation of the economic opportunity that the country presents and how to unlock this value.

Also activity across government departments and agencies is not coordinated in pursuit of the goal of attaining competitiveness. There is, for example, lack of alignment between the government's social policies, especially education, and its economic, foreign and defence policies. Furthermore, policy inconsistencies between successive governments have left little room for the private sector to innovate and generate fresh ideas. This lack of coordination is exacerbated by an over-reliance on foreign assistance and policy prescriptions from multilateral agencies.

What can be done? Sustainability, environmentally conscious, inclusive growth from the bottom up and global competitiveness are all interconnected. Yet, much of the thinking and work being done today is not looking at the inclusive approach for growth. Policy-makers are thinking in pieces as unique problems that can be addressed separately. The overall economic, political and social canvas needs to be addressed in a coordinated fashion for Pakistan to take advantage of its growth opportunity. There are four key areas where action should be taken.

First, the private sector should help generate a national debate on the need to develop a shared mindset across government, industry, the media and other key stakeholders to attain competitiveness. This will serve as a signal not only to the international community but also to the country's public sector administration, business community and labour force that Pakistan is serious about competing.

Second, the government should be willing to pull all the levers at its disposal to implement such vision. This involves creating an environment that gives foreign and domestic companies a reason to invest and stay in Pakistan. This in turn could be achieved through a realignment of tax and investment policies, especially in sectors where investment is a critical precursor to long-term structural change.

Third, a global media campaign targeted at international as well as domestic investors should, be launched, highlighting the trade and investment opportunities in Pakistan and the government's agenda of reform.

Fourth, the government's social and economic policies including education, transport, infrastructure, energy and communications must be aligned with this vision. This coordinated approach should extend to Pakistan's defence and foreign policies, which should also reflect Pakistan's aspirations of rapid economic progress.

*Improve Governance.* The problems of governance stem from the inability of governments and public sector institutions to deliver public services in the face of rising demands and expectations.

As this is discussed elsewhere in this volume it is sufficient to emphasise that without improved governance, delivery systems and effective implementation, Pakistan will find it difficult to educate its citizens, build infrastructure, increase agricultural output and ensure that the benefits of economic growth are efficiently distributed.

*Improve infrastructure.* Pakistan's infrastructure constraints are evident in the present power crisis, lack of a modern railroad system, shortage of low- to middle-income housing, congestion on urban roads and main highway systems and an inadequate port capacity. There is grossly inadequate primary, secondary and higher education and healthcare facilities. Pakistani companies suffer as a consequence of these factors, for example, by experiencing production delays in exports due to limited port capacity and cumbersome customs procedures. The lack of availability of a well-trained, healthy and productive work force further inhibits business potential. In addition, poor logistics and transportation also hamper the movement of inventory between farm and market or factory and market.

If Pakistan's growth continues at an average rate of 7–8 per cent in the coming decade, this will fuel the demand for energy, transport, logistics, communication, healthcare, housing, water, education and communication. Urbanisation is also increasing. Almost a third of the population now lives in four major urban centres. A 2 per cent in-migration rate means that this number will grow by over half in the next twenty-five years. These unprecedented levels of urbanisation present challenges but can also bring opportunities as vast numbers of people can have access to information, services, communication facilities as well as standards of living which do not exist in the rural areas. Official estimates of new infrastructure requirements in terms of ports, railroads, hospitals, schools, low income housing and energy are approximately $30 billion in the next five years just to sustain current levels of growth.

So there is a dual problem: the current infrastructure is inadequate and future growth is burdened by lack of resources and poor planning. Obvious examples include: the current energy shortage, which is the consequence of neglect of the power sector by successive governments, and the shortage of trained technical staff and engineers—impediments to any rapid infrastructure roll out. Lastly future growth is hampered by the challenges of security. Building dams in Khyber Pakhtunkhwa, mining coal in Baluchistan or establishing a modern port capacity on the southern coastline are all dependent on the security of human capital.

What can be done? First and foremost, Pakistan needs to resolve its financing issues, Pakistan needs to further develop its capital markets as well as create market access for long term foreign capital inflows. A vibrant and liquid corporate bond market, the ability to source fresh equity from the domestic and international equity markets, deregulation of the insurance and pensions markets, and a stable banking system are all areas for greater focus. Previous governments have achieved some measure of success in this regard to the extent that the country was able to tap international markets for debt and also improve its international credit rating. Pakistan has also set up the Infrastructure Project Development Facility (IPDF) that needs to be better utilised to bring about more robust public-private partnerships in energy, health care, transportation, agriculture and education.

It is also important to focus on infrastructure projects, which can be more easily delivered by a combination of government initiatives, foreign assistance or domestic private investment. Examples include projects for low-income housing, a modern irrigation system, high yield crops and development of human capital with particular focus on skills needed to help existing and new industries grow.

*Becoming the region's food reservoir.* Even though the setback from the floods may in the near term affect Pakistan's ability to feed itself, a country that has been self-sufficient in food should be able to effect a recovery. The country's major agricultural products include cotton, wheat, rice, sugarcane, fruits and vegetables while its livestock and dairy resources provide ample milk, beef, mutton and eggs. It is, however, essential for Pakistan to improve its agricultural output levels and productivity. Agriculture generates around 22 per cent of the GDP while employing 45 per cent of the labour force. Almost two thirds of the population is dependent on agriculture for their livelihood—hence changing the complexion of the agricultural sector through a focused investment drive would help to radically change the complexion of Pakistan's economy.

Over the past twenty years land under cultivation has remained relatively static and yields per hectare have only improved marginally. Intensive farming and environmental degradation have resulted in soil erosion. These factors will continue to impede agricultural growth as urbanisation results in a loss of arable land.

To enable Pakistan to become the granary of the region, not only productivity, but also scale, quality, continuity and reliability of agrifood production needs to be ensured. The world's largest distributors of food in the region, which include Wal-Mart, Nestlé, Unilever, Metro, Sears, Carrefour and Spinney can then be persuaded to increase investment in downstream production which feed agri food businesses in the region. Investment, particularly in better seeds and new technology, is required to raise yields.

Second, agriculture needs to be deregulated to allow greater degree of commercialisation and economies of scale. Eliminating price controls, restrictions on inter-provincial movement of goods and strict curbs on smuggling of food products to neighbouring countries will allow greater flexibility to farmers to sell directly to the organised retail sector.

Third, a comprehensive national agricultural policy needs to be evolved to offer incentives to indigenous and foreign investors. To promote sustainable R&D in the sector, that policy should encourage joint ventures between global and local companies. In particular, large local landowners should be encouraged to forge alliances to enable 'contract farming' which invites expertise, technology and finance with an enhanced regional market focus to boost both production and productivity. However, the current system of land holdings, price controls and lack of legal enforceability may inhibit the entry of new players, technology and expertise into Pakistan. To overcome such obstacles, a combination of removal of subsidies and public sector investment could act as a catalyst for growth.

Fourth, due to the small size of farm holdings, there should be a comprehensive programme of education for farmers at the basic level about better agricultural practices, information and availability of better seeds, use of fertiliser and crop patterns. The village farmer is the key to increased agricultural productivity.

*Raise education standards.* Pakistan's abysmal literacy figures need to be frontally attacked by a national policy. This is discussed in the next chapter.

*Build a skilled work force.* Reaping the demographic dividend will depend on having a skilled workforce. The present size of approximately fifty-five million people means that Pakistan's labour force is the ninth largest in the world, and growing by at least two to three million workers a year. In addition to education initiatives, it is critical to unleash a parallel effort aimed at bridging the skills gap.

There are several problems here. First, the skills needed for low-paid agricultural jobs are very different from the skills needed for higher-paid jobs such as in healthcare, plumbing or construction. While vocational training centres have been established in different parts of the country, there is insufficient effort to identify and provide the skills that are needed. Second, the higher education institutes that produce doctors, engineers and business graduates are not numerous enough to churn out enough trained professionals. Some studies have shown that there is an exodus of trained manpower nearly the size of fresh incoming graduates particularly in the field of engineering. These trends are alarming and need to be reversed.

This means first, a list of skills that are required across sectors should be developed. Some of these skills may be common but others may be sector specific. In this regard, the government sponsored National Vocational and Technical Education Commission (NAVTEC) can be used to upscale its programs to give technical and vocational training a quantum jump and ensure that standards of attainment improve.

Second, a public-private partnership should be set up by the Ministry of Technology to bring together all the technical manpower resources in the country and use this as a pool to harness technology, expertise and ideas. These can then be commercially applied in areas and sectors in which Pakistan ought to focus to achieve competitive

214

strength. Such a pool can also be applied to build the capacity of highly skilled technical managers needed to produce and disseminate high-middle- and low-end technologies and products.

One area where highly and technically skilled manpower exists is in the Pakistan Armed Forces. This 'hidden' talent reserve has a demonstrated ability to absorb and learn the use of new technologies. This resource ought to be leveraged by the private sector to 'leap-frog'. Corporate leaders could join hands with leading technology experts in the Armed Forces in a joint effort to identify those areas that could provide the basis for export driven growth in areas where the industrial sector can be transformed. A case in point is Brazil where government policy has over the last three decades helped to make Brazil among the largest exporters of defence technologies and equipment by combining technological expertise in their domestic auto sector with defence expertise.

It is important for Pakistan to align its labour market policy with a sound policy for competitiveness in industry, agriculture and the service sector. One initiative that attempts to identify indicators on skills and wages using labour market force data is the Pakistan Employment Trends Report produced by the Ministry of Labour and Manpower in collaboration with the International Labour Organisation (ILO). More specifically the report has looked at the technical and vocational training capacity in the country and how this can improve competitiveness. The key message here is greater investment in education and training, particularly for young people and women.

While government and private sector initiatives are focusing on upgrading the infrastructure in both these areas, much more needs to be done to create alignment between those industries and sectors which are being targeted for export growth and the skills and education levels which are required for people entering the labour market to be employed at levels which allow them to climb the income curve.

*Boost exports.* Pakistan has never had a consistent, coherent and well-articulated export-focused growth strategy. Indeed, exports are often treated as a residual after-thought once the domestic market has been catered for. This is inexplicable given that the country has had a persistently large trade deficit, which has been increasingly difficult to finance each year. While exports have been rising, economic growth, per se, has never been driven by exports. Nor has building a dynamic export sector been at the forefront of any government's economic strategy. Although domestic demand has to remain an important cornerstone of the overall growth story and firms have to be competitive domestically to survive, the focus of policy has to shift from being inward looking to one which is outward looking, focused more on export growth than just on domestic demand.

Comparison with other countries reinforce the lesson that trade openness has been an important factor in driving economic growth in successful countries. Openness has helped economic transformation. Aside from the benefits of having a more competitive environment, which induces firms to become more efficient, unblocking the access to export markets that were not accessible before also provides opportunities for economies of scale in industrial production.

Pakistan's export to GDP ratio is relatively low and its exports per capita are among the lowest when compared to other Asian economies. If one looks at the export mix, it is apparent that sectors that are low technology and low value are the ones that have grown. Broadly speaking exports fall into two categories: textiles and other Small and Medium Enterprise (SME) industries across different sectors such as leather, chemical, medical goods and agricultural products.

The challenge for Pakistan is to diversify this portfolio by implementing policies that contribute to successfully exporting new and more sophisticated products both within textiles and the SME sectors. A closer look at textiles and SMEs is telling.

*Transform textiles.* Pakistan is the fourth largest producer and the third largest consumer of cotton in the world. The downstream textile and garments sector, considered to be low value addition, has grown the most and today this sector represents the single largest industrial sector. It employs approximately 38 per cent of the total manufacturing labour force, supports about 1.5 million farmers and contributes about 9 per cent to the country's GDP. It is also consistently responsible for between 50 and 70 per cent of the country's exports. During the past several decades, textiles have attracted the highest share of total capital investment.

Significant progress has been made by an increase in upstream cotton cultivation and the downstream industry has developed from being a fabric producer and yarn exporter to exporting products with a higher value added content. Problems however remain. Cotton yields lag behind those of competing countries, irrigation methods are antiquated, and cotton picking, storage and transportation facilities continue to be poor resulting in contamination of cotton. The cotton produced remains of low quality, which restricts the types of products that can be made from it.

This is evidenced by the value added sector where Pakistan has visibly slid down the value chain with gains in the low value added sectors and setbacks in the higher value added segments. Globally, Pakistan's value added segments find it hard to compete effectively with goods from China, India, Bangladesh and Sri Lanka. This is further compounded by a poor policy framework, political turmoil, and the high cost of energy and transport. Despite the existence of a Ministry of Textiles, problems are faced by producers due to the shortage of qualified, skilled labour, absence of research and development, weak marketing capabilities and a general apathy to address problems proactively at the official level.

This situation needs to be urgently addressed. As a core industry Pakistan's textiles have the ability to transform its economic future. The sector has been mismanaged and misunderstood for decades. Pakistan's natural advantage as a cotton producing country has thus been undermined while nations like Bangladesh, China, India, and Sri Lanka have been able to lower costs, attain higher exports and capture world market share without cotton-growing being the backbone of their economies. While some of the large Pakistani business groups have emerged amongst the most competitive textile producers in the world, this is not true for the textile sector as a whole, which remains fragmented. The more successful groups are those that are vertically integrated and have successfully positioned themselves in foreign markets, earning a significant percentage of their export revenues from value added products.

The key to transforming the textile industry is to add value to cotton by better organisation and coordination from cotton ginning to the finished product which can add a new edge to the sector's competitiveness. This could involve policies to support the import of plant and machinery, access to favourable financing terms, support to cotton growers, incentives for proper transportation and logistics and greater focus on penetrating export markets. This would assist producers to get to the finished goods stage with greater ease and allow greater economies of scale to develop.

A hypothetical example to demonstrate the payback of value addition is as follows. If Pakistan were to utilise its cotton to produce high-quality shirts and trousers its exports could surge. Pakistan produces twelve million bales of cotton each year. Each bale contains 480 pounds of cotton. The production of one shirt and trouser combined consumes approximately two pounds of cotton. If Pakistan produced nothing but shirts and trousers, and sold one trouser and one shirt collectively for $25 in the international market, then, Pakistan could earn $72 billion in export earnings each year. Pakistan's current textile and apparel exports are $10 billion. A textile strategy which encourages value addition, could therefore transform Pakistan's economic landscape.

One step in the right direction has been the introduction of the new National Textile Policy 2009–2014 announced by the Ministry of Textiles in 2009. This establishes an investment fund that aims at incentivising investments in specific areas including modernisation of machinery and technology, removing infrastructural bottlenecks, enhancing skills, better marketing and use of information and communication technology. The fund provides generous sector-specific and general rebates, re-financing schemes and grants. That said, such a policy falls short on implementation, as it has not resulted in the level of capital investment required to grow value added textiles to the level where they can start to make a meaningful contribution across the board for the economy as a whole.

*SME Sector.* Often the official pre-occupation with the textile sector blindsides the government to other 'value added' exports in the SME sector. Whilst textile exports traditionally account for as much as 70 per cent of annual exports, remaining exports include SME sectors including food, petroleum products, leather, pharmaceuticals, engineering goods, cement, sports goods, carpets, surgical equipment, furniture, gems and jewellery. Most of these sectors are high value added, high margin and have a higher demand propensity in export markets. The key hurdle is that they account for a smaller percentage of Pakistan's total exports and hence command little attention from government policy-makers.

SME manufacturing enterprises generate 35 per cent of Pakistan's manufacturing output, 85 per cent employment for non-agricultural labour and 25 per cent of exports. These are impressive statistics, yet they remain in the backwater of mainstream economic policy. What is urgently needed is a sustained and vigorous policy-driven growth in these sectors with strong forward and backward inter-industry linkages using the 'inclusive' growth model. With labour-input, a large component of capital and output, rapid SME growth can have a salutary impact on wages, employment, living standards and alleviating poverty.

Much needs to be done to achieve this outcome. The government has large bureaucracies dealing with SME in all provinces but it is unclear what they do. Surveys of activity in this sector are undertaken, sometimes as infrequently as fifteen years, and a rather imprecise growth rate is calculated. This figure is then put into the National Income Accounts and repeated year-after-year until the next survey. The growth rate of the SME sector has been determined to be as low as 2.5 per cent per annum and has averaged between 7.5 per cent and 7.8 per cent per annum for the last five years. This is not the true rate of growth of the SME sector; rather it is a 'plug in' number, which economic managers use, in the GDP economic model. In Pakistan's National Accounts, the SME growth rate and that of large scale manufacturing together combine to yield the total manufacturing sector growth. Perhaps with more accurate documentation, it would be possible to generate a more accurate assessment of growth rates for SME.

So what is first needed is more and better information on what is going on in the SME sector from which most exports emanate. Second, growth in these SME sectors can be enhanced by technology inputs, trained labour and manufacturing or service capacity to scale up production as well as the marketing expertise in order to penetrate global markets. This can create a virtuous cycle of growth, employment creation, learning about new products and development.

Second, the incentive structure needs to favour exports through judicious adjustment in trade, tax, finance and tariff policies. Special incentives should be given to exporters. If this 'tilt' is sustained, new exports can surge. An examination of the rather non-descript category of 'Miscellaneous Exports' in the official export data turns up some surprising high-value items that Pakistan exports to some very sophisticated markets but the amounts are small and their year-on-year growth is fairly erratic.

Third, the non-price determinants of exports need to be strengthened by emulating 'best-practice' techniques employed by the world's leading exporters. Fourth, domestic and FDI proposals that are aimed at exports should be given the highest priority and placed on a fast track for approval. FDI inflows offer the best route to securing discrete upward shifts in the technological progress function in the SME sector, simultaneously bringing in better managerial and marketing skills critical for exports.

Fifth, at the firm level, companies have to find a uniquely Pakistani way to develop a game plan for themselves. To be successful, Pakistani firms have to build market shares in sectors where they have the ability to produce better and cheaper goods for international markets.

## The Importance of Harnessing Entrepreneurial Talent for SME Development

According to the MIT Entrepreneurship Centre at MIT Sloan School, it is imperative for rapidly developing economies to review the importance of supporting entrepreneurship as an urgent matter of public policy. In a similar vein, an Economist Intelligence Report emphasised the importance of government investment in education and Research and Development by highlighting that 'waves of technically trained young people—steeped in the latest theories and techniques, and honed by some of the smartest minds in science and technology—do more to raise a country's industrial competitiveness than all the tax breaks, development aid and government initiatives put together'.

Pakistan's SME Development Vision as spelled out by the SME policy is 'SME-led economic growth resulting in poverty reduction, creation of jobs and unleashing the entrepreneurial potential of the people of Pakistan'. The SME policy has a vast institutional network consisting of institutions like the Small and Medium Enterprise Authority (SMEDA), the National Productivity Organisation, the Pakistan Software Export Board (PSEB) and the Competitiveness Support Fund. Whilst these organisations have developed a great deal of capacity and can launch a number of high impact programs to encourage entrepreneurship, much more needs to be done in terms of coordination, impact and results.

One of the main concerns is that growth of small and medium sized businesses is still constrained due to limited access to financing, bureaucracy, and the absence of a skilled worked force with the tool kit for setting up a successful small business. Wherever such initiatives are underway, they suffer from limited funding, uneven and insufficient government support and lack of coordination. If properly harnessed, small enterprises have the ability to increase the per capita income to a level of US $10,000 in the next ten years.

Whilst an institutional network exists, some of the key initiatives that need further capacity and focus are as follows. First, set up and fund training programs for small businesses in vocational schools and universities in urban and major rural areas. Second, banks should ensure adequate funding for small enterprises, which is based on cash flow lending versus asset-based models. Third, the government should fund an early stage equity fund to provide seed capital for early stage start up ventures where the fund is managed on a private enterprise basis which could be sector specific such as high growth information technology, human development, agriculture, services, and industry. Fourth, efforts should be directed to encourage ideas, progress and innovation through the formation of clusters. Clusters inherently evolve because of entrepreneurship. For example, the technology cluster in Pakistan is Lahore and the textile cluster in Pakistan is Faisalabad and Karachi. Most successful businesses in Pakistan are founded by entrepreneurs who are located in a particular area; the cluster forms around these entrepreneurs. Therefore, focusing on entrepreneurship in clusters can have a significant impact, which reinforces the idea of an inclusive growth model that involves the private sector and focuses on investing in education, vocational training and entrepreneurship.

*Define a Coherent Exchange Rate Policy*

A 'stable' exchange rate is always thought to be a reflection of how 'well' the economy is being managed. Indeed, governments frequently intervene in exchange rate management matters and ask that the exchange rate is kept stable in nominal terms or only fluctuates around a tight band. An appreciating exchange rate is greeted with applause. Devaluation is always deemed to be bad. The reality is more nuanced. An exporter is interested in the 'real' value of the dollar s/he earns per unit of exports, not the 'nominal' amount. Thus the nominal exchange rate needs to be corrected for inflation—or more specifically, relative inflation—meaning Pakistan's inflation vis-à-vis the inflation rates of our trading partners and competitors yields a Real Effective Exchange Rate (REER). Empirical studies show that exports do respond to changes in the REER because it is an important—albeit not the only—determinant of export success.

Historically, and even now, there has been a strong anti-export bias in Pakistan with the REER tending towards an appreciation, which means the exporter is getting fewer and fewer real dollars per unit of exports. If exporters see that the improvement in real export profitability is likely to be fleeting or dissipate through future inflation or by changes in government policy, they will have little incentive to export and would prefer to sell in the domestic market.

One way of forestalling REER appreciation is to allow for greater downward flexibility in the nominal exchange rate so as to yield a constant on rising REER. A better way is to reduce our adverse relative inflation differential as opposed to our trading partners and competitors. However, this would require highly disciplined macroeconomic policies (small fiscal deficits and a tight monetary policy stance with positive real interest rates) that can be sustained over time. Unfortunately, this is something that Pakistan has not been able to do. Brief periods of price stability have given way to extended periods of high inflation rooted in lax macroeconomic indiscipline.

Successful exporting countries, specifically in Asia, and more notably China, keep the REER slightly depreciated thus giving their exporters a lasting competitive edge. China is a good example. By keeping the Renminbi at a significantly lower level than that which would be dictated by market forces and the size of China's foreign exchange reserves, China has emerged as an unstoppable export juggernaut. Of course in following such an exchange rate regime China has come in for a lot of criticism, especially from the US, because of its large and growing trade deficit with China which the US claims robs their economy of millions of jobs.

To establish if Pakistan would benefit from a similar policy it is important to examine some of the key economic data related to exchange rates, balance of payments and inflation. For purposes of analysis, the exchange rate over a three year period, between January, 2007 and July 2010, where the Pakistani Rupee underwent significant depreciation against the US dollar and other major currencies, will be taken as an example. From a level of Rs. 60.7/USD in January 2007 to Rs. 85.6/USD in July 2010, the value of the Pakistani Rupee had eroded by 38.5 per cent. Chiefly responsible for this sharp decline was the supply side shock from global commodities, in particular crude oil which shot up from approximately $80 per barrel to $140 per barrel. Being an oil importing country, the trade deficit burgeoned to $15.3 billion while Forex reserves dropped to just $6.7 billion. Inflation hit a peak of 25 per cent as the entire consumer basket was jolted by commodity prices and massive deficit financing from the central bank. During the same period exports grew from $17.3 billion in FY07 to $19.6 billion in FY10, while imports jumped from $27 billion to $31 billion. In simple terms the increase in oil prices thus fuelled the deficit in the balance of trade and the consequent devaluation of the Pakistani Rupee.

Would a policy of forced and greater devaluation have helped Pakistan in the medium to long term scenario? The problem with such a strategy is Pakistan's unfavourable terms of trade. The terms of trade is the export price index relative to the import price index and helps gauge capital inflow and outflow in terms of 100 indices. In fact, a close examination of the terms of trade suggests that Pakistan's terms of trade are not only unfavourable but also deteriorating for all major categories except food and live animals which improved significantly in FY09. These have declined from 73.6 in FY05 to 63.8 in January 2007 to 54.9 in nine months FY10. This indicates that in FY05, for every unit of import Pakistan exported 73.6 per cent of the index value, and by nine months FY10 export unit relative to the import unit had dropped to 54.9 per cent. These figures reveal that if Pakistan devalues its currency, the incremental cost paid for imports will be more than the additional benefit earned from exports on a relative time basis.

The key point is that the Real Effective Exchange Rate (REER) is what really matters to exports rather than the nominal exchange rate. From January 2007 the Pakistani Rupee has significantly depreciated, in nominal terms, against the USD. This indicates that the PKR has weakened against the USD and thus Pakistan's exports to the US and other trading partners should have become more competitive, as they had become cheaper in units of foreign currency. However the REER paints a different picture; it takes the nominal exchange rate, adjusted for foreign price levels and then deflates it by domestic inflation. This index had during the same period appreciated and the PKR had strengthened by 5.8 per cent since January 2007. As a result instead of Pakistani exports getting cheaper, exports have become more expensive in the international market and hence less competitive.

The primary reason for this is domestic inflation. In FY08, CPI was 12 per cent, which spiked to 20.8 per cent in FY09 before settling down to 11.7 per cent in FY10. Essentially the domestic cost of manufacturing, transporting and selling our goods abroad has risen to such an extent that it has neutralised the advantage of a weak currency.

The skewed structure of Pakistan's imports and the infrastructural inefficiencies inherent in the domestic economy prevent Pakistani exporters from benefiting from a weaker currency. This is partly because Pakistan is an oil-importing country with 34 per cent of the total import bill attributed to the import of crude and refined petroleum. A weaker PKR means a higher import bill, higher prices for transportation (7.5 per cent of CPI basket) and energy (7.5 per cent of CPI basket) not to mention the indirect effect on perishable food items, house rent, recreation and other components of the inflation basket. Higher costs not only erode the margins of exporters who already suffer from power shortages, security threats and high interest rates but force them to pass on the price increase to their international customers. Given that most Pakistani exports are low value added items, they also suffer from demand inelasticity. This means that a price decrease does not increase volumetric demand by enough to offset the revenue loss from lower prices.

While it is tempting to think that a policy of deliberate PKR devaluation would improve export competitiveness, the reality is that domestic inflation, supply bottlenecks and fiscal indiscipline, would result in real appreciation as witnessed over the last three years and, in fact, make exports less competitive. The solution to increasing exports lies, therefore, in stabilising the macroeconomic environment, providing adequate infrastructure and security, access to credit, investment in product quality and value addition which are longer term policy objectives, all necessary conditions to complement a policy of maintaining a competitive exchange rate.

The converse of this is to keep a stable exchange rate, which is what happened during the period, 2002–2007. During this period, Pakistan saw its exports rise from $9 billion to $17 billion. A stable currency policy allowed a steady build up of reserves and investment flows. Investment rates climbed to as high as 23 per cent as foreign direct investment felt more confident that future returns would not be eroded by a weak currency. This allowed the liquidity cycle to ease up leading to a benign interest rate environment, reduced debt servicing. All good news for GDP growth as compared to previous years where low reserves encouraging dollarisation, low investment rates and relatively low growth.

So does a successful export-driven economy mean that Pakistan needs to use the exchange rate more aggressively? The focus has to be the Real Effective Exchange Rate, rather than the nominal exchange rate. Keeping REER competitive is a necessary but insufficient condition. If Pakistan can maintain a competitive REER, Pakistan can recoup lost competitiveness by focusing on supply side issues which control inflation or it can continue to play 'catch up' and do what is being done now which is a constant downward adjustment of the nominal exchange rate hindering export competitiveness.

## Control Inflation

There is growing consensus among central bankers that medium- to long-term price stability is the overriding goal of monetary policy. Research has shown that maintaining low and stable inflation has helped economies to grow, as businesses, households and individual consumers are able to make better investment, savings and wage contract decisions. If inflation gets out of control either due to an overheating of the economy or supply side factors, central banks have generally resorted to monetary tightening as a means to control inflation. This has the knock on effect of reducing aggregate demand and feeding into slower growth.

The State Bank of Pakistan (SBP)—an independent institution with full autonomy on monetary policy—has delicately balanced two opposing objectives, an anti-inflation policy and a pro-growth policy. There has been an impressive array of reforms in this regard, including the Fiscal Responsibility Act and Debt Limitation Act of June 2003, yet the reform agenda needs to be boosted further in the current macroeconomic environment.

While inflation was not an issue in 2002–2008, the current challenges are more testing. In order to achieve the 7 per cent growth trajectory the SBP needs to keep inflation low. The recent monetary tightening in response to rising inflation has not been preferred strategy, not only because it is politically unpopular but also because it results in increasing debt servicing and could result in further weakness in the currency and another bout of inflation. With Pakistan's high debt to GDP ratio as well as a growing fiscal deficit, control of inflation becomes a pressing priority to induce confidence in the business community and public at large about future price stability. The SBP alone cannot control inflation without the presence of a coordinated fiscal policy which requires support from the Ministry of Finance. The budget announced in June 2010 was a step in the right direction as it signalled a more responsible fiscal stance by the government. This would entail the government sticking to an agenda where unnecessary current expenditures are severely curtailed along with a clear policy for revenue enhancement.

Recent indicators suggest that inflation is on the rise. This has been precipitated by the government's decision to increase electricity tariffs, fuel prices, elimination of food subsidies and the imposition of a new 'Reformed General Sales Tax'. Further tariff increases and rises in taxation have been announced by the government, partly driven by the additional resources required for rehabilitation and relief for flood affectees. The SBP is also pointing to aggregate demand picking up, led mainly by public sector consumption, while prospects for aggregate supply remain weak due to energy shortages and the poor law and order situation. These developments together with the rising total debt reinforce the need to have renewed efforts to keep inflation and the fiscal deficit under control.

What can be done? First and most fundamentally, the government should announce a 'Medium Term Financial Strategy' (MTFS) for the next five years where a coordinated fiscal and monetary policy having a target band for inflation should form a cornerstone of the government's approach. Setting an inflation target or a band for inflation would certainly help to engender positive expectations across the economy and help to reinforce a 'mindset' that the government is serious about controlling inflation. Given that the vast majority of people are sensitive to rising prices, the very poor and low income groups, as well as business and industry, lose from higher input and capital costs in a rising inflation scenario.

Inflation-targeting is also an appealing choice as it has worked in both developing and advanced countries. It is not an end in itself, but a means to an end, which is achieving price stability that can be defined as low and stable inflation. The real point is to get inflation down to, in line with, or maybe even below its major trading partners and competitors. If Pakistan can achieve this, then policy-makers will not need to depreciate its nominal exchange rate and play catch-up with the adverse relative inflation differential. Getting that adverse inflation differential down is therefore key. The target range within such a context should be between 5 to 8 per cent over the next five years.

Secondly, this strategy should be supplemented by having a closely aligned industry and trade policy, and a clear policy on raising the level of productivity for capital and labour in key export sectors as well as those sectors where capacity constraints result in price increases of goods and services. Examples of these sectors would include food, housing and energy—which collectively account for over 60 per cent of the consumer price index. In particular, at a time when most nations globally are scrambling for food security, Pakistan's government would reap significant future dividends if it were to have a strong agricultural policy to encourage investments that enhance agricultural output and productivity. Increased attention to Research and Development would need to be an integral part of a productivity enhancement drive, particularly in agriculture and the SME sectors, which are export oriented. This is another way of improving competitiveness, which aims at cutting unit costs by raising productivity of capital and labour. To have a stable exchange rate raising productivity in the export sector is the only way to cut costs and increase export profitability. This would not only help to curb inflation but also allow an export surplus which would help in improving long term macroeconomic indicators.

Thirdly, the official consumer price index could be reconstituted to reduce the weight of food and energy which are dependent on exogenous factors and a global pricing mechanism which is beyond the control of governments. This would leave other items in the CPI basket such as wages, rent, medical care, transportation, textile and apparel goods prices intact and would be a more significant monitor of how successful the government is in terms of achieving its inflation target.

Fourthly, to reinforce the stable price 'mindset', the government could enact an Act of Parliament which compels subsequent governments to adhere to a consistent policy of bringing inflation within the target band. In the context of an Act of Parliament, caveats can be structured for unexpected natural disasters such as the 2010 floods that produced a sharp increase in the price of food and other necessities, which offset the benefits of an inflation targeting policy.

## Conclusion

Despite turbulent economic and political headwinds over the last three decades Pakistan's economy has not only avoided collapse but has recorded an average growth rate of over 5 per cent per annum. Pakistan's medium and longer-term future will be driven by key demographic and economic trends. As the focus of much international attention, Pakistan has the opportunity to push ahead on key structural reforms. Coupled with a steady flow of loans, assistance and investments, this has the potential to hedge any economic downturn in the short to medium term. The list of things Pakistan needs to do is not new. Yet they are difficult things to achieve and require a clearly defined implementation framework and the full support of government bureaucracy, industry, businesses and the public at large with priority given to those measures that can create jobs to accommodate new people entering the work force each year.

While the full extent of damage emanating from the floods in Pakistan is not known at the time of writing this chapter, billions of dollars will be required for rebuilding and reconstruction. Whilst the floods have caused much misery and devastation the disaster can act as a catalyst to formulate a clear economic vision. The need for better governance, for creating social safety nets for the poor and for accelerating growth can become pressing national issues. This, in turn, can force the government in power to become more transparent and accountable to the public.

There are two scenarios that can emerge. The best-case scenario is one where economics prevails over geo-political risks, and a collective will under the leadership of a credible government is created to transform the economic landscape of Pakistan. This can result in a change in perception about Pakistan, trigger an investment cycle targeting growth in infrastructure and propel Pakistan into the 7–8 per cent growth trajectory.

The second scenario is one where future growth is unstable and low. Political and geo-political instability continues to weaken an already fragile economy and investment rates remain low due to the poor internal security situation. In this scenario, Pakistan's population, instead of being a natural advantage, could turn into a crisis if young people are unable to find economic opportunities and where unmatched expectations result in discontentment, unemployment and growing disparities between the top and bottom end of the social pyramid.

Pakistan's record in reform and policy implementation to achieve long-term economic development has at best been marked by missed opportunities and failures. The risks of failure are much greater today than at any time in the past, but so too are the rewards of meaningful reform.

*Acknowledgements*

I would like to express my gratitude to the many people who saw me through this chapter; to all those who provided support, talked things over, read, wrote, offered comments, allowed me to quote their remarks and assisted in the editing, proof reading and design.

First, I would like to thank Dr Maleeha Lodhi for inviting me to contribute this chapter and for her patience and outstanding guidance throughout; Dr. Meekal Ahmad for his invaluable comments and assistance; my wife, Saira, who helped despite her commitments as a lawyer and a dedicated mother of our daughters, Nuraiya and Zeyna; Abid Hasan who provided valuable ideas; and my dedicated team of research analysts, including Hamad Aslam and Mustafa Pasha at BMA Capital for their unstinting support. Above all I would like to thank my mother and father, Shehla and Mazhar, who have got me this far, supported and encouraged me to write this chapter, which I dedicate to them.

12

# TURNING ENERGY AROUND

## Ziad Alahdad

Pakistan's energy sector is in crisis. Its problems seem insurmountable. Although positive initiatives have been implemented over the years many opportunities have been lost. The result is the current predicament.

Power outages of up to eighteen hours a day disrupt the lives of people and threaten the economy in an unprecedented way. Despite abundant installed capacity the power system is mired in critical operational issues including a pervasive circular debt. Payment arrears between various entities has jammed the flow of funds through the power supply-chain, and deprived fuel suppliers and independent power producers of cash to the extent that their viability and therefore output is jeopardised. Demand is outstripping supply at a time when the country's security situation imposes obvious constraints. But if the energy deficit is not urgently tackled it contains the seeds of dangerous social unrest. Equally disquieting is the fact that energy policy initiatives being promoted today are the same as those proposed some thirty years ago, indicating little implementation progress in the intervening years while the crisis deepened.

How can this situation be remedied? In light of overwhelming evidence that the absence of a coordinated energy policy remains a fundamental constraint, an integrated approach needs to be established together with an institutional structure that supports it. This was partially implemented in Pakistan in the 1980s but faded away subsequently with the increasing fragmentation of policy institutions and functions. Without integration, decision-making remains inherently flawed and policy initiatives are reduced to shooting in the dark.

The country has the capacity to speedily revive the integrated approach together with the first steps of a supporting institutional structure. The rest of the institutional changes can be phased in gradually. This will enable policy-makers to rapidly tackle, on an informed basis, the urgent and longer-term problems facing the sector, replacing the current ad hoc approach which reacts to, rather than averts, crises. It will help pave the way for the recovery of the energy sector that can then aid the economic rebound. It is not so much the availability of resources but how they are managed which makes the difference between success and failure.

## State of the Energy Sector

Pakistan's policy-makers have done a reasonably good job of articulating (repeatedly through several five-year planning cycles) policy objectives for the energy sector.[1] The broad objective is to develop the sector to support an expanding economy. Developing indigenous resources, importing energy at competitive prices to meet deficits, expanding delivery infrastructure and improving energy efficiency and reliability, would enhance energy supplies. Security of energy supply would be increased by greater reliance on national resources thus reducing import dependence, and by diversification of energy supplies to manage risks and external shocks. Long-term viability of the sector would be supported by a shift in the role of government from owner to that of policy-maker and regulator, encouraging the private sector to own and run the energy companies through appropriate incentives, including attracting foreign and local private capital and deploying competitive processes. Also, the objectives contain consumer-oriented, eco-friendly and pro-poor elements, promoting service-provision, environmental protection and affordable energy for the underprivileged.

Despite these laudable objectives the sector is in a dire state. The problem is not a lack of clarity on *what* needs to be done but *how* it is to be done.

Before considering solutions, it is essential to briefly review the state of the sector, the gravity of issues, and why the situation has become so serious. The official Pakistan Energy Yearbook 2009[2] lays out the supply and consumption picture. Total primary energy supply in Pakistan is 63 MTOE (Million Tons of Oil Equivalence) of which natural gas accounts for 48 per cent, oil 32 per cent, hydroelectricity 11 per cent and coal around 7 per cent. Nuclear, LPG and imported electricity make up the remaining 2 per cent. Pakistan imports a third of its energy requirements mainly in the form of oil and coal, despite huge proven reserves of coal and a significant exploration potential of oil. Over 80 per cent (17 MTOE) of Pakistan's oil requirements are imported at a prohibitive cost of $12 billion a year, and over 60 per cent (3 MTOE) of its coal supplies come from overseas.[3]

The official figure for total energy consumption is 37 MTOE[4], the difference between supply and consumption being the losses in conversion, processing, transmission, distribution, as well as non-technical losses, which is a euphemism for theft. The industrial sector is the dominant consumer with over 40 per cent of the market. The transport sector consumes just over 30 per cent and households around 22 per cent. The remainder consists mainly of commercial and agricultural consumers.

The Hydrocarbon Development Institute of Pakistan (HDIP) in the Ministry of Petroleum and Natural Resources produces an impressive document, the Energy Yearbook, based on input from various energy-related ministries and agencies. The quality of information and analysis is testament to the fact that, despite the serious brain drain from Pakistan, islands of excellence remain. This offers hope for the future and gives pause to those who maintain that the situation is beyond redemption.

There is, however, a glaring omission, which reflects the preoccupation of policy-makers. The data pertains only to commercial energy, i.e., energy for consumers connected to national grids and billed for services.

Estimates of non-commercial or traditional forms of energy are missing. Data in this area is sporadic and much less reliable, mainly because of the conspicuous lack of attention accorded to it. If non-commercial energy is included, the supply picture changes dramatically. Traditional biofuels (fuelwood and other biomass) head the list, followed, in descending order, by natural gas, oil, hydro and coal.[5] On the consumption end, again, a starkly different picture emerges.[6] Households become the primary consumer using 50 per cent of the mix. Biofuels account for over 85 per cent of household energy use, of which fuelwood is the largest component followed by biomass, and crop residues.

The most egregious aspect of the omission is that non-commercial energy use accounts for nearly half of the overall demand for energy in Pakistan. By including non-commercial energy in the calculations, policy-makers will be forced to consider major shifts in emphasis. Supply and consumption patterns are presented in Table 1 below.

Table 1: Pakistan energy supply and consumption 2009

1.1: Primary commercial energy supply

| Energy source | MTOE | Percentage |
|---|---|---|
| Share natural gas | 30.3 | 48% |
| Oil | 20.1 | 32% |
| Hydro | 6.6 | 11% |
| Coal | 4.6 | 7% |
| Nuclear, LPG, imported power | 1.0 | 2% |
| Total | 62.6 | 100% |

1.2: Commercial energy consumption

| Consumption sector | MTOE | Percentage share |
|---|---|---|
| Industry | 14.8 | 40% |
| Transport | 11.4 | 30% |
| Household | 8.1 | 22% |
| Commerce, agriculture, govt. | 3.0 | 8% |
| Total | 37.3 | 100% |

1.3: Total energy consumption: commercial plus non-commercial

| Consumption sector | Percentage share |
|---|---|
| Household | 50% |
| Industry | 26% |
| Transport | 19% |
| Commerce, agriculture, govt. | 5% |
| Total | 100% |

Note: Non-commercial primary energy supply not shown due to inadequate data.

In one sense, the historical neglect of non-commercial energy seems understandable. Commercial energy is a key ingredient for national growth and *prima facie* warrants the lion's share of attention, particularly if growth has been stymied, as has often been the case in Pakistan, and there is pressure on policy-makers to jump-start the economy. There is an inherent fallacy in this approach. While commercial energy consumers contribute significantly to GDP growth, neglected non-commercial consumers drag down national output over the longer-term by unregulated and unchecked practices and technologies, which waste energy and denude forestry resources by harvesting beyond the maximum allowable cut, i.e. beyond the level at which the forestry resource becomes unsustainable. Although the economic, social and environmental implications of the neglect requires a separate detailed study, we only need to look around us to see the disastrous effects on the degradation of forests and eco-systems, and the poverty that this approach has engendered over the past sixty-four years.

In evaluating the state of the sector in relation to the economy, three other parameters are significant. First, data from the Energy Yearbook and the Economic Survey clearly show that growth in energy consumption and economic growth have followed almost identical patterns for the last decade and a half, reaffirming that energy fuels the economy and its shortage curbs growth. The second is Pakistan's per capita energy consumption, which at 0.49 TOE is significantly lower than the world average of 1.78. This reflects the country's level of development.[7] As energy availability is a key determinant in the standard of living, this parameter is also indicative of the high incidence of poverty. The third is Pakistan's energy consumption per dollar of GDP growth, which is around 0.82 against the world average of 0.32. This illustrates the relative inefficiency of energy use in Pakistan and highlights the pressing need to strengthen policy initiatives that encourage greater utilisation efficiency.[8] In a constrained energy supply situation, any improvement in efficiency means adding to the supply.

The above figures are based on commercial energy but if non-commercial energy is included, the comparisons are likely to be even more pronounced. Moreover, the household sector, which is the largest consumer and where waste is greatest, would become the focus of improving energy efficiency. By excluding non-commercial energy, the industrial sector appears as the largest consumer and therefore the focus of attention. This does not imply that the industrial sector should be overlooked. There are many low-cost and no-cost initiatives that can be implemented here. But it is important to strike the right balance between available financial resources and the concentration of effort.

Pakistan's energy resource potential is substantial and remains largely unharnessed although not all of it is currently financially or technically exploitable. This potential is in the form of depleting fossil fuels (oil, gas, coal) as well as renewables (hydro, solar, wind, woodfuels and agricultural residues). Among fossil fuels, in the petroleum (oil and gas) sub-sector, Pakistan has a large prospective area (or, in geological language, sedimentary basin) covering 830,000 square kilometres. Probable reserves are estimated at twenty-seven billion barrels of oil and 282 trillion cubic feet (TCF) of gas.[9]

Of this, 936 million barrels of oil had been confirmed and 609 million barrels produced till 2007, leaving 327 million barrels of proven reserves yet to be recovered. The reserves-to-production ratio stands at fourteen, critically low considering the high and growing level of oil imports, and compared with the worldwide ratio of forty.[10] For natural gas, 53 TCF have been confirmed, of which 23 TCF were produced till 2007, leaving 30 TCF of proven reserves. The reserves-to-production ratio is twenty-one—uncomfortably low given Pakistan's heavy dependence on natural gas as the primary commercial fuel, and in comparison with a worldwide ratio of 59.[11]

Till early 2009, 725 exploratory wells had been drilled which resulted in over 219 oil and gas discoveries. This works out to a drilling density of 1.99 wells per 1,000 square kilometres—far lower than the world average of ten. However, the success rate of 1:3.3 is much better than the world average of 1:10.[12] The success rate coupled with the large sedimentary basin implies that if the exploration level is increased, there are good chances of significantly raising the level of proven reserves and, consequently, production of oil and gas. This, however, is proving difficult since vast portions of the sedimentary basin lie in areas where security deters any significant exploration— more so as such activity is usually carried out by international oil companies with their own manpower and risk capital.

Pakistan's indigenous coal reserves are huge, estimated at 186 billion tons, of which the Thar deposit of 175 billion tons is the fifth largest in the world. Proven reserves stand at 1,980 million tons and at the present production level the reserves-to-production ratio is well over 400. This signals the need to enhance production significantly. However, most of this coal is of low quality (high sulphur and ash content) and is located in remote areas. Its exploitation therefore requires expensive excavation, treatment and transport infrastructure, in areas where security is a concern.

Renewable energy sources are also significant. Hydroelectric potential in Pakistan is an impressive 41,700 MW of which only 6,600 MW or 16 per cent has been harnessed till today. For mini-hydro (units up to 5 MW capacity), the potential is about 1500 MW of which only 60 MW (4 per cent) has been tapped. Pakistan's almost entirely untapped wind energy potential, according to the USAID Renewable Energy Lab, is estimated at 41,000 MW of power generation based on areas of favourable wind regimes.[13]

Solar energy is abundant and remains unharnessed except for a few isolated projects. If only 0.25 per cent of the land area of the province of Balochistan were covered by solar panels of 20 per cent efficiency, this would be enough to provide electricity to the entire country.[14] However, the feasibility of generating large quantities of wind and solar power (while improving with continuing research) is highly questionable. Estimates for non-commercial sources, mainly woodfuels, are less reliable. These resources are considerable and constitute 45 per cent of the energy supply mix for the country. However, there is ample evidence that in several parts of the country, unregulated harvesting of this poorly managed resource is severely impairing its sustainability.

The current state of the energy deficit and its projected growth is even more worrisome for the future. Data from the Planning Commission, although ignoring non-commercial energy, illustrates the magnitude of the crisis ahead.[15] It projects an annual energy demand increasing from the present level of around 60 MTOE to 198 MTOE by the year 2025. This is based on an annual economic growth of 6.5 per cent. While not consistent with recent trends, this could be envisioned over the longer term, with an abating global financial crisis and a cautiously optimistic view of Pakistan's economic regeneration.

The total indigenous supply over the same period increases from around 40 MTOE to only 75 MTOE. Oil and gas supplies are assumed to increase only slightly in line with constraints on future exploration activities. In contrast, indigenous energy from coal, hydroelectricity, nuclear and non-traditional renewable sources, are assumed to increase significantly in an attempt to offset limitations in oil and gas. The resulting deficit grows from the already disquieting level of around 20

MTOE to a staggering 122 MTOE by 2025. These figures, perhaps more than any other, underscore the fragility of the energy sector, implying a long-term dependence on external sources. This is neither a viable nor affordable scenario.

Three characteristics of Pakistan's energy sector take on special significance. First, the indigenous resource potential is substantial, notwithstanding some critical exploitation issues. Two, the energy deficit is prohibitively large and expanding. Three, nearly half the population, mainly the rural poor, is not connected to the commercial grids and relies on non-commercial energy. This combination often tempts policymakers to promote the harnessing of all forms of energy available. This is a common trap, particularly in a severely cash-strapped environment such as Pakistan. In this approach, for example, undue priority is given to renewable forms such as solar and wind, since they are considered free and able to reach poor, remote localities. Such forms of energy are indeed 'free' since they are constantly renewable, but they are not necessarily cheap. Moreover, they do little to close large deficits. Even compared with nuclear power generation, itself an expensive option, wind power is around 60 per cent more expensive and solar about 30 per cent. Nevertheless, to support poverty alleviation objectives under severe budgetary constraints, all options should be on the table but a mechanism needs to be in place to strike an affordable balance. The degree of departure from the optimum can make the difference between success and failure of energy policy.

How did we get here? How this dire state of affairs came about is analysed in a noteworthy work, which traces the history of the downward spiral and milestones along the way.[16] The path is characterised by 'stop-go' reforms, policy reversals, bureaucratic delays and missed opportunities and, over the last decade or so, a growing security crisis. Through all this, there were some sound and well-intentioned policy initiatives and concerted efforts towards implementation. However, these efforts could not yield the desired results in a policy environment, which lacked the necessary fundamentals.

A few examples illustrate the dilemma.[17] In the early 1980s, there were four international oil companies, which had been granted concessions for exploration in Pakistan. Such companies commonly deploy their own capital for exploration, relying on satisfactory profit sharing or production-sharing agreements with the government to recoup their expenditures once commercial production begins. Drilling conditions were difficult and expensive with deep wells in high-pressure areas but discovery prospects were good. However, a major oil company, on the verge of a significant discovery, decided to suspend drilling operations and leave the country. The net effect was to discourage further exploration at a time when at least ten companies were considering the possibility of exploring in Pakistan with their own capital for the first time—a possibility that could have turned around the country's energy future.

A combination of factors led to the oil company's departure. Among them was the inflexibility of the bureaucracy to address glaring anomalies in the tax structure, which severely eroded the cash flow of the company especially in areas with high exploration costs. The second, more significant reason was that, under the prevailing policy regime, oil and gas prices could only be negotiated after commercial discovery. This was a major disincentive for a company deploying its own capital in expensive operations. Rising expenditures in an uncertain post-discovery regime was enough to warrant a pullout even on the verge of discovery, to the detriment of Pakistan's economy. Pakistan's policy-makers failed to understand that the country was competing with others across the world in attracting scarce exploration risk capital. For this, it needed to make its pricing regime as attractive as possible. If there had been a mechanism to rapidly assess the economic penalty of the policy, which traded immense long-term benefits for short-lived financial gains, the story would have been different. It is a credit to subsequent policy-makers that these retrogressive policies were amended. This is now reflected in the government's exploration promotion[18] and investment promotion documents.[19] However by the time this was done conditions had changed. The security situation became a key deterrent to exploration. This underscores a lost opportunity, one of many policy actions offering too little, too late.

At around the same time, another petroleum company involved in a joint venture with the government had decided to sell to the government its shares in a natural gas field development operation, which provided valuable nitrogen-rich gas feedstock to the fertilizer industry. It took over a year to negotiate the sale price and government interlocutors were able to reduce the purchase price by a significant amount. This could be considered a major gain but for one serious repercussion. Through the protracted negotiations, the field expansion program was put on hold, resulting in immense losses in revenue to the joint venture itself, as well as to the fertilizer industry, and in terms of lost agricultural productivity due to lack of fertilizer. Again, a mechanism to assess the penalty could well have prompted speedier negotiations with less immediate financial gains but with vastly greater financial and economic benefits in the longer term.

Perhaps the most significant example of lost opportunities relates to Central Asia in the early to mid-90s when all six of the newly independent republics, under immense internal economic pressures, were actively seeking avenues to export their surplus energy. Strong consideration was given to the southern corridor through Pakistan to tap the large energy-starved South Asian market as well as gain access to ports on the Arabian Sea for further extending export. This was well before the security situation in Afghanistan had begun to deteriorate. As expected, there were competitors promoting alternative routes. The Great Game was on again, being played with higher stakes and at electronic speed.

Central Asian authorities and international consortia made several attempts to pursue discussions with Pakistani authorities but progress was elusive. One thing was evident. The level of interest and effort of the competitors drowned out the lukewarm response of the Pakistani government and private sector. The rest is history. One can only surmise how the trade corridors, had they been established, would have transformed the regional scenario. Revenue from trade and from transporting energy across the region would have brought immense benefits to Afghanistan and Pakistan. Both countries, as well as India, would have also benefited from greatly enhanced energy supplies. The resulting prosperity and trade links would certainly have strengthened interdependence among the three countries and helped mitigate the conflict which currently engulfs the region.

## Integrated Energy Planning

Energy analysts and policy-makers alike agree that energy sector planning and policy formulation need to be carried out on an integrated basis. The appropriate mechanism to achieve this is known by various acronyms. This chapter refers to it as IEP (Integrated Energy Planning). The concept and principles of IEP presented here are those advocated in 'Integrated National Energy Planning in Developing Countries', amended to reflect conditions in Pakistan.[20] In practice, as is the case in Pakistan, investment planning and pricing are often carried out on an ad hoc, crisis-driven, sub-sector basis. Typically, as also happens in Pakistan, electricity and oil sub-sector plans are prepared largely independent of each other, as well as of other energy sub-sectors. Moreover, the powerful electric power sub-sector often dominates policy decisions on pricing, subsidies and investment priorities, which are inevitably skewed in its favour to the detriment of other sub-sectors, and the economy as a whole. In times of cheap energy, the repercussions could be relatively benign. However, with rising and volatile international oil prices and acute energy shortages, as is the case today, IEP becomes vital.

IEP, as an integral part of economic planning, enables optimum use of energy resources to achieve socio-economic development. Since energy affects every part of the economy, the energy sector is analogous to the financial sector. Some analysts describe energy as the physical counterpart of money. IEP develops a coherent set of policies covering: energy needs to meet growth and environmental targets; optimum fuels mix; conservation; energy security through diversification and reducing dependence on external sources; energy needs of the poor; foreign exchange savings; trade deficit management and revenue generation to finance sector development. IEP integrates the policies and plans of the energy sector with national economic objectives, while ensuring close coordination and consistency between each of the energy sub-sectors.

Figure 1: The Integrated Energy Planning Process

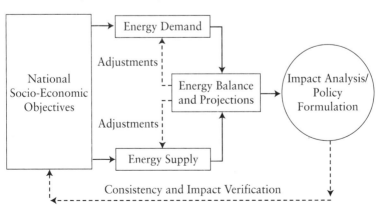

IEP is a five-stage process (Figure 1): Establishing the socio-economic background and national objectives; analysing energy demand; identifying supply options; constructing the energy balance; and formulating policy and analysing its impact. The energy balance, the core of IEP, assigns specific energy sources to corresponding uses. It stipulates the supply of various forms of energy, its conversion and losses and the net available for consumption, broken down by sector. IEP yields a set of detailed energy policies and plans (including policy tools and investment) for the short, medium, and long term, under various scenarios, tested for impact on the economy. The success of IEP depends upon establishing a separate ministry or department for energy with overarching responsibility for the sector and access to top policy levels. As an interim measure, an integrated energy cell can be set up in a central agency such as a planning ministry.

'Integration' under IEP does not signify the revival of central planning or building a more intrusive or manifold bureaucracy. On the contrary, the mechanism is designed to facilitate coordination, and the concomitant institutional structure streamlines and considerably reduces bureaucracy and red tape. This can become contentious because of the reluctance of concerned ministries, agencies and individuals to accept realignment of the power structure that must accompany such changes—hence the importance of political will.

*International Experience*

The concept of IEP was introduced in the 1970s and successfully applied in a wide range of countries, amended to suit individual country conditions. However, in the 1990s, in the wake of a major push by international development agencies to promote market economies in the developing world, it began to wane on the assumption that the free market will determine appropriate policy choices. This assumption does not hold for most countries in the developing world. It might have been ideologically motivated to counter the 'Gosplan' heritage of the newly independent states of the former Soviet Union. Fast-forward to today. The World Bank is preparing a global energy sector strategy.[21] Feedback from countries has identified the absence of long-term energy planning as an emerging issue—signalling the importance of reverting to coordinated long-term planning for those countries that may have discarded the model and suffered as a consequence. Common sense seems to be prevailing over ideology to achieve a practical balance.

Through all this, most developing countries maintained some form of integrated energy planning. Success was characterised by three ingredients: comprehensive coordinated analysis; supporting institutional arrangements at the policy level, and sound implementation. Analytical sophistication varied, but institutional structures have evolved into a central energy policy institution, configured in one of two ways: a stand-alone integrated energy ministry or an integrated energy department/agency within a central ministry. A few examples of countries which fall into one or other of the two arrangements (both supportive of IEP) include: Indonesia, Malaysia, Thailand, Philippines, Poland, Bulgaria, Romania, Hungary, Slovakia, Czech Republic, Cambodia, Viet Nam, Russia, Ukraine, Belarus, Turkey, Tajikistan, Kyrgyzstan, Uzbekistan, Uganda, and Kazakhstan.[22]

Two countries with well-managed energy sectors, which can serve as examples for Pakistan are Turkey and Kazakhstan, in terms of an integrated line ministry model and well coordinated and successfully implemented policies.

*IEP in Pakistan*

Many analysts have drawn attention to the lack of energy policy coordination. 'The Weight of History: Pakistan's Energy Problem'[23] which focuses on commercial energy, emphasises the need for a comprehensive approach. On traditional fuels, 'Energy, Poverty Reduction and Equitable Development in Pakistan'[24] states: 'it is imperative that government policies and strategies recognize' the 'near invisibility of the role of traditional fuels', for which it advocates 'better inter-sectoral policy coordination, and integrated development approaches' maintaining that 'the costs of inaction are high.'

The absence of comprehensive integrated energy planning has also evoked international comment. Quoting an executive, the *New York Times* wrote: 'There is nobody in Islamabad who is working on a coherent, integrated plan. The discussion just keeps going in circles.'[25] USAID's energy assessment of Pakistan[26] listed, as the first item, the following shortcoming: 'The ability to perform system-wide planning in the electricity and energy sector as a whole, both in terms of technical analysis and ability to develop and implement plans of action.'

Building capacity requires coordinated interventions at three levels: training at the individual level; building appropriate institutions to effectively utilise trained manpower; and establishing a policy environment which provides incentives for institutions to function efficiently. In the energy sector Pakistan has relatively good access to training both within the country and overseas. Despite the gradual erosion of trained manpower, the sector retains a modicum of quality. Weaknesses in the policy environment have been discussed. What warrants a closer look is the organisational structure of policy institutions especially the lead ministries, main regulatory bodies and planning institutions in the energy sector.[27] The Ministry of Petroleum and Natural Resources heads the oil, gas and coal sub-sectors. The Oil and Gas Regulatory Authority regulates petroleum product distribution including CNG for vehicles, sets safety standards and equalises prices across the country. Coal exploration and development are undertaken by the Pakistan Mineral Development Corporation through leases granted to the private sector, administered by provincial governments. The Ministry for Water and Power is responsible for the electric power sub-sector. The Pakistan Atomic Energy Commission oversees nuclear power generation. The National Electric Power Regulatory Authority is charged with ensuring fair competition and consumer protection. The Private Power and Infrastructure Board was set up to improve investment incentives in the power sector as a one-stop facility for investors.

The Ministry of Urban Affairs, Forestry and Wildlife oversees the woodfuels sub-sector. The Ministry of Food, Agriculture and Livestock handles other biomass including agricultural residues. The Alternative Energy Development Board is the central national body for renewable energy and is also charged with rural electrification in areas remote from the power grid. The SAARC Energy Center is being set up to address regional issues, to facilitate energy trade within SAARC and promote more efficient energy use within the region. The Ministry of Finance, Planning and Economic Affairs is involved in energy pricing and taxation policies. The Ministry of Production and the Ministry of Industries deal with industrial energy conservation in the public and private sector, respectively.

Thus, responsibility for the energy sector is highly fragmented and there are major overlaps. This is clearly not conducive for IEP, despite the best efforts of HDIP to compile and analyse data or of the Planning Commission to coordinate plans emerging from so many institutions.

IEP is not unknown in Pakistan. To trace its history, it is necessary to turn the clock back to the early 1980s when it was introduced, albeit partially and briefly.[28] The government of the time was firmly committed to establishing IEP and, as an interim step, had established a planning unit within the Directorate General of Energy Resources (DGER) in the Ministry of Petroleum. Recognising that this location strengthened the dominance of the petroleum sub-sector over other vital areas such as non-commercial energy, a decision was taken to move the expertise to a central neutral location. The ENERPLAN Cell was created in the Planning Division and charged with the national energy planning function. Relevant government administrative orders were issued and budgets approved.[29] Funding was secured for training and technical assistance to start the analytical work. An Energy Policy Board,[30] with top-level representation from all energy-related ministries, was instituted to provide 'a central coordination forum for policy decisions, program guidelines, monitoring and evaluation of all components of ENERPLAN'. Integration with national plans was to be carried out at this level. Decisions having nation-wide impact were to be referred to the National Economic Council or the Cabinet.

This was a good start. However, the risk was that the location in the Planning Division would eventually dilute the importance of the energy sector, given the Planning Division's involvement with the whole economy. These arrangements were intended as interim measures till a ministry of energy emerged. For a while the arrangements worked but then began to falter. International institutions such as the World Bank continued to provide loans and advice to the energy sector but policy reform had slowed down. Emphasis on IEP was lost perhaps because of the misplaced notion that market forces would compensate. It is significant that the World Bank's last comprehensive energy sector review for Pakistan dates to the early 1980s,[31] despite the recognition that energy is a critical impediment to economic development. Even the last sub-sector (oil and gas) review dates to 2003.[32] USAID did issue an energy sector assessment in 2007,[33] identifying the absence of integrated planning as a primary weakness. However, it did not elaborate on what steps needed to be taken.

The unraveling of IEP was inevitable since there was no follow-through on the necessary organisational changes. Instead of moving towards a simple integrated structure, there was a gradual expansion of the network of policy institutions, compounding the complexity and confusion. So the situation in the energy sector today should come as no surprise. Under these conditions, the ineffectiveness of seemingly well-conceived and well-intentioned policy initiatives was inevitable.

IEP now needs to be re-introduced, this time in a comprehensive manner, supported by an appropriate institutional framework. The seeds of IEP remain in Pakistan and can be revived quite rapidly to restart the process. Documents establishing the various bodies are in the records, together with elaborate administrative and technical studies to back them up. Moreover, many of the processes and skills already exist, such as sophisticated national planning and budget processes and the know-how for preparing energy balances. The expertise in HDIP can be transferred to an energy planning cell in the Planning Division, strengthened by expertise from the Ministry of Forestry, the Ministry of Agriculture and Livestock and the Alternative Energy Development Board, to give due importance to non-commercial and other renewable forms.

The necessary institutional restructuring can take place on a phased basis to minimise disruption. The first phase of restructuring, the establishment of a planning cell with access to top policy levels, can be done very rapidly. At the same time, plans would need to be initiated towards forming the ministry of energy with the planning cell at its core, and amending the structure, functions and decision-making processes of the current energy-related policy bodies to facilitate the initiative. While maintaining the independence of regulatory institutions, they should be put under one roof to facilitate coordination. To minimise disruption, these changes would need to be carefully designed and phased in. A firm commitment towards this end, cemented with an up-front public announcement, is vital. The cost of not doing so could, once again, result in an unraveling of the process and history will repeat itself.

IEP is not the panacea for Pakistan's energy problems. It is the essential starting point without which informed policy decisions in this sector cannot be made. It provides the ingredients of good data, information and analysis, eliminating guesswork and lobbying by special interests, which have tended to dominate the scene. Pakistan can finally begin to optimise the sustainable exploitation and utilisation of energy within its financial constraints and economic aspirations, addressing overwhelming issues such as prohibitive and ever-widening energy deficits.

## How IEP Can Address Pakistan's Special Issues

Several issues in Pakistan's energy sector, similar to those found in other parts of the developing world have been discussed earlier. IEP provides an analytical platform to address these and to test out the

246

efficacy of a range of policy options. Some other special issues are dealt with below.

## Circular Debt

This very complex and convoluted problem can be explained, in simple terms, as follows. The government-owned electric power system pays for its expenses from sales revenues collected from consumers and the government makes up any deficit. The latter practice runs counter to the declared objective of moving towards profitable operations and eventual privatisation of entities in the sector. Consumer tariffs are insufficient to pay for expenses and the government coffers are over-stretched. This results in prohibitive levels of arrears, including non-payments to suppliers of fuel as well as to private independent power producers (IPPs). It also gives rise to a chain of outstanding arrears through the generation, transmission and distribution entities within the power system itself. While tariff increases and injection of govern-ment capital might be the quickest short-term remedy, these are only stop-gap measures. Notwithstanding recent price adjustments, tariff levels have not increased sufficiently to cope with spikes in petroleum prices or low rainfall, which depresses hydel generation. Tariff increases are, understandably, hampered by affordability issues.

The other side of the equation is the cost of power delivery. Here a host of issues appear, involving system management and structure, maintenance levels, load balancing, plant utilisation and efficiency, system losses including an inordinate level of theft, tariff collection performance and related corruption, lack of regional interconnections, and so on. System losses are a prohibitive 25 per cent of net generation and consumer payment arrears are an unacceptable 30 per cent of the amount billed.[34]

In short, the power system is financially unviable and operationally impaired. It relies on heavy government capital injection in the form of unaffordable subsidies, which increases the fiscal deficit, promotes defi-cit financing and loss of reserves, and leads to the inevitable deprecia-tion of the currency. Despite periodic capital injection, circular debt continues to grow. It is difficult to get an accurate figure of the net out-standing debt because of significant overlaps and because it is a mov-ing target. To give some idea of magnitude, the gross receivables in the energy sector are currently estimated at $6 billion.[35] By some estimates, the net figure has grown from approximately \$3.5 billion in June 2009 to \$4.8 billion today. In addition to the state-owned power system and IPPs, it affects virtually all entities in the commercial energy sector. For the state-owned power system alone, the government is now contemplating a \$1.3 billion injection to close the current arrears gap.[36]

Some critics consider this crisis to be self-inflicted and stemming from lack of payment discipline but, when seen through the lens of IEP, its causes can be attributed, in large part, to the absence of the IEP mechanism. This would explain the conspicuous lack of a long-term integrated approach and the reliance on stop-gap measures. The result is that, while power system capacity in Pakistan is 19,855 MW and the peak demand is 14,500 MW, the power system can only meet 70 per cent of the peak demand;[37] hence the acute shortages, brown-outs and black-outs.

IPPs, embroiled in the circular debt issue, deserve special mention. Following the adoption of the 1994 Private Power Policy, nineteen IPP projects achieved financial closure in record time for which Pakistan was internationally acclaimed. The US Energy Secretary, after a visit to Karachi in September 1994, described it as the best energy policy in the entire world. By 1998, however, termination procedures had been initiated for eleven of the projects on technical grounds and allegations of corruption, causing a major reversal of Pakistan's image at a particularly problematic time for the economy. A long and painful process of renegotiating the projects was started.

The technical causes were wide-ranging and complex. In retrospect, some simple lessons can be drawn.[38] First, while incentives for private power generation alleviated power shortages in the short term, too much capacity was contracted with insufficient attention to least cost expansion. In times of depressed demand, the liability of the government-owned power system becomes particularly prohibitive. Under the provisions of the Power Purchase Agreements, the system is obligated to take the power or pay for it, guaranteeing the IPPs an agreed minimum plant factor.[39] Second, the magnitude and nature of private investment was not in synch with the level of sector reform and national socio-economic and governance reforms. Third, it would have been prudent to stagger the competitive bids over a number of years to enable bidders to better assess the risk and reduce their bids. Rapid response times inevitably impose upward pressures on bids. Fourth, staggering IPP bids, thereby reducing capacity requirements, would allow the power system operator to reassess demand and adjust contracted capacity and timing of subsequent projects. Fifth, a more trans-parent and politically acceptable approach in accommodating changing country conditions would have helped. Finally, contracts should be open to a mutually acceptable re-negotiation process.

It is evident that many of the above issues, particularly those relating to demand and supply considerations and optimal system expansion, would have been preempted had an IEP system been in place.

One of the most significant benefits of IEP is the ability to quantify the cost penalty or the opportunity cost of pursuing sub-optimal plans—vital for a country confronted with so many issues, for which less-than-optimal choices often become necessary. A prime example is Pakistan's need to address issues of poverty and inequitable income distribution. Access to and affordability of energy is a critical concern among the urban and rural poor. This inevitably leads in the shorter term to subsidies and cross-subsidisation. Some might question the use of sophisticated planning techniques if, in the end, substantial 'devia-tions' from the optimal scenario would be necessary. This is a fallacy. There is nothing wrong with subsidies if their design meets certain basic criteria. Subsidies should be clearly targeted to the poor through a system of means testing. They must be affordable to the national economy. If not, their inevitable withdrawal would have dire conse-quences for the very group they were meant to benefit. They must be transparent, i.e. not concealed in quasi-budgetary transactions. The moral hazard of encouraging waste would need to be minimised. IEP, complete with a range of scenarios and impact analyses, provides the tool to assess the impact of subsidies in the energy sector and to the national economy as a whole and thus make informed choices.

Pakistan is not unique in excluding non-commercial energy in its analyses. There are two main reasons for this. First, data on non-commercial energy is less reliable and errors in estimation could lead to a significant bias in the energy balance because of the large share of non-commercial energy in the total mix. Second, the primary energy equivalence for non-commercial fuels is particularly misleading because in general, they are burned at much lower efficiencies than commercial fuels and their share in useful energy consumption is consequently lower. However these are not plausible reasons for the omission. With-out traditional energy, meaningful policy and investment priorities cannot be established for the sector as a whole. IEP would highlight the need for significantly upgrading non-commercial energy data and for focusing on the utilisation efficiency of non-commercial energy.

Energy consumption in particular sectors such as households has been defined as the energy delivered to that sector. It does not take into account the efficiency of utilisation of the delivered energy, known as end-use efficiency. IEP, in promoting conservation measures and defining conserved energy as adding to energy supply, forces energy planners to focus on end-use efficiency rather than on delivered energy alone. In Pakistan this will inevitably lead to measures such as the dissemination of higher-efficiency, tested and tried cook-stoves rather than the reliance on traditional wasteful methods such as 'three-stone' fires.

With nearly half of Pakistan's total requirements met by non-conventional sources such as fuelwood, the current neglect means ignoring nearly half of the country's energy supply source and half of its population—hardly justifiable for a country fighting the scourge of poverty and trying so hard to improve its lagging social indicators.

In the light of the evidence presented above, the conclusion is simple. The elusive fundamental in Pakistan's energy sector reform is IEP and the imperative of adopting this is unquestionable. With it, Pakistan's policy-makers can finally go beyond *what* needs to be done to *how* it is to be done. Moreover the time to act is now. Necessary skills exist in Pakistan and, with political will and a modicum of external assistance, the recovery of the energy sector can be undertaken fairly swiftly. On that will depend the country's economic revival.

13

# EDUCATION AS A STRATEGIC IMPERATIVE*

*Shanza Khan and Moeed Yusuf*

Education lies at the heart of Pakistan's multiple challenges. If Pakistan is to emerge as a stable, moderate polity able to reap dividends from its burgeoning population it must be able to provide the young and future generations both personal safety and a decent livelihood. This requires relative peace, an environment conducive for economic growth, and a workforce that can power progress. Vital to such a turnaround is a well-educated population. Only through massive quantitative and qualitative gains in education can Pakistan produce the skill set required to drive the economy efficiently and produce a critical mass of well-informed and visionary leadership it so badly needs. Equally important, it is only through high quality, value-neutral education that Pakistan can challenge the salience of the Islamist discourse that threatens to radicalise society and drive youth energies towards destructive—often violent—channels.

This means that education should not only be a development priority but also a strategic one. Pakistan's education performance is a tale

* This paper partly builds upon earlier work by Moeed Yusuf on the issue of youth radicalization in Pakistan. Some of the discussion in the paper borrows heavily from his earlier publication: 'Prospects of Youth Radicalization in Pakistan: Implications for U.S. Policy', *Brookings Institution*, Analysis Paper no. 14, Oct. 2008, pp. 3–7; 15–18.

of unfulfilled expectations which has caused disaffection and alienation among vast segments of society. The immediate future needs to be seen as a corrective phase that requires holistic interventions in the education sector. The chapter begins by outlining the conceptual underpinnings of the empirical analysis to follow. This is followed by consideration of the Pakistani education sector's performance and implications for society. In the final section concrete steps are identified that can help bring about the required transformation.

## Education as an 'Expectation Builder'

Modern societies grasped the importance of a well-educated polity very early on. In recent decades however, investment in human capacity has become a top priority for international, multinational, and national efforts. Conventional wisdom suggested that education was critical for a society to produce a skilled labour force that could operate as productive members of the economy. Over time, education has increasingly been seen as a force multiplier capable of having a much broader impact—both positive and negative—on societies than merely producing a skilled work force. High quality education can provide the means of social mobility and act as a source of contentment to people. It can contribute to peace, drive societal narratives and thus mould the very outlook of communities positively, as well as inculcate a civic sense among citizens. On the other hand, poor educational standards or agenda-driven education can contribute to a sense of alienation and deprivation, lead to internal discord and violence, and channelise societal energies in unproductive directions.

The discussion here draws on the 'expectations' literature. Education is seen as an 'expectation builder'; it raises anticipations at three distinct stages. To begin with, demand for education creates expectations among parents and children that the state would be able to provide opportunities for acquiring education. Once access to education is provided, consumers begin to expect qualitative improvements. The third stage of expectations stems from the fact that the schooling process itself has attached to it hopes of finding commensurate employment.

The literature talks of 'unfulfilled expectations' as a major worry. A failure to fulfill expectations in terms of access to or quality of education could be a function of state incapacity, deliberate policies that exclude certain segments of society, or education content that is ill-suited to the requirements of modern economies and societies. Regardless, it implies that those who miss out are not fit to contribute to the economy optimally. Moreover, they tend to feel aggrieved and may become alienated and marginalised from their communities. Alienation, deprivation, and marginalisation of youth are in turn linked to radicalisation and discord.[1]

However, the failure of education does not have to be absolute to cause alienation. Particular segments of societies can be at a loss even if the rest of the society is progressing. In fact, the literature argues that feelings of alienation and marginalisation are often harboured when access to opportunities is unequal rather than absent. Discussing young males in particular, Collier (2000, p. 94) supports the relative deprivation hypothesis.[2] Kaplan (1996) concurs with this view, arguing that discrimination against specific segments of society can cause the disadvantaged to resort to violence.[3] Indeed, global studies on the linkage between education and violence point to a correlation between conflict outbreak and persistence and low educational attainment. Countries with the lowest rates of primary school enrolment show greater incidence of conflict.[4] Secondary education is also believed to be inversely related to prevalence of internal conflict.[5]

Educational content can also be used deliberately to pursue a particular agenda or create a sense of deprivation among students. Learning materials can emphasise a particular version of history or a worldview that may create an exclusionary and discriminatory mindset. Curricula, learning materials, and teaching methods that promote narrow-minded outlooks and intolerance are least suited to peaceful co-existence. Much too often, communities that have experienced extreme forms of conflicts have had divisive education systems. Rwanda, Nazi Germany, and South Asian countries like Sri Lanka, India and Pakistan are all cases in point.

The problem of perceived alienation or deprivation is compounded in contexts already ridden by violence and extremism. Here, the frustration caused by low educational attainment, agenda-driven content, or a mismatch between education and economic opportunities provide a perfect opportunity for militants to recruit cadres.

Grounding the argument in the 'education as an expectation builder' premise, the following discussion examines the Pakistani case in some detail. It argues that the Pakistani education sector has led to unfulfilled expectations at each of the three mentioned stages: there has been a failure to provide enough education, to provide good quality education, and to provide amicable livelihoods to the educated. Consequently, a vast proportion of the Pakistani population is ill prepared for a modern economy and is vulnerable to internal discord and violence.

*Recounting 'Expectation Failures' in Pakistani Education*

*Stage I: Failure to Provide.* Pakistan has made progress with regard to most education indicators over time. The total net primary enrolment rate has increased from 33 per cent in 1991 to 66 per cent in 2008.[6] The ratio of female to male primary enrolment has increased from 52 per cent to 83 per cent.[7] Meanwhile, the total primary completion rate as a percentage of the relevant age group has risen from 50 per cent to 60 per cent in the corresponding period.[8] The total adult literacy rate has also increased from 26 per cent in 1981 to 54 per cent in 2008.[9] Recent developments have yielded somewhat greater progress exemplified by the fact that youth literacy at 68.9 per cent is 15 per cent higher than adult literacy.[10]

But progress remains poor both in absolute terms as and relative to the rest of the South Asian region and other lower middle-income developing countries. With the exception of Afghanistan, Pakistan has the lowest education outcomes in the region. Half of Pakistan's population is illiterate, the country has the second highest number of out-of-school children in the world (9.5 million in 2005), it suffers from high drop-out rates even at the primary level, and there is substantial gender disparity at every education level. In fact, despite overall quantitative gains the gender gap has widened between 1981 and 2008 from 20.6 to 26.8 per cent.[11] Rural-urban and interprovincial disparity also continues to persist. Interprovincial disparity in youth literacy is just as high as in adult literacy.[12]

It is evident then that the Pakistani education system has failed to reach a large proportion of its eligible population. The problem is principally a supply side one. For one, the difficulty of accessing educational facilities keeps children away. A number of surveys register complaints about having to travel long distances to reach schools, especially for girls in rural areas. Lack of basic facilities in schools such as electricity, drinking water and toilets are additional deterrents to school attendance. Out of 163,914 public schools (including 10,651 mosque schools), 10.5 per cent operate without a building; 6.1 per cent are *kacha*

Table 1: Disparities across gender, region and provinces

| | Adult literacy rate | | | Percentage of population (aged 10 years and older) that has completed primary level or higher | | | Population (aged 10 years and older) that has ever attended school | | |
|---|---|---|---|---|---|---|---|---|---|
| | Male | Female | Total | Male | Female | Total | Male | Female | Total |
| *Urban Areas* | 78 | 61 | 70 | 70 | 57 | 64 | 80 | 66 | 73 |
| Punjab | 78 | 65 | 71 | 70 | 60 | 65 | 81 | 69 | 75 |
| Sindh | 79 | 62 | 71 | 71 | 57 | 65 | 81 | 65 | 74 |
| KP | 73 | 41 | 58 | 72 | 38 | 52 | 78 | 49 | 64 |
| Balochistan | 74 | 36 | 57 | 65 | 32 | 49 | 75 | 41 | 60 |
| *Rural Areas* | 57 | 26 | 41 | 52 | 23 | 36 | 63 | 32 | 48 |
| Punjab | 58 | 33 | 45 | 48 | 30 | 40 | 66 | 40 | 53 |
| Sindh | 50 | 12 | 33 | 50 | 11 | 28 | 54 | 17 | 37 |
| KP | 61 | 18 | 39 | 42 | 17 | 35 | 68 | 26 | 47 |
| Balochistan | 47 | 10 | 31 | 52 | 8 | 23 | 49 | 13 | 33 |
| *Overall* | 65 | 38 | 52 | 35 | 35 | 46 | 69 | 44 | 57 |
| Punjab | 65 | 43 | 54 | 56 | 40 | 49 | 71 | 50 | 60 |
| Sindh | 66 | 39 | 54 | 57 | 36 | 47 | 68 | 43 | 56 |
| KP | 63 | 22 | 42 | 57 | 21 | 38 | 70 | 30 | 50 |
| Balochistan | 54 | 17 | 37 | 42 | 14 | 29 | 55 | 20 | 39 |

schools; 61 per cent lack electricity; 36.5 per cent lack drinking water; 42.4 per cent lack latrines; 44.3 per cent lack boundary walls; 3.8 per cent are declared dangerous while another 16.5 per cent are in need of major repair.[13] Almost 10,000 schools are officially designated as non-functional. Vacant teacher posts and absenteeism are also high across all provinces.[14] Unaffordable costs, lack of interest in education, and for females, cultural sensitivities are other commonly cited reasons for children being out of school.

The present situation represents a failure on the part of the state to deliver on its fundamental duty to provide basic educational opportunities to its citizens. Those left out are people who will at best be suboptimal participants in the economy during their productive work life. Their sheer numbers represent a massive lost opportunity for Pakistan. Also, the current situation is bound to engender frustration and disaffection across the board. This is especially the case for a society like Pakistan's where demand for education is very high. In a Population Council (2002) survey whose findings have persistently been confirmed by subsequent research, 80 per cent of the young males and over 70 per cent of their female counterparts included in the survey expressed a desire to be educated at secondary and tertiary levels.[15] The supply-demand gap then is an obvious alienating factor. Internal tensions become even more likely when one considers that gender and geographical location within Pakistan are significant determinants of access to education.

A number of reasons can be adduced for this dismal state of affairs. The 2009 National Education Policy correctly identifies the two primary reasons as the 'commitment gap' and the 'implementation gap'.[16] The commitment gap is reflected in the low resource allocation to the sector. In 2009–10, public expenditure on education was 2 per cent of GDP, the lowest in South Asia.[17] This is representative of Pakistan's average educational spending; in the last fifteen years, average education expenditures have been a mere 2.1 per cent of GDP. Even within education, the bulk of the investment has been channelled to a few well-maintained higher education institutions implying that the benefits of the public subsidy of education are primarily availed by the higher income groups.[18] The primary and secondary education tiers which are believed to be crucial to developing human capacity en mass have been neglected.

The implementation gap directly affects governance of the sector as well as the allocation and utilisation of resources. The lack of a planning culture and capacity and weaknesses in administrative capacity and accountability mechanisms result in only 20 to 30 per cent of the allocated funds being utilised effectively.[19] Corruption, manifested in funds siphoned away for personal gain, influence in the allocation of resources, in the recruitment, training and posting of teachers, in selection of textbooks, and in the conduct of examinations and assessments are significant implementation challenges that decision-makers have struggled to address.

*Stage II: Failure to deliver quality.* Pakistan's education sector is anomalous in that it has three parallel and largely unconnected systems of education operating simultaneously. These are the public and non-elite private schools, the elite private schools, and the religious seminaries—the *madrasahs*. Approximately 67 per cent of the school going children are enrolled in public schools, close to 29 per cent are in private schools—the majority of these are in the non-elite variant—and 4 per cent attend *madrasahs* (see table 2).[20] The three systems follow their own curricula, teaching methods, and examination processes. Consequently, quality of education and the type of student body in each vary greatly. Only the public education system is fully regulated by the government.

Table 2: Parallel streams of education

| | No. of institution | No. of students enroled | No. of institutions as a % of total | % of total students enroled |
|---|---|---|---|---|
| *Public* | 179,022 | 24,657,819 | 71.0 | 67.0 |
| *Private* | 60,827 | 10,541,089 | 24.1 | 28.7 |
| *madrasahs* | 12,276 | 1,588,075 | 4.9 | 4.3 |

Source: AEPAM, 2008.

The three education systems are broadly stratified along three dimensions: socio-economic, qualitative, and ideological. The *madrasahs* system largely caters to children from the poorest segment of society. The majority of public school and non-elite private school students belong to the lower-middle to middle socio-economic groups. Elite private schools apply stringent socio-economic screening and are reserved exclusively for the rich. So isolated are these systems that students go through their school life (and even adult life) without having the opportunity to engage intellectually across systems. The education sector therefore ends up producing three distinct cohorts from within the Pakistani youth, each quite cutoff from the other.

In terms of quality, *madrasahs* have the greatest mismatch with the requirements of modern economies. They are essentially geared towards producing cadres suitable only for the clerical sphere; this makes them misfits for mainstream employment opportunities. The public education and a large proportion of the non-elite private schools—together account for the overwhelming majority of Pakistani students—also suffer from extreme qualitative shortcomings. This is manifested in the learning outcomes, curricula, textbooks and other learning materials, assessments, teacher quality, and the learning environment. Although they teach all subjects expected of modern school systems, they follow fixed syllabi, which encourage rote learning—memorisation. The medium of instruction in public schools is predominantly Urdu; they even lack the capacity to develop a minimum level of proficiency in the English language, which is necessary for most white-collar jobs. The relatively small number of elite private schools are the only ones that provide decent quality education. They use English as the medium of learning and are ahead of the others in terms of teaching standards and learning outcomes. Most of them encourage objectivity and creative thinking among students. It is hardly surprising then that parents who send their children to private schools are found to be far more satisfied than those whose kids attend public schools or formal *madrasahs*.[21]

The third layer of stratification is ideological. Though there is considerably greater overlap across systems in this case, in general one can attribute distinct and often irreconcilable world visions across the three systems. Pakistani *madrasahs* may not be actively engaged in producing militants as the West has suspected for long but they do produce graduates with narrow-minded ideological biases. In her research on *madrasahs*, Christine Fair (2006; 2007) argues that these cadres are much more likely to sympathise with Islamists where they are welcomed and given a positive identity.[22] The syllabi of the public schooling system are closely managed by the state and provide a highly skewed historical narrative that is nationalistic and creates a siege mentality by portraying Pakistan as being perpetually under threat from all corners. The content also meshes Islam with nationalism and presents the two as being intrinsically linked. The roots of this anomaly lie in the 1980s when agenda-driven education was deliberately used as a political tool and textbooks were rewritten to inject a definitive anti-India and pan-Islamic bias.[23] The elite private schools, while being bound by the state to follow the prescribed narrative in subjects such as Pakistan Studies, have more leeway given their unregulated nature. In addition, the economic stratum their students belong to allows them more physical and informational exposure to the Western style of life and leaves them less susceptible to accepting the curriculum biases at face value.

The divergent outlooks of these three cohorts are evident from who they look up to and which direction they want their country to take. *Madrasah* students tend to be amenable to the extremist world-view. Students from the public schools, who are perhaps most representative of mainstream society, idealise legendary Muslim historical figures but do retain some admiration for figures known for their anti-West outlook. Products of the private schools talk fondly of Hollywood stars, personalities in the arts and theatre, international sportsmen and the like.[24] Overwhelming majorities of private school-educated youth seem to view Turkey as a model for Pakistan to replicate. This is fundamentally different than the preference of their less privileged counterparts who are more likely to mention Iran or Saudi Arabia.[25]

Frustration, alienation, internal discord and polarisation are built into the education system. The isolation and divergent outlooks of the three variants make for a divided polity. Indeed, the perceptions of the country's youth validate this. Children of the elite are highly dismissive of their Urdu medium counterparts and intolerant of young rural men, especially those from lower socio-economic backgrounds. A sizable segment from within the elite schools considers itself superior and more progressive than the rest. *Madrasah* students on the other hand blame the elite for having robbed them of necessary resources and causing hardship for the rest of society. Their sense of alienation and deprivation is shared by the public school, and to a lesser extent non-elite private school students and provides an opening to Islamists to cash in on a 'haves versus have nots' narrative.[26] These disparate visions also make it virtually impossible to forge a consensus on a national narrative in Pakistan.

*Stage III: Failure to provide livelihoods.* Educational attainment is a double-edged sword. While lack of education disqualifies youth from attaining economic mobility and is thus undesirable, high level of education without the requisite outlet to apply skills raises expectations which, if unfulfilled for long, can create an 'expectation-reality disconnect'. Again, the latter makes the excluded disgruntled with the system, which not only keeps potentially productive human capacity from engaging in constructive endeavours but also acts as a violence-inducing factor.

Surveys suggest that an overwhelming majority of young men and women in Pakistan want to work provided suitable opportunities—commensurate with their educational attainment—are made available.[27] Unfortunately, access to desirable employment in Pakistan is as unequal as provision for high quality education. While Pakistan's labour market has expanded, and the unemployment rate has declined to an impressive 5.32 per cent, the improvement is unable to keep up with the large pool of employable youth. In fact, youth employment has only dropped marginally since 1990 and even many who were employed at one time fell back into the unemployed category.[28] To be sure, the majority of non-elite young citizens can only find relatively menial jobs and are thus underemployed. The public sector is inherently corrupt and job openings are rarely awarded on merit. Children of the poor, with generally little access to the corridors of power and already disadvantaged by the poor skill set developed in public schools, are invariably the first to be denied these prized positions.

The private sector has expanded tremendously in recent years and presents many more lucrative opportunities. Ironically however, the combination of the private sector's growth and a virtual breakdown of the public sector act to increase the inequality in opportunities for graduates of private versus public schools. Private sector firms solicit employees with diverse exposures, a broad knowledge base, good English language skills, and robust analytical ability. The only young adults that fit the bill are products of elite private schools or foreign colleges (the latter are exclusively members of elite households). In fact, so blatant is the bias against public, non-elite private, and *madrasah* graduates that recruiters explicitly put a premium on foreign and elite local degrees. A disproportionate amount of entry level positions thus end up going to the already rich, leaving those from lower socio-economic classes underemployed. For educated (even if poorly) young men, underemployment ends up having just as much of an alienating effect as unemployment.

There is evidence aplenty of the coming crisis. Increasingly, reasonably eloquent, post-secondary degree holders are seeking financial help—that is to say, begging—on the streets of urban towns in Pakistan. These are young men very different from the stereotypical beggars that dot the streets of Pakistani cities and have been forced to the street by the labour market crunch. Detailed discussions with such individuals reveal great contempt for a state that cannot provide opportunities. There is also envy and resentment against the elite who are believed to have deliberately created entry barriers for the poor, and there is a sense of alienation from the larger society.

*Reversing Failure*

Inability to reverse these failures will not only limit Pakistan's economic growth but carries the potential of rupturing the very fabric of society though polarisation and unrest. While there is very little hard evidence for education having contributed directly to terrorism in Pakistan, anecdotal evidence combined with profiles of most actors involved in terrorist attacks does suggest a linkage. Indeed, it would be naïve to believe an absence of any correlation. The mechanisms through which this connection would be playing out are aptly described by Winthrop and Graff (2010) as:

(i)   Poor education causing grievances for those left out.
(ii)  Education creating narrow world views.
(iii) Education failing to instil civic citizenship.
(iv)  The context providing opportunities for militant recruitment.[29]

Future challenges in terms of reversing the identified failures in education are likely to be even more daunting than in the past. A major reason is the severe demographic pressure. Pakistan possesses one of the largest youth bulges in the world. Over sixty-five million are between ages zero and fourteen and are thus either currently at school or will enter school life in the coming decade. Furthermore Pakistan is only half way through its demographic transition and the current rate of 3.8 births per female is set to carry Pakistan's youth bulge well beyond 2025.[30] This implies an extremely large cohort whose educational needs will have to be met if Pakistan is to extract positive demographic dividends. According to Mahmood (2009), barring accelerated improvement Pakistan confronts a situation where 28.2 million of its citizens will be out of school in the year 2030.[31]

The economic signs are not encouraging for the short to medium term either. Pakistan will have an additional four million employable youth by 2030 taking the total number to twenty-one million.[32] The stock of unemployed youth will have reached six million in 2030 unless unemployment is kept below 4 per cent, which is virtually impossible in the near term according to official estimates.[33] The increased pace of urbanisation adds to the conundrum as expectant youth will move to the cities to find livelihoods, only to be frustrated by the modest absorptive capacity of Pakistani towns. The literature on the subject suggests that such a development encourages urban youth radicalisation.

Simply put, Pakistan faces a monumental task in halting and then reversing the decline in the education sector. Failure is not an option given that the state of education will determine Pakistan's economic progress, its overall societal outlook, magnitude of internal tensions, and most importantly, the state's ability to provide citizens with personal safety and an environment favourable to sustainable progress.

*Stage I: Correcting the failure to provide.* The ultimate goal for policymakers is to provide a level playing field for students irrespective of their caste, creed, location, family's economic capacity and religion. Not only must access to education improve, but it must be spread evenly across the entire citizenry. This will be challenging as Pakistan's present youth development statistics suggest high disparity across socio-economic strata, schooling systems, and physical location.[34] All future policies must remain cognizant of the explosive ramifications of neglecting underprivileged citizens in peripheral areas.

Financial outlays for education must increase significantly in the coming years. Successive governments have committed themselves to increasing spending on education but progress has been slower than planned. No matter how politically challenging, education's share as a proportion of GDP must be enhanced to at least the developing country average in the immediate term. In addition, conscious effort must be undertaken to ensure a better balance on spending between administrative and development expenditures within the sector.

Better governance and transparency are buzzwords repeated *ad nauseam* in discussions of institutional reform. The challenge is great and lacks an immediate solution. But there is no alternative to generating the political will and capacity for better management of the education sector and ensuring that educational allocations are made efficiently. Institutional duplication and organisational inefficiencies need to be addressed across the board. As a start, the ambiguities about the different roles of the Federal and Provincial governments in education need to be mapped and clarified. Policy continuity is also essential.

As a complementary policy strand, there is need for greater empowerment of those with a direct stake in education. The idea of establishing functional School Management Committees (SMCs) is correct provided they are given the needed authority and independence to ensure that schools function, teachers are present, and students attend regularly. The SMCs now in place are largely ineffectual.

Given that dropout and completion rates are significantly correlated to poverty, reduction in tuition fees in public schools and increased allotment of need-based scholarships and free textbooks and uniforms should be encouraged. The Punjab government undertook such a program with mixed results.[35] While the program was subsequently rolled back, its experience can be studied and improved upon as a similar initiative is launched across Pakistan.

Conditional cash transfer programs have increasingly become popular and shown to raise school enrolment and retention in a number of countries such as Mexico, Colombia, Nicaragua and Brazil.[36] Pakistan has introduced a few demand size incentives such as involving communities in social service delivery but the explicit use of cash transfers to ensure higher school attendance is largely missing. Moreover, the programs that do involve communities are small relative to the size of the problem, focus on particular provinces, are not integrated, and their targeting and administration is weak.[37] International best practices could be used to improve Pakistan's efforts in this realm.

A positive development in recent years has been the mushrooming of non-elite private schools, especially in Punjab and Sindh. These schools are playing an increasingly significant role in extending educational services particularly in rural areas where the largest growth in private schools is occurring.[38] Further encouragement of private schools along with innovative public-private partnerships where the public sector is found wanting is a desirable policy intervention.

*Stage II: Correcting the failure to deliver quality.* Qualitative improvements in education are bound to lag behind quantitative gains but efforts must strive to keep this gap as narrow as possible. The key lies in transforming the public school system and ensuring its uplift so that it can match its elite counterpart. Areas that need attention include the development of new teaching methods that promote creative thinking, qualitative benchmarks for student learning, and standards for teacher recruitment, among others. The concrete steps required are well understood and rehearsed. The political will to implement them is often lacking and needs to be evolved.

Largely at the behest of donors, Pakistan has paid substantial attention to teacher professional development. The effort should be reinforced from within. A step in the right direction has been made with the establishment of the National Professional Standards for Teachers in Pakistan. Efforts must be made to ensure the quality of teacher education and implementation of the standards.[39]

In the short run, a stop-gap measure could entail setting up a program to bring in a significant number of foreign teachers or those from Pakistan's substantial diaspora in the West, especially ones trained to teach English language and basic mathematics and sciences. These teachers could be placed across the various levels of public schooling throughout the country.

To complement these efforts, stronger public-private partnerships have to be forged to help overcome some of the capacity constraints in the public sector. The government has initiated programs like 'adopt a school' whereby non-government organisations are encouraged to take over management of public schools.[40] There is significant interest but the scope of such efforts is very limited at present. A well-crafted incentive structure needs to be put in place and bureaucratic hurdles removed to encourage more non-government entities to consider adopting schools.

The *madrasah* education system needs urgent reform to allow it to prepare students for modern economies while retaining their faith-based focus. The agenda to transform the existing ones is oft expressed but political constraints and fear of resistance have prevented the government from doing anything significant. A more realistic alternative may be to set up parallel *madrasahs* run either by the public or private sector that utilises teachers able to offer balanced theological study in combination with teaching modern subjects.

With regard to public sector education syllabi, the emphasis should be on revising textbooks with the aim of reverting to the content used prior to Islamisation during the 1980s. The aim is not secularisation of the curricula—as that would meet resistance from a deeply conservative society. Rather, the aim should be to remove distortions of history and material that engenders extremist mindsets. Moreover, the curricula would benefit from greater emphasis on 'peace education' and teaching that instills a strong civic sense.

Finally, the government is encouraging private schools to offer 10 per cent of admissions to needy students from underprivileged backgrounds.[41] This is a step in the right direction and can go a long way in removing the isolation of students among the three systems. The private sector must be urged to rigorously enforce this regulation, which is not the case at present.

*Stage III: Correcting the failure to provide livelihoods.* Pakistan's principal weakness in economic planning has been an overriding focus on high macroeconomic growth and not the quality or distributional effects of that growth. The model has not been inclusive and it is only recently that pro-poor growth has become part of the mainstream policy discourse. Strong and sustained macroeconomic growth is imperative to increase the size of the national pie. To complement this however, initiatives geared to equitable income distribution need to be taken. This also means providing job opportunities to the educated unemployed, many of whom come from disadvantaged social backgrounds.

The government's social safety net initiatives will remain central to its ability to providing the disenfranchised the requisite livelihood opportunities. It is encouraging to see an emphasis on employment schemes and small scale business promotion by the present authorities. The allocations for such initiatives should be further increased and the institutional shortcomings that continue to undermine these programs should be corrected. Special efforts should be made to make these schemes transparent, perhaps by giving civil society a formal role in monitoring and accountability.

Vocational training stands out as an obvious avenue to explore in order to improve opportunities for the uneducated or the poorly educated. While there has been significant donor and government attention, there are still just a limited number of vocational training centres in urban areas while rural Pakistan lacks these facilities. Even where they exist, they do not seem to have been instituted under any coherent policy framework. Moreover, the quality of training is inadequate. Presently, there is lack of congruity between the local industries and training available at the institutes. Very little attempt has been initiated to involve the end users in the operation, management, and program delivery as well as to align the course contents to the needs of the industry. The lack of interactions between industries and Technical and

Vocational Education Training (TVET) institutes has therefore resulted in the marginalisation of the TVET institutions with employers demonstrating little interest in extending cooperation to the institutions. This is an area where the donor community has relatively greater experience given its success in other countries. It could treat this as a priority by coordinating its efforts to correct the stated shortcomings.

Perhaps the most executable option to ease Pakistan's labour force burden in the next decade or two is to find adequate opportunities for labour migration abroad. Pakistan has used this safety valve to good effect in the past by sending a large number of its skilled and unskilled labour force across the world. While economic constraints in recipient countries and the 'extremist' tag attached to Pakistan in global perception has dented the traditional outflow of labour, the international community could help Pakistan in providing fresh avenues for labour absorption. To enhance the prospects, Pakistan's vocational training could be tailored to the future demand of various countries projected to have a labour shortage. Friendly countries could consider special arrangements to allow inflow of employable Pakistanis.

Education remains central to Pakistan's recovery. Given the current circumstances, hoping for return to stability without improving education substantially is a misnomer. The challenge confronting Pakistan is a daunting one. The state must begin to see education as a right, not a favour to its people. Even then, the suggested policy measures cannot bring change overnight. The next decade or so ought to be approached as a corrective period during which the essential policies will be put in place. Progress will likely be frustratingly slow but if executed properly these steps will prepare the ground for more accelerated and visible improvement in the decade that follows. Should this effort be made, the Pakistan of 2030 has every prospect of being more and better educated, with its society empowered by a better sense of civic responsibility—a country able to provide job opportunities to all its citizens. This, in turn, would serve as the essential base on which economic progress and prosperity can be predicated.

14

# PAKISTAN AS A NUCLEAR STATE

*Feroz Hassan Khan*

Has the advent of nuclear weapons calmed down anxieties and brought about a level of national confidence in Pakistan to enable the state to meet other challenges? What role do nuclear weapons play in a nation's destiny? The 1998 nuclear test ought to have reinforced a simple lesson for security thinkers in South Asia. It should focus national leadership into calming crises and preventing wars. Yet even after twelve years of demonstrating its nuclear capability, there are continuing strategic anxieties in Pakistan even if there is also increased faith in nuclear weapons as the final arbitrator of the nation's survivability.

Based on what has so far been known about Pakistan's nuclear program and policy-making, scholars have understood Pakistan's development of a nuclear deterrent entirely as a function of its level of insecurity.[1] Though useful, this explanation is a partial one. Pakistan's creation of an operational nuclear deterrent is more adequately explained as a response to competing threat analyses and conceptions about national security, which were constructed, articulated, and defended, by various Pakistani politicians, scientists, and military leaders over a four-decade period.

This chapter assesses how Pakistan's national security evolved as a result of its nuclear policies and the trajectories ahead. It explains why the Pakistani leadership initiated a nuclear bomb program, how it

267

went about making weapons and delivery systems, and what steps it has taken to create a nuclear doctrine, command and control system, signalling strategy, and other elements required for a safe, secure, and robust nuclear deterrent.[2]

Pakistan's acquisition of nuclear weapons is the subject of immense curiosity amongst international political and security analysts. The country is facing crises—both internal and external—that challenge both its nuclear and conventional deterrent and which no other nuclear nation has faced in contemporary history. Were it not for nuclear weapons, Pakistan's response to multiple security challenges—especially in the war against terrorism since 2001—would have been significantly more complicated. Though nuclear weapons allow Pakistan to balance multiple security challenges they do not play any role in deterring and redressing the character of threat which Pakistan faces internally and on its Western borderlands.

Yet in the broader canvas of its security landscape and nation's history, Pakistan's survival would have been questionable without the nuclear capability. At least on five occasions since the mid-1980s conventional war with India was averted. This convinced several security analysts on the war-preventing role of nuclear capability.[3]

In 1946 Bernard Brodie had famously pronounced nuclear weapons as 'Absolute Weapons', whose possession changed the role of the military from 'fighting and winning wars to averting them'. This truism has seemingly evaded the security thinking in India—Pakistan's most enduring threat. As new security doctrines to fight conventional war under a 'nuclear shadow' are conceived and contemplated in India, there is correspondingly increased belief in the efficacy of the nuclear deterrent in Pakistan. This disconnect has dangerous implications for strategic stability in the region. Coercive military mobilisations and deepened crises have occurred on the pretext of terrorism and each was eventually defused through international intervention and/or fear of escalation to the nuclear threshold. Pakistan's security thinkers fear India's linking of sub-conventional to conventional war as a deliberate attempt to conflate international terrorism with unresolved regional security issues (Kashmir being at the core of all) and justify conventional war with its long time adversary.

This chapter therefore examines the realistic role of nuclear weapons in the national security of Pakistan and its future. The first section will review the contours of five decades of efforts to attain the nuclear deterrent, explaining in the process the political and technical challenges, decisions and eventual demonstration of the nuclear capability. The second section analyses how the deterrent was made operational in testing times and how a robust command and control system evolved over time. The third section explains Pakistan's emerging force, postures and efforts to maintain strategic stability in the region. The last section concludes with future trajectories and pathways, which nuclear Pakistan might undertake in the next decade or so.

*Security Dilemma and Strategic Options: 1947–1998*

Despite mounting security challenges in Pakistan's first decade, nuclear weapons did not figure in the country's security calculus. In the first phase, which began with the country's independence in 1947 and ended with the military *coup d'état* orchestrated by General Ayub Khan in 1958, no Pakistani leader showed any interest in the atomic bomb. After a brief experiment with non-alignment, Pakistan joined the US-sponsored anti-communist alliance. It also established the Pakistan Atomic Energy Commission (PAEC) and sent scores of scientists and engineers overseas for nuclear training but no effort was made to initiate a nuclear bomb program. During the next period, when the Army ran the government from 1959 through 1971, and when it was apparent that India was creating the capability to manufacture nuclear weapons, a few senior scientists and bureaucrats advanced the need to acquire a nuclear capability but the military leadership doubted its feasibility and utility and believed that national defence was best met through the modernisation of conventional forces and continued alliance with the West.

The next phase of Pakistan's nuclear history was decidedly different. Following the loss of East Pakistan in December 1971, Pakistan again reverted to civilian rule under the leadership of Zulfikar Ali Bhutto, an advocate of nuclear deterrence since the early 1960s. In January 1972 Bhutto urged the PAEC to begin preparing for a nuclear bomb program, but there was no urgency until India tested its first nuclear explosive device in May 1974. Following France's cancellation of the sale of a plutonium reprocessing plant under US influence, Pakistan shifted its resources to a uranium centrifuge program under the direction of Abdul Qadeer Khan.

The nuclear program experienced significant challenges during the decade after General Zia-ul-Haq deposed Bhutto (in July 1977) and then executed him. But this was also the period when Pakistan eventually obtained bomb-grade material, assembled its first nuclear explosive device, and fashioned a rudimentary deterrence strategy. Despite—and in part because of—a barrage of non-proliferation pressures from the West, virtually every senior Pakistani civilian and military official internalised the criticality of nuclear weapons to national security.

These policies were further institutionalised during the next decade under the civilian rule of prime ministers Benazir Bhutto and Nawaz Sharif. It was during this period that the nuclear program achieved its highest and lowest points. The crowning achievement came when Pakistan detonated its first nuclear explosive devices and subsequently declared itself a nuclear weapons state just a few weeks after India conducted a series of surprise nuclear tests on 11 and 13 May 1998. The low watermark came when diffusion of power at the apex of national governance led to loose oversight and poor regulation of the nuclear program, which enabled A. Q. Khan to secretly and illicitly transfer nuclear materials, technology, and know-how to Iran, Libya, and North Korea.

During the final phase of Pakistani nuclear policy, which coincides with President Pervez Musharraf's rule from 1999–2007, the nuclear arms program was placed under tight military control; A. Q. Khan was fired and placed under *de facto* house arrest; a National Command Authority was established along with a comprehensive command and control system; and Pakistan's deterrence strategy was refined and proven effective under fire when India refrained from attacking it after Delhi's comprehensive mobilisation for war in 2002.

Since the return of civilian rule in 2008 the content of Pakistan's nuclear policy has remained unchanged: Islamabad is more than ever committed to nuclear weaponry as the ultimate guarantor of national security. Its nuclear policy remains of tight command and control, minimum credible deterrent posture and ambiguity in doctrine of use and force postures for the foreseeable future.

In the second decade of the twenty-first century, Pakistan's attachment to nuclear weapons is further reinforced as it faces numerous sources of security threats against which nuclear weapons can only play a limited role. Pakistan's nuclear policy is affected by the discriminatory treatment, especially after the US forged a special civilian nuclear deal for India. To add insult to injury, some quarters in Washington engaged in hostile propaganda against its nuclear security.

## The 1998 Nuclear Tests

In the spring of 1998, for the first time in India's history, Hindu nationalist parties under the Bharatiya Janata Party (BJP) received a plurality of the national vote and came to power with a mandate to declare India as an overt nuclear power and push their traditional hard line on Pakistan. On 11 and 13 May 1998, India conducted a series of nuclear tests. As in 1974 the US response, after absorbing the initial shock, focused on how to prevent Pakistan from following suit. Even as international pressure mounted on Pakistan not to reciprocate, rhetoric from the Indian Home Minister L. K. Advani menacingly urged Pakistan to 'realise the change in the geo-strategic situation in the region, roll back its anti-India policy, especially with regard to Kashmir' and threatened that 'India would undertake hot pursuits to chase insurgents from Kashmir back into Pakistan'.[4]

Pakistani leaders faced a stark choice. If it joined India in the international doghouse Islamabad would have to pay relatively greater economic costs, which the nearly bankrupt economy could barely afford.[5] On the other hand, if it refrained from conducting its own nuclear tests, the Sharif government would face domestic opposition and also risk the erosion of its nuclear deterrence. Although Sharif wavered for a few days, he soon agreed with the military leadership that demonstratively proving nuclear deterrence was much more important to Pakistan's wellbeing than forgoing another round of economic sanctions.[6] Pakistan responded by ignoring the diplomatic pressure, pulling out its own nuclear weapons, and conducting a reciprocal series of nuclear explosive tests.

The period from the 1970s until the nuclear tests in 1998 provides four major insights about Pakistani security policy. First, as belief in nuclear weapons grew more popular, it became institutionalised among all relevant government agencies. The quest for nuclear weapons evolved from a modest and ambiguous political directive into the highest national priority and ultimately the core of its national security. The hallmark of that period was Pakistan's determination to stick to its nuclear objectives despite the certainty of US sanctions. In contrast, before 1971, fear of US opprobrium was viewed as a compelling reason for Pakistan not to pursue a full-blown nuclear program. Pakistan preferred sanctions, economic embargoes, and conventional force degradation to any move to neutralise its deterrent capability.

Second, Pakistan developed its nuclear capability at a time when it was a crucial American ally against the communist threat. For the United States, the goal of bleeding the Soviet Union through asymmetric means was greater than Pakistan's nuclear activity and democratic deficit. As the end of the Cold War made US interests in the region wane Pakistan continued with the same regional policies to advance its objectives in Afghanistan and Kashmir. Throughout the two decades since the late 1970s, Pakistan followed a nuclear policy of denial and ambiguity, as its scientific establishment vigorously continued to procure nuclear materials and technology from all possible sources.

Third, despite all the trouble and hardship that Pakistan experienced to obtain nuclear weapons, they ironically did not play a major role in the country's security calculus beyond enhancing a vague notion of deterrence during deep crises with India in the 1980s and 1990s. Military thinking in Pakistan remained focused on conventional war fighting. Even with the possession of an existential nuclear deterrent capability, defence planners preferred to rely on asymmetric strategies that were deemed to be cheaper options in Kashmir and Afghanistan via the Taliban. Pakistani planners failed to understand the implications of pursuing a proxy war strategy in their own neighbourhood. Supporting these insurgencies under the nuclear shadow as a regional policy had the risk of blowback. This strategy was dangerous given the fact that the possession of nuclear capabilities itself was isolating Pakistan and evoking sanctions.

Lastly, Pakistan's policy of acquiring nuclear weapons by any means had an unprecedented consequence for nuclear proliferation. Pakistani policy-makers did not expect their lax nuclear oversight would create the permissive environment, which enabled A. Q. Khan and his colleagues to establish his far-reaching nuclear supply network. The Pakistani ambition was to secure its interests along its borders, relaying on a nuclear capability to deter a far superior adversary from escalating a low-intensity conflict. Pakistan paid and continues to pay a heavy price for following this policy.

*Operational Deterrent*

Musharraf took over as Army Chief in October 1998 in tense regional and domestic circumstances. Pakistan was under international sanctions because of the nuclear tests. Relations with India were tense due to the ongoing Kashmir uprising and arrival of the Hindu nationalist party. Domestically Pakistan was also in a burgeoning crisis. The Sharif government was trying to gain absolute dominance by waging political war on multiple fronts, including the Presidency, the Judiciary, and the Parliament (opposition parties). The economy was faltering due to extravagant economic policies and corruption. And civil-military relations were under severe strain following the removal of Musharraf's predecessor Army Chief Jehangir Karamat.[7]

After a summer of high-intensity conflict in Kargil and breakdown of civil-military relations, the military finally took over power on 12 October 1999. Nuclear weapons played a prominent role in President Pervez Musharraf's policy focus and strategic orientation. Because nuclear weapons provide assurance in the prevention of war and containment of crises, Musharraf relied on this capability as a buffer in time and space to focus on strengthening other elements of national power. The economic revival of Pakistan became his singular focus. After the catastrophic attacks on the US in September 2001 when Pakistan again became a front line state he saw an opportunity to jumpstart the economy with new aid and cash flows. In a few years, he had turned the economy around evident in Pakistan's 8 per cent annual GDP growth by 2006.[8]

Immediately after 9/11, when confronted with the choice of reversing course on Afghanistan and abandoning the Taliban, preserving Pakistan's strategic assets was a key factor in his decision to join the US-led coalition.[9] Subsequently, and especially after the 13 December 2001 attack on the Indian Parliament, he changed Pakistan's strategic orientation toward India from active hostility to a process of dialogue and conflict resolution. Despite these changes, however, Pakistani domestic politics continued to remain fragile and civil-military relations worsened during his tenure.

Before the coup Musharraf had taken command of a conventional army that now had proven nuclear weapons though the nuclear arsenal was not under military command. Musharraf made major changes in the Army's leadership and brought a more proactive approach to address the Army's problems and low morale.

On the suggestion of his new military command, Musharraf approved a plan to secretly occupy positions vacated by India along the LoC, specifically in the Kargil sector. Exploiting vacant positions and jockeying for tactical dominance has been an ongoing practice between the two militaries along the LoC since the mid-1980s, beginning with India's 1984 occupation of the Siachen Glacier. Musharraf briefed Prime Minister Nawaz Sharif who in turn visited the military command area in late January and February 1999. On the one hand, Sharif was in knowledge if not actually having approved the Kargil operation; on the other hand, he was making peace overtures to India. By the spring of 1999, less than a year after Pakistan's nuclear tests, Pakistan embarked upon two contradictory approaches. As Pakistani soldiers were crossing the LoC, occupying abandoned positions, and reaching out deeper to interdict a strategic highway, Sharif received the Indian Prime Minister after a dramatic bus ride to Lahore. This led to an upbeat summit culminating in an agreement that promised peace and security.[10]

By the summer of 1999, a mini-war had broken out on the Kargil heights, bringing the two nuclear neighbours to the brink of major conflict. With mounting fears of an eventual nuclear exchange, the international community intervened to bring an end to the crisis. Pakistani soldiers were forced to withdraw, which brought a humiliation of sorts. This eventually produced further deterioration in the country's civil-military relations and paved the way for the coup in October 1999. Kargil underscored incoherence in Pakistani governance and strategic decision-making. This was a very shaky beginning for Pakistan as a nuclear power.[11]

Among the multiple challenges that Musharraf faced was the problem of managing an overtly nuclear armed Pakistan. As revealed by the Kargil episode Pakistani strategic thinking was still dominated by conventional military logic. As was the experience during the early phase of the Cold War, the true meaning of the nuclear revolution took many years to mature. India and Pakistan may be facing an even greater time lag in reaching this understanding. Kargil was a learning experience for Musharraf. As head of state he adopted a pragmatic and mature approach, which was later demonstrated during the 2002 military standoff with India—a crisis that also risked escalation to full-scale war and with it the possibility of nuclear use. This parallels to some degree the US experience of the Bay of Pigs followed by the Cuban Missile Crisis.

Musharraf issued a directive to study the implications of Pakistan's overt nuclear status. Confronted with a choice between declaring a nuclear command authority or a nuclear use doctrine, he eventually approved the former. To Pakistani defence a planner declaring command and control was a reflection of responsibility. The underlying motivation was to quash the perception of nuclear irresponsibility. At the same time, neither the military nor the civilian bureaucracy had any experience in dealing with the critical questions raised by being a nuclear power. The military had no acquaintance with issues such as nuclear force planning, strategy, targeting, integrating conventional forces, or developing a command-control infrastructure. The civil bureaucracy had been conducting nuclear diplomacy for decades but did not understand the nuances of international relations as a declared nuclear power. Pakistan was still at an early point along a steep nuclear learning curve.

On 2 February 2000, Musharraf announced Pakistan's command and control setup, making its Secretariat the Strategic Plans Division (SPD), located at the Joint Services Headquarters. The Pakistani war direction is conducted from the National Military Command Center (NMCC), which houses in it the civil and military leadership and integrates operations and intelligence of conventional armed forces. The nuclear command-control set up is an overlay of the existing national command structure and has two segments. The apex body is the Employment Control Committee, a senior leadership group comprising both military and civilian policy-makers, which gives policy direction and is the authority over strategic forces. The subordinate body is the Developmental Control Committee, which is comprised of military and scientific elements and which is tasked to optimise the technical and financial efficiency of the whole program to implement the goals set by the Employment Control Committee.[12]

The foremost decision taken early on by the Pakistani government was to determine the purpose of nuclear weapons. Nuclear weapons are for deterrence purposes, but deterrence is not believed to come automatically. Deterrence requires a mixture of credible force, demonstrative capability and a manner to convey its will to the opponents. Further, Pakistanis recognise that deterrence works primarily in the eye of the beholder, and as a political weapon, nuclear force can only be credible once it is perceived as militarily usable. For over a decade now, after three major crises, Pakistan's National Command Authority has matured in formulating strategic doctrines, thresholds, targeting, and survivability techniques.

Pakistan's strategic forces continue to grow. Its fissile material consists mainly of highly enriched uranium; but the PAEC also has developed the capability to produce weapon-grade plutonium on a small scale.[13] On the delivery side, Pakistan's mainstay consists of ballistic missiles, especially solid-fuel ballistic missiles such as Hatf-3 (Ghaznavi) and Hatf-4 (Shaheen) with ranges from 290 to 650 kilometres respectively. Further, for deeper targets Pakistan has the Hatf-5 (Ghauri) and Hatf-6 (Shaheen 2), which can target key Indian cities and garrisons, and which have estimated ranges of up to 1,250 kilometres and 2,200 kilometres, respectively.[14]

As the Pakistan force posture grew under a coherent development plan based on an array of strategic assessments, the primary belief that nuclear weapons are essential for national security, was deeply internalised in the Pakistani state by this time. Nuclear weapons had been tested and the financial costs had already been paid. However, the auxiliary assertions about the role of nuclear weapons were still in flux. What were the 'influencing' dimensions of being a country that obtains a political status of becoming a nuclear power, especially in terms of regional and international affairs? Further, for Pakistan it was unclear how to determine the military feasibility of nuclear weapons, especially how to integrate these capabilities into its conventional war planning and deterrent postures.

In terms of nuclear policy planning and strategic thinking, after the 1998 nuclear tests Pakistan had only a vague notion of an existential nuclear deterrence. Under the leadership of Lt. Gen. Khalid Ahmad Kidwai, the SPD proceeded to develop clearer concepts and guidelines on force structure and planning and on prioritising force goals within the parameters of financial and resource constraints. Though the command and control system is still evolving its functioning and efficacy is still shrouded in secrecy. During the 1999 and 2002 crises, nuclear weapons were not openly brandished though some preparations or passive dispersive measures for survivability may have been taken.[15] During this period, Pakistan also developed the art of signalling deterrence through declaratory statements and ballistic missile testing,[16] but nuclear weapons did not play an overt role during the 1999 and 2002 crises. Nevertheless, the nuclear arsenal did play its primary deterrent role: crises remain limited in action, and escalation to general war was avoided.[17] There were however other factors, such as US intervention, which probably played a critical role in easing India-Pakistan tensions.

Musharraf inherited a nuclear program that had developed sufficiently but lacked a coherent direction. Worse, an uncontrolled procurement network had unravelled under his watch. The command and control system was made more effective after the firing of A. Q. Khan, with rapidly upgraded security and oversight and the enactment of export control legislation.[18] Meanwhile, the nuclear arsenal continued to grow both in quantity and quality. Pakistan's delivery means were expanded and diversified, including in the arena of cruise missiles, which were tested recently. American defence analyst John H. Gill describes Pakistan's current nuclear strategy concisely: 'Pakistan seeks to maintain sufficient conventional and nuclear strength to deter an Indian attack, or if deterrence fails, to prevent a catastrophic defeat long enough for the international community to intervene and halt the conflict.'[19]

Nuclear weapons are now so deeply embedded in Pakistani security thinking that any attempt to dissuade it from this path—towards disarmament or towards a weapon-free world—would be met with stiff resistance from the entire spectrum within the state. Today, the Armed Forces, civilian bureaucracy, scientific community, and entire political spectrum, from the religious right to liberal left, all support Pakistan's continued nuclear weapons capability. Also, there is a strong consensus that Pakistan's nuclear weapons are under threat from hostile countries, which include the United States, Israel and India. Pakistanis believe that their nuclear arsenal remains vulnerable to preventive or preemptive attacks and thus even a slight hint of threat or rumour prompts the Armed Forces to take precautionary measures. The West often accused Pakistan of issuing nuclear threats as during Kargil. This tendency has existed since the mid-1980s when reports about a joint Indo-Israeli attack against Kahuta circulated inside Pakistan, only to be later confirmed when it became evident (at least to Pakistani defence planners) that India seriously contemplated such a plan.[20]

Today, the Pakistani Armed Forces, which are custodians of the nuclear arsenal, have taken significant steps to integrate nuclear weapons into their war plans and deterrence strategy. However, other Pakistani elites have contested the military's limited conception of the role of nuclear weapons. Religious opposition parties, such as Jamaat-e-Islami (JI), articulate the role of nuclear weapons in a different light and have demonstrated nuclear symbolism by placing models of missiles in prominent public places.[21] The party's think-tank contends that the value of Pakistan's nuclear deterrent extends beyond countering India. According to JI Senator Khurshid Ahmad:

Pakistan as an Islamic state has a responsibility to the broader Umma...
Pakistan's nuclear weapons will inevitably be seen as a threat by Israel, and
therefore Pakistan must include Israel in its defense planning...Under the circumstances, the future of the Muslim world depends on Pakistan.[22]

To date, no serious planning has occurred in Pakistan that would
indicate that the Islamic myth of nuclear influence had taken hold or
that the government is thinking in terms of extending deterrence or
proliferating nuclear weapons in order to profit from their value as an
ideological weapon. However, the rhetoric that Pakistan was the first
Muslim country to acquire nuclear weapons remains a popular notion
in domestic political culture.

*Emerging Force Postures*

Pakistani anxiety did not dissolve even after demonstrating its nuclear
weapon capability in 1998. India's conventional forces and its advanc-
ing nuclear capability continue to make Pakistan vulnerable to Indian
coercion. Pakistan's nuclear force posture evolved under military
doctrines, military force mobilisations in crises and a calculus of conventional force imbalance. Indeed the most important factor is the
correlation of Pakistan's strategic force posture with India's conventional force postures and military crises.

The twin military crises in 1999 (Kargil) and 2001–2002 (Paraka-
ram) were catalysts for conceptualising Pakistan's national security
thinking and integration of nuclear force planning and conventional
force planning at the Strategic Plans Division. There was seemingly
little realisation in India that coercing a conventionally weaker adversary that had newly demonstrated its nuclear weapon capability would
only speed up the process of making nuclear weapons operational.
India ought to have known that the central premise of Pakistani going
nuclear was to redress the strategic imbalance and to seek a way to
deter hostile India from attacking its weaker neighbour.

The 2001–2002 crisis might well have been another Indian effort to
display superior military might in a bid to force Pakistan into submission. The timing of this coercive deployment were seen as exploiting
the post-9/11 environment, especially when Pakistan was engaged
along its western frontier due to US operations in Afghanistan. India
clearly posed a two-front dilemma for Pakistan. More importantly
what remains an enigma for Pakistani security planners was the funda-

mental assumption that Indian military planners could start, control and win a limited war without escalating into nuclear tripwires. The 2001–2002 military standoff was another grim reminder of the perpetuity of the existential threat from India, reinforcing the significance of nuclear weapons in deterring India from 1971-like adventures. There appeared a lack of sober recognition in India's security thinking that the advent of nuclear weapons means that war should not even be contemplated. Pakistan therefore has to prepare to counter the threat of Indian mobilisation each time it occurs in response to terror attacks in India.

As Pakistan lacks comparable resources, nuclear deterrence would be the only recourse to rely on. The more innovation in conventional military doctrine against Pakistan is contemplated and the more new technologies (subsurface cruise missiles, space based surveillance, and ballistic missiles defence for example) are acquired by India, the greater the challenge to strategic stability in the region. As new challenges to internal stability emerge for Pakistan, and its security forces are drawn into multiple contingencies, there would be even more reason to depend on nuclear deterrence to deal with the threat from India.

Nuclear deterrence does not come about automatically, especially against an adversary that seeks opportunity and space to threaten war. Strategic forces must be structured to create deterrent forces. Pakistan had no clear models to emulate. Its force-structuring model was *sui generis*. This meant weighing its vulnerabilities and strengths to determine force-planning parameters. Its geo-physical vulnerability, especially the lack of depth and proximity of communication centres to Indian military thrusts were all key considerations. Conversely, this weakness from short distances enabled Pakistan to draw up plans for rapid mobilisation for defence and implied that Indian offensive forces would stand to lose surprise and travel a greater distance. Next, denying escalation control would force India to calculate the risk of any misadventure.

The Strategic Plans Division (SPD) announced four explicit thresholds, which alone or in combination would constitute redlines: space, destruction, economic strangulation and abetting domestic violence. Under President Musharraf, a unified command system existed in the country, which provided the Pakistan National Command Authority (NCA) a semblance of coherence in planning and decision-making—thus clearly articulating objectives and force goals. The Strategic Plans

Division (SPD) established at the Joint Services Headquarters in 1999 was tasked to act as a secretariat for the NCA.

Beginning in spring 1999, strategic planning commenced with a net threat assessment and appraisal of conventional capabilities. Simultaneous studies of several models for force planning provided a base for organisational and operational planning. The crucial determining factor was the financial and technical resources that would impact the minimum deterrence requirement but also the force structuring goals. It was therefore important to develop such organisational models for strategic force commands and operational procedures that Pakistanis were familiar with. Within a short span SPD was tackling a complex set of issues of nuclear management, which included developing procedures for preparing nuclear warheads and delivery vehicles, survivability, security, safety and other mechanism for command and control. Even as these processes were growing it was ultimately the 2001–2002 military standoff that brought about the final shaping of nuclear forces when dispersal and mating plans were actually tested under extremely trying conditions of a physical threat from an enemy. India inadvertently provided Pakistan a chance to refine its procedures with an environment of real-time threats.

By the end of the crisis in October 2002, Pakistan had a well-exercised and functioning Strategic Force Command (SFC) under the Pakistan Army with ballistic missile units and Strategic Air Commands operating with The Pakistan Air Force (PAF) all operating under a centralised command, control, communication and intelligence (C3 I) system at the Joint Services Headquarters. The Nuclear Command Authority (NCA) comprised the highest-level of civilian and military decision-makers. While nuclear force planning and development was done under the Chairman Joint Chief of Staff's Committee, the Prime Minister, Cabinet Ministers and four service chiefs formed the Employment committee of the NCA, which is the apex body that invites the heads of the scientific organisations to facilitate NCA decisions.

The institutional response to manage the ultimate weapons and threats helps to keep an eye on developments and advances in India. But it does not mitigate the stark reality of resource constraints, which determines the force posture. Matching all Indian advances is not necessary to maintain the strategic parity with India. Periodic review by the NCA for qualitative match and force goal ceilings as well as oversight of safety, security and survivability of arsenals will remain a regular feature in Pakistan's nuclear future.

Pakistani arsenals are maintained in non-deployed form. The NCA maintains centralised control of the assets. An elaborate system of security and safety has been employed though the Security Division, which ensures physical security of storage and transport. Security is tight with strict access control within each organisation and a personnel reliability program has been instituted much on the lines of Western countries.

It is extremely important for Pakistan to keep the safety coefficient high in normal peacetime. But the system must respond to the rapid changing strategic environment, which takes little time to change. As has been witnessed, a Mumbai type attack can lead to a speedy deterioration of the situation. The NCA is charged with assuring readiness in the event of a sudden strike or conventional war breakout.

*Future Trajectories*

Pakistan is well on its way to field a nuclear triad in the future. Land-based forces will principally rely on a mix of solid- and liquid-fuelled ballistic and cruise missiles (Babur), which is likely to be the mainstay for the foreseeable future. The air-based deterrent will improve as Pakistan develops its air defences for both conventional and strategic delivery. Research and development continues on a sea-based deterrent. In the long run a submarine based cruise missile deterrent will ensure a second strike stability. Meanwhile improvement in command and control with information, surveillance and reconnaissance capability (C2ISR) will continuously be enhanced. A rejuvenated Space and Upper Atmosphere Research Commission (SUPARCO) will have new tasks in this regard. Launching a Pakistan satellite in the next decade will give dedicated data; guidance and space based accuracy as well as enhance C2ISR. Early warning can win nearly half the battle.

The likely role of nuclear weapons in Pakistan's regional policies and international engagements will primarily depend on the trajectories of regional security dynamics. Four developments would affect Pakistan's security policy. The first will be the outcome of the so-called War on Terrorism in Afghanistan and its impact on Pakistan's security interest. The second would be the shaping of the regional power balance between India and Pakistan. Would strategic balance lead to peaceful resolution of conflict or would continued arms build up and modernisations increase tensions bringing in more crises and wars? The third factor will be the policy course that United States might follow in Asia and the Muslim world. US security policy, particularly with respect to China and Iran, Pakistan's two important neighbours, as well as towards the Islamic world, will necessitate a role for Pakistan. Finally, most importamt will be the outcome of how Pakistan tackles its internal stability situation and emerges out of the current domestic crises. Depending on these developments, Pakistan's nuclear policy is likely to evolve into one of two futures.

The first course is moderate and pragmatic and would occur if Pakistan has a stable government that achieves balanced civil-military relations. This course would perpetuate the national security establishment's perception of nuclear force as purely a national security instrument. Even with changing regional dynamics it will likely follow the predictable pattern that has been seen in the past. It would continue to rely on a combination of internal and external-balancing techniques to meet emerging threats. Pakistani nuclear and conventional forces would grow in tandem with India's force modernisation. Pakistan's external balancing would probably rely on China, Muslim countries, and the United States. If Pakistan's economy grows and if relations with India improve, the likelihood will be high of repeating the Cold War nuclear experience of arms control and confidence-building measures with India.

The other nuclear future is a radical shift away from Pakistan's traditional approach to international relations. Such an outcome is more likely if a radical right-wing government assumes power. A domestic change of this nature could shift the emphasis of nuclear weapons from a purely national security tool to a more ideologically based power instrument. This would result in confrontation with Pakistan and the West. Such a future would grossly complicate Pakistani security dilemmas.

# 15

# REVERSING STRATEGIC 'SHRINKAGE'

*Munir Akram*

Pakistan has been a strategically challenged state from the moment of its creation—facing hostility from its separating neighbour, India; gross inadequacies in the military, financial and bureaucratic structures, and a huge refugee influx. Pakistan survived those early years against all odds, due to the iron will of its founder, Mohammad Ali Jinnah, and the enthusiasm of its Muslim population for a state free not only from British rule but also the threat of Hindu subjugation and the dream of reviving the glory of Islam's millennia of rule in the subcontinent.

Today, despite the prognostications of its detractors, Pakistan's existence as a sovereign state is not in question. Pakistan has acquired its unique identity; all the country's major power centres and provinces—despite periodic dissent—have a vested interest in its existence; its armed forces are determined to defend its independence and territory; and the acquisition of nuclear weapons capability has provided the presumption of immunity from external aggression of the sort that led to the separation of East Pakistan. But, as always in its short history, Pakistan still confronts serious strategic challenges, short and long term, which, if not wisely confronted and overcome, could become life threatening.

Several of these challenges are internal—mis-governance, extremism and terrorism, economic stagnation and social breakdown. Most of these internal challenges are inextricably linked to, and the consequences of, external causes and developments.

The immediate challenges facing Pakistan are visible and imposing in themselves: the violent attacks by the Tehrik-i-Taliban Pakistan (TTP) in the Khyber Pakhtunkhwa province and major cities; Pakistan's costly and unpopular involvement in Afghanistan, the alienation of many Baloch, economic stagnation—manifest in the power crisis—and the growing poverty and social deterioration affecting the vast majority of Pakistan's population. The combination of political turbulence and incoherence, growing extremism, ethnic and social violence, terrorist attacks and economic stagnation, have created a dangerous mood of national pessimism, bordering on despair.

The first priority is to overcome these immediate challenges. Despite the confused political circumstances and inadequate governance, a start has been made towards confronting some of these challenges. This start—as so often in Pakistan's history—has been initiated, directly or indirectly, by the Pakistani Army.

*Fighting the TTP*

In 2009 the Army made the vital determination that the foremost priority was to confront and defeat the TTP and its affiliates, which pose the most direct challenge to Pakistan. The US was asked to use its drones to target the TTP, not only the Afghan Taliban, to prove the credibility of its alliance with Pakistan. While placing action against the Afghan Taliban on the backburner, massive military operations were launched in Swat and, later, in South Waziristan, Orakzai and other Agencies. These operations were made possible in large measure due to the emergence of a general public consensus in Pakistan that the TTP's violence and acts of barbarism were unacceptable from both a national and Islamic viewpoint and that it must be crushed. The Armed Forces were also motivated by considerable evidence of support to the TTP from the Tajik-led Afghan intelligence and their Indian mentors. By all accounts, these military operations have been fairly successful and, in Swat, the large displaced civilian population has been able to return home. The TTP is not obliterated; its attacks continue. But the organisation and its leadership have been severely mauled and remain under pressure from the air and on the ground.

A conclusive success against the TTP will require isolating it—together with al Qaeda—from the tribes and other militant groups from which the TTP draws recruits and support. In particular, de-linking the pro Kashmiri groups from the TTP is vital as these groups too will have to be suppressed. Over the longer term, pacification of the tribal regions will be possible only through the restoration of effective governance, a fair justice system and the creation of economic and employment opportunities. The anticipated withdrawal of US-NATO forces from Afghanistan will diminish the 'jihadi' appeal of the TTP and assist in the pacification of these regions.

### Pacifying Afghanistan

Progress has also been made in preserving Pakistan's interests in Afghanistan. This required the Army and the ISI to play 'hardball' over the last two and a half years. India had to be convinced that its interventions in Balochistan and the Federally Administered Tribal Areas (FATA) were not cost-free. Certain Afghan Taliban groups were targeted where essential; in other instances action was held back when it served Pakistan's interests. The 'capture' of a string of Taliban leaders, including Mullah Baradar, in 2010 could not all be 'accidental', as some US officials and the Western media asserted.

Importantly, the US has become convinced that it can execute its current military strategy in Afghanistan and evolve a framework for peace that would enable an honourable US-NATO withdrawal, only with cooperation and support of Pakistan's Armed Forces. The red carpet treatment accorded the Pakistan Army Chief during rounds of the Pakistan-US 'strategic dialogue' in March and October 2010 reflected this recognition in Washington. Success or failure in Afghanistan will have critical implications for President Barack Obama's re-election.

There is now greater convergence between Pakistan and the US on Afghanistan, and on fighting the TTP and al Qaeda, then at any time since 9/11. However, neither side has as yet clearly identified its final objectives in Afghanistan, nor the process by which these are to be achieved. The US Administration is still clarifying a strategy for negotiating peace with the Taliban. Pakistan seems hesitant to act decisively until it knows US objectives and strategy. Meanwhile, President Karzai seems to be playing all sides to ensure his own survival. He has alternately supported and denounced US-NATO military operations. He has opened contacts with some of the Taliban and with Gulbuddin Hekmatyar. He has sought Pakistan's cooperation to negotiate with the Taliban, but told the US that Pakistan is impeding such talks. Simultaneously, President Karzai has reportedly told Iran and India that Pakistan is pushing him into these negotiations. India is alarmed by the prospect of a Taliban return to power (which would terminate its strategic gains in Afghanistan), and is busy reconstructing its old alliance with Iran and Russia to resurrect the Northern Alliance and others opposed to accommodation with the Taliban.

It is so far unclear how this tangled web will be unraveled. Without strategic clarity and political determination, Pakistan could lose the tactical space it has secured. Islamabad needs to evolve its own plan for peace in Afghanistan, establish the required contacts with the Afghan insurgents and persuade the US to endorse this path to peace and an honourable US-NATO exit from Afghanistan.

### Reviving the Economy

For four consecutive years until 2007, Pakistan recorded encouraging, if uneven, economic growth. But it failed to address fundamental economic problems—poverty and human development, job creation, infrastructure and economic efficiency and productivity. The political turmoil of the following two years, mounting terrorist attacks, erosion of business confidence and the impact of the concurrent global economic crisis pushed the Pakistan economy into a severe and fundamental crisis. This crisis cannot be overcome without significant external financial support. Unfortunately, despite promises of a 'democracy dividend', Western assistance has been extended in dribs and drabs and often with unacceptable conditions e.g. those reflected in the Kerry-Lugar Bill. Simultaneously, Pakistan's traditional friends—China, Saudi Arabia, and UAE—have been halting in their commitments due to doubts about the political leadership in Pakistan. Yet, perhaps what has been most lacking is a clear and comprehensive Pakistani plan to address the economic challenge.

With the improved prospects for a period of political equilibrium, if not stability, in Pakistan, the new national determination to confront anti-state terrorism and the growing international consensus that Pakistan needs to be rescued economically for the sake of regional stability, there is now scope for reviving Pakistan's economic fortunes. The rescue plan will need to encompass: fiscal stabilisation, with generous international support, improved revenue generation and budget discipline; major investments, especially in physical infrastructure, including energy, and social development, particularly health and education; and rapid growth and job creation through a stimulus package to support expansion in manufacturing, agriculture, services and exports.

There is no reason why Pakistan cannot achieve fairly high growth rates within the next few years. The primary need is for honesty, clarity and coherence in Islamabad, and readiness to utilise all available diplomatic leverage with the international community.

## Balochistan

Apart from the economy, a credible effort is required to heal the festering sore in Balochistan. Ending the violent attacks and disaffection in the province is vital for national cohesion, political stability and economic growth. Balochistan's untapped natural resources and its strategic location will be essential elements of Pakistan's future economic growth and political importance. Prospects for ending violence in Balochistan will greatly improve once India is stopped from aiding the Balochistan Liberation Army (BLA) insurgents through Afghanistan. Targeted action against recalcitrant elements will need to be accompanied by effort at political accommodation with the major tribal and political groups and a fair resolution of legitimate Baloch grievances.

It is vital, however, that the pressing challenges of today do not deflect attention from the more enduring and fundamental strategic challenges that confront Pakistan.

## The Pervasive Challenge from India

As ever, the most enduring and formidable of these challenges emanate from India. The hostility between Pakistan and India has deep historical and popular roots in both countries. Despite cultural, linguistic and ethnic affinities, the mutual hostility between the Muslims and Hindus of the sub-continent is real and endemic. It was the *raison d'être* for the creation of Pakistan. The history of the last sixty years has, if anything, further intensified this hostility and given it structural expression in the relationship between the two states. The Kashmir dispute, in essence, is but one expression of this divide and hostility. (Bangladesh's relationship with India displays the same dynamic.) Thus, even if outstanding issues, like Kashmir, are resolved, and some semblance of civility restored between Pakistan and India, their relationship will remain competitive for the foreseeable future. Those who argue that, with goodwill and conflict resolution, peace and harmony can descend on the sub-continent are either ignorant or self-serving.

Today, unlike the early years, India's objective is no longer to undo Partition and absorb the territories of Pakistan. The cost would far outweigh the benefit (of course, many Indians—and their friends, including some in Pakistan—endorse the vision of the Bharatiya Janata Party's L.K. Advani of a South Asian Confederation led by India). Today, India's ambition, propelled by its self-perception and Western encouragement, is to emerge as the supreme regional power and eventually a global power to rival China. Pakistan stands in the way of this ambition. It resists India's presumption of South Asian dominion. It blocks India's geographical access to Central and West Asia. It reminds the world of Indian oppression of Muslim-majority Kashmir and exposes the fallacy of Indian secularism. It neutralises a large part of India's military power. It gnaws at India's Achilles' heel—Kashmir. It diminishes India's nuclear weapons status by demanding nuclear parity.

To realise its regional and global ambitions, New Delhi believes that Pakistan's capacity and will to resist Indian domination must be broken. To achieve this, India is pursuing a well thought out strategy on multiple fronts. The Indian strategy encompasses: the defamation and denigration of Pakistan and especially its Armed Forces—through its diplomacy and the media—as the 'epicentre of terrorism'; the political, economic and strategic encirclement of Pakistan by building India's strategic and economic links with Iran, Oman, the Central Asian States and, more recently, even with Pakistan's closest friends, Saudi Arabia and Turkey; the promotion of subversion and insurgency in Balochistan; infiltration of the TTP to support attacks against Pakistan's security forces and civilian centres; the build up of India's Armed Forces to overwhelm Pakistan in a conventional conflict; efforts to delegitimise Pakistan's nuclear weapons capability through propaganda about nuclear proliferation from Pakistan, including to terrorist organisations; acquisition of the option to economically strangle Pakistan, for example, through constraints on Indus water flows. It is visible to any perceptive Pakistani that this Indian strategy has already made several gains and is progressively eroding Pakistan's vital national interests and objectives.

This Indian success is mainly due to its expanding economy and large market which offers opportunities for profit to other nations and their companies. It is built on the perception, assiduously propagated by New Delhi, that given its growing economic and military prowess, India is destined to emerge as the regional super-power and can serve as a strong force for stability in South Asia and the Indian Ocean. Simultaneously, India promotes the converse perception of Pakistan as a violent and turbulent state afflicted with the twin evils—terrorism and nuclear proliferation—that are the West's current phobias. In Washington, and other Western capitals, the consensus emerged during the Bush Administration that India is their 'natural partner' to confront 'Islamic terrorism' and to 'balance' the rising power of China. Thus, India's 'great power' status was proclaimed even before it has been realised. The faucets of arms, advanced technology, investment, and trade, have been opened for India, even as they have become mostly closed for Pakistan. Without this Western endorsement and support, India's ambition of regional domination and great power status would be most difficult to realise.

*The Cost of Counter-Terrorism*

It is ironic that Pakistan's strategic decline took place during the period of the post 9/11 'alliance' with the US. Pakistan-US relations have witnessed several such periods of tactical convergence: for example, during the early years of the Cold War and in the anti-Soviet Afghan war of the 1980s. Unfortunately, each time, as US strategic priorities shifted, these alliances of convenience turned into estrangement and even hostility. While the Pakistani governments and leaders of the time benefited from US support, any objective cost-benefit analysis would reveal the fundamental damage done to Pakistan—political, economic, and strategic—as a consequence of these periodic alliances with and dependence on the US. Thus, the Cold War alliance with the US evoked Soviet hostility, its veto against Kashmir and its support for India's break up of Pakistan in 1971. Pakistan's participation in the anti-Soviet Afghan war contributed directly to the rise of religious extremism, sectarianism, violence and terrorism in Pakistan.

The past nine years of Pakistani cooperation with the US against al Qaeda and the Taliban in Afghanistan have no doubt provided Pakistan important US political and economic support, although the benefits of US patronage have been grossly under-utilised by the previous and present Pakistani governments. But this period of the counter-terrorism alliance has also witnessed some of the most serious strategic reversals for Pakistan. These include:

- The replacement of the 'friendly'—though internationally unacceptable—Taliban regime in Kabul by a hostile Panjsheri—Tajik-dominated government.
- The migration of Afghan Taliban and al Qaeda leaders into Pakistan and progressive escalation of Pakistan's military involvement against them, shifting the locus of the war from Afghanistan to Pakistan.
- The neutralisation of the Kashmiri freedom struggle, as Pakistan was obliged, under US pressure, to halt cross-border support to them.
- The emergence of a coalition between radical Pakistani groups under the umbrella of the TTP, the spread of their influence, even control in parts of FATA and adjacent areas and bold attacks against Pakistan's security forces and civilian centres.
- India's growing role and influence in Afghanistan, and its utilisation of Afghan territory and intelligence services to support subversion in Balochistan and the north western regions.
- The unjust depiction of Pakistan as the 'safe haven' for al Qaeda and global terrorists, accompanied by mounting US pressure on Pakistan to 'do more' in its fight against them, leading to the deployment of 150,000 Pakistani troops on the Western border, inevitably diminishing Pakistan's defence capabilities against India, and provoking attacks against Pakistan's security forces, leaders and civilian population.
- The Western campaign, actively supported by India, to de-legitimise Pakistan's nuclear programme, including US pressure for sensitive information and access after the A.Q. Khan proliferation scandal; questions raised regarding the safety and security of Pakistan's nuclear weapons and their possible takeover by 'Islamic' radicals; and the 'de-hyphenation' of the nuclear relationship between Pakistan and India.

Even as Pakistan's strategic interests, and its internal stability and cohesion, were eroded as a consequence of the US 'alliance', India's strategic position progressively improved. Apart from the closure of the Kashmiri militancy and opening of the Afghan avenue for subversion against Pakistan, this period saw the crystallisation of the Indo-US 'strategic partnership', manifested in the Indo-US civilian nuclear agreement; US and Western offers of the most advanced military equipment and technologies to India, including fighter aircraft, anti-ballistic missile systems, early warning, satellite and space capabilities, are all barred to Pakistan. This was done, under the banner of 'de-hyphenating' US relations with Pakistan and India, without regard for the strategic consequences for Pakistan. Indeed, to rub salt in Pakistan's wounds, open declarations were made by US officials that Pakistan was not eligible, deserving or capable of receiving the materials or access offered to India. US 'officials' and the Western media joined with the Indians to portray Pakistan as the 'epicentre' of terrorism and nuclear proliferation.

Obviously, the domestic vulnerability and weakness of Pakistani leaders, and their almost complete dependence on the US for survival, made it possible for Washington and its allies to act so blatantly against Pakistan's vital national interests. This did not end with the change of government in 2008. On the contrary, US efforts to control Pakistan's security and domestic affairs visibly intensified, as evident from the conditionalities incorporated in the Kerry–Lugar Bill and the demand that Pakistan shift its military focus from deterring India to fighting the Taliban. Washington fully expected Pakistan's leadership to do its bidding.

*The Difficult Road Back to Strategic Assertion*

It was the sharp reaction within the higher echelons of the Pakistani Army to the Kerry–Lugar 'conditionalities', and the brazen attempt to assert control over Pakistan's Armed Forces and the ISI and dictate Pakistan's security priorities, which signalled that 'the worm had turned'. This was followed by a period of 'inaction' by the Pakistani Army on Afghanistan. As the TTP and the Afghan Taliban made advances, strident statements emanated from Washington, issuing the improbable warning that Islamabad itself could be overrun by the Islamic radicals 'only sixty miles away'.

When the Pakistan Army's operation was launched in Swat, the Western media presumed it was in response to American pressure. In fact, it was undertaken only when the local political leaders gave up their naïve bid for accommodation with the TTP and public opinion in Pakistan turned against the militants due to their acts of brutality and barbarism. There was minimal coordination with the US. The operations focused only on the TTP not the Afghan Taliban. Later, Pakistan's high command clearly communicated that it would not relent in its priority aim of deterring India and responding to its conventional and nuclear arms build up. The declaration issued by the National Command Authority on 13 December, which, among other things, demanded restoration of nuclear equality with India and opposed any early negotiations on a Treaty to halt fissile material production, was an important public reflection of Pakistan's newly revived national assertiveness, at least on security issues.

The 'red lines' drawn by the Pakistani Army resulted in a series of intense consultations between it, the US military and political officials. US emissaries made private amends to the ISI for earlier 'rogue agency' insults. These consultations coincided with, and no doubt contributed to, the comprehensive policy review on Afghanistan and Pakistan conducted by the Obama Administration. This review, by all accounts, led to the conclusion that, after a final escalated military effort to put the Afghan insurgency on the defensive, the US should seek an honourable way to withdraw most, if not all, it's forces from Afghanistan before the next US Presidential elections, including through negotiations with the Afghan Taliban. An equally important, though less publicised, conclusion was that Pakistan's role would be critical in implementing both the military and political components of the new Afghanistan strategy and Islamabad's legitimate national concerns and interests would need to be accommodated.

The ensuing overtures to Pakistan culminated in the 'Strategic Dialogue' held in Washington in March 2010. For this dialogue, Pakistan reportedly conveyed a fifty-eight-page document listing the outcomes it sought from the dialogue. Significantly, the preparations for the dialogue, and the most important meetings in Washington, were conducted by the Pakistan Army Chief.

In Pakistan's ruling circles, there is evidently considerable satisfaction at the progress in the Washington dialogue and the subsequent interaction between the Pakistani delegation and President Obama in the October round in Washington. There is a belief in Islamabad that the American strategic outlook on Pakistan has changed fundamentally; that it is now responsive to Pakistan's national concerns on Afghanistan, India, the nuclear issue and economic and trade issues. Thirteen sectoral groups have been discussing specific areas for cooperation and reporting to the principals.

Hopefully, Pakistan's civilian and military leadership will not allow the warm words and courtesies extended by US leaders to create undue euphoria and unrealistic expectations. Islamabad must make a realistic evaluation of what is likely to be achieved through this latest attempt at close engagement with Washington. Pakistan-US convergence can be achieved on Afghanistan, al Qaeda and the Taliban. The US needs Pakistan to execute a politically acceptable exit strategy from Afghanistan. In turn, Pakistan requires US cooperation to construct a post-American order in Afghanistan which is not inimical to Pakistan's national interests. Pakistan-US cooperation against al Qaeda and the TTP is similarly essential for both. Yet, even in the context of counter-terrorism, there may be limits and difficulties as evident from the fall-out of the May 2010 Times Square bombing attempt, with the US attempt to shift the goal posts with Pakistan after this incident by demanding early operations in North Waziristan.

It was very clear from the two rounds of the Washington dialogue that the US is neither able nor inclined to assist Pakistan on India, Kashmir or the nuclear issue. Vague promises were conveyed by US officials. Quiet US advice may have led to the Thimpu meeting between the Pakistani and Indian Premiers. But India has not been persuaded to resume the broad based 'composite' dialogue; nor shown the slightest inclination to address the Kashmir dispute or arms control and security issues.

At the 'Nuclear Summit' in April 2010 President Obama scrupulously avoided past demonisation of Pakistan. Nevertheless, Pakistan was asked to agree to the start of negotiations on the Treaty to ban fissile material production, apparently in exchange for the unnecessary and non-deliverable demand made by Pakistan that the US 'recognise' its nuclear 'status'. Pakistan already has recognition as a de facto nuclear weapon state. It does not need, nor will it get, de jure recognition from the US, or the international community, in the foreseeable future. Nor will any 'recognition' by the US imply that the overt and covert attempts to constrain and neutralise Pakistan's nuclear deterrence capabilities will end.

Clearly, within the present US strategic parameters, it is unlikely that it will help Pakistan to address the more fundamental challenges posed by India—Kashmir, the conventional military balance, credible nuclear deterrence. On these issues, Pakistan will need to formulate and implement its own independent responses to protect and promote its national interests. A policy change on these issues in New Delhi, Washington and other capitals will come about only once Pakistan displays its determination to assert its own interests.

*Kashmir*

Jammu and Kashmir remain vital for Pakistan for multiple reasons:

- Identity: as a Muslim majority area of British India which, according to the criteria for Partition, should have been a part of Pakistan.
- Territory: gain or loss of an area bigger than Belgium.
- People: ethnically, religiously, culturally and historically linked to the people of Pakistan rather than India.
- Strategy: the only direct land link to Pakistan's ally, China.

Nowhere is Pakistan's strategic decline more visible than on the Kashmir dispute. Due to a series of policy mistakes, India's palpably unjust position on Kashmir now evokes greater international understanding and sympathy than the legally and morally correct position traditionally taken by Pakistan, i.e. that the future of Kashmir should be decided by the Kashmiri people, through a free and fair referendum conducted by the UN, as prescribed by several UN Security Council resolutions.

The Kashmiri revolt against Indian oppression that erupted in December 1989 was a golden opportunity for Pakistan to press for a fair and durable solution for the dispute. It was lost. Pakistan, still under the heady aura of the 'jihadi' victory over the Soviets in Afghanistan, opted to support religiously motivated groups to spearhead the Kashmiri freedom struggle. Soon, these groups assumed a life and agenda of their own, often inimical to the aspirations and culture of the Kashmiris. Indian intelligence infiltrated these groups. The acts of barbarism perpetrated by some of them e.g. the Al-Faran incident in the early 1990s were duly exploited by India to press for the delegitimisation of the Kashmiri freedom struggle. Following 9/11, and the attack on the Indian Parliament, Pakistan was obliged, under US pressure, to halt 'cross-border' support to the Kashmiris. No concessions were secured from India in exchange for this commitment.

Although it is axiomatic that negotiations pursued from a position of weakness cannot yield a fair result, an ill-considered endeavour was launched—through back-door diplomacy entrusted to a close aide of President Pervez Musharraf with no knowledge of India-Pakistan relations or Kashmir—to seek a compromise that, we know now, would have confirmed the status quo, if not worsened it. Fortunately, India delayed acceptance of this 'compromise'. The political turmoil in Pakistan after the 2007 Chief Justice crisis, rendered the exercise infructuous.

Pakistan's ability to negotiate a just solution for Kashmir is no better today than five years ago. A credible freedom struggle cannot be revived quickly. For the sake of its international image, its internal stability and its socio-economic aspirations, Pakistan has no choice but to suppress the violent proclivities of the jihadi groups.

At the same time, there is also no compulsion on Pakistan to concede its traditional position on Kashmir. Pakistan cannot impose a Kashmir solution on India. But nor can India impose a solution on Pakistan. The persistence of the status quo may not be a desirable situation, particularly for the oppressed Kashmiris. But they have displayed remarkable resilience. They have not given up their aspiration to be free of Indian rule. Pakistan can do no less than to respect their aspirations. Sooner or later, the Kashmiris will revolt again against India's rule. Pakistan should be in a position to help them at such time to achieve their aspirations. Meanwhile, India's occupation of Kashmir locks up almost a third of its land force, enhancing Pakistan's ability to balance India's numerically larger army.

Pakistan's policy on Kashmir should go back to the future. Islamabad should: one, reaffirm its fundamental position, i.e. a resolution of Kashmir can come about only through the free exercise of the right of self-determination by the people of Jammu and Kashmir; two, express open and active support for the Kashmir groups and leaders who favour integration with Pakistan or separation from India and help to unite them under a common and coherent political platform, hence Pakistan should not fear the call for Kashmiri independence, since an independent Kashmir, however unlikely, will always be pro-Pakistan; three, assert its moral, political and legal right to support the Kashmir freedom struggle against India; four, denounce terrorism against civilians and non-combatants and break all links with groups which resort to terrorism; five, instead of pleading for a dialogue which is not likely to be successful, refrain from a dialogue until India halts its human rights violations and oppression in occupied Kashmir (and its subversion in Pakistan); six, publicise and hold India accountable, in international forums and the media, for its continued suppression of the Kashmiris and its gross violations of human rights in occupied Kashmir.

A bolder stance on Kashmir, based on international principles and the support of the Pakistani people, will not escalate the danger of a conflict so long as Pakistan's conventional and nuclear deterrence capabilities remain credible. It will have several other advantages:

enhance the rapport between the government and the people of Pakistan and between Pakistanis and Kashmiris; create a disincentive for India's subversion within Pakistan; generate the political motivation for the major powers to intercede in evolving a just settlement for Kashmir and other issues that plague Pakistan-India relations.

## The Conventional Military Balance

So far, Pakistan has managed to maintain an effective conventional defence capability against India, due in part to better strategic planning and acquisitions, mainly from China, and lethargy and mistakes in India's defence acquisition and development programmes.

However, India has embarked on a major arms build-up which includes plans to acquire 120 plus advanced strike aircraft, nuclear submarines, AWACs (Airborne Warning and Control systems), antiballistic missiles, satellite and space capabilities. These plans were outlined by India's military chief in December 2009 when presenting India's new military doctrine. He identified five 'thrust areas' for the Indian military build up: (1) the ability to fight a two-front war against Pakistan and China; (2) optimise the capability to counter 'asymmetric and sub-conventional threats'; (3) enhanced capabilities for 'strategic reach' and 'out of area' operations 'from the Persian Gulf to the Malacca Straits'; (4) acquisition of strategic and space-based capabilities, including missile defence; and (5) maintenance of a 'technical edge' over adversaries (Pakistan and China). The Indian Army Chief also propounded the so-called Cold Start strategy to mobilise and strike, within hours, at Pakistan 'under a WMD overhang'.

India, no doubt, foresees that, with its growing financial capacity and access to the most advanced equipment and technologies, not only from Russia but also the US, Israel and other Western countries, it can, over the next several years, acquire the capacity to overwhelm Pakistan in a conventional conflict. If it can simultaneously neutralise Pakistan's nuclear deterrent capability, through political or military means, it would be able, finally, to dictate terms to Pakistan and establish its regional hegemony over South Asia.

There are some defeatists among Pakistan's political and economic elite who believe that India's regional domination, and rise to global power status, is inevitable and Pakistan would do well to accept this emerging reality. Perversely, some of them argue that this would help end the military's preeminent role in Pakistan. But, acceptance of

Indian domination would virtually extinguish the *raison d'être* for the creation of Pakistan as a separate and independent homeland for the Muslims of South Asia, free of Hindu domination. Such surrender clearly would not be acceptable to the vast majority of the people of Pakistan. It would mock the enormous sacrifices of preceding Pakistani generations for freedom. In any event, Indian hegemony is not inevitable and can continue to be resisted by a determined and resilient Pakistani nation so long as it has the conventional and nuclear capability to deter Indian aggression.

It is vital for Pakistan to retain the capacity to resist and repel India by conventional means. In the absence of credible conventional defence, Pakistan will be obliged to rely almost exclusively, and immediately, on its nuclear and strategic weapons, significantly lowering the threshold for nuclear escalation in any future conflict.

Obviously, Pakistan cannot afford to match India's military build-up. Its response will have to be defensive and asymmetrical. The development and acquisition of such defensive capabilities must remain a high priority for Pakistan. It can be achieved only through closer strategic cooperation with China.

Such a defensive military response should be accompanied by vigorous diplomatic efforts to prevent a destabilising and expensive arms race in South Asia. India's defence suppliers should be confronted with the prospect that their quest of quick profits from major arms sales to India will entrench New Delhi's refusal to negotiate a fair solution for Kashmir and other outstanding disputes with Pakistan. It would increase the danger of a conventional conflict and its possible escalation to the nuclear level. It is thus in the best interest of the global community to prevent, not fuel, an Indian arms build-up. In particular, the US, if it wishes to see peace, stability and prosperity in South Asia, must exercise self-restraint in its arms sales to India and persuade other Indian suppliers—Israel, France and Russia—to do so as well. Such a diplomatic campaign is desirable even if its chances of success are not bright. It will, at least, justify Pakistan's response.

## Credible Nuclear Deterrence

It is self-evident that, given India's larger conventional forces, Pakistan will need to rely on its nuclear-strategic capability to credibly deter Indian aggression and military adventurism. This capability was acqui-

297

red through the dedicated efforts of Pakistani leaders, scientists, soldiers and diplomats in the face of the concerted and discriminatory campaign waged by the major powers over the previous decades to prevent Pakistan from acquiring, demonstrating and deploying its nuclear and missile capabilities. Today, unquestionably, Pakistan is a credible nuclear weapon state, with capabilities that match and, in some areas, surpass those of India.

But Pakistan cannot afford to be complacent. The credibility of its nuclear deterrence could be eroded in several ways.

Unlike India, Pakistan continues to be subjected to discriminatory restraints on the transfer of advanced technologies and equipment and on civilian nuclear cooperation on the basis of assertions that it contributed to nuclear proliferation and that its nuclear materials, facilities and weapons are susceptible to capture or attack by 'Islamic terrorists'. There is no legal or political basis for penalising Pakistan for the past. All the nuclear weapon states have been involved in outward or inward nuclear proliferation at some stage, otherwise nuclear weapons could not have been acquired by most of them. Dr A.Q. Khan had many distinguished predecessors. In fact, Pakistan's nuclear programme, which is under tight military control, is less susceptible to capture or attack by 'terrorists' than the less vigorously (civilian) guarded weapons, materials and facilities in India, or the 'loose nukes' and fissile material scattered in various parts of the former Soviet Union.

Pakistan's recent demand for recognition of its nuclear weapon status, while understandable, is irrelevant and unlikely. Not even India has been accorded formal recognition. Informal recognition already exists. The real challenges are different and will arise in the future.

The current restrictions against Pakistan on the transfer of advanced technologies which are now available to India, will enable India, over time, to acquire offensive and defensive capabilities that are more sophisticated than Pakistan's, both in the nuclear and conventional fields, such as space-related weapons, satellites, nuclear powered submarines, anti-ballistic missiles, and information technology. These capabilities could significantly neutralise Pakistan's capacity for conventional and nuclear deterrence.

In the context of nuclear deterrence, there are three aspects that require attention: size and quality of Pakistan and India's nuclear weapons arsenals, and the credibility of Pakistan's nuclear offensive capabilities and the effective protection of these capabilities.

With the access to nuclear fuel imports, opened up by the Indo-US civilian nuclear agreement and the NSG waiver, India can significantly enlarge its nuclear weapons arsenal by fully diverting its indigenous uranium to its weapons programme. While absolute parity is not essential for nuclear deterrence, India's larger arsenal—combined with its future qualitative edge—could erode the credibility of deterrence. Thus, Pakistan will need to acquire sufficient stocks of fissile material, especially plutonium, to build a larger number of warheads required to respond to India's offensive and defensive capabilities. It cannot, therefore, accept the proposal to ban fissile material production, at least for the next several years. Pakistan must also assess whether India has developed thermo-nuclear weapons, e.g. with designs provided by another nuclear weapons state or Israel. India may conduct further nuclear weapons tests to validate its new weapons designs. Obviously, Pakistan will need to respond in kind.

Second, India's acquisition of anti-ballistic missile capabilities, early warning systems and satellite and space systems, can significantly compromise the ability of Pakistan's missiles and strike aircraft to penetrate Indian defences, substantially eroding the credibility of Pakistan's nuclear deterrence. Without the financial and technological ability to match India qualitatively, Pakistan will have to respond by deploying a larger number of nuclear-armed missiles. For this too, continued fissile material production is vital.

Third, advanced Indian capabilities could also enable it to undertake pre-emptive counter force strikes to eliminate Pakistan's offensive systems at the outset of a conflict. Even more ominously, in the event of an Indo-Pakistan conflict, the major Western powers, and Russia, are likely to make all possible efforts to prevent Pakistan from threatening a resort to the nuclear option. If political pressure does not work, they could launch operations to capture or take-out Pakistan's nuclear and strategic capabilities, or resort to military actions or threats thereof, to prevent Pakistan, even when facing defeat, to threaten the use of its nuclear capability. To deter an Indian preemptive strike or major power intervention, Pakistan will need to put its nuclear weapons delivery systems on higher alert, place some missiles in hardened and dispersed silos, and acquire one or more nuclear submarines as a survivable platform for a retaliatory second-strike.

*Strategic Marginalisation*

An even more complex challenge is to reverse Pakistan's progressive and significant political, economic and diplomatic marginalisation in regional and global power relations. Being de-hyphenated from India and equated with Afghanistan are the most visible signs of this decline in global status. This is the result of several years of strategic confusion, internal discord, economic weakness, external dependency as well as the reversals imposed on Pakistan by the War on Terrorism and India's active diplomacy.

The vital ingredients to reverse strategic marginalisation will be: economic revival, political stability, national confidence and self-respect and hard diplomacy. Other countries—friends and foes—must perceive that Pakistan is determined to boldly defend its own national and strategic interests and is prepared to utilise all the leverage it can muster—military, political, economic—to defend and uphold these interests. In inter-state relations, as in physics, every action must produce a reaction. Actions by other states which help or hurt Pakistan's national interests must be reciprocated. Despite its current economic vulnerabilities, Pakistan possesses sufficient leverage to ensure that other powers do not ride rough shod over its national interests. The principal requirement is that Pakistan's leadership develop a coherent vision of the country's strategic interests, goals and priorities and pursue a well-planned campaign to achieve these.

In this context, the most urgent objectives should be to revive and build relations with several key countries: China, Saudi Arabia, Iran and Russia.

China has been Pakistan's principal geo-political partner. While defence cooperation with China remains on track, trade and economic cooperation is constrained by incoherent efforts, corruption, bureaucratic inertia and failure to provide adequate security to Chinese workers in Pakistan. Periodic problems have occurred because of the presence of Uighur rebels among the Islamic militants in the border areas. Meanwhile, despite its strategic alignment with Pakistan, China's trade and economic relationship with India has expanded exponentially. China is being drawn into partnerships with India in several emerging groups to promote specific convergent interests—the G-3 (Russia, China, India), BRIC (Brazil, Russia, India, China), the G-20 (major economies). All of these exclude Pakistan.

It is largely up to Pakistan to leverage its strategic relationship with China to advance its national interests and objectives. China has a strategic interest in supporting Pakistan's resistance to Indian domination. China is now in an even better position then in the past to assist Pakistan, economically and strategically. Instead of preoccupation with the whims of Washington, Islamabad should focus on the opportunities offered by Beijing. A new and comprehensive plan is needed to revive and invigorate the Pakistan-China strategic relationship.

## Saudi Arabia

The nature of Pakistan's relationship with Saudi Arabia has also changed. It is now less equal and reciprocal. On the one hand, Pakistan's dependence on Saudi Arabia has grown for financial support, oil supplies and even domestic political accommodations. Meanwhile, Saudi Arabia has broadened its strategic horizons—seeking to diversify and strengthen its regional and global support base, mainly against Iran's expanding influence and power in the region. Saudi Arabia has been wooed assiduously by India. The value for Riyadh of Pakistan's informal nuclear umbrella appears to have decreased. An erosion of Saudi support on Kashmir and the economy is visible. Pakistan needs to build a more balanced relationship with the Kingdom based on mutual interest and reciprocal support.

## Iran

The relationship with Iran is critical. Its cooperation is vital for peace in a post-American Afghanistan. Its present strategic alignment with India is hugely negative for Pakistan. There are areas of convergent interests which should be strengthened—pacifying Afghanistan and both sides of Balochistan, gas supplies to Pakistan, preventing an Israeli (and/or US) military strike against Iran, ending nuclear discrimination against Muslim countries. Existing problems—suspicion in Tehran that Pakistan serves as a US proxy; past power rivalries in Afghanistan; Iran's role with Shi'a groups in Pakistan—need to be openly addressed on the basis of reciprocity and mutual accommodation.

## Russia

At the end of the Cold War, Pakistan failed to exploit possibilities to build a new and friendlier relationship with Russia, which continues to play an important role in Pakistan's neighbourhood. The major problems with Moscow are: Russian memories of Pakistan's contribution to the Soviet defeat in Afghanistan; opposition to the perceived sympathy within Pakistan for the Afghan Taliban and other Islamic groups, including those active in Central Asia and the Caucusus; and Moscow's close military relationship with India. Each of these problems can be addressed. Pakistan's commitment to combating Islamic militants can now be more readily established, even if pragmatic accommodations may be required with the Afghan Taliban. Pakistan's policy independence from the US global and regional agenda is also likely to become more visible once it asserts its national interests. Moscow's military ties with India should not pose an insuperable obstacle to economic and even some limited military cooperation with Russia once a measure of mutual trust is built.

*A New Strategic Paradigm*

Pakistan's endeavour to reverse its political marginalisation would become much easier if it can change the strategic paradigm regarding South Asia that emerged over the last decade. This change can emanate mainly from a shift in the security parameters and perceptions of the United States and its allies.

Increasingly, the Obama Administration, in its declarations at least, has displayed refreshing honesty and realism in analysing the major security threats and challenges to the US in the 'broader Middle East'. It has rightly concluded that Israeli intransigence on the Palestinian issues threatens US policies towards the entire Muslim world, generates the widespread hostility against it and contributes to Islamic radicalism and terrorism. President Obama has also placed emphasis on developing a relationship of cooperation rather than containment towards China and 'resetting the button' on relations with Russia. More pertinently for Pakistan, he has determined that military solutions are unlikely in Iraq and Afghanistan and that most, if not all, US forces should be withdrawn as soon as possible from these two theatres of war.

This new realism in Washington offers Pakistan an opportunity to reshape the strategic environment in South Asia. To this end, Islamabad should make a concerted effort to convince Washington to endorse the following strategic premises regarding South Asia:

First, while desirous of expanded economic and trade relations with India, the US should no longer be pre-occupied with building India as a counterweight to 'balance' or contain China. This is not only unnecessary but also likely to generate the competitive Chinese reaction which Washington wishes to avoid. Indeed, in the future, India could itself emerge to challenge US interests in the region.

Second, India is not the best partner for the US in combating Islamic extremism or terrorism. This fight has to be fought and won within the Islamic countries and, critically, by Pakistan. India's support may be functionally useful; but with its own continuing record of suppressing the Kashmiris and discriminating against its own Muslims, its credentials to contribute to reversing the rise of extremism in the Muslim world are questionable. What America needs is a 'new deal' with the Muslim world; it is Pakistan, not India, which can help to promote this.

Third, India is not a factor for regional stability, as advertised. On the contrary, it is the principal cause of political turmoil in South Asia. It is not a 'status quo' power seeking stability. India seeks a new role as the regional hegemon. It is India's ambitions and interference which have destabilised all its neighbours—Sri Lanka, Nepal, Bangladesh and parts of Pakistan. It is India which refuses to accept fair solutions to disputes with every one of its neighbours. It is India's suppression of the Kashmiris that keeps alive the threat of terrorism. It is India's quest for dominance which is likely to fuel a conventional and nuclear arms race with Pakistan and retard prospects of rapid development and regional economic cooperation in the region.

The United States—working together with China, Europe and Russia—is in a position to create a security and political paradigm in South Asia that can promote sustainable peace and improve the prospects for prosperity. Although Pakistan and India are unlikely to discard mutual hostility, their competitive relationship can be 'managed' in directions which are constructive and stabilising. Such a new paradigm could be built within the following parameters: one, a balance in conventional forces between Pakistan and India maintained at the lowest possible levels. This would involve acceptance by India and Pakistan of restraints on the development and acquisition of certain destabilising weapons systems, e.g. anti-ballistic missiles, and a progressively less threatening deployment of forces; two, formal global acknowledgement of the nuclear weapons status of both India and

Pakistan and application of a non-discriminatory nuclear regime to both, accompanied by agreements by them to restrain the expansion of their nuclear and strategic capabilities, build mutual transparency and confidence to ensure against deliberate or accidental nuclear use, and commitments by both to respect and contribute to the nuclear non-proliferation regime; three, the commencement of a genuine dialogue on Kashmir and other outstanding issues, such as the water dispute between India and Pakistan—and similar disputes with India's other South Asian neighbours—expressly supported and encouraged by the international community through the UN or another collective forum; four, the creation of a South Asia free trade zone, with adequate measures to protect the economies of the smaller countries and ensure a 'level playing field'; five, following progress on the preceding, the establishment of transit agreements, allowing India access to Central and West Asia, and Pakistan access to Nepal and Bangladesh, with international financial and technical support to build the required infrastructure.

Such a new South Asian paradigm would serve the interests of the peoples of Pakistan, India and other regional states as well as the international community. It could transform South Asia from an area of instability and danger into the latest Asian economic miracle.

Much depends on how well Pakistan and its leaders confront the present and emerging strategic challenges to the country and build clear and bold responses to overcome these challenges.

16

# THE AFGHAN CONUNDRUM

## *Ahmed Rashid*

In Afghanistan: a war going in the wrong direction, a fatally flawed election, reconstruction at a standstill and a growing political vacuum that the Taliban is filling even as some NATO countries contemplate withdrawing their troops.

In nuclear-armed Pakistan: a long-running multidimensional crisis, political and ethnic strife, an unprecedented economic depression, and growing local Islamic extremism which plays host to al Qaeda and the Afghan Taliban; despite these mounting domestic challenges, Pakistan is still vying for influence in Afghanistan in anticipation of an eventual Western withdrawal.

In Washington and European capitals: growing doubts about the viability of the US-led military campaign in Afghanistan, continuing suspicions about the intentions of Pakistan's military, the inability to push ahead with a regional strategy or engage with Taliban moderates, and a lack of a credible government in Kabul.

The disastrous legacy that President Barack Obama inherited in Afghanistan is primarily the fault of former President George W. Bush and his failure to deliver sufficient political, military and economic resources to both the country and the region writ large. But lest we think revisiting the past is an unnecessary detour into mistakes no longer relevant, it is fixing these missteps that are key to preventing a complete radicalisation of the region.

The descent of Afghanistan to the brink of anarchy was solidified in 2009. It was the result of eight years of blunders, miscalculations and wanton neglect. It was the Bush team's lack of a strategic agenda for Afghanistan in three critical areas that led to an inevitable escalation of violence. There were woefully insufficient US troops and no comprehensive strategy that would have integrated US military and civilian activity to help the Afghan government increase capacity, improve governance and speedily build its security forces. Instead the US armed and financed rapacious warlords, many of them members of the former Northern Alliance, which antagonised the Pashtuns and Pakistan.[1] For several years the Pashtun belt was treated as a war zone as US Special Forces hunted for al Qaeda and US aircraft carried out indiscriminate bombing.

Within weeks of winning the victory in Afghanistan, US troops were training for the invasion of Iraq. Afghanistan became a stepchild as the Bush administration preserved US resources, money and troops for the invasion of Iraq. But the insurgency could never have taken off in the way it did without the Taliban having safe sanctuaries in Pakistan. After losing between 12,000 to 15,000 men the remnants of Taliban fighters and its leadership who had escaped capture or death arrived in Pakistan and found a safe haven there. Key figures from the former Taliban regime constituted a new Taliban Shura in Quetta where many lived with their families.

Second, there was no comprehensive diplomatic or regional approach to Afghanistan's six direct neighbours, a necessary precondition if Bush's team was to come to grips with the complex history of these states' interference and battle for influence in Afghanistan. Two of them, Iran and Pakistan, were clandestinely backing the Taliban. Still, Pakistan's military ruler, then-President Pervez Musharraf, remained Bush's hero. And Afghanistan's influential distant neighbours Russia, India and Saudi Arabia were also ignored.

Last, there was no political strategy for state building and improving governance by dealing comprehensively with President Hamid Karzai, government ministers, warlords, tribal elders, governors, the parliament and other players. Setting out clear benchmarks for Karzai and his government to adhere to should have increased Afghan effectiveness, but Bush's regular telephone calls to the president were largely wasted on fireside chats.

This culminated in a critical deterioration. In the spring of 2008, large tracts of Afghanistan in the south and east, and for the first time

306

provinces around Kabul, were under the control of the Taliban, which began to appoint its own governors, courts, police and tax collectors to run these areas. The Taliban's two greatest assets became its safe havens in Afghanistan and Pakistan, particularly the recruiting and logistic bases in Pakistan's tribal areas and Balochistan province, and the uninterrupted flow of money from the likes of donations, drug sales and kidnappings.

More than half of the country's thirty-four provinces turned into no-go areas for Afghan government officials, foreign aid workers and even some NATO forces who were not allowed by their governments to fight the Taliban. For the first time since losing its regime, the Taliban had broken out of its traditional Pashtun ethnic power base in the south, making it easier to deploy guerrillas to the north and the west in 2009.

The Taliban expansion in 2008 was matched by its extraordinary progress in improved military tactics: more sophisticated ambushes, suicide car bombs, mine warfare, multiple urban terrorist attacks, and targeted killings and kidnappings to demoralise the Afghan public and Western civilians. In 2009 the Afghan Taliban had all but become a countrywide movement.

The role Pakistan played from 2001 onwards was critical in shaping the outcome. The Army which had been deployed in and around FATA after 9/11 withdrew many of them in early 2002 because of the build-up of tensions with India, after the storming of the Indian parliament by Kashmiri militants. For much of that year tensions with India preoccupied the army allowing al Qaeda and the Taliban to move around at will in FATA and create new allies among the local Pakistani Pashtun tribes and other extremist groups in Punjab.

Pakistan's security agency continued to give tacit support to the Taliban. This was a result of the Army's fear that by backing the US invasion of Afghanistan, it had inadvertently helped bring to power the former Northern Alliance, which the military detested because of the support it had received from Pakistan's regional rivals India, Iran and Russia. The NA held most of the important ministries in the Karzai government. The Army was also deeply perturbed at the sudden influx of Indians into Kabul. The Bush administration did little to avert the build up of tensions.

Moreover, the US focus on Iraq and lack of commitment to rebuilding Afghanistan convinced the Pakistan military that the US would soon pull out of Afghanistan. Pakistan believed it would be left dealing with an unstable Afghanistan as it was in 1989 after the Soviets and the US withdrew from the region. For President Musharraf it made more sense to hold the Taliban in reserve as a proxy force for Islamabad to influence future events in Afghanistan, while mistrust between Pakistan and India and the US, further convinced the military that its policies were the right ones. In particular the military were deeply riled by the nuclear deal agreed to by the US and India which legitimised India's nuclear weapons program.

Nevertheless, the ISI did move against al Qaeda, cooperating with the CIA to arrest several leading figures who were hiding out in Pakistani cities including Khalid Sheikh Mohammed, the planner of the 9/11 attacks and Abu Zubaydah, a key recruiter for al Qaeda. In retaliation al Qaeda enlisted local Pakistani extremist groups to try and assassinate Musharraf. Two unsuccessful suicide attacks were made on his life in December 2003 but even these attacks failed to convince the military that they now faced a growing threat at home from the newfound alliance of al Qaeda, the Pakistani and Afghan Taliban and extremist groups in Punjab. The Army had sidelined these groups after Musharraf ordered their activities in Indian Kashmir to be wound down and he began a back channel peace process with India. There was no attempt by the Army to demobilise the Punjabi extremist groups.

In April 2007 Lt. Gen. Karl Eikenberry who commanded US and NATO forces became the first US general to publicly tell the US Congress, the White House and NATO that it could not win in Afghanistan without addressing Taliban sanctuaries in Pakistan.[2] Pressure on the Musharraf regime began to mount, just as Musharraf himself entered a volatile political situation at home with rising opposition to his rule.

The stepped-up US pressure led to greater intelligence cooperation between the ISI and the CIA which led to the deaths of several top Taliban commanders including Mullah Akthar Usmani who was killed in December 2006 and Mullah Dadullah in May 2007. Mullah Obaidullah was arrested in March 2007 and later freed by the Pakistanis. These losses led to the elevation of Mullah Abdul Ghani Baradar, a close companion of Mullah Omar, who now presided over the Taliban's military committee in Quetta. Brader became the de facto field commander of the Taliban as Mullah Omar remained largely in hiding.

The Taliban and Pakistan were seeking to outlast the presence of Western forces and to some extent they were succeeding. As long as the Karzai government failed to govern effectively or provide services and jobs to the people while allowing corruption and drug trafficking to take place, the Taliban were winning by default. Despite the growing US and NATO pressure on the military which faced growing threats from its own Pakistani Taliban, the Pakistan Army refused to abandon the Afghan Taliban leadership in Quetta.

In 2008–9 the Taliban moved out of their southern strongholds and expanded into the provinces around Kabul and to Kunduz in the northeast and Herat in the south west. The Taliban were now a national, countrywide movement even though their base remained among the Pashtun tribes. By late 2008 the Taliban controlled some 164 Afghan districts out of a total of 364, compared to control of just thirty in 2003. NATO said the Taliban had shadow governors in thirty-three out of thirty-four provinces.[3]

## *The Obama Administration and Pakistan*

Immediately on assuming office, President Barack Obama conducted several rapid reviews of policy towards Afghanistan and Pakistan and unveiled his first plan on 27 March 2009. The new policy promised major attention to be paid to what was now termed Af-Pak and the region. Obama appointed veteran diplomat Richard Holbrooke as the Special Envoy for Af-Pak, while General David Petraeus took charge of the US Central Command headquarters. A new US Army doctrine now accepted that stabilising war-torn countries and securing the population was more important than chasing insurgents. There was to be much more covert and overt pressure on Pakistan to cooperate on curbing Taliban activities on its soil.

The US poured 21,000 marines into southern Afghanistan in the spring of 2009 including 4000 military trainers to speed up the building of the Afghan army and police. However much of the year was taken up preparing for the presidential elections and ensuring its security. Nevertheless the Afghan government, undermining both the international community and Karzai, who was the overall winner, heavily rigged the August elections.[4] The US was now left without an effective Afghan partner with whom it could work to stabilise the country.

The Taliban took full advantage of this. According to the UN in 2009 there were, on average, 1,200 attacks a month by the Taliban—a 65 per cent increase from the previous year. The Afghan civilian death toll reached 2,412, an increase of 14 per cent. In addition, US and NATO combat deaths rose 76 per cent, from 295 in 2008 to 520 in 2009.[5]

The appointment in 2009 of General Stanley McChrystal as the commander of US and NATO forces, signaled the new counterinsurgency strategy and also the US military's conviction that it could not win the war through military means which would eventually mean holding talks with the Taliban. Karzai's representatives had already met with some Taliban figures in Saudi Arabia in early 2009 and their dialogue continued. By the end of 2009 the US and the West had endorsed a 'reintegration' plan to bring in Taliban soldiers and commanders by offering them an amnesty and a compensation package. However, there was still US reluctance to follow Karzai's lead on offering 'reconciliation' with the Taliban leadership until they had demonstratively broken their links with al Qaeda.

After three months of deliberation on 1 December 2009, Obama revisited his Afghan strategy at a speech at West Point military academy. He promised 30,000 more troops and a civilian surge in rebuilding the country, but he gave the US Army just eighteen months to diminish the Taliban threat because in July 2011 he would start handing over areas of responsibility to the Afghan government and start withdrawing US troops. Talks with the Taliban now took on a greater momentum.

By 2010 the prevailing view in Washington became that many Taliban fighters in the field could eventually be won over, but that the US troop surge that Obama had ordered had to roll them back first, reversing Taliban successes and gaining control over the population centres and major roads. According to the American strategy that emerged that year, the US military had to weaken the Taliban before negotiating with them. So US strategy aimed only to peel away Taliban commanders and fighters and resettle them without making any major political concessions or changes to the Afghan constitution.

There was another way of looking at the crisis that began building up during 2009–2010. Despite their successes, the Taliban reached the height of their power. They did not control major population centres—nor could they, given NATO's military strength and air power. The vast majority of Afghans did not want the return of a Taliban regime despite their anger at the Karzai government and the general international failure to deliver economic progress. This situation offered a critical opportunity to persuade the Taliban that this was the best time to negotiate a settlement, because they were at their strongest since 2001 when US military action ousted them from power.

While Washington remained deeply divided about talking to the Taliban leaders the Taliban began to show the first hint of flexibility. The earliest sign came in a ten-page statement issued in November 2009 for the religious festival of Eid. The Taliban leader Mullah Omar, while urging his fighters to continue the jihad against 'the arrogant [US] enemy', also pledged that a future Taliban regime would bring peace and non-interference from outside forces, and would pose no threat to neighbouring countries—implying that al Qaeda would not be returning to Afghanistan along with the Taliban. Sounding more like a diplomat than an extremist, Omar said, 'The Islamic Emirate of Afghanistan wants to take constructive measures together with all countries for mutual cooperation, economic development and good future on the basis of mutual respect.'

Many considered the Taliban could just sit it out until the Americans started to leave and then lay siege to Kabul. There were several factors that were now forcing the Taliban to talk to Kabul and the US. The Taliban were exhausted after nine years of war and the high toll of casualties they have suffered. They realised they could not govern the country alone even if they regained total power and they wanted to break their dependence on al Qaeda and Pakistan.

As the US military surge got under way in early 2010 in Helmand and Kandahar provinces, there was increasing US pressure for Pakistan to do more to 'capture or kill' Afghan Taliban leaders. The Army, which was now fully convinced that it had to eliminate the Pakistani Taliban in FATA, and deployed 140,000 troops to do so, but it still refused to go after Haqqani's base in North Waziristan.

Pakistan said it was too busy dealing with its own acute problems with the Pakistani Taliban and a growing number of terrorist attacks by various insurgent groups. Its forces were overstretched, it had little money, and it would oblige the Americans only when it was ready to do so. In fact, Pakistan resisted any military offensive against the Afghan Taliban leaders since it long viewed them as potential allies in a post-American Afghanistan, when the US was expected to ditch Pakistan as well.

At the same time the Army remained fearful of a hasty US withdrawal from Afghanistan, which could result in civil war, mayhem in its backyard or the former Northern Alliance retaking power in Kabul.

The Army was also convinced that the US would do nothing to stem India's presence in Afghanistan, which grew at Pakistan's expense.

Pakistan fully supported the idea of talks between the Taliban and Karzai but on its own terms. In February 2010 the ISI and CIA arrested several leading Taliban figures in Pakistan, including the Taliban second-in-command Mullah Abdul Ghani Barader. However the US and other allies were not convinced that the arrests represented a major U-turn by the Pakistani military. Instead it appeared that the Pakistan military and ISI were hardening their terms for a major say in any future dialogue with the Taliban. Barader and other Taliban leaders were at odds with the ISI—wanting to open a dialogue with Kabul but by bypassing the ISI, which is why they used Saudi Arabia as a venue.

The military feared being superseded in any future negotiations in the belief that it had more at stake in Afghanistan than any other neighbouring country. It wanted a major role in any peace talks and aimed to convince the Americans of that. However, the Obama administration is still far from accepting the idea of negotiating with the Taliban leadership. US politicians and officials insisted that the Taliban had to be significantly diminished through military offensives over the coming year before any such talks could take place, although the US military believed that talks should start sooner. All US officials agreed that the Taliban has to first make a decisive break from their operational alliance with al Qaeda.

## Pakistan's Strategic Interests: The Weight of History

What were Pakistan's strategic interests in Afghanistan that played such a determining role in Islamabad's policy towards Afghanistan for three decades? How meaningful are those strategic interests today?

The relationship between the two countries has been a roller coaster ride but never reached the pitch of antagonism that relations with India did. In 1947 Afghanistan had refused to accept the border between the two countries and was the only nation to oppose Pakistan's entry into the United Nations. Diplomatic relations were severed twice in 1955 and 1962 following border skirmishes as Kabul laid claim to large parts of the North West Frontier (NWFP) and Balochistan provinces, which Kabul said the British had illegally seized and later incorporated into present day Pakistan.

Intermittently between 1947 and the late 1980s Kabul supported and patronised left wing Pashtun nationalist and autonomist parties in the NWFP and Balochistan who aspired to creating a Kabul-centred 'Greater Pashtunistan'. In turn, in the 1970s Pakistan sponsored Afghan Islamists who belonged to the Ikhwan and worked for an Islamic revolution in Afghanistan. On the border both countries maintained a balance of power tensions by paying off Pashtun tribes to retain their loyalties.

At the same time, with Afghanistan landlocked and totally dependent on Karachi for its port, trade and people-to-people relations remained excellent. For the Pashtun tribes there was no apparent border and they criss-crossed the region freely. Afghanistan remained neutral in Pakistan's frequent wars and skirmishes with India—a great boon to the military—while the Afghan royal family's intermarriages with Pakistan's feudal elite brought the ruling classes together.

However, the end of the monarchy in 1973 and the seizure of power by the King Zahir Shah's cousin Mohammed Daud saw the revival of the Pashtunistan issue. President Daud, who was allied to the Soviet Union, gave sanctuary to leftist Pashtun and Baloch rebels who in the 1970s were in conflict with Prime Minister Zulfiqar Ali Bhutto. The Afghan communists who seized power from Daud in 1978 pursued the same policies.

Thus on the eve of the Soviet invasion the Pakistan military, which itself had seized power, was deeply concerned about threats from Afghanistan. It is therefore not surprising that President Zia was to articulate a major Pakistani strategic interest in the future of Afghanistan, when it came to eliciting aid from the Reagan administration in 1981. Zia was determined that Kabul-backed irredentist movements between Pakistan's Baloch and Pashtun should never again threaten Pakistan. Pakistan needed a friendly government in Afghanistan that would recognise the Durand Line, cease laying claim to Pakistani territory and stop providing sanctuary to Pakistani dissidents.

One way to ensure this was to back Islamists within the Afghan and Pakistani Pashtuns. The Bhutto government had already pursued this end—training leading members of the Afghan Ikhwan. That the Afghans articulated their struggle against the Soviet occupation as a jihad rather than a modern war of national liberation gave further scope to Zia's ambitions. Both Pakistan and the US were to stretch the jihadi factor further when they turned the Afghan insurgency into a global jihad inviting Muslim fighters from dozens of countries to Peshawar and expanding the war into Soviet Central Asia.

The *Mujahideen* had no ethnic agenda to divide countries or claim territory because they viewed ethnicity as anathema and the entire Muslim world as a single *ummah*. For the Army the same *mujahideen* could be later used to fight Pakistan's overt war in Indian Kashmir. Zia envisaged a wide zone of influence for Pakistan stretching into Soviet Central Asia as an outcome of the anti-Soviet war. Pakistani Pashtuns were encouraged to take part in the Afghan jihad laying the seeds for the future Pakistani Taliban.

Zia also promoted the idea of Afghanistan offering 'strategic depth' to Pakistan—a military doctrine conceived as a counter to an Indian attack with the Pakistan Army having little geographical depth to wage a counter attack from. Elements of the Pakistan Army could retreat or regroup in Afghanistan where Pakistani aircraft and even some of its nuclear arsenal and rockets could be kept out of harms way. (The latter was seriously considered by military officers after the Taliban captured Kabul.)

However, the theory of strategic depth was so thoroughly rubbished in the 1980s by critics—including retired generals—that it disappeared, until it was resurrected in 2009 by the present Army Chief General Ashfaq Kayani, who described it not as military doctrine but as political justification to show Pakistan's need for a friendly government in Kabul. However with India and Pakistan now nuclear powers such conventional warfare talk of territory, geography and safe havens had become even more meaningless. A conventional war that led to Pakistan's defeat would almost certainly lead to the use of nuclear weapons.

Pakistan's second strategic claim since the Soviet occupation has been the desire to influence and control the Afghan Pashtuns who should rule Afghanistan but not eye Pakistan's Pashtun territories. In any future peace settlement this will remain a key demand of the Pakistan military—to ensure that the governors and police chiefs in the southern and eastern provinces are not openly anti-Pakistan. Never again, however, will Pakistan enjoy the kind of acquiescence it received from the Taliban regime in the 1990s.

All these advantages were seemingly lost when US pressure forced President Musharraf to help the West oust the Taliban after 9/11. Yet Pakistan was to retain its options, first by winning US support in helping defeat the Taliban and then giving Taliban leaders an escape hatch and sanctuary in Pakistan. The subsequent US failure to develop Afghanistan or send in sufficient troops to secure the country while it prepared for the war in Iraq made the US turn a blind eye to Musharraf's double game. As long as the Army continued to help detain al Qaeda militants on its soil, the Americans asked no questions about the Afghan Taliban until 2007.

The Pakistani Army's desire to have some control over future events in Afghanistan was also due to its strategic aim of avoiding encirclement by India; but it was also a result of the setbacks it had received since 2001. The military is still smarting from former President Bush's decisions to allow the anti-Pakistan Northern Alliance to take Kabul in 2001, to ignore Islamabad's later requests for consultations on US strategy in Afghanistan, and to treat all Afghan Pashtuns as potential Taliban. This helped radicalise Pakistan's own Pashtun population, which is more than twice the size of Afghanistan's. (There are twelve million Pashtuns in Afghanistan and twenty-seven million in Pakistan.)

The third strategic interest first outlined by Zia was to never allow India a foothold in Afghanistan. India had remained a staunch ally of the Afghan communist regime and the Soviets, but their diplomatic presence in Kabul ended once the *mujahideen* and later the Taliban took over. Throughout the 1990s there was no Indian presence in Afghanistan and the army had considered this a victory. Pakistani and Kashmiri militants were able to train and fight in Afghanistan free of international harassment. Many of these same fighters were to end up as the Punjabi Taliban in 2008, willing to take on their benefactors—the Army—in a bloody war for dominance.

The India factor has now returned with vengeance for the Pakistan Army. When India did return to Afghanistan after 9/11 it found its non-Pashtun allies within the government as it had aided the Northern Alliance in the civil war. It also found many allies among secular and educated Pashtuns who rejected the Taliban and were sick of ISI manipulation. India swiftly developed an extremely well-conceived aid program investing approximately US$1.2 billion that spread Indian projects and largesse across all ethnic groups, built key infrastructure projects, set up the transport system in Kabul and contributed to important social programs like health. Unlike Western aid agencies, 80 per cent of Indian money was actually spent on projects as Indian NGOs had low expenditures.

Pakistan's military believes that India is rapidly expanding its influence across the very same region—Afghanistan and Central Asia—that Zia had first hoped to do so, thereby attempting to encircle Pakistan with a ring of hostile states. Pakistan believes India is also financing and training the renewed Baloch insurgency as several key Baloch leaders now live in exile in Kabul. Pakistan accuses Indian intelligence or RAW of working with Afghanistan's spy agency the National Directorate for Security (NDS) to help the Baloch insurgents.

Pakistan has declined to offer any concrete evidence about any of these claims either to the public or to the Americans. The ISI has also spread enormous amounts of patently exaggerated propaganda about the extent of the Indian presence, such as claiming that there are a dozen or more Indian consulates in Afghanistan, in order to win over Pakistani public opinion. Even more damaging to relations since 2006 have been the repeated attacks on the Indian embassy, its consulates and road-building projects by Taliban linked to the Jalaluddin Haqqani group, which has a close working relationship with the ISI. The devastating attack on Mumbai in 2008 by Pakistan's Lashkar-e-Taiba, which led to nearly 170 people being killed including many foreigners, was also blamed by India on the ISI, although it is unlikely to have been the case. For more than a year India ceased all dialogue with Pakistan and insists that LeT has to be eliminated before meaningful talks can go ahead.

Clearly, a key element of Pakistan's future demands will be based on eliminating India's presence in Afghanistan—a maximalist demand which would be more likely watered down to a lesser demand of asking for a reduction of India's aid and diplomatic presence on the Pakistan border and the reduction or even closing down of Indian consulates in Jalalabad and Kandahar. However, vital for this is an Indo-Pak dialogue on their mutual interests and competition in Afghanistan and how these can be contained and made more transparent to the other side.

India poses a real dilemma for the Pakistan Army as it battles the Pakistani Taliban on its own soil. The Army has refused to go up against the key forces that it controls or once controlled that are visibly anti-India—the forces of Haqqani in North Waziristan and the Punjab-based groups such as LeT. The Army and the government remain in deliberate denial that there is a terrorist threat in Punjab despite dozens of bomb blasts in the province. The reason is that groups like LeT are still maintained by the military as the first line of defence against any Indian attack, as potential fifth columnists who can sow havoc inside India at a time of war and who are loyal to the Army's *raison d'être* to confront India.

## Conclusion

Pakistan has legitimate security interests in Afghanistan, but so do other immediate neighbours like Iran, the Central Asian states and near neighbours like India, China and the Arab Gulf states. All of them would likely step up their interference in Afghanistan if they see Pakistan dominating the peace talks. Moreover, too overt a Pakistani role is likely to be rejected by Karzai, the Northern Alliance and Afghan civil society groups and even by many Taliban who would like to end their dependence on Pakistan. The Pakistan military which continues to run the country's Afghan policy despite an elected civilian government now faces its biggest test—whether it can help bring an end to the war in Afghanistan, gain its minimum strategic interests and not turn the entire region into a cauldron of competition as existed in the 1990s. At the same time, the military has to comprehensively defeat the Pakistani Taliban and their extremist offshoots that continue to wreak havoc in cities across the country.

17

# THE INDIA FACTOR

*Dr Syed Rifaat Hussain*

Can Pakistan and India move away from their enduring rivalry and make peace? Can the shadow of the November 2008 Mumbai terrorist attacks be removed by sustained diplomatic engagement between the two countries?

This chapter seeks to answer these questions by reviewing the record of diplomatic efforts and identifying the obstacles in the path of progress while underscoring the importance of a peace process whose absence can provide determined spoilers on both sides ample opportunity to push the nuclear-armed adversaries toward deadly confrontation.

## Is a Peace Process in Place?

A peace process can be defined as concerted efforts by parties in dispute to seek a resolution of their conflict through dialogue and negotiations. The initiation of a peace process normally follows incidents of armed conflict between the parties in dispute. Usually it takes place with the support of interested third parties. The onset of the peace process, while reducing escalatory pressures for violence, does not guarantee that peace will necessarily follow. In fact, the failure of the peace process to yield positive results may enhance possibilities for the outbreak of violent conflict.

Table 1: Important Indo-Pak agreements (1948–2009)

| Number | Date and Place | Issues | Status | Comments |
|---|---|---|---|---|
| 1. | 27 July 1949 Karachi | Ceasefire Line in Jammu and Kashmir | Operational | Gave rise to Siachin dispute |
| 2. | 8 April 1950 | Minority Rights | Operational | Communal harmony |
| 3. | 22 January 1957 New Delhi | Trade and Commerce | Contested | Spawned Most favoured nation controversy |
| 4. | 9 September Karachi | Water Rights (Indus Water Basin) | Operational | Potential for conflict |
| 5. | January 1966 Tashkent | Peace Making after 1965 War | Overtaken by events | Third Party Mediation |
| 6. | 2 July 1972 Simla | Peace and Security after 1971 War | Contested | Framework for normalisation |
| 7. | 27 August 1973 New Delhi | Prisoners of War | Implemented | Trust Building |
| 8. | 14 April 1978 New Delhi | Design of the Salal Hydro electric plan | Contested | Source of discord |
| 9. | 31 December 1988 Islamabad | Cultural Cooperation | Lapsed | Important for people-to-people contacts |
| 10. | 31 December 1988 Islamabad | Prohibition of attack against nuclear installations and facilities | Operational | Vital Nuclear CBM, Trust Building |

| | | | | |
|---|---|---|---|---|
| 11. | 6 April 1991 New Delhi | Advance notice on military exercises and troop movement | Operational | Important military CBM |
| 12. | 17 August 1992 New Delhi | Prevention of space violations and Over flight rights | Operational | Important CBM |
| 13. | 23 June 1997 Islamabad | Joint Working Groups for Composite Dialogue | Sidelined in 2010 after several interruptions | Framework for dialogue process |
| 14. | 20 February 1999 Lahore | Peace and Security (Lahore Declaration, Joint Statement and MoU nuclear CBMs) | Operational | Core Principles of conduct |
| 15. | 6 January 2004 Islamabad Joint Statement | Cross-Border Terrorism, Dialogue Process | Operational | Reassurance, Reciprocity |
| 16. | 20 June 2004 Joint Statement | Nuclear CBMs. The statement described nuclear capabilities of each other as a 'factor for stability' and called for regular meeting 'among all the nuclear powers to discuss issues of common concern'. | Operational | Joint commitment to work towards strategic stability |
| 17. | February 16–18, 2006 Islamabad | Composite Dialogue Schedule | Operational | Vital for Substantive Dialogue |

| | | | |
|---|---|---|---|
| 18. | 17 September 2006 Havana Joint Statement | Resumption of Composite Dialogue Process, Cross-border terrorism and Kashmir | Operational | Vital for ongoing dialogue |
| 19. | 16 July 2009 Sharm el-Sheikh Joint Statement | Both sides recognised Dialogue as the only way forward and declared terrorism as the common enemy. Action on terrorism should not be linked to the Composite Dialogue process and these should not be bracketed. | Operational | Provided impetus for resumption of stalled peace process |

Source: Compiled by the author.

The existence of an India-Pakistan peace process is evidenced by several factors. First, both countries have regularly engaged in bilateral talks to resolve differences on a wide range of issues: border demarcation, boundary adjustment, water distribution, trade and commerce issues, protection of minorities, Kashmir, conventional and nuclear confidence building measures (CBMs). Since 1997 all these issues have been discussed as part of the composite dialogue involving eight issues: Peace and Security including CBMs; Jammu and Kashmir; Siachin; Sir Creek; Tulbul, Wullar, Baghlihar and Kishenganga water projects; terrorism and drug trafficking; economic and commercial cooperation; promotion of friendly exchanges in various fields. Second, India-Pakistan bilateral talks have yielded a large number of agreements that have a fairly good compliance record by each country (see Table 1).

Three, despite lack of agreement on Kashmir, both countries have since the mid-1990s made conscious efforts to push the peace process forward. Four, since their overt nuclearisation in May 1998, the world community has repeatedly called upon the two nations not only to exercise restraint but also to forego use and the threat of the use of force in settling differences. All the four nuclear crises between India and Pakistan—1986–87 Brasstacks, the 1990 Kashmir crisis, the 1999 Kargil conflict, and the 'compound crisis' of summer 2002—were defused with the help of Washington as a third party.

*Roadblocks to Peace*

At least four factors can be identified as the sources of the enduring enmity between Islamabad and New Delhi. First, there is a clash of opposing ideologies in the conflict between the diametrically opposed philosophical systems of Islam and Hinduism. As pointed out by S.M. Burke, 'Centuries of dedication to such diametrically opposed systems as Islam and Hinduism could not but nurture an utterly different outlook on the outside world among their respective followers.'[1]

The second source of tension arises from Pakistan's fear of India's sheer size and the pair's strategic and economic asymmetry. As noted by Howard Wriggins:

However unjustified Indian leaders may have thought it, Pakistan's overriding concern vis-à-vis India' is the 'fear of India's size, the size of its army... and fear compounded out of not infrequent public statements by prominent Indians regarding the tragedy of partition and reiterating the inherent unity of the subcontinent.[2]

The third factor contributing to a state of perpetual hostility is the legacy of the trauma of partition. This has carried over in the mindsets of those who took over the administration of the two countries. Leo Rose and Richard Sisson comment: 'Most of the political and social concepts that dominated the ideology and psychology of the narrow elites that controlled these two movements survived into the independence period and have not disappeared.'[3]

Last, but not least, is the unresolved issue of Kashmir. Besides being the fundamental cause of the first two wars between India and Pakistan, and a trigger for the May–July 1999 conflict in Kargil, Kashmir is now universally recognised as a nuclear flash point and a serious international security issue. Between 2004 and 2007, New Delhi and Islamabad used back channel links to develop a shared understanding in the form of a 'non-paper' for a final resolution of the dispute.[4] Media reports indicated that both sides had reached a broad agreement on five elements of the Kashmir settlement. The agreed points were:

(1) No change in the territorial layout of Kashmir currently divided into Pakistani and Indian areas.
(2) The creation of a 'softer border' across Line of Control (LoC).
(3) Greater autonomy and self-governance within both Indian and Pakistani controlled parts of the state.
(4) A cross-LoC consultative mechanism.
(5) The demilitarisation of Kashmir at a pace determined by the decline in cross border terrorism.'[5]

This understanding failed to materialise due to the fall of the Musharraf regime in 2008.

Because of the divisive impact of these factors relating to ideology, the violent legacy of partition, images of the enemy, and the unresolved issue of Kashmir, India and Pakistan have been constrained to pursue their security policies within the framework of unilateral security, where intended gains for one side are supposed to result in an equivalent loss for the other. But this unilateralist way of thinking about security has become untenable in the wake of South Asia's passage to overt nuclearisation in May 1998.

*Nuclearisation and Impact of 9/11*

On 11 and 13 May 1998, India conducted five nuclear tests codenamed 'Shakti' and proclaimed it to be a nuclear weapon state.[6] The

Indian nuclear tests created a great sense of alarm in Pakistan. Pakistan's Foreign Minister Gohar Ayub Khan described them as a 'death blow to the global efforts at nuclear non-proliferation' and called upon the international community to issue a strong condemnation.[7] Reacting to international appeals that Islamabad should exercise restraint in the face of India's provocative action, Prime Minister Nawaz Sharif stated that 'as being a sovereign state Pakistan has every right to undertake measures for national defence and security.'[8] Belligerent statements by Indian leaders which warned Islamabad to roll back its anti-India policy and vacate Azad Kashmir not only aggravated Pakistani threat perceptions but also convinced Islamabad that the Shakti tests threatened to tilt the strategic balance in India's favour.[9]

Characterising the Indian action as a qualitative change in its security environment, Islamabad brushed aside international urgings not to conduct a rival nuclear test. In a 13 May statement Foreign Minister Gohar Ayub Khan categorically stated, 'Indian actions pose an immediate and grave threat to Pakistan's security and these will not go unanswered.' To review Pakistan's security options Prime Minister Nawaz Sharif convened a meeting of the Defence Committee of the Cabinet. Joining strident calls for an immediate tit-for-tat response by the small but powerful pro-bomb lobby in Pakistan, Leader of Opposition, Benazir Bhutto called on the government to 'immediately respond to the Indian test.' Two weeks later, on 28 and 30 May, Pakistan conducted five nuclear tests in the Chagai Hill range in Balochistan.

In the wake of the South Asian nuclear tests, the relationship between military and political stability has become absolutely critical. In fact, military stability will not be achieved without political stability. As nuclear-armed states, India and Pakistan do enjoy 'security' in the basic sense of the word, that is, security stemming from a lack of incentives on either side to resort to war as a rational choice. Notwithstanding some specific imbalances that go against Pakistan in the overall force relationship between the two sides, a military balance that discourages any direct military confrontation does exist today.[10] As pointed out by E. Sridharan:

... explicit nuclearisation with a demonstrated missile capability has assured Pakistan's security in a way that reduces the sensitivity to relative gains in the military sphere ... Pakistan is more secure vis-à-vis a possible Indian military threat than ever before ... Therefore, it has less to fear and much to gain from greater economic engagement with India.[11]

In response to Pakistani nuclear tests President Clinton imposed Congressionally mandated sanctions under which all American bilateral and multilateral economic assistance to Pakistan was cut off. Because of its economic vulnerability, the Pakistani economy was severely hit by the withdrawal of international financing and by the indirect effects of this withdrawal on other capital inflows to Pakistan.

As part of its three-pronged strategy of 'damage control' which aimed at preventing any escalation of a nuclear and missile race between India and Pakistan, minimising damage to the non-proliferation regime and promoting dialogue between India and Pakistan, the US called upon New Delhi and Islamabad to comply with the benchmarks set out by the Security Council in its resolution 1172 passed on 6 June, 1998. These included such steps as: signing and ratifying the CTBT; halting all further production of weapon-usable fissile material and joining the negotiations on a fissile material treaty at the Conference on Disarmament in Geneva; limiting development and deployment of delivery vehicles for weapons of mass destruction and resuming bilateral dialogue on resolving long-standing tensions and disputes.

India-Pakistan ties suffered a marked decline in the wake of their rival nuclear tests. Following press reports[12] that Indian war planes had violated Pakistani airspace on 1 August 1998 Kashmir Affairs Minister, Lt. Gen. (Retd) Abdul Majeed Malik told a news conference that Pakistan was ready to 'give a befitting reply to any armed conflict imposed on it by India.'[13] A day later, Prime Minister Sharif accused India of 'taking South Asia to the brink of war'[14] and called upon the international community to take notice of Indian aggression. Responding to these statements, Indian Prime Minister Atal Bihari Vajpayee warned Islamabad 'India would use a firm hand to respond to any attack on its border.' He expressed the resolve of his government to 'fully back' the efforts of the Indian Army to 'repulse the nefarious designs of Pakistan.'[15]

The escalation in verbal hostility was coupled with intensive firing by both sides along the volatile Line of Control (LoC) in Kashmir. This generated considerable international concern. On 3 August 1998 Washington reportedly sent 'urgent messages' to Islamabad and New Delhi asking them to 'refrain from proactive actions and rhetoric', to 'resume the senior level dialogue.'[16]

Motivated partly by their shared interest to avoid the risks of inadvertent escalation and partly by the need to respond to international pressure, both New Delhi and Islamabad expressed their willingness to resume the stalled talks. In October 1998 Foreign Secretary level talks were resumed. These paved the way for a summit meeting between the Prime Ministers which was held in Lahore on 20–21 February 1999.

The Vajpayee-Sharif summit resulted in three agreements: a joint statement, the Lahore Declaration and the Memorandum of Under-standing. The MoU dealt with nuclear issues and committed both sides to adopt a wide-range of confidence-building measures aimed at avoid-ance and prevention of conflict. But hopes of better India-Pakistan relations generated by the Lahore Summit were dashed by the May–July 1999 Kargil crisis, which brought the two countries to the brink of war. Angered by Pakistan's military incursion, which endangered its vital supply routes to Leh and the Siachin, New Delhi threatened to impose a war on Pakistan in order to restore the status quo. India also effectively mobilised world opinion against Pakistan.

Caving in to mounting international pressure for withdrawal, Prime Minister Nawaz Sharif made a dash to Washington on 4 July and signed a joint statement with President Clinton, which called for the restoration of the 'sanctity' of Line of Control in accordance with the Simla Agreement. Riding the wave of world sympathy unleashed by the Kargil episode, India adopted an uncompromising attitude toward Pakistan. In August 1999 India shot-down a Pakistan navy aircraft 'Atlantique', killing all nineteen people on board after the ill-fated plane went astray during a training flight in Balochistan. Shunning Pakistani and international calls for the resumption of India-Pakistan 'dialogue', New Delhi declared that it will not talk to Islamabad unless the latter committed itself to severing links with Kashmiri militants and stop its alleged support for 'cross-border terrorism' in Indian-held Kashmir. Pakistan's retreat from democracy after the 12 October 1999 military coup in Pakistan intensified Islamabad's regional and international iso-lation, as strong world disapproval followed this development.

In America the return of the Republicans led by George W. Bush to power in 2001 intensified Clinton's opening to India.[17] Taking a 'less absolutist' view of New Delhi's nuclear aspirations, the Republican Party platform described India as 'one of the great democracies of the twenty-first century' and raised expectations that the Bush Administra-tion would be 'more sensitive to Indian security concerns, and more willing to accommodate India's own aspirations to be a great power.'[18]

The terrorist attacks of 11 September 2001 offered New Delhi a golden opportunity to further deepen its security links with Washington. New Delhi promptly endorsed Bush's declaration of a 'War on Terrorism' and pledged full cooperation. In doing so 'New Delhi hoped to turn the war on terrorism to its advantage as a lever to end Pakistan's decade-long covert support for the anti-India insurgency in disputed Kashmir.'[19]

Relations between India and Pakistan reached their lowest ebb after the 13 December 2001 terrorist attack on India's parliament, in which over a dozen people, including five security guards, were killed. Despite Islamabad's swift and strong condemnation of the attack, Prime Minister Vajpayee accused Islamabad of supporting Kashmir militant groups Lashkar-e-Taiba (LeT) and Jaish-e-Mohammed (JeM), whom he blamed for carrying out the attack. Islamabad denied the allegations and accused New Delhi of 'stage-managing' the attack to discredit the Kashmiri struggle for freedom, and also to give a bad name to Pakistan as a state supporting terrorism.

New Delhi initiated a full-scale military mobilisation, and in May 2002, war between India and Pakistan seemed a distinct possibility. Faced with the nightmare scenario of an India-Pakistan shooting war turning into a nuclear conflagration—with devastating consequences for the region and the American anti-terror campaign against al Qaeda—Washington exerted intense diplomatic pressure on New Delhi and Islamabad, asking them to pull back from the precipice.

Amid warlike noises from New Delhi President Musharraf announced a sweeping reform agenda in his address to the nation on 12 January 2002. Condemning radical Islamists who had unequivocally set up a 'state within a state',[20] he declared his determination to rid Pakistani society of their pernicious influence. He announced a ban on all sectarian activity, and set up speedy trial courts to punish terrorists. Most significantly, he banned six extremist Islamic groups involved in sectarian campaigns in the country, including LeT and JeM, both of which had already been designated as terrorist groups by the US State Department.

Signaling a qualitative shift in Pakistan's involvement in militancy in Kashmir, President Musharraf said, 'No organisation will be able to carry out terrorism [under] the pretext of Kashmir.'[21] Two days before President Musharraf's landmark speech, Islamabad announced the setting up of National Kashmir Committee, under the presidency of moderate Sardar Muhammed Abdul Qayyum Khan, a former President of Azad Kashmir. The purpose of this committee was to continue the struggle for the rights of the Kashmiri people by new means. Islamabad's sweeping measures to curb Islamic militancy in Pakistan and to end armed support to the insurgents in Kashmir, however, failed to dissipate the clouds of war. Fearing that war with India was imminent, Pakistan withdrew more than 50,000 troops it had deployed along its border with Afghanistan to prevent al Qaeda and Taliban forces from entering its territory. Islamabad also informed Washington that in the event of an India-Pakistan war, it would have to reclaim some of the airfields that it had allowed the United States to use for its operations in Afghanistan.

To prevent a looming India-Pakistan war from playing havoc with its anti-terror campaign Washington launched a frantic diplomatic campaign to defuse the India-Pakistan crisis. Following the visit of Deputy Secretary of State Richard Armitage to New Delhi and Islamabad in June 2002, both countries agreed to step back.

In response to President Musharraf's pledge that he would 'permanently'[22] end his country's support for armed militancy in Indian-held Kashmir, New Delhi lifted some of the diplomatic and economic curbs imposed on Islamabad in the wake of the December 2001 attack on the Indian parliament. Musharraf's decision to limit Islamabad's strategic support for the militancy in Kashmir, although greeted with howls of 'sell out' by Islamic hard-liners in the country, evoked a positive response from India in May 2003. Prime Minister Vajpayee told the Indian parliament on 2 May 2003 that he was willing to make his 'third and final' effort at peace by agreeing to hold 'decisive talks'[23] with Pakistan.

Two weeks earlier, during a visit to Kashmir, he had said that he wanted to extend a 'hand of friendship'[24] to Pakistan. Taking advantage of this offer, Pakistan's Prime Minister Mir Zafarullah Khan Jamali called Mr Vajpayee on 28 April 2003. This broke the ice. Following their telephonic conversation both sides announced the return of diplomats to each other's capitals, and agreed to re-establish communication and sporting links. Under constant prodding from the world community the feuding neighbours slowly but steadily began to move towards rapprochement.

In a remarkable reversal of Islamabad's verbal strategy on Kashmir, President Musharraf publicly stated on 17 December 2003 that even though 'we are for United Nations Security resolutions... now we have left that aside.'[25] He pledged in a joint statement issued in Islamabad following his meeting with Prime Minister Vajpayee, on 6 January

2004 that he would 'not permit any territory under Pakistan's control to be used to support terrorism in any manner.'[26] This statement was meant to mollify New Delhi's concerns relating to the issue of alleged 'cross-border' infiltration from Pakistan.

By dropping its longstanding demand for a UN-mandated plebiscite over divided Kashmir, and by assuring New Delhi that Islamabad would not encourage violent activity in Indian-held Kashmir, President Musharraf created much-needed political space for New Delhi to substantively engage with Islamabad to find a workable solution to the festering Kashmir dispute. Following the 6 January meeting between Musharraf and Vajpayee, the first round of official talks between the two countries was held in Islamabad from 16–18 February. The joint statement issued in Islamabad on 18 February announced that both sides had agreed to resume their stalled composite dialogue.[27] It also mentioned that the foreign ministers of both countries would meet in August 2004 to review the overall progress of the composite dialogue.[28] Meanwhile the surprise victory of the Congress Party, led by Sonia Gandhi, in the May 2004 Indian national elections further raised hopes of a permanent peace between India and Pakistan.

*Composite Dialogue*

India and Pakistan resumed their stalled peace process in February 2004. This has yielded tangible but varying degrees of progress on all eight issues that have been on the agenda. This progress is summarised in Table 2.

Indian Prime Minister Manmohan Singh put forth the Five Working Groups proposal at the Second Jammu and Kashmir Round Table in Srinagar on 25 May 2006. The proposal sought to involve local Kashmiris in the following areas:

1. Confidence-building measures across segments of society in the State
2. Strengthening relations across the Line of Control
3. Economic Development
4. Ensuring Good Governance
5. Strengthening relations between the State and the Centre

The positive steps jointly taken by India and Pakistan to improve their relations through the mechanism of the composite dialogue include the following:

- The November 2003 ceasefire along the LoC, which terminated armed hostilities after thirteen years, continues to hold. Despite occasional outbreaks of violence along LoC, the ceasefire continues to hold.
- The conclusion of several nuclear confidence-building measures (CBMs), including an agreement to establish a permanent hotline between their foreign secretaries and the decision to conclude an agreement with technical parameters on pre-notification of missile flight tests.
- The initiation of discussions and conclusion of agreements on reducing the risks of nuclear accidents and the unauthorised use of nuclear weapons as well as on preventing incidents at sea.
- Resumption of a bus line between Srinagar, the capital of Jammu and Kashmir (J&K), and Muzaffarabad, the capital of Azad Jammu and Kashmir (AJK) in April 2005.
- Opening of LoC at five points after the October 2005 earthquake in AJK to facilitate the provision of humanitarian assistance as well as meetings between divided families.
- Launching a truck service on the Srinagar-Muzaffarabad route in May 2006.
- Launching of the second cross-Kashmir bus service, linking Poonch in J&K with Rawalakot in AJK in May 2006.
- Reopening of additional rail and road links across the international border between the two countries. These include: a bus service linking Sikhism's holiest city, Amritsar in India, with Nankana Sahib, the birthplace in Pakistan of Sikhism's founder. A railway link between Munnabao in Rajasthan and Khokhrapar in Sindh from January 2006.
- Resumption of bilateral trade through Wahgah at the international border.
- Agreement to restart shipping routes.
- Reactivation of the Joint Economic Commission and Joint Business Councils to promote commercial activity between the two sides.
- Setting up of the Joint Working Group to explore prospects for Iran-Pakistan-India gas pipeline.
- Creation of an India-Pakistan anti-terrorism institutional mechanism to identify and implement counter-terrorism initiatives and investigations.

Table 2: India-Pakistan composite dialogue (June 2004–2008)

| Agenda Item | Status of Negotiations | Progress Achieved | Sticking Points | Prospects | Indian Views | Pakistani Views |
|---|---|---|---|---|---|---|
| 1. Peace and Security including CBMS | Four round held but stalled after Mumbai attacks | Agreements on secure hotline, missile test notification; Consultations on security concepts and nuclear doctrines; Agreement to implement the 1991 Agreement on Air Space Violations; hold monthly Flag meetings between local commanders; speedy return of inadvertent Line crossers; periodic review of existing CBMS<br><br>April 2006 Agreement on pre-notification of flight testing of Ballistic Missiles and the operationalisation of the hotline between the two foreign secretaries to prevent misunderstanding and reduce risks relevant to nuclear issues; February 2007 Agreement on reducing the risks from nuclear accidents | Permanent relocation of strike formations in forward positions. No nuclear first use versus non use of force | Good | Current moves must pave the way for a Treaty of Peace, Security and Friendship between the two countries | Without resolving the core issue of Kashmir, peace between India and Pakistan would remain elusive |

| 2. Jammu and Kashmir | Four rounds held including active back channels links. Stalled after Mumbai attacks | Observance of ceasefire along LoC since November 2003. No visible progress towards resolution of Kashmir problem. Floating of new ideas and proposals—self-governance, demilitarisation and joint management. New Delhi-Srinagar roundtable discussions. Five Working groups proposal* to seek Kashmiri support for Indian policies in Kashmir. Back channel discussions yielded a blueprint for the resolution of Kashmir conflict. It had five key elements: no changes in territorial layout of Kashmir; creation of soft-borders across LoC; greater autonomy and self-governance within both Indian and Pakistani controlled parts of the state; across LoC consultative mechanism; the demilitarisation of Kashmir at a pace determined by the decline in cross-border terrorism | Adherence to Stated Indian and Pakistani positions. 'No redrawing of borders.' 'Territorial status quo unacceptable to Pakistan' | Good if talks continue and their ambit is expanded to include Kashmiris from both sides of the divide | Termination of cross-border infiltration from Pakistan as a pre-requisite for progress on Kashmir | Indian unwillingness to embrace Pak proposals regarding demilitarisation zones, self-governance and joint management of Kashmir. This betrays lack of seriousness on the part of New Delhi to make substantive progress on the resolution of the Kashmir issue |

| Agenda Item | Status of Negotiations | Progress Achieved | Sticking Points | Prospects | Indian Views | Pakistani Views |
|---|---|---|---|---|---|---|
| 3. Siachin | Several rounds of talks held but stalled after Mumbai attacks | Ceasefire since November 2005 | Delineation of LoC beyond NJ9842. Authentication of present positions of occupation versus evolving a framework for troop withdrawal to create complete zone of disengagement | Stalemate | Pak must agree to authentication of existing Indian position before troop withdrawal to an agreed location can take place | Both sides must work for troop withdrawal and agree not to violate the de-limited zone |
| 4. Sir Creek | Technical level talks held but stalled after Mumbai attacks | May 2006 agreement to conduct a joint survey of Sir Creek and the adjoining region; Joint survey completed in March 2007 | Differences relating to the termination points of the land boundary in the Sir Creek area have yet to be ironed out | Promising | Negotiate a fixed boundary around the middle of the Creek along the 1914 resolution map | Seek arbitration if bilateral efforts do not lead to delimitation of maritime boundary |

| | | | | | | |
|---|---|---|---|---|---|---|
| 5. Tulbul/Wullar, Baglihar and Kishenganga | Several rounds of talks held but stalled after Mumbai attacks | Agreement on design modification | Conflicting interpretation of Indus-Water Treaty | Progress hinges on the overall state of Indo-Pak relations | India not violating Indus-Basin Treaty as Tulbul is a navigational project | Indus-Water Treaty forbids a water storage yielding barrage on the river Jhelum. India International mediation sought to determine if Indus-Basin Treaty is being violated |
| 6. Terrorism and Drug Trafficking | Several rounds of talks held but stalled after Mumbai attacks | Reiteration of commitment to combat terrorism in all its forms and work toward its elimination; 2006 Agreement on Joint anti-terrorism mechanism MoU on counter-narcotics emphasising closer cooperation between drug enforcement agencies. Agreement to create India-Pakistan anti-terrorism institutional mechanism to identify and implement counter-terrorism initiative and investigations | Pakistan must discontinue its support for cross-border terrorism activity of the banned jihadi outfits such as LeT | For terrorism not very promising. For anti-drug trafficking, the prospects seem promising | Without addressing the issue of cross-border terrorism no meaningful bilateral cooperation against terrorism is possible | Pakistan is doing all that it can to bring cross-border terrorism under control. India must share its intelligence with Pakistan. India is using cross-border terrorism to deflect attention from its state-sanctioned violence in Indian-held Kashmir. |

| Agenda Item | Status of Negotiations | Progress Achieved | Sticking Points | Prospects | Indian Views | Pakistani Views |
| --- | --- | --- | --- | --- | --- | --- |
| | | | | | | India-Pakistan must evolve an institutional mechanism to jointly investigate acts and incidents of terrorism |
| 7. Economic and Commercial Cooperation | Several rounds of talks held but stalled after Mumbai attacks | Revival of Indo-Pak Joint Commission; India-Pakistan Joint Working Group to study the feasibility of Iran-Pakistan-India Gas Pipeline Project; Draft proposal for a Shipping protocol. Agreement on steps to boost bilateral trade from $2 billion to $10 billion by 2010 | India's demand for most favoured nation; Implementation of SAFTA | Promising | Pakistan must immediately grant MFN status to India; Economic cooperation should not be held hostage to resolution of the Kashmir dispute | Without achieving progress towards resolution of Kashmir dispute, prospects for economic cooperation will remain limited |

| 8. Promotion of Friendly Exchanges in various Fields | Several rounds of talks held but stalled following Mumbai attacks | Resumption of bus service between Srinagar and Muzaffarabad; Operationalisation of Bus service between Amritsar-Lahore and Amritsar-Nankana Sahib; Operationalisation of Poonch-Rawalakot Bus service and a truck service between Muzaffarabad and Srinagar; Munabao-Khokarapar train service; Proposal for a Karachi-Mumbai ferry service; MoU between PMSA (The Pakistan Maritime Security Agency) and ICG (Indian Coast Guard) to enhance communication links | Lack of liberal visa regime | Promising | Friendly exchanges are a vital tool for peace-building between the two countries | Friendly exchanges per se have limited value. Resolution of Kashmir dispute must be accorded the highest priority |

*The Mumbai Setback*

On 26 November 2008 a band of ten well-armed terrorists launched an onslaught on India's commercial capital, Mumbai, which led to the slaughter of 166 people including twenty-five foreign nationals from eight different countries. The attacks occurred at a time when Pakistan's Foreign Minister, Shah Mahmood Qureshi was visiting India to discuss issues relating to the ongoing dialogue process including Kashmir, the Chenab River water and trade ties between the two countries. The instantaneous effect was a sharp downturn in India-Pakistan relations. The peace process launched in 2004 was suspended amid mutual recriminations as India blamed Pakistan for the outrage and Pakistan denied responsibility.

Relations between India and Pakistan had begun to lose their positive momentum in the months preceding the Mumbai attacks. Musharraf was beset by two major crises in the summer of 2007. The Lal Masjid (Red Mosque) episode involved a military assault on a mosque in Islamabad that had become a centre of violent radicalism in the heart of the country. The operation caused a large number of deaths (including those of civilian hostages held in the mosque) and sharply reduced the President's credibility. It was, moreover, followed by a rapid rise in terrorist attacks, including a spate of suicide bombings. Musharraf's difficulties were compounded by the campaign of angry protests launched by the lawyer's community against his decision to dismiss the Chief Justice of the Supreme Court of Pakistan, Iftikhar Chaudhry. Serious doubts arose about his ability to remain in power.

As Musharraf's internal legitimacy began to erode in the wake of country-wide political protests spearheaded by the lawyers, New Delhi became extremely sceptical of his ability to forge a national consensus to implement his 'out of the box' thinking on Kashmir. As a consequence, the planning for a landmark visit by Prime Minister Manmohan Singh to Islamabad in March 2007 during which both leaders were to announce a comprehensive peace settlement aimed at burying the hatchet over Kashmir had to be shelved.[29]

According to Prime Minister Manmohan Singh, 'I and General Musharraf had reached an agreement, a non-territorial solution to all problems but then General Musharraf got into difficulties with the chief justice... and therefore the whole process came to a halt.'[30] The assassination on 28 December 2007 of opposition leader Benazir Bhutto with whom President Musharraf had cut a power-sharing deal in July 2007 to pave the way for her return to the country, raised more questions about political stability. The PPP's advent to power following the February 2008 elections and the abysmal showing of the Pakistan Muslim League (Q)—known as the 'King's party'—against its principal political rival, Nawaz Sharif's Pakistan Muslim League (PML-N), forced Musharraf into a tight political corner.

Meanwhile, the tension between India and Pakistan kept growing. Pakistan increasingly viewed India's growing involvement in Afghanistan as antagonistic to its interests.[31] A series of ceasefire violations across the Line of Control (LoC) led to accusations and counter-accusations of bad faith between the two sides.[32] On 7 July 2008, the Indian embassy compound in Kabul was hit by a powerful blast in which fifty-eight people including two senior Indian officials were killed. Afghan President Hamid Karzai was quick to blame Pakistan for the attack.[33] India's National Security Advisor M. K. Narayanan asserted 'we do not suspect but have a fair amount of intelligence' on the involvement of the Pakistani military's Inter-Services Intelligence (ISI).[34]

In the shadow of this event, the fifth round of the composite dialogue got under way in New Delhi with foreign secretary-level talks on 21 July. However no schedule for meetings on the various subjects it covered was announced. Indian foreign secretary Shivshankar Menon observed, 'India's peace process with Pakistan is under stress.'[35] Pakistan's foreign secretary Salman Bashir acknowledged India's 'misgivings' but denied any culpability and rejected Indian accusations.[36] In September 2008, India denied visas to a Pakistani hockey team. Thus, on the eve of the Mumbai terrorist attacks, the peace process had already become stagnant under the twin pressure of Pakistan's domestic turbulence and new sources of tensions between the neighbours.

Initially, India did not blame the civilian government in Pakistan for being directly involved in the Mumbai attacks but accused the LeT of perpetrating the crime. But Pakistani responsibility was underlined by the Minister for External Affairs Pranab Mukherjee, who held 'some elements' in Pakistan for being responsible and demanded that Islamabad not permit the use of its territory for terrorism against India.[37] On 1 December, India handed over two demarches to Pakistan. In the first, India accused 'elements from Pakistan' of carrying out the terrorist attack and said it expected Islamabad to take 'stern action against the groups that could have been involved in the attack.'[38] The second demarche was more specific and sought the extradition of three people—Maulana Masood Azhar, Tiger Memon and Dawood Ibrahim. It also urged action against the Jamaat-ud-Dawa (JuD). India's Minister of State for External Affairs Anand Sharma told the Agence France-Presse that the Mumbai attacks had dealt a 'grave setback' to relations. Sharma said the gunmen were 'all from Pakistan' and stressed that it was time Islamabad delivered on its promise to prevent its soil being used for attacks on India.[39] On 9 December 2008, the Mumbai police released the coordinates of nine terrorists involved in the attacks—all belonging to Pakistan.

While condemning the Mumbai attacks as 'detestable' and 'heinous', Islamabad asked India to avoid 'knee-jerk' reactions and provide proof.[40] The Pakistani strategy was to deny culpability, insist that both countries were victims of terrorism and assert that the attacks could not have occurred without 'local' assistance.[41] It was also pointed out that India was raising 'the convenient Pakistan bogey' to divert attention from its own security lapses and that 'India has a massive problem of domestic terrorism.'[42]

Immediately after the Mumbai outrage, India handed Pakistan a list of twenty persons allegedly involved in terror incidents in India and demanded their extradition to India for trial. Pakistan's response was tactically legalistic. Islamabad pointed out that there was no extradition treaty between the two countries and asserted that if India insisted on anyone being handed over, Pakistan too would ask for the perpetrators of the Samjhauta Express blast to be extradited.[43]

India accused Pakistan of being uncooperative. In response, Pakistan arrested LeT leader Zaki-ur-Rehman Lakhvi and twelve other activists. On 10 December, a United Nations Al-Qaida and Taliban Sanctions Committee under UN Security Council Resolution 1267 banned three organisations operating in Pakistan: the Jamaat-ud-Dawa (JuD), the al-Rashid Trust and the al-Akhtar Trust. The Committee also added four leaders of JuD to a list of people and groups facing sanctions for ties to al Qaeda or the Taliban including a freeze in their assets, travel ban and arms embargo.

Pakistani resistance to pressure from India and the global community took different forms. Though the government did act against the JuD, the crackdown was not swift and comprehensive. It took the Punjab government more than two months after the Mumbai attacks to take over the JuD's headquarters at Muridke, which it did on 25 January. This effectively gave the organisation time to create a different identity for itself under the name Falah-e-Insaniat Foundation. The military also applied pressure on the US to indicate that Pakistan could be distracted from its effort to fight the Taliban.[44]

Dissatisfied with the Pakistani response, Indian Prime Minister Manmohan Singh in a speech in Parliament on 12 December called Pakistan 'the epicentre of terrorism' and pointed out that the restraint exercised by New Delhi should not be 'misconstrued' as a sign of weakness while demanding that 'the infrastructure of terrorism' in Pakistan be dismantled.[45] India also put in a formal request to the UN Security Council seeking a ban on the JuD. On 19 December, Mukherjee, who had earlier ruled out military action, stated that New Delhi would 'consider the entire range of options'.[46] India's new Home Minister, P. Chidambaram, warned that Pakistan would have to pay an 'enormous price' if another attack took place.[47]

While raising this pressure the Indian government also began to engage with Islamabad. On 5 January it handed over a sixty-nine-page dossier of 'evidence' on the Mumbai terror attacks.[48] This included telephonic transcripts between the gunmen and their LeT commanders, decoded Skype calls over the Internet, a list of weapons recovered after the 26/11 carnage, and the interrogation report of Ajmal Kasab. India also used the dossier in its diplomatic offensive to convince the international community of its case.

In the first week of January 2009, Home Minister Chidambaram made plain the view that the high degree of sophistication in training and equipment displayed by the terrorists reflected the involvement of the Pakistani state.[49] Prime Minister Singh repeated the allegation.[50] Fearing another escalation of tensions and the risk of war, the US tried simultaneously to defuse the tension and to put pressure on Pakistan to respond to Indian demands. The American ambassador to New Delhi described the evidence contained in the Indian dossier as 'credible'.[51]

Calling for more evidence from India Islamabad forwarded a set of thirty-two questions to aid the investigation process.[52] On 13 March, India provided information in reply to questions raised.[53] But the process of cooperation remained uneven, with each side periodically calling on the other to do more. In June 2009, JuD leader Hafiz Saeed, who had been under house arrest for six months, was set free by the Lahore High Court for lack of sufficient evidence.[54] Pakistani calls for more information were met by Indian accusations of stonewalling.

But some cooperation nonetheless continued. In July, President Zardari distanced himself from the previous government by admitting publicly that Pakistan had, in the past, 'deliberately created and nurtured' extremist groups for 'short-term tactical objectives'.[55] Soon after, Prime Ministers Singh and Gilani met on the sidelines of the Non-Aligned Movement summit in Sharm-el-Sheikh, Egypt. Their joint statement agreed that 'terrorism is the main threat to both countries' and that 'dialogue is the only way forward'.[56] India also made a major concession: that 'action on terrorism should not be linked to the composite dialogue process'.[57] Pakistan informed India that it had arrested, along with others, Zaki-ur-Rehman Lakhvi, a senior LeT leader identified by Kasab as the mastermind of the Mumbai attacks.[58] On 17 July, Prime Minister Gilani said that the joint declaration signed by the two prime ministers 'underlines our concerns over India's interference in Balochistan and that Pakistan would give India proof about this.[59]

The Sharm el-Sheikh statement evoked a harsh negative reaction in India. Describing this as 'surrender', BJP deputy leader in the Lok Sabha, Sushma Swaraj said, 'Once terrorism-related issues are de-linked, there will be nothing composite about the dialogue.'[60] On 29 July Dr Singh clarified during a Lok Sabha session that 'terrorism has not been de-linked from the composite dialogue with Pakistan'. He said, 'As neighbours, it is our obligation to keep our channels open. Unless we want to go to war with Pakistan, dialogue is the only way out. But we should do it on the basis of trust, but verify'. He also refuted reports that Pakistan had handed over at Sharm el-Sheikh a dossier about India's involvement in Balochistan.[61] Faced with stiff domestic opposition, New Delhi decided to ignore repeated Pakistani pleas for a meeting at the level of the two foreign secretaries and went on a diplomatic offensive by claiming that Pakistan-based militant groups were planning fresh attacks against New Delhi. On 17 August, Prime Minister Manmohan Singh claimed that there was 'credible information' that Pakistan-based militant groups were planning fresh attacks on India. He said, 'Coming to specific challenges, cross-border terrorism remains a most pervasive threat.'[62]

Worried that the opening for resumption of the peace dialogue provided by Sharm el-Sheikh meeting might be lost, the US-led international community pressed both sides to resume talks as soon as possible. On 16 July, US Assistant Secretary Robert Blake said Washington wanted to see 'greater understanding and progress particularly on the issue of

Pakistan moving forward with prosecution of those responsible for the Mumbai attacks.'[63] On 18 July Hillary Clinton, in an interview, urged India to help Pakistan fight terrorism, saying that this would augment India's standing as a global power.[64] On 27 September Prime Minister Manmohan Singh said that India had supplied sufficient evidence to Pakistan to bring to book those involved in the Mumbai attacks.[65] Two days later China asked India and Pakistan to resolve the Kashmir issue amicably and offered to play a 'constructive role' in settling the 'bilateral issue'. Hu Zhengyue, Assistant Minister for Foreign Affairs, in charge of Asia, said, 'As a friend China will be happy to see such progress [in the peace process] and we will be happy if we can play a constructive role in resolving the issue [Kashmir].'[66]

Reacting strongly to the Indian pressure Islamabad accused New Delhi of stoking terrorism in Balochistan and Pakistani areas bordering Afghanistan. On 2 November at a press briefing top officials disclosed that Pakistan had tangible proof of India's involvement in militancy in South Waziristan and had decided to take up the matter with New Delhi.[67]

During President Barack Obama's visit to China in November, Washington underscored the need for progress in India–Pakistan ties to achieve the goals of 'peace, stability and development' in South Asia. The joint statement issued at the end of President Obama's visit states:

They (US and China) support the efforts of Afghanistan and Pakistan to fight terrorism, maintain domestic stability and achieve sustainable economic and social development, and support the improvement and growth of relations between India and Pakistan.[68]

On 21 November, prior to his first state visit to Washington under the Obama Administration, Dr Singh said in an interview that India was set to resolve all outstanding issues with the Pakistan on the condition that it would not permit its territory to be used against its neighbour. It was a 'tragedy' he added that Pakistan has come to the point of using terror 'as an instrument of state policy'.[69] On 25 November he called on the international community to put 'combined pressure' on Pakistan to ensure that 'ghastly attacks' such as Mumbai would not take place again.'[70] On 28 November, Minister of State for External Affairs Shashi Tharoor said that India cannot negotiate with Pakistan while having a gun pointed at its head.[71]

This indicated India's no-talks posture ahead. On 22 December, India turned down Pakistan's proposal for the resumption of the composite dialogue process till the perpetrators of the 26/11 Mumbai terror attacks were prosecuted. Tharoor said: 'Our PM has said very clearly you [Pakistan] take the first step, we will reach you more than half-way. That first step has not been taken.'[72] On 6 February, the United States said it had been encouraging measures by both India and Pakistan to decrease tension and augment cooperation.[73]

Blake, who urged the two countries to resolve their differences through peaceful means, reiterated this call.[74] Reacting to mounting international pressure to resume the stalled peace talks, Indian Foreign Secretary Nirupama Rao invited her Pakistani counterpart to visit New Delhi on 25 February for talks. The dialogue failed to produce any tangible result. Both sides used the occasion to reiterate their stated positions. On 3 March, Foreign Minister Qureshi said that Pakistan went to the talks with an open mind but 'engaging in talks for the sake of talks will serve no purpose....[unless] India change(s) its approach towards Pakistan which continues to be anchored in the Cold War mindset.[75] On 2 March, India's Home Minister criticised Pakistan for allowing JuD chief Hafiz Saeed to make 'provocative' speeches against India instead of acting against him.[76] Responding to Indian allegations of inaction, Islamabad declared that the new dossiers from India did not contain actionable intelligence and were not enough to arrest Hafiz Saeed.[77] On 13 March Minister Malik claimed there was solid evidence of the Indian involvement in acts of terror in Balochistan and the government was taking up this matter diplomatically with India.[78]

On 13 April, the Indian and Pakistani prime ministers met each other at the US-hosted Nuclear Security Summit in Washington. Their gesture of shaking hands was seen as a positive move but soon after Dr Singh declared at a news conference that there could be no talks with Pakistan until it cracked down on the perpetrators of the Mumbai attacks.[79] On 3 May 2010 an Indian court convicted Kasab on charges of murder and waging war against India.[80] India's Home Minister described the verdict as a 'message to Pakistan that they should not export terror to India'.[81] On 29 April deputy special representative for Afghanistan and Pakistan at the State Department, Paul Jones said that President Barack Obama believed that reducing tensions between India and Pakistan is a 'high priority' for the United States. But this 'is best done in a quiet fashion'.[82]

Washington described the resumption of India-Pakistan dialogue as 'encouraging'. Commenting on the India-Pakistan thaw at the SAARC summit at Thimpu, a senior American official P. J. Crowley said:

We have encouraged the leaders of Pakistan and India to restore direct dialogue that has been characteristic of the relation between those two countries within the last few years. We're encouraged that they are taking steps to do that...[83]

## Looking Ahead

After a hiatus of nearly eighteen months the peace engagement recommenced. Looking ahead beyond the day-to-day management of the relationship the list of issues competing for attention has grown longer. Apart from the eight elements of the composite dialogue, it now includes such divisive issues as water, intensifying Indian and Pakistani competition for influence in Afghanistan, Pakistani apprehensions about Indian involvement in Balochistan and the Indian belief that Pakistan has not irreversibly altered its policy of using jihadi militant organisations to wage what it describes as proxy war against India. Prioritising these different issue areas and converting them into shared core concerns around which negotiations can take place will be the biggest procedural hurdle for both sides. By jettisoning the composite dialogue framework, New Delhi and Islamabad have not only opened the door for engaging in debilitating 'talks for talks' but have also run the enormous risk of losing all the gains made during four rounds of composite dialogue held since January 2004. Finding a way to preserve these gains and building on them through a sustained peace engagement will not be an easy task.

Following the Mumbai terrorist attacks, New Delhi has made a conscious effort to 'recast the dialogue around the issue of terrorism'[84] and this narrow focus works to Islamabad's detriment as it denies Pakistan the negotiating space to discuss all outstanding issues between the two countries. Apart from according terrorism the highest priority and using engagement as a lever to 'get Pakistan to up the level of its cooperation on terrorism',[85] the Indian approach toward the dialogue with Pakistan is also informed by the belief that given Pakistan's serious domestic problems including a fragile economy, poor governance and rising terrorism, Islamabad is not in a position to extract any meaningful concessions from New Delhi especially on Kashmir. As argued by K. Subrahmanyam, 'Given the military, economic and demographic equation between the two countries, there is no possibility of Pakistan succeeding in changing the status quo by force...Therefore, India does not need any incentive to engage Pakistan in a peace process.'[86] In the same vein, Bharat Karnad, has pointed out that:

Accounting for 72 per cent of the population, 72 per cent of the region's land space and, by late 1990s, 75 per cent of the wealth produced in South Asia, India in the new century is in a decisively better situation...the widening economic and resource gap renders the prospect of Pakistan as a serious competitor, let alone rival, to India meaningless and militarily and economically unsustainable.[87]

Another factor influencing the Indian diplomatic calculus vis-à-vis Pakistan is the growing Western endorsement of New Delhi's geopolitical outlook as a rising major power. 'The Quadrennial Defense Review' released by the Pentagon in February 2010, after noting India's rising 'economic power, cultural reach and political influence', and its worldwide military influence through counterpiracy, peacekeeping, humanitarian assistance and disaster relief efforts, described it as a 'net provider of security in the Indian Ocean and beyond'.[88] 'The National Security Strategy' unveiled by the White House in May 2010, while valuing 'India's growing leadership on a wide array of global issues', pledged that Washington 'will seek to work with India to promote stability in South Asia and elsewhere in the world'.[89]

Since 2000, India has increased the number of countries with which it has defence-specific agreements from seven to twenty-six by the end of 2008. Bilateral and multilateral exercises are also an increasing feature of India's expanding defence relations as it 'seeks to find new technologies to transform its military from Cold War era weapons to 21st century capabilities through such opportunities.'[90] In July 2005 India and the United States entered into a civil-nuclear cooperation agreement which committed the United States to allow the export of nuclear material and technology to India for peaceful civilian purposes and made an exemption for India from the application of the provisions of the Atomic Energy Act of 1954. The subsequent approval of the US-India deal by the Nuclear Supplier Group has opened the floodgate of civil nuclear cooperation with India. Pakistan has viewed the Indo-US nuclear deal as an effort by Washington to rewrite the rules of international nuclear commerce favour India, which has the net effect of enabling 'India to produce significant quantities of fissile material and nuclear weapons from un-safeguarded nuclear reactors', and thereby 'igniting an arms race and having implications on strategic stability in South Asia'.[91]

Delhi's rising diplomatic stock and its expanding influence in the global arena have direct ramifications for the India-Pakistan peace process. Three are noteworthy: first, faced with the spectre of a rising India, Pakistan may turn inward to put its own house in order. This internal balancing act would require a long truce with India and would augur well for enduring peace between the two countries. Second, to play the prohibitively costly game of strategic competition with India, Islamabad might revive its atrophying links with jihadi groups to use against its archrival. This option would not only put the two countries on the path to military confrontation with nuclear overtones but would have devastating blowback consequences for Pakistan.

Third, Islamabad might bandwagon with New Delhi to take advantage of India's high economic growth and especially tap into a huge Indian market for its goods. The pursuit of this option would require Islamabad and New Delhi to bury their hatchet over Kashmir and become friendly neighbours. None of these options are a foregone conclusion. A lot would depend on how India and Pakistan negotiate their way out of current challenges. The resumption of the peace process, while reflecting their sensitivity to 'reputational risks', which do not allow them to keep their peace talks in a state of permanent freeze, underscores the fact that the long-term sustainability of their dialogue depends on achieving tangible progress towards narrowing down their differences on the core issue of Kashmir. Without achieving any tangible progress on this, the India-Pakistan dialogue will not only remain devoid of substance but also perennially vulnerable to attempts by various kinds of spoilers to derail it.

# CONCLUDING NOTE

The contributors to this volume have offered a number of policy recommendations that address Pakistan's systemic and fundamental challenges to assure the continuing viability and vitality of the state. These may, it is hoped, prove to be key elements of a reform agenda that will help Pakistan's leaders to turn the country around and guarantee its long-term stability.

Today's turmoil and turbulence are such that there is no concerted official effort to plan for Pakistan's future. But both the urgent and the essential must be addressed if the country is to be transformed into a strong state responsive to the welfare of its people and not merely its privileged elites. Dysfunctional politics, unresolved structural economic problems, internal security threats and the governance deficit all have to be tackled simultaneously and not in isolation from one another as together they have contributed to the systemic crisis.

But first urgent actions have to be taken to deal with the country's security situation and the crisis in public finances to enable the pursuit of other critical goals. Prioritsation is necessary to push forward an enforceable reform agenda.

Effective governance is what makes the difference between successful states and struggling ones. Improving the quality of governance is therefore central to the effort to move Pakistan beyond the 'crisis state'. This volume has identified both short- and longer-term reform measures needed to enhance the capabilities of public institutions, institute checks and balances and create a more competent civil service. Yet none of these policies can be undertaken without articulating a vision and the mechanism to implement it.

What this book has also emphasised is the need to bring the country's politics in sync with the social, economic and technological

349

changes that have been transforming the national landscape and creating a more 'connected' society. Electoral and political reforms that foster greater and more active participation by Pakistan's growing educated middle class will open up possibilities for the transformation of an increasingly dysfunctional, patronage-dominated polity into one that is able to tap the resilience of the people and meet their needs.

In re-designing the polity the central principle that should be applied is that democracy cannot function without the rule of law. This means strengthening the judiciary to operationalise robust checks and balances. It also means ensuring the availability of justice to citizens by reforming the judicial system, especially at the lower levels.

Stable civil-military relations are essential for political stability to be maintained. The Armed Forces can contribute towards a viable national polity by subjecting themselves to civilian oversight and control. This will have to be matched by civilian leaders who should abide by the Constitution and refrain from dragging in the Army to settle political disputes.

The goal of economic revival will have to be comprehensively targeted with emergency actions, short term measures and long term reforms, all of which will have to be pursued simultaneously. Immediate steps to restore macroeconomic stability and the fiscal and financial balance need to be accompanied by efforts to mobilise resources to power Pakistan's economic development. Broadening the revenue base by taxing the rich and the powerful and bringing exempted sectors such as agriculture into the tax net should be the crucial elements for setting up an equitable and efficient tax regime.

The state has to play a central and active role to create an enabling environment for economic growth and job creation. This means addressing the infrastructure deficits, especially in power, evolving a fair regulatory framework for economic activity and halting the haemorrhaging in the public sector enterprises that is fuelling the budget deficit and crowding out private investment.

A coherent strategy to revive the agriculture sector should include new investment in the rural infrastructure, appropriate pricing and incentives, land reclamation, focused research and development, application of modern technology and utilisation of international market rules and opportunities. These measures should aim to turn the country into the region's food reservoir.

Policies to promote industrial growth and expansion should entail greater support to small and medium enterprises, and identification and encouragement of manufacturing in sectors where Pakistan has or can acquire the greatest competitive advantage and where demand is rising rapidly. A key policy objective should be the country's integration into global production chains and manpower training and skills development.

The highest priority needs to be given to human development. A crash programme should be implemented to educate Pakistan and meet the target of achieving universal primary education in the next ten years through higher government spending and public-private partnerships. Meeting the education and health needs of citizens, alleviation of poverty and steps to end discrimination against women should be part of a comprehensive human development strategy.

It is also critical to address the challenge of a rapidly growing population and youth bulge by implementing a mix of policy measures that include a programme to reduce fertility and a far-reaching literacy campaign focused on the rural areas and women to achieve higher primary school enrolment. Skills training and increasing female labour participation will also be needed to reap a demographic dividend and turn the country's human capital into an engine for economic growth.

Restoring internal security and order will require a holistic approach that deals with the multifaceted challenge of terrorism and violence. An overwhelming reliance on military means has distracted attention from the need to deal with the ideological and political aspects of the militant challenge and may even have dispersed rather than diminished the threat. Evolving a counter-narrative, forging a political consensus and mobilising public support against militancy must be part of the strategy to stop the flow of recruits to militant organisations in order to break the cycle of radicalisation. A multilayered, multipronged strategy is needed that includes efforts to engage in the battle of ideas and address the factors—including issues of governance and injustice—that create the breeding ground for militancy.

To promote its vital short and long term national objectives and regain lost strategic space, Pakistan needs to adjust its foreign policy and invigorate its diplomacy within the current and emerging political and economic environment.

Its priority goals should include promoting peace in Afghanistan through an inclusive political settlement based on that country's realities while working to end terrorism and extremism within Pakistan and the region. A modus vivendi with India should be sought which

351

maintains Pakistan's policy independence including for Kashmir's legitimate aspirations and preserves credible conventional and nuclear deterrence while exploiting the potential for mutually advantageous trade and economic relations.

Vastly expanded strategic and economic relations should be pursued with China which offer Pakistan the best hope for the realisation of its security and economic objectives. A balanced and stable relationship with the US should be built on mutual accommodation of legitimate national interests, respect for Pakistan's sovereignty and expanded cooperation in areas of benefit to both sides.

Pakistan should also seek to revive historic and mutually supportive relationships with key Islamic nations especially Saudi Arabia, Turkey and the Gulf states, as well as Malaysia, Iran and Indonesia.

This is not an exhaustive list of all that is contained in the volume but an identification of the critical priorities on which a national consensus needs to be fashioned. None of this is possible without political will on the part of a political leadership that commits itself to the larger good rather than just its own interests. Political will can only be effectively asserted when leaders enjoy authority as well as power and pursue goals regarded as fair and legitimate by the wider public.

Only such an assertion of political will can help to revive the vision and hope that accompanied Pakistan at its inception. Executing this game plan for success may seem a daunting task but Pakistan's people deserve no less.

# NOTES

## 1. THE PAST AS PRESENT

1. Arnaud de Borchgrave (2010), 'Paranoidistan', *The Washington Times*, 2 Feb.
2. Sadanand Dhume (2010), 'Why Pakistan Produces Jihadists', *The Wall Street Journal*, 3 May.
3. Shuja Nawaz (2009), 'The Battle for Pakistan', *The Wall Street Journal*, 19 Oct.
4. Syed Irfan Ashraf and Faizullah Jan (2009), 'Prisoners of a Jihadi Past', *Dawn*, 25 Feb.
5. See Ayesha Jalal (1985), *The Sole Spokesman: Jinnah, the Muslim League and the Demand for Pakistan*, Cambridge: Cambridge University Press, passim.
6. Cited in Ayesha Jalal (1990), *The State of Martial Rule: The Origins of Pakistan's Political Economy of Defence*, Cambridge: Cambridge University Press, p. 128.
7. Saadat Hasan Manto (2008), 'Letters to Uncle Sam' in Khalid Hasan (ed. and tran.), *Bitter Fruit: The Very Best of Saadat Hasan Manto*, New Delhi: Penguin, pp. 612, 614, 623–24, 628.
8. Hussain Haqqani (2005), *Pakistan: Between Mosque and Military*, Lahore: Vanguard, attributes the close nexus between the military and the mosque after the 1980s to the early years of Pakistan.
9. 'Pakistan Comes Back to Earth', *The Economist*, 24 May 1952, p. 522.
10. See Vali Nasr (2000), 'The Rise of Sunni Militancy in Pakistan: The Changing Role of Islamism and the Ulama in Society and Politics', *Modern Asian Studies*, vol. 34, no. 1 (Feb.), pp. 139–180 and Muhammad Qasim Zaman (1998), 'Sectarianism in Pakistan: The Radicalization of Shi'i and Sunni Identities', *Modern Asian Studies*, vol. 32, no. 3 (Jul.), pp. 689–716.
11. Ahmed Rashid (2008), *Descent into Chaos: The United States and the Failure of Nation Building in Pakistan, Afghanistan, and Central Asia*, New York: Viking, Chapter 13.

## 2. WHY JINNAH MATTERS

1. Mohammad Ali Jinnah (1948), *Speeches of Quaid-i-Azam Mohammad Ali Jinnah as Governor General of Pakistan*, Karachi: Sind Observer Press, pp. 9–10.
2. Ibid., p. 10.
3. Ibid., p. 10.
4. Jamil-ud-din Ahmad (ed.) (1976), *Speeches and Writings of Mr. Jinnah*, Lahore: Sh. Muhammad Ashraf, pp. 408–409.
5. Stanley Wolpert (1984), *Jinnah of Pakistan*, New York: Oxford University Press, pp. 337–340.
6. Liaquat H. Merchant (1990), *Jinnah: A Judicial Verdict*, Karachi: East-West Publishing Company, p. 12.
7. Liaquat H. Merchant (1990), pp. 10–11.
8. Rajmohan Gandhi (1986), *Eight Lives: A Study of the Hindu-Muslim Encounter*, Albany, NY: State University of New York Press, p. 178.
9. Mohammad Ali Jinnah (1989), *Quaid-i-Azam Mohammad Ali Jinnah: Speeches and Statements 1947–48*, Islamabad: Government of Pakistan, Ministry of Information and Broadcasting, Directorate of Films and Publications.
10. Z.H. Zaidi (1993), *Jinnah Papers: Prelude to Pakistan*, vol. I, parts I and II, Islamabad: Quaid-i-Azam Papers Project, part I, p. 760.
11. Ibid., p. 760.
12. Mohammad Ali Jinnah (1989), *Quaid-i-Azam Mohammad Ali Jinnah: Speeches and Statements 1947–48*, Islamabad: Government of Pakistan, Ministry of Information and Broadcasting, Directorate of Films and Publications, p. 272.
13. Ibid., p. 96.
14. Ibid., p. 275.
15. Ibid., p. 67.
16. Ibid., p. 273.
17. Z.H. Zaidi (1993), *Jinnah Papers: Prelude to Pakistan*, vol. I, parts I and II, Islamabad: Quaid-i-Azam Papers Project, appendices, vol. 1, part II, p. 647.
18. Mohammad Ali Jinnah (1989), *Quaid-i-Azam Mohammad Ali Jinnah: Speeches and Statements 1947–48*, Islamabad: Government of Pakistan, Ministry of Information and Broadcasting, Directorate of Films and Publications, p. 39.
19. H.M. Seervai (1990), *Partition of India: Legend and Reality*, Bombay: Emmenem Publications, p. 134.
20. Ibid, p. 134.
21. Rizwan Ahmed (1993), *'Sayings of Quaid-i-Azam': Mohammad Ali Jinnah*, Karachi: Quaid Foundation and Pakistan Movement Centre, pp. 99–100.
22. Jamil-ud-din Ahmad (ed.) (1976), *Speeches and Writings of Mr. Jinnah*, Lahore: Sh. Muhammad Ashraf, pp. 419–420.

23. Ibid., p. 20.
24. Rizwan Ahmed (1993), p. 101.
25. Mohammad Ali Jinnah (1989), *Quaid-i-Azam Mohammad Ali Jinnah: Speeches and Statements 1947–48*, Islamabad: Government of Pakistan, Ministry of Information and Broadcasting, Directorate of Films and Publications, p. 128.

## 4. BEYOND THE CRISIS STATE

1. Based on interviews in May 2010 with Ishrat Husain, former Governor of the State Bank of Pakistan and Shahid Javed Burki, former Vice President of the World Bank and Finance Minister of Pakistan. See also paper by Ishrat Husain, 'Recent Economic Developments and Future Developments'. Burki subsequently put the size of the middle class at even more—30 per cent of the population in 'The Middle-class millions', *Dawn*, 2 Nov. 2010.
2. This pre-occupation is captured in Pervez Musharraf (2006), *In the Line of Fire*, New York: Simon & Schuster.
3. Many outsiders have commented on this change. See, for example, William Rhodes (2007), 'Pakistan middle class, beneficiary of Musharraf, begins to question rule', *New York Times*, (25 Nov.), and William Dalrymple (2008), 'A New Deal in Pakistan', *The New York Review of Books*, (3 Apr.). See also the interesting material assembled on the blog, Haq's Musings, at http://www.riazhaq.com.
4. *Biradaris* are extended kinship groups. An excellent study by Steven Holtzman has shown the key role they have played in electoral politics in the Punjab, which can be traced to British colonial rule. The study finds that administrative and constituency boundaries drawn by the British deliberately encouraged representational politics based on *biradari* ties. See 'Biradaris and Elections in the Punjab: Colonial Roots and Post-Colonial Implications'.
5. Figure provided by an IMF official in an interview in Washington DC in March 2010.
6. This discussion draws greatly on the work of Ayesha Jalal and on excellent accounts in a number of books including Ayesha Jalal (1995), *Democracy and Authoritarianism in South Asia: A Comparative and Historical Perspective*, Cambridge: Cambridge University Press; Shahid Javed Burki (1999), *Pakistan: Fifty years of Nationhood*, Boulder, CO: Westview Press; Khalid B. Sayeed (1980), *Politics in Pakistan: The Nature and Direction of Change*, New York: Praeger; Marvin Weinbaum (1999), 'Economics: Misplaced priorities, Missed opportunities' in Selig S. Harrison (ed.) *India and Pakistan: The First Fifty Years*, Cambridge: Cambridge University Press; and the issues raised in Veena Kukreja and M.P. Singh (2005), *Pakistan: Democracy, Development and Security Issues*, SAGE Publications Pvt. Ltd.
7. Ayesha Jalal (1990), *The State of Martial Rule: The Origins of Pakistan's Political Economy of Defence*, Cambridge: Cambridge University Press.

8. For a brilliant account of the 'insider-outsider clash' see Shahid Javed Burki (1996), *Pakistan Under Bhutto, 1971–77*, New York: Macmillan.

9. The literature is vast. For a review see Herbert Kitschelt (2000), 'Linkages between Citizens and Politicians in Democratic Polities', *Comparative Political Studies*, vol. 33, no. 6–7.

10. See the interesting discussion in John R. Schmidt (2009), 'The Unravelling of Pakistan', *Survival*, (Jun.-Jul.), vol. 51, no. 3.

11. Writer and journalist Zahid Hussain has written extensively on this. See, for example, his seminal article, 'House of Feudals', *Herald*, (Karachi, Apr. 1985) which is still relevant today.

12. Economic data from the Ministry of Finance, Government of Pakistan provided by the Embassy of Pakistan in Washington DC. Much of the data that follows has been drawn from official Pakistani publications of the Finance Ministry and the State Bank.

13. Report of the Task Force on Reform of Tax Administration, (14 Apr. 2001).

14. Related by economist Shahid Kardar who then served as Finance Minister in the Punjab and is currently the Governor of the State Bank of Pakistan.

15. See report in *Dawn*, 17 Jun. 2010 citing the principal adviser to the Finance Ministry, Saqib Shirani.

16. Much of this discussion draws on a series of interviews with Dr Muhammad Yaqub, Governor of the State Bank of Pakistan (1993–2000).

17. Report of the Task Force, p. 2.

18. Vali Nasr (2009), *Forces of Fortune*, New York: Free Press, provides a good account of these developments. See also Hilary Synnot (2009), *Transforming Pakistan*, London: Routledge.

19. Pakistan ICT Indicators (Statistics Division, Government of Pakistan, undated).

20. Ibid.

21. See the account in Zahid Hussain (2010), *The Scorpion's Tail*, New York: Free Press, Chapter five.

22. Author's own notes from the period of serving as Pakistan's High Commissioner to the UK.

23. Ibid.

24. Interview with an official of the Election Commission of Pakistan, Islamabad.

25. See, for example, Dr Ijaz Shafi Gilani (2009), 'Weak State Strong Nation: A survey of surveys, 2008–09', (Islamabad Pakistan Institute of Legislative Development and Transparency)

26. Jason Burke (2010), 'Letter from Karachi', *Prospect*, Issue 169 (Apr.).

## 5. ARMY AND POLITICS

1. Talk at Brookings Institution, Washington DC, 19 June 2000. Quoted in Shuja Nawaz (2008), *Crossed Swords: Pakistan, Its Army, and the Wars Within*, Oxford: Oxford University Press, pp. xxvii-xxviii.

## 6. PRAETORIANS AND THE PEOPLE

1. For a theoretical discussion on constitutionalism and various facets of liberal democracy, see Mark F. Plattner (2010), 'Populism, Pluralism and Liberal Democracy', *Journal of Democracy*, vol. 21, no. 1, (Jan.), pp. 81–92.
2. For a detailed analysis on the concept, see Peter D. Feaver (1996), 'The Civil-Military Problematique: Huntington, Janowitz and the Question of Civilian Control', *Armed Forces & Society*, vol. 23, no. 2, pp. 149–178.
3. Rahimullah Yusufzai (2006), 'No End in Sight', *Newsline*, (Apr.) [Last accessed on 21 Aug. 2010].
4. Pakistani news media widely reported General Kayani and Corps Commanders' opposition to the Bill, see *Dawn*, Lahore, 7–9 Oct., 2009. For an informative analysis, see Zahid U. Kramet (2010), 'Kerry-Lugar bill a Catch-22 for Pakistan', *Asia Times Online* [Last accessed on 20 Aug. 2010]. In June 2010, Pakistan and China signed a nuclear deal, whereby China agreed to provide two civilian nuclear reactors. The deal was criticised by the US and India. For details see, 'China says Pakistan nuclear deal "peaceful"', *BBC News Online*, 17 Jun. 2010, [Last accessed on 20 Aug. 2010].
5. According to media reports and government spokespersons, over fourteen million people have been displaced and crop damage is estimated to the tune of $1–3 billion. Infrastructure damage and property loss is yet to be calculated. UN Secretary-General, Ban Ki-moon, visiting the food hit areas of the country described it as 'heart wrenching', *Dawn*, Lahore.
6. For an excellent analysis on the subject, see John K. Cooley (1999), *Unholy Wars: Afghanistan, America and International Terrorism*, London: Pluto Press, pp. 57–64.
7. Saeed Shafqat (2002), 'From Islam to Islamism: The Rise of Dawat-ul-Irshad and Lashkar-e-Taiba' in Christophe Jaffrelot (ed.) *Pakistan: Nationalism without a Nation?* (London: Zed Books) pp. 131–147.
8. Ibid.
9. For an informative analysis and details on the scale of cooperation on these matters, see, C. Christine Fair and Peter Chalk (2006), *Fortifying Pakistan: The Role of U.S. Internal Security Assistance*, Washington, DC: USIP Press Books.
10. For information and updates visit, http://www.centcom.mil/en/pakistan/ [Last accessed on 22 Aug. 2010].

11. For a detailed analysis see, Shafqat Saeed (1997), *Civil-Military Relations in Pakistan: From Zulfikar Ali Bhutto to Benazir Bhutto*, Boulder, CO: Westview Press, pp. 225–254.

12. For the text of the Legal Framework Order, 2002, see, http://www.dawn.com/2002/08/22/top3.htm. Through this order Pervez Musharraf introduced twenty-nine amendments in the 1973 constitution—giving powers to the president to dismiss PM, restricting the powers of the parliament and public officials and creating the National Security Council. Musharraf got himself elected through a Referendum Order No. 12, on 30 April 2002 for five years.

13. 'CJ suspended, escorted home', *Dawn*, Lahore, 10 Mar. 2007, see also *Dawn*, 10 Nov. 2007.

14. Joshua Partlow (2009), 'Pakistani Ruling Rebukes Ex-Leader', *Washington Post*, (11 Nov.).

15. 'Benazir Survives Midnight Carnage: Twin Blasts cast shadow over homecoming', *Dawn*, Lahore, Oct. 19, 2007.

16. Nick Schifrin (2008), 'Benazir's Will Made Public', *ABC News*, (5 Feb.).

17. Salman Masood (2008), 'New Pakistan Army Chief Orders Military Out of Civilian Government Agencies, Reversing Musharraf Policy', *New York Times*, (13 Feb.).

18. For text summary, President's speech and signing in ceremony, see *Dawn*, 19 Apr. 2010.

19. 'Pakistan, With Confidence, New Prime Minister Vows to Fight Terrorism', *Radio Free Europe Radio Liberty*, 29 Mar. 2008.

20. 'US silent on visit of Asfandyar', *Dawn*, Lahore, 10 May 2008.

21. For a list of various meetings held in this capacity, see 'Latest Embassy Press Releases, 2008', Embassy of the United States: Islamabad, Pakistan.

22. Tanveer Ahmed (2008), 'Economy Woes Real Test of President Zardari', *Daily Times*, (7 Sept.).

23. Policy analysts and Op-eds have been extremely critical of how government has handled the flood situation in the country—undermining the faith in party government and the working of democratic set up. See, for example, S. Akbar Zaidi (2010), 'A drowning State', *Dawn*, (20 Aug.) and Mushtaq Gaadi (2010), 'Engineering failures', *Dawn*, (16 Aug.).

24. However, the decision has generated considerable debate in Pakistani media and among policy analysts on granting of extension, many argue that extension is unwarranted and should not have been given.

25. That is what the Constitution lays out and in case of General Kayani's extension most likely happened.

26. For an interesting and insightful analysis on General Kayani and his views and orientation from an Indian perspective see, Praveen Swami (2010), 'General Kayani's quiet coup', http://www.thehindu.com/opinion/lead/article548266.ece?homepage=true, (3 Aug.), [Last accessed on 20 Aug. 2010]. For a balanced and sympathetic assessment of General Kayani, see

Yousafzai, Rahimullah (2007), 'General Kayani's rise from humble begin-nings', www.thenews.com.pk/top-=11425 (28 Nov.), [Last accessed on 20 Aug. 2010].

27. *Time Magazine*, 1 May 2009, listed General Kayani among the 100 most influential leaders of the year. For a biographical sketch and detailed career profile, see http://www.globalsecurity.org/military/world/pakistan/ashfaq-parvez-kayani.htm [Last accessed on 21 Aug. 2010].

28. Since he was heading ISI at that point the incident was widely reported in Pakistani press, see *Dawn*, Lahore, 10 Mar. 2007.

29. In March 2010 while preparing for a visit to the US for a strategic dia-logue meeting, the COAS called a meeting of the federal secretaries at GHQ Rawalpindi, see *Dawn*, Lahore, 16 Mar. 2010.

30. Following the Mumbai attacks by Lashakar-e-Taiba in December 2008 President Zardari had announced to send DG, ISI to India, however, the move was quickly squashed by General Kayani and the visit never mate-rialised. See Ganguly, Sumit (2010), 'General Kayani—A Musharraf in the Making?', http://timesofindia.indiatimes.com/world/pakistan/General-Kayani—A-Musharraf-in-the-making/articleshow/5704978.cms (20 Mar.), [Last accessed on 21 Aug. 2010].

## 7. IDEOLOGICALLY ADRIFT

1. Ayesha Jalal (1990), *The State of Martial Rule*, Cambridge: Cambridge University Press, p. 16.
2. Khalid bin Sayeed (1968), *Pakistan: The Formative Phase*, London: Oxford University Press, pp. 198–99.
3. *Quaid-i-Azam Mohammad Ali Jinnah's Speeches as Governor-General of Pakistan 1947–48*, (1964), Karachi: Government of Pakistan.
4. Ardeshir Cowasjee (2003), 'In the Name of Religion', *Dawn*, (5 Oct.), http://www.dawn.com/weekly/cowas/20020310.htm.
5. Ardeshir Cowasjee (2000), 'The Sole Statesman—3', *Dawn*, (2 Jul.), http://www.dawn.com/weekly/cowas/20000702.htm.
6. Husain Haqqani (2005), *Pakistan: Between Mosque and Military*, Wash-ington, DC: Carnegie Endowment for International Peace, p. 46.
7. Ayesha Jalal (2008), *Partisans of Allah: Jihad in South Asia*, Cambridge: Harvard University Press.
8. A. R. Siddiqui (1996), *The Military in Pakistan: Image and Reality*, Lahore: Vanguard Books, p. 107.
9. Report of the Court of Inquiry constituted under Punjab Act II of 1954 to enquire into the Punjab Disturbances of 1953 (Lahore: Government Print-ing Press, 1953), pp. 215–18.
10. The following analysis of Generals Ayub and Yahya Khan's attempts to develop Pakistan's Islamic ideology draws on the afore-cited Husain Haqqani (2005).

11. Mohammed Ayub Khan (1960), 'Pakistan Perspective', *Foreign Affairs*, vol. 38, no. 4, (Jul.), p. 547.

12. Ayub Khan (1967), *Friends Not Masters*, London and Karachi: Oxford University Press, pp. 196–97.

13. Ibid., p. 183.

14. Huseyn Shaheed Suhrawardy (1957), 'Political Stability and Democracy in Pakistan', *Foreign Affairs*, vol. 35, no. 3, (Apr.), p. 425.

15. A. R. Siddiqui (1996), pp. 163–64.

16. Ibid., pp. 204–206.

17. Michael Hornsby (1971), 'President Yahya Dashes Hopes of Reconciliation', London: *The Times*, (3 Jul.).

18. William L. Richter (1979), 'Political Dynamics of Islamic Resurgence in Pakistan', *Asian Survey*, vol. 19, no. 6, (Jun.), p. 549.

19. 'The Islamic Bomb', *Time*, (9 Jul. 1979), http://www.time.com/time/magazine/article/0,9171,920461,00.html.

20. 'General Zia ul-Haq's Address to the Nation on July 5, 1977', quoted in Hasan-Askari Rizvi (1986), *The Military and Politics in Pakistan 1947–1986*, Lahore: Progressive Publishers, pp. 289–93.

21. Stephen Cohen (2004), *The Idea of Pakistan*, Washington, DC: Brookings Institution Press, p. 171.

22. President Zia-ul-Haq's interview to Ian Stephens (6 Jan. 1979), in President of Pakistan General Mohammad Zia-ul-Haq—Interviews to Foreign Media, vol. II (Islamabad: Government of Pakistan, undated), pp. 2–6. Quoted in Husain Haqqani (2005), p. 135.

23. Ziaul Islam Ansari (1990), *General Muhammad Zia ul-Haq: Shaksiat aur Karnamay* [Man and His Achievements], Lahore: Jang Publishers, p. 24. Quoted in Haqqani, Husain (2005), p. 193.

24. 'From U.S., the ABC's of Jihad', *Washington Post*, 23 Mar. 2002, http://www.washingtonpost.com/ac2/wp-dyn/A5339–2002Mar22?language-printer.

25. *Sectarian War: Pakistan's Sunni-Shia Violence and Its Links to the Middle East*, event summary, Woodrow Wilson Center (Washington, DC), 2 May 2007, http://www.wilsoncenter.org/index.cfm?fuseaction-events.event-summary &event-id-231933.

26. 'Musharraf Speech Highlights', *BBC*, 12 Jan. 2002, http://news.bbc.co.uk/2/hi/south-asia/1757251.stm.

27. Pervez Musharraf (2004), 'A Plea for Enlightened Moderation', *Washington Post*, (1 Jun.), http://www.washingtonpost.com/wp-dyn/articles/A5081–2004May31.html.

28. For more on militancy in Punjab, see Aysha Siddiqa (2009), 'Terror's Training Ground', *Newsline*, (Sept.), http://www.newsline.com.pk/News-Sep2009/coverstorysep.htm.

29. 'Sufi Advisory Council Set Up', *The News*, 7 Jun. 2009, http://www.thenews.com.pk/daily-detail.asp?id-181907.

30. Jane Perlez (2009), 'Pakistan Attacks Show Tighter Militant Links', *New York Times*, (15 Oct.), http://www.nytimes.com/2009/10/16/world/asia/16pstan.html?-r-1&hp.

31. See Aysha Siddiqa (2009), 'Faith Wars', *Dawn*, (14 Feb.), http://www.dawnnews.tv/wps/wcm/connect/dawn-content-library/dawn/the-news paper/columnists/faith-wars-yn.

32. Pervez Hoodbhoy (2009), 'The Saudi-isation of Pakistan', *Newsline*, (Jan.), http://www.interfaithstrength.com/images/Pervez.htm.

## 8. BATTLING MILITANCY

1. Hassan Abbas (2005), *Pakistan's drift into extremism: Allah, the Army, and America's War on Terror*, New York: M.E. Sharpe, p. 201.

2. International Crisis Group (ICG) report, 'Pakistan: Madrasas, extremism and the military', (Jul. 2002).

3. Ibid.

## 9. RETOOLING INSTITUTIONS

1. World Bank (1992), 'Governance and Development', Washington D.C., World Bank.

2. Overseas Development Institute (2006), 'Governance Development and Aid Effectiveness: ODI Briefing Paper', London, (Mar.).

3. G. Hyden, J. Court and K. Mease (2004), *Making Sense of Governance*, Boulder, Co: Lynne Rienner.

4. Transparency International which carries out Perception Surveys on corruption across a large cross-section of countries has consistently ranked Pakistan among the most corrupt countries. Although the actual ranking has varied the direction remains unchanged. World Bank Governance Indicators, Economist Intelligence Unit (EIU) Index, Failed State Index, International Country Risk Guide (ICRG) Heritage Foundation, Economic Forum Index all corroborate the decline in the various indicators of governance and institutional strength.

5. Ishrat Husain (1999), *Pakistan: The Economy of an elitist state*, Karachi, Oxford University Press.

6. Arun Shourie (2010), *We must have no price*, New Delhi, the Express Group.

7. A. Alesina (1997), 'The Political Economy of high and Low Growth', *World Bank Annual Conference on Development*.

8. A. Alesina et al. (1996), 'Political Instability and Economic growth', *Journal of Economic Growth*, vol. 1, no. 2, (Jun.).

9. Governance Indicators: World Bank Institute (Washington D.C. World Bank various years).

10. Most of the discussion on the governance and institutional reforms that follows is derived from the 2008 Report of the National Commission for

Government Reforms (NCGR) and the 2010 Pay and Pension Commission Report, both of which were Chaired by the author. Both these reports are based on extensive research, field visits throughout the country, observations and consultations with the civil servants, academia and civil society.

11. International Crisis Group (2010), Reforming Pakistan's Civil Service: Asia Report No 185, *ICG Report* (15–16 Feb.).

12. See, for example, a thorough but independent study by Social Policy Development Centre (2008), 'Social Development in Pakistan 2006–07: Devolution and Human Development', Annual Review 2006–2007, Karachi, Social Policy Development Centre.

13. The material in this section is drawn from an earlier paper: Husain, Ishrat (1999), 'Institutions of Restraint: The Missing Element in Pakistan's Governance', Pakistan Development Review vol. 38, no. 4, Islamabad, PIDE.

## 11. BOOSTING COMPETITIVENESS

1. Stephen Cohen (2006), *The Idea of Pakistan*, Brookings Institution. In this book Stephen Cohen outlines much of the broader and specific issues facing Pakistan which have the potential to create further destabilisation in Pakistan.

2. Goldman Sachs (2007), BRICs and Beyond, *Goldman Sachs Economic Group*.

3. Much of the economic data in this chapter has been taken from Government of Pakistan publications of various years including State Bank of Pakistan Annual Reports and Ministry of Finance, Annual Economic Survey.

4. Central Intelligence Agency, World Factbook and IMF working papers.

5. Economic data used in the chapter is sourced from various Annual Reports of the State Bank of Pakistan and the Government of Pakistan's various annual publications entitled 'Economic Survey'.

6. BMA Capital Research Reports, 2000–2010.

7. Global Competitiveness Report (2009), World Economic Forum.

## 12. TURNING ENERGY AROUND

1. 'Medium Term Development Framework: 2005–10', Pakistan Planning Commission.

2. 'Pakistan Energy Yearbook 2009', Hydrocarbon Development Institute of Pakistan, Ministry of Petroleum and Natural Resources.

3. Akthar Awan (2008), Presentation on 'Renewable Energy and Pakistan', Member, (Energy) Planning Commission, Islamabad.

4. Hydrocarbon Development Institute of Pakistan, 'Pakistan Energy Yearbook 2009', Ministry of Petroleum and Natural Resources.

5. Sabira Qureshi (2007), 'Energy, Poverty Reduction and Equitable Development in Pakistan', in Robert M. Hathaway, B. Muchhala and M. Kugel-

man, *Fueling the Future: Meeting Pakistan's needs in the 21st Century*, Document by Woodrow Wilson International Center for Scholars: Asia Program, (Mar.).

6. Ibid.
7. Akthar Awan (2008), Presentation...
8. Ibid.
9. Oil and gas theoretical reserves, confirmed reserves and production figures from Ministry of Petroleum and Natural Resources, 'An Overview of Fossil Fuel Energy Resources of Pakistan' in 'Pakistan Energy Yearbook 2008'.
10. American Scientist Interview with David Goldstein, author of *Out of Gas*.
11. 'International Energy Outlook 2008'.
12. Ministry of Petroleum and Natural Resources (2009), 'Successful Past and a Brighter Future' in 'Opportunities in Pakistan's Upstream Oil and Gas Sector'.
13. Akthar Awan (2008), Presentation...
14. Miriam Katz (2008), 'The Feasibility of Renewable Energy in Pakistan', *Triple Bottom Line Magazine* (16 Mar.).
15. 'Medium Term Development Framework: 2005–10', Pakistan Planning Commission.
16. Shahid Javed Burki (2007), 'The Weight of History: Pakistan's Energy Problem' in (eds) Robert M. Hathaway, B. Muchhala and M. Kugelman, *Fueling the Future: Meeting Pakistan's needs in the 21st Century*, Document by: Woodrow Wilson International Center for Scholars: Asia Program, (Mar.).
17. The examples relate to periods during which the author was the World Bank's advisor on energy projects in Pakistan, and later, the Bank's coordinator of energy operations in Central Asia.
18. Ministry of Petroleum and Natural Resources (2009), 'Petroleum Exploration and Production Policy 2009', (Mar.).
19. Ministry of Petroleum and Natural Resources (2009), 'Opportunities in Pakistan's Upstream Oil and Gas Sector'.
20. Mohan Munasinghe (1980), 'Integrated National Energy Planning in Developing Countries', *World Bank Reprint Series*, no. 165.
21. 'World Bank Group Energy Strategy Feedback and Discussion Points', Jul. 2010.
22. Very recently Kazakhstan's integrated line ministry structure suffered a setback when, for work-load reasons, the electricity sub-sector was moved to the Ministry of Industry.
23. Shahid Javed Burki (2007).
24. Sabira Qureshi (2007).
25. Sabrina Tavernise (2010), 'Pakistanis Living on Brink and Often in the Dark', *New York Times*, (27 Apr.).
26. USAID (2007), 'Energy Sector Assessment for USAID/Pakistan', (Jun.).

27. Ziad Alahdad (2008), 'Institutional Structure for Integrated Energy Planning: The Case for Pakistan', paper presented at Seminar on Pakistan's Energy Needs in Washington by the UET Alumni Association, (11 Oct.).

28. At the time, the author was the World Bank's advisor on energy projects in Pakistan.

29. 'Administrative Approval and Expenditure Sanction in Respect of Energy Planning and Development Project (ENERPLAN)', Planning and Development Division directive no: Energy/ENP/19(1)PC/84, (1 Oct. 1984).

30. Gazette Notification No: 12 (29–1) Energy/PC/83, Government of Pakistan, (26 Sept. 1984).

31. 'Pakistan: Issues and Options in the Energy Sector', World Bank Report No. 2953-PAK, (5 Jun. 1980).

32. 'Pakistan Oil and Gas Sector Review', World Bank Report No: 26072-PK, (10 Jul. 2003).

33. USAID (2007).

34. Vladislav Vucetic and Achilles Adamantiades (2009), 'Power Sector Reform in Pakistan: Issues and Challenges', in (eds) Robert M. Hathaway, B. Muchhala and M. Kugelman, *Fueling the Future: Meeting Pakistan's needs in the 21st Century*, Document by Woodrow Wilson International Center for Scholars: Asia Program, (Mar.).

35. Dow Jones Report (2010), 'Managing the Energy Sector Financial Gap', (4 Jul.).

36. Dow Jones Report (2010), 'Ensuring Energy Security through Diversified Strategies', (3 Jul.).

37. Bashir A. Syed (2010), 'Pakistan's Energy Crisis, Causes, New Policies, and Plausible Solution', *The London Post*, (19 Jun.).

38. Julia M. Fraser (2005), 'Lessons from the Independent Private Power Experience in Pakistan', *World Bank*, (May).

39. Achilles Adamantiades (2006), 'Pakistan Electricity Sector Profile', (Mar.).

## 13. EDUCATION AS A STRATEGIC IMPERATIVE

1. The 'grievance' literature argues that individuals or groups that feel discriminated against or alienated from broader society have a greater likelihood of joining armed insurrections. Examining the case of Sierra Leone, Paul Richards has argued that youth violence in the country is a rational 'attention seeking behavior' under circumstances where young people have been alienated due to a failed education system and lack of income earning opportunities. Paul Richards (1996), *Fighting for the Rain Forest: War, Youth & Resources in Sierra Leone*, Oxford: James Currey.

2. Paul Collier (2000), 'Doing Well Out of War: An Economic Perspective' in Mats Berdal and David M. Malone (eds.), *Greed and Grievance: Economic Agendas in Civil Wars*, Boulder and London: Lynne Rienner, p. 94.

3. Robert D. Kaplan (1996), *The Ends of the Earth: A Journey at the Dawn of the 21st Century*, New York: Random House.

4. Rebecca Winthrop and Corinne Graff (2010), 'Beyond Madrasas: Assessing the Links between Education and Militancy in Pakistan', Center for Universal, *Brookings Institution*, working paper 2, (Jun.), p. 21.

5. Jeffrey Dixon (2009), 'What Causes Civil Wars? Integrating Quantitative Research Findings', *International Studies Review*, vol. 11, no. 4, pp. 707–35.

6. World Development Indicators, World Bank, 2009.

7. Ibid.

8. Ibid.; Ministry of Education, Government of Pakistan (2005), as cited in Center for Poverty Reduction and Income Distribution, 'Pakistan Millennium Development Goals Report 2005', Planning Commission, Islamabad, (Sept.), p. 19.

9. World Development Indicators, World Bank, 2009.

10. UNESCO Institute for Statistics, http://stats.uis.unesco.org/unesco/Table Viewer/document.aspx? ReportId=143&IF_Language=eng.

11. World Development Indicators, World Bank, 2009.

12. There are broad disparities in youth literacy not only across provinces but also within provinces; this points to the uneven access to education for students depending on their physical location. Even in Punjab, the most prosperous province, youth literacy rate varies from a low of 28 per cent in Ranjanpur to a high of 80 per cent in the districts of Chakwal, Jhelum, and Rawalpindi (which also have the lowest incidence of poverty). In Sindh the district of Karachi has a youth literacy rate of 80 per cent but more than half of the districts stand at less than 40 per cent. Balochistan and Khyber-Pukhtunkhwa have the lowest rates of youth literacy with only 15 per cent of the youth in districts such as Kohistan, Musa Khel and Dera Bugti being literate. 'Attaining the Millennium Development Goals in Pakistan: How Likely and What Will it Take to Reduce Infant Mortality, Child Malnutrition, Gender Disparities and to Increase School Enrollment and Completion', *World Bank*, South Asia Human Development Sector Discussion Paper Series, Report no. 8, May 2005 [data used in the report is from the 1998 national census of Pakistan].

13. Academy of Educational Planning and Management (2008), 'Pakistan Education Statistics 2006–07', National Educational Management Information System, Ministry of Education.

14. In Punjab out of 362,073 sanctioned posts only 309,083 are filled. In Balochistan, 39,867 posts out of the 42,887 sanctioned are filled. Academy of Educational Planning and Management, 'Pakistan Education Statistics 2006–07', 2008.

15. Population Council (2002), 'Adolescents and Youth in Pakistan 2001–02: A National Representative Survey', project sponsored by UNICEF, p. 56.

16. Ministry of Education (2009), 'National Education Policy 2009', Government of Pakistan, (1 Aug. [revision]).

17. India's education expenditures amounted to 3.3 per cent of GDP, Bangladesh's stood at 2.6 per cent, Nepal's at 3.2 per cent, and Iran's at 5.2 per

cent. Ministry of Finance (2010), 'Pakistan Economic Survey 2009–10', Government of Pakistan, Islamabad.

18. Ghulam R. Memon (2007), 'Education in Pakistan: The Key Issues, Problems and the New Challenges', *Journal of Management and Social Sciences*, vol. 3, no. 1, pp. 47–55.

19. Ministry of Education (2009), 'National Education Policy 2009'.

20. These figures vary somewhat depending on the source consulted. *Madrasah* figures are especially contentious and range between 0.5–5 per cent.

21. M. Younas Khalid et al. (2010), 'Social Audit of Local Governance and Delivery of Public Services', *UNDP Pakistan*, (Apr.), p. 119.

22. C. Christine Fair (2006), 'Islamic Education in Pakistan', *Trip Report, United States Institute of Peace*, http://home.comcast.net/~christine_fair/pubs/trip_report.pdf; C. Christine Fair (2007), 'Militant Recruitment in Pakistan: A New Look at the Militancy-Madrasah Connection', *Asia Policy*, no. 4, pp. 107–34.

23. For a detailed account of the bias in Pakistani education curricula, see A.H. Nayyar and Ahmed Salim (eds) (2004), 'The Subtle Subversion: The State of Curricula and Text-books in Pakistan', project report, *Sustainable Development Policy Institute, Pakistan*, pp. 9–72.

24. This information is based on a series of random informal discussions with students from various backgrounds over the past four years in the city of Lahore, Karachi, and Islamabad, and rural areas in Swat, NWFP. The discussions were not meant to be rigorous and respondents were not selected through any formal methodology.

25. Ibid.

26. In his seminal work on youth attitudes in Pakistan, Tariq Rehman argues that the idea of 'haves versus have nots' is present in the jihadi propaganda of virtually all Islamist outfits. Tariq Rehman (2003), 'Pluralism and Tolerance in Pakistani Society: Attitudes of Pakistani Students Towards the Religious Other', http://www.tariqrahman.net/language/Pluralism%20and%20Intolerance%20in%20Pakistani%20Society.htm. Paper presented at conference on pluralism at the Aga Khan University-Institute for the Study of Muslim Civilization, (25 Oct.).

27. Population Council (2002), 'Adolescents and Youth', pp. 67–68.

28. G.M. Arif and Amena Urooj (2009), 'Absorption of Growing Labor Force in Pakistan' in *Pakistan's Demographic Transition in the Development Context*, Islamabad: Population Council, (Nov.), p. 30.

29. Winthrop and Graff (2010), pp. 34–47.

30. Ministry of Finance, Government of Pakistan (2007), 'Pakistan Economic Survey 2006–07', Islamabad, p. 190.

31. Naushin Mahmood (2009), 'Demographic Transition and Dividend: A Perspective on Educational Attainment Effects in Pakistan', in *Pakistan's Demographic Transition*, pp. 20–21.

32. Arif and Urooj (2009), p. 28.

33. Official estimates suggest that Pakistan will have to grow at a rate of 6.35 per cent on average to keep unemployment at the current level of 5.32 per cent but that any attempt to push growth rates above 5.45 per cent over the next five years will be unsustainable and will cause a balance of payments crisis at some point. Planning Commission (2010), *Medium-Term Development Imperatives and Strategy for Pakistan*, final report of the Panel of Economists, Government of Pakistan, (Apr.), p. 26.

34. Faizunna and Ikram (2004) develop a comprehensive 'Youth Development Index' for Pakistan and come up with this as a major finding. See Azeema Faizunnisa and Atif Ikram (2004), 'Determinants of Youth Development in Pakistan', *Lahore Journal of Economics*, vol. 9, no. 2.

35. The program, *Parha Likha Punjab* was launched by the then Chief Minister Ch. Pervez Elahi in 2006.

36. 'Attaining the Millennium Development Goals', *World Bank* (2005).

37. Ibid.

38. Ibid.

39. For details of the institutional setup and performance of the teacher education and professional development programs in Pakistan, see UNESCO and USAID (2006), 'Situation Analysis of Teacher Education: Towards a Strategic Framework for Teacher Education and Professional Development—Pakistan', http://unesco.org.pk/education/documents/step/SituationAnalysis-StrategicFrameworkforTeacherEducation.pdf. Shanza N. Khan was one of the main contributors to this report.

40. A number of adopt-a-school schemes are currently operational across Pakistan. See 'Public Private Partnerships in the Education Sector: Education Sector Reforms Action Plan 2001–2005: Policy, Options, Incentive Package and Recommendations', Ministry of Education, Government of Pakistan (2004).

41. Ministry of Education (2009), 'National Education Policy 2009'.

## 14. PAKISTAN AS A NUCLEAR STATE

1. According to realism theory in international relations, approach to nuclear proliferation is treated as a state's decision to build nuclear weapons primarily as function of levels of insecurity. See Benjamin Frankel (1993), 'The Brooding Shadow: Systemic Incentives and Nuclear Weapons Proliferation', in Zachary S. Davis and Benjamin Frankel (eds), *The Proliferation Puzzle: Why Nuclear Weapons Spread and What Results*, London: Frank Cass, pp. 37–78; and Bradley A. Thayer (1995), 'The Causes of Nuclear Proliferation and the Utility of the Nuclear Nonproliferation Regime', *Security Studies* vol. 4, no. 3, pp. 463–519.

2. See Feroz Hassan Khan and Peter R. Lavoy (2008), 'Pakistan: The Dilemma of Nuclear Deterrence' in Muthiah Alagappa (ed.), *The Long Shadow: Nuclear Weapons and Security in 21st Century Asia*, Stanford: Stanford University Press, pp. 215–240.

3. See, for example, Kenneth Waltz and Scott D. Sagan (eds), (2003), *The Spread of Nuclear Weapons: A Debate Renewed*, New York: W.W. Norton & Company, Inc., pp. 88–155. Also see Ganguly, Sumit and Hagerty, Devin (2005), *Fearful Symmetry: India-Pakistan Crises in the Shadow of Nuclear Weapons*, New York: Oxford University Press.

4. George Perkovich (2000), *India's Nuclear Bomb: The Impact on Global Proliferation*, New York: Oxford University Press, pp. 422–423.

5. Dennis Kux (2001), *The United States and Pakistan 1947–2000: Disenchanted Allies*, Washington DC: Woodrow Wilson Center Press and Johns Hopkins University Press, p. 345.

6. Sartaj Aziz (2009), *Between Dreams and Realities: Some Milestones in Pakistan's History*, New York: Oxford University Press, pp. 190–196.

7. Nawaz Sharif's personalised style of governance and lack of institutional decision-making had come under intense criticism. In an address to the Naval War College in the first week of October 1998, Army Chief Jehangir Karamat emphasised the need for an institutionalised decision-making process in national security matters and suggested implementation of the previously mooted concept of a National Security Council. Nawaz Sharif reacted by calling for Karamat's resignation over the latter's public advice, and the Army Chief was sent home unceremoniously, lowering the morale of the Armed Forces.

8. For several months, Pakistan has appeared as an emerging Market. See 'Emerging-market Indicators', *Economist*, 378, no. 8468, (11–17 March 2006), 89. For a detailed analytical study see Shahid Javed Burki (2007), *Changing Perceptions, Altered Reality: Pakistan's Economy Under Musharraf, 1999–2006*, New York: Oxford University Press, Also see Pervez Musharraf (2006), *In the Line of Fire: A Memoir*, New York: Simon &Schuster, pp. 181–196.

9. When he announced his controversial policy reversal on Afghanistan in a 19 September 2001 speech to the nation, President Musharraf indicated that any other decision could have caused 'unbearable losses' to the security of the country, the health of the economy, the Kashmir cause, and to Pakistan's strategic nuclear and missile assets.

10. See the contents of the 1999 India-Pakistan Lahore Agreement, accessed on 15 Apr. 2006.

11. The Kargil crisis is comprehensively analysed in Peter R. Lavoy (2007) (ed.), *Asymmetric Warfare in South Asia: The Causes and Consequences of the Kargil Conflict*, Cambridge: Cambridge University Press.

12. For details, see Feroz Hassan Khan, 'Pakistan Nuclear Future', 164–5.

13. Pakistan has an indigenously built power reactor at Khushab and a pilot-scale reprocessing facility under the PAEC. Pakistan has the capability of producing up to ten kilograms of bomb-grade plutonium per year.

14. John H. Gill (2005), 'India and Pakistan: A Shift in the Military Crisis?' in Ashley J. Tellis and Michael Willis (ed.) (2005), *Military Modernization: In an Era of Uncertainty*, Seattle: The National Bureau of Asian Research, p. 257.

15. Strobe Talbott (2004), *Engaging India: Diplomacy, Democracy, and the Bomb*, Washington, D.C.: Brookings Institution Press; and Bruce Riedel (2002), 'American Diplomacy and the 1999 Kargil Summit at Blair House', Center for the Advanced Study of India, University of Pennsylvania, *Policy Paper Series*.

16. Rahul Roy-Chaudhury (2004), 'Nuclear Doctrine, Declaration Policy, and Escalation Control', and Feroz Hassan Khan (2004), 'Nuclear Signaling, Missiles, and Escalation Control in South Asia', both in Michael Krepon, Rodney W. Jones and Ziad Haider (eds), *Escalation Control and the Nuclear Option in South Asia*, Washington D.C.: Henry L. Stimson Center, pp. 75–118.

17. Ganguly and Hagerty, *Fearful Symmetry*.

18. A. Q. Khan was removed from Khan Research Laboratory in March 2001 and fired from his government position as Scientific Advisor after the exposure of his network in 2004. Pakistan enacted export control legislation in 2004 and earlier established the Pakistan Nuclear Regulatory Authority.

19. Gill, 'India and Pakistan: A Shift in the Military Crisis?', p. 253.

20. Based on Indian sources, Scott Sagan informs that India had planned 'to build a situation for a fourth war' with 'contingency plans to take out its nuclear program in a preventive strike'. See Scott D. Sagan and Kenneth N. Waltz (2003), *Spread of Nuclear Weapons: A Debate Renewed*, New York: W.W. Norton & Company, Inc., pp. 92–95. Also in an interview by the author with General Mirza Beg, in Rawalpindi, 1 September 2005, he asserted that Pakistan had credible information of India's planning a preventive attack in the early 1980s and he, as Chief of General Staff at General Headquarters, had to plan the defence of Kahuta. Since then fear of sudden strike at nuclear installation has remained a permanent threat hypothesis in Pakistan.

21. Sharif government had placed replicas of missile and nuclear test sites in main rotaries in Islamabad as symbols of nuclear nationalism. The Musharraf government had removed most of these replicas from the capital's streets in deference to Indian Prime Minister Vajpaee's visit to Islamabad in January 2004 (a few are still seen in Islamabad).

22. Khurshid Ahmad (1998), 'Nuclear Deterrence, CTBT, IMF Bail-outs and Debt Dependence', *Tarjuman al-Qur'an*, (Dec.); cited in Sohail H. Hashmi (2004), 'Islamic Ethics: An Argument for Nonproliferation', in Sohail H. Hashmi and Steven P. Lee (eds), *Ethics and Weapons of Mass Destruction: Religious and Secular Perspectives*, New York: Cambridge University Press p. 341.

## 16. THE AFGHAN CONUNDRUM

1. Ahmed Rashid (2000), *Taliban, Islam, Oil and the New Great Game in Afghanistan*, London: I.B.Tauris; Connnecticut: Yale University Press. This

book has been reissued in April 2010 with an updated section. The second book is, Ahmed Rashid (2009), *Descent into Chaos: The world's most unstable region and the threat to global security*, Penguin.

2. Lt. Gen Karl Eikenberry's testimony was given at a hearing of the Senate Armed Services Committee, Washington DC, 13 Feb. 2007.

3. Anthony Cordesman (2009), 'More Troops, Fewer Caveats. Let's Get Serious', *The Times* London, (10 Aug.).

4. This was widely reported in the media, including for example, *The Economist* (2009), 'Elections in Afghanistan: Re-rigging Hamid Karzai', (10 Sept.); Jeremy Page (2009), 'Abdullah Abdullah throws down election gauntlet to President Karzai', *The Times*, (15 Aug.).

5. Anthony Cordesman (2009).

## 17. THE INDIA FACTOR

1. S.M. Burke (1975), *Mainsprings of Indian and Pakistani Foreign Policies*, Karachi: Oxford University Press, p. 22.

2. Howard Wriggins (1977), 'The Balancing Process in Pakistan's Foreign Policy', in Lawrence Ziring et al., (eds), *Pakistan: The Long View*, Durham, N.C.: Duke University Press, pp. 303–4.

3. Richard Sisson and Leo Rose (1992), *War and Secession: Pakistan, India and the Creation of Bangladesh*, Karachi: Oxford University Press, p. 35.

4. In these secret talks, Pakistan was represented by President Musharraf's principal secretary, Tariq Aziz while India was represented, first by J.N. Dixit, Prime Minister Manmohan Singh's national security adviser and following his death by former Ambassador Satinder Lambah. According to noted journalist Steve Coll, the 2007 version of the 'non-paper', laid out several principles for a settlement: 'Kashmiris would be given special rights to move and trade freely on both sides of the Line of Control. Each of the former princely state's distinct regions would receive a measure of autonomy.... Providing that violence declined, each side would gradually withdraw its troops from the region. At some point, the Line of Control might be acknowledged by both governments as an international border.' Steve Coll (2009), 'The Back Channel', *The New Yorker*, (2 Mar.).

5. Farhan Bokhari and Jo Johnson (2007), 'Political wrangles dim the prospects of deal with India', *The Financial Times*, (29 May).

6. According to official Indian statements, these tests ranged from sub kiloton devices to 43-kiloton thermonuclear devices. The purpose of these tests was to generate additional data for improved computer simulation for design and for attaining the capability to carry out some critical experiment if necessary. For text of these statements see *The News* (International) 12 May and 14 May 1998.

7. *The News* 13 May 1998.

8. Ibid.

9. Mr S. Singhal, head of the Vishwa Hindu Parishad party declared that a 'war would be a better step to teach Pakistan a lesson'. 'A War is needed to

teach Pakistan a lesson: Singhal', *Asian Age* 24 May 1998. Similarly Home Minister of India, Mr. K. L. Advani stated on 19 May 1998 that 'Islamabad should realise the change in the geo-strategic situation in the region and the world and roll back its anti-Indian policy, especially with regard to Kashmir. India's bold and decisive step to become a nuclear weapon state has brought about a qualitatively new stage in Indo-Pakistan relations, particularly in finding a solution to the Kashmir Problem.' See *The News* 20 May 1998.

10. According to Brigadier Naeem Ahmad Salik, Director of the Arms Control and Disarmament Directorate at the Strategic Plans Division, Joint Staff Head Quarters, 'Although the balance is clearly tilted in India's favor, what is generally overlooked is the fact that India's conventional advantage is by means overwhelming, and Pakistan has so far been able to maintain a manageable ratio of forces and is capable of holding its own for a considerable time.' Naeem Ahmad Salik (2003), 'Regional Dynamics and Deterrence: South Asia', *Security Studies*, p. 217.

11. E. Sridharan, 'Improving Indo-Pakistan relations: international relations theory, nuclear deterrence and possibilities for economic cooperation', *Contemporary South Asia*, vol. 14, no. 3 (September 2005), p. 322.

12. Umer Farooq, 'Indian war planes intrude Pakistani air space as LoC shelling intensifies', *The Nation* August 2, 1998.

13. 'Aggression will be foiled', *Dawn* August 2, 1998.

14. Net Express, 'Sharif Speaks of War as Border Firing continues', http://www.indianexpress.com/ie/daily/19980803/21550734p.html.

15. 'India warns Pakistan against any attack', *The News*, 4 August 1998.

16. Shaheen Sehbai (1998), 'Washington concerned over LoC fighting', *Dawn* (4 Aug.).

17. In her influential article 'Promoting National Interest', Condoleezza Rice stressed the need for maintaining close cooperation with India. She argued that the United States 'should pay closer attention to India's role in the regional balance. There is a strong tendency conceptually to connect India with Pakistan and to think only of Kashmir or the nuclear competition between the two states. But India is an element in China's calculation, and it should be in America's, too. India is not a great power yet, but it has the potential to emerge as one.' Condoleezza Rice (2000), 'Promoting National Interest', *Foreign Affairs* (Jan.-Feb.), p. 56. Echoing Ms Rice's characterisation of India as a rising great power which the United States must take seriously, Robert B. Zoellick wrote: 'India, the world's largest democracy and before long its most populous nation, will play an increasingly important role in Asia. To grow and prosper, it will need to adjust to the global economy. To contribute to its prosperity and regional security, India will need to lower the risk of conflict with its neighbors. And to have influence with India, America must stop ignoring it. A more open India, possessing a broader understanding of its place in the world, could become a valuable partner of the United States in coping with the Eurasia's uncer-

tainties. In addition to proposing trade and investment liberalisation, the United States should open a regular, high-level security dialogue with India on Eurasia and the challenges to stability.' Robert B. Zoellick (2000), 'A Republican Foreign Policy', *Foreign Affairs* (Jan.-Feb.) p. 75.

18. Robert M. Hathaway (2002), 'The US-India Courtship: From Clinton to Bush', The *Journal of Strategic Studies*, vol. 25, no. 4 (Dec.), p. 10.
19. Dennis Kux (2002), 'A Remarkable Turnaround: U.S.-India Relations', *Foreign Service Journal* (Oct.), p. 20.
20. Text of President General Pervez Musharraf address to the nation on Radio and Television in *Dawn*, 13 Jan. 2002.
21. Ibid.
22. Ibid.
23. *Times of India*, 3 May 2002.
24. *The Hindu*, 6 April 2002.
25. *Dawn*, 18 December 2003.
26. For the text of the 6 January Joint Statement, see http://www.satp.org/satporgtp/countries/india/document/papers/indo_pak-6jan04.htm
27. The following schedule of meetings was announced after the February meeting in Islamabad: 1. Foreign Secretaries would meet in May/June 2004 for talks on peace and security including CBMs; and Jammu and Kashmir; 2. Talks on Siachin; Wullar Barrage/Tulbul Navigation Project; Sir Creek; Terrorism and Drug-trafficking; Economic and Commercial Cooperation; and Promotion of Friendly Exchanges in various fields would be held at the already agreed levels in July 2004. It was also agreed that the following technical level meeting would be held between the two sides: 1. Meeting between the Director General, Pakistan Rangers, and the Inspector General, Border Security Force, in March/April 2004; 2. Expert level talks on nuclear CBMs in the latter half of May 2004; 3. Committee on Drug-trafficking and Smuggling in June 2004.
28. Text of Indo-Pak Joint Statement, 18 February 2004 as quoted in *The News*, 19 February 2004.
29. This account of the Mumbai terrorist attacks draws heavily upon Rajesh Basrur et al. (2009), 'The 2008 Mumbai Terrorist Attacks: Strategic Fall-out', RSIS Monograph No. 17, pp. 20–28.
30. 'Pakistan and India were close to an agreement', *The Daily Times*, 2 May 2009.
31. Barnett Rubin and Ahmed Rashid (2008), 'From Great Game to Grand Bargain', *Daily Times*, 12 November.
32. 'Rivals Trade Blame over Kashmir', *BBC News*, 29 July 2008.
33. *The Daily Times*, 8 July 2008.
34. 'ISI involved in Indian Embassy bombing: NSA', *The Times of India*, (New Delhi), 14 July 2008. This may have been information obtained from US intelligence, which is reported to have drawn this conclusion. See Mark Mazzetti and Eric Schmitt (2008), 'Pakistanis Aided Attack in Kabul, U.S. Officials Say', *New York Times*, (1 Aug.).

35. *The News*, 22 July 2008.
36. 'Tough Talking Accusations', *Daily Times*, 22 July 2008.
37. 'Initial information suggests Pak hand in Mumbai attack: Pranab', *Times of India*, 28 November 2008; 'Mumbai attacks to hurt Indo-Pak ties: Pranab Mukherjee', *Times of India*, 28 November 2008.
38. 'India Demands Strong Swift Action', *News*, 2 December 2008.
39. Ibid.
40. 'Lashkar-i-Taiba Denies Role', *News*, 28 November 2008.
41. 'Troika Meets', *Nation*, 30 November 2008; 'No state institution involved in terrorism: FO', *News*, 2 January 2009; 'The Blame Game' *News*, 29 November 2008.
42. Ibid.; 'Fighting Terror Jointly', *Dawn*, 29 November 2008.
43. The Samjhauta Express, a bi-weekly train carrying passengers between the two countries, was struck by a bomb attack some 90 km from Delhi on the night of 18 February 2007. The majority of the sixty-eight killed were Pakistani citizens. 'Dozens Dead in India Train Blasts', *BBC News*, 19 February 2007.
44. Rina Chandran (2008), 'India, Pakistan Simmer over Mumbai Attacks', *Reuters*, (29 Nov.).
45. 'Much More Needs to Be Done: Singh', *News*, 12 Dec. 2008.
46. 'India to Consider All Options, Warns Pranab', *News*, 20 Dec. 2008.
47. 'Pakistan Must Give Cast Iron Guarantees: Chidambaram', *Times of India*, 4 Jan. 2009.
48. For the text of the dossier, see 'Mumbai Terror Attacks—Dossier of Evidence' *Hindu*, n.d., <http://www.hindu.com/nic/dossier.htm> [Last accessed 24 Jul. 2009].
49. Jawed Naqvi (2009), 'Mumbai Attacks: India Blames "State Actors"', *Dawn*, (5 Jan.).
50. 'Pak "Official Agencies" Supported Mumbai Attacks: PM', *Indian Express*, 6 Jan., 2009.
51. 'Terror Evidence in Indian Dossier Credible: US', *Times of India*, 7 Jan. 2009.
52. Syed Irfan Raza (2009), 'Thaw at Last: Mastermind Lakhvi in custody, Eight named in FIR, 30 questions given to India', *Dawn*, (13 Feb.).
53. Qudssia Akhlaque (2009), 'Kasab's Confessional Statement Missing in Indian Response', *Dawn*, (16 Mar.).
54. 'Hafiz Saeed Set Free', *Daily Times*, 3 Jun. 2009.
55. Nirupama Subramanian (2009), 'Pakistan Admits to Creating Militant Groups', *Hindu*, (9 Jul.).
56. 'Full Text of India-Pakistan Joint Statement', *Zee News*, 16 Jul. 2009 <http://www.zeenews.com/news547571.html> (accessed 24 Jul. 2009).
57. Ibid.
58. 'Noose Tightens around Lashkar Commander Lakhvi', *Times of India*, 20 Jul. 2009.

59. 'India interfering in Balochistan, says Gilani', *Tribune*, Chandigarh 19 Jul. 2009.

60. Neena Vvas (2009), 'We will not accept delinking: BJP', *The Hindu*, (18 Jul.).

61. Venkatesh Kesari (2009), 'PM Pak Policy: Trust but, Verify', *The Asian Age*, (30 Jul.).

62. Vinay Kumar (2009), 'Pakistani terrorist groups planning more attacks: Manmohan', *The Hindu*, (18 Aug.).

63. Ashish Kumar Sen (2009), '26/11, US wants Pakistan to speed up trial', *The Tribune*, (17 Jul.).

64. 'Secretary Clinton's Interview with Frankly Speaking', 18 Jul. 2009, <http://www.america.gov/st/texttrans-english/2009/July/20090719112338ptellivremos0.4464642.html>.

65. 'Pakistan must give up terror as state policy: Manmohan', *The News*, 27 Sept. 2009.

66. 'China urges peaceful solution of Kashmir', *The Nation*, 29 Sept. 2009.

67. 'Proof of India's involvement in militancy found', *Dawn*, 3 Nov. 2009.

68. 'Obama wants China to play role in Indo-Pak Ties', *The News*, 18 Nov. 2009.

69. 'Pakistan based terrorist groups plotting more attacks: Manmohan', *The Hindu*, 21 Nov. 2009.

70. 'Manmohan: Pakistan not doing enough to punish 26/11 culprits', *The Hindu*, 26 Nov. 2009.

71. 'Remove gun from our head to restart talks, Pak told', *The Tribune*, Chandigarh, 29 Nov. 2009.

72. 'India turns down dialogue offer', *The Tribune*, Chandigarh, 23 Dec. 2009.

73. 'US encouraging Indo-Pak peace moves', *The News*, 6 Feb. 2010.

74. 'US wants Pakistan, India to cultivate stable relationship', *Dawn*, 21 Feb. 2010.

75. 'India following strategy of 'talks for the sake of talks': Qureshi', *Daily Times*, 4 Mar. 2010.

76. Ashok Tuteja, 'Inaction against Saeed', *The Tribune*, Chandigarh, 3 March 2010.

77. 'Dossiers no basis to arrest Saeed: Pak', *The Tribune*, Chandigarh, 5 Mar. 2010.

78. 'Solid evidence of Indian involvement in Baluchistan terror acts: Malik', *The News*, 13 Mar. 2010.

79. 'PM: Talks with Pak only after action against 26/11 culprits', *The Tribune*, Chandigarh, 15 Apr. 2010.

80. Erika Kintetz, 'India court convicts Pakistani in Mumbai siege', *Associated Press*, 3 May 2010.

81. 'Mumbai attacks conviction a message to Pakistan', *Dawn*, 4 May 2010.

82. Anwar Iqbal and Masood Haider (2010), 'Reducing Indo-Pak tension US high priority', *Dawn*, (30 Apr.).

83. 'US encouraged by resumption of Indo-Pak talks', *The Hindu*, 30 Apr. 2010.

84. Maleeha Lodhi (2010), 'Limits of coercive diplomacy', *The News*, (9 Feb.).

85. Siddharth Varadarajan (2010), 'India's embrace of dialogue remains limited, reluctant', *The Hindu*, (12 Feb.).

86. K. Subrahmanyam (2010), 'Peace process with Islamabad: It is better to involve Pakistan Army', *The Tribune*, Chandigarh, (8 Feb.).

87. Bharat Karnad (2009), *India's Nuclear Policy*, London: Praeger Security International, p. 112.

88. *Quadrennial Defense Review* (2010), Washington, DC: Feb., p. 60.

89. National Security Strategy (2010), Washington, DC: May, pp. 43–44.

90. Brian K. Hedrick (2009), 'India's Strategic Defense Transformation: Expanding Global Relationships', *The Letort Papers*, Carlisle, PA: U.S. Army War College, Strategic Studies Institute, Nov., pp. v-vi.

91. Iftikhar A. Khan (2007), 'US-India deal may ignite arms race: Civil N-power a priority: NCA', *Dawn*, (3 Aug.).

# REFERENCES

*Chapter 2*

Ahmad, Jamil-ud-din (ed.) (1976) *Speeches and Writings of Mr. Jinnah*, Lahore: Sh. Muhammad Ashraf.

Ahmed, Rizwan (1993) *'Sayings of Quaid-i-Azam': Mohammad Ali Jinnah*, Karachi: Quaid Foundation and Pakistan Movement Centre.

Gandhi, Rajmohan (1986) *Eight Lives: A Study of the Hindu-Muslim Encounter*, Albany, NY: State University of New York Press.

Jinnah, Mohammad Ali (1948) *Speeches of Quaid-i-Azam Mohammad Ali Jinnah as Governor General of Pakistan*, Karachi: Sind Observer Press.

Jinnah, Mohammad Ali (1989) *Quaid-i-Azam Mohammad Ali Jinnah: Speeches and Statements 1947–48*, Islamabad: Government of Pakistan, Ministry of Information and Broadcasting, Directorate of Films and Publications.

Merchant, Liaquat H. (1990) *Jinnah: A Judicial Verdict*, Karachi: East-West Publishing Company.

Seervai, H.M. (1990) *Partition of India: Legend and Reality*, Bombay, Emmenem Publications.

Wolpert, Stanley (1984) *Jinnah of Pakistan*, New York: Oxford University Press.

Zaidi, Z.H. (1993) *Jinnah Papers: Prelude to Pakistan*, vol. I, parts I and II, Islamabad: Quaid-i-Azam Papers Project.

*Chapter 10*

Amjad, R. (2006), 'Employment Strategies and Labour Market Policies: Interlinkages with Macro and Sectoral Policies', in *Pakistan: Decent Employment Generation and Skills Development*, Papers, Synthesis and Recommendations of the National Tripartite Forum on Employment and Skills, jointly organised by the Ministry of Labour, Manpower and Overseas Pakistanis, and ILO, 25–26 April 2006, Islamabad.

APAX Partners and The Economist Intelligence Unit Report: 'Understanding Technology Transfer', Spring 2005.
BMA Capital Research Reports, 2000–2010.
Central Intelligence Agency, World Factbook and IMF working papers.
Cheema, Ali (2004), 'Stabilization Policy: Less Mythologizing More Reality', *Dawn*, (24 Nov.).
Cohen, Stephen (2006), *The Idea of Pakistan*, Brookings Institution. In this book Stephen Cohen outlines much of the broader and specific issues facing Pakistan which have the potential to create further destabilisation in Pakistan.
Economic data used in the chapter is sourced from various Annual Reports of the State Bank of Pakistan and the Government of Pakistan's various annual publications entitled 'Economic Survey'.
Global Competitiveness Report 2009–10, World Economic Forum.
Goldman Sachs Global Economics Department (2005), *BRICs and Beyond*. Goldman Sachs.
Government of Pakistan publications, including State Bank of Pakistan Annual Reports and Ministry of Finance, Annual Economic Survey.
IMF News Brief No. 00/23 (28 Apr. 2000), 'IMF Executive Board Reviews Pakistan Misreporting, Remedial Steps'. Pakistan was required to promptly repurchase SDR 18.95 million in outstanding debt to the IMF and voluntarily repurchase another SDR 22 million for a total 'fine' of SDR 40.95 million for misreporting.
Iqbal, Zubair (2007), 'Pakistan—Sustainability of the Current Economic Boom' Paper Presented to the IPP, (Sept.).
Social Policy and Development Center, 'An Overheating Economy?', Annual Review June 2005.
Yaqub, Muhammad (2003), 'Political and Economic Aspects of Banking Sector Reforms in Pakistan', South Asia Region Internal Discussion Paper No. IDP-188, The World Bank, (May).

# INDEX

Advani, L. K.: 271
Afghanistan: 17, 39, 68, 79, 206, 240, 272, 300, 305–6, 351; and India, 315; border of, 61, 83, 120; civilian death toll, 309–10; education outcome rate in, 254; government of, 92, 309; Indian presence in, 18; Kabul, 290, 305, 307, 309, 311, 313, 315, 339; military of, 309; National Directorate for Security (NDS), 316; NATO presence in, 65, 285–6; Operation Enduring Freedom (2001–), 1, 6, 19, 49–50–1, 65, 75–6, 88, 131, 178, 205, 278, 285–6, 301, 306; opposition to Pakistan's entry into UN (1947), 312; population of, 315; presence of Pakistan-based insurgent groups in, 137; refugees from, 48; Soviet invasion of (1979–89), 15–16, 59, 62, 85, 101, 122–4, 129, 135–6, 140, 143, 145, 174, 205, 281, 289, 294, 308, 313–14; Taliban presence in, 8, 65, 137, 290–1, 302, 307, 309, 311; training of Pakistani militants in, 143
Ahl-i-Hadith: 15
Ahle-Hadith Conference: 101
Ahmad, Qazi Hussain: family of, 54; former Amir of Jamaat-e-Islami, 54

Ahmadi: declaration as non-Muslims (1974), 15, 116–17, 119; excommunication of, 15; ideology of, 116
Akbar the Great Mughal: symbolism of, 24–5
al Banna, Hasan: founder of Muslim Brotherhood, 134, 144
al Qaeda: 8, 62, 69, 125, 131, 284, 289, 293; 9/11 attacks, 16, 59, 133, 179, 205, 273, 278, 285, 294, 314, 327; and Taliban, 310; growth of, 132; influence of, 83, 138–9; operatives, 127, 141, 143–4; supporters of, 108, 140, 308
al Zawahiri, Ayman: 145
Armitage, Richard: Deputy Secretary of State, 329
Asian Development Bank: 184; estimate of Indus River flood damage, 197
Ata-ur-Rehman: background of, 142; founder of Jundullah, 142
Atatürk, Mustafa Kemal: 27
Aurangzeb: death of (1707), 24; last Great Emperor of Mughal Empire, 24–5
Australia: population of, 36
Awami National Party (ANP): 54, 80, 101, 107; and Asif Ali Zardari, 106; member of coalition in

379

Gandhi, Rajiv: and Benazir Bhutto, 18
Gandhi, Sonia: leader of Indian Congress Party, 330
Germany: 40
Gilani, Yousuf Raza: 109; administration of, 54, 72–3; family of, 73; granting of three-year extension to General Ashfaq Parvez Kayani (2010), 110
Goldman Sachs: Next-11 concept, 203
Grant, Mark Lyall: High Commissioner, 68; meetings with Pervez Musharraf, 68–9

Harakat-a-Jihad-al Islami (HJI): emergence of, 136
Harakat-ul-Mujahideen (HuM): emergence of, 136; presence in Afghanistan, 137; recruits, 142
al Hawsawi, Mustafa Ahmed: capture of (2003), 144
Hekmatyar, Gulbuddin: 285; leader of Hizb-e-Islami, 120
Hidayatullah, G. H.: correspondence of, 29
Himalayas: 1
Hinduism: 22, 29, 117, 283, 287, 297, 323; and India, 10–11, 114; minority population in Pakistan, 28, 32
Hindustan: 10
Hizb-e-Islami: led by Gulbuddin Hekmatyar, 120; supported by ISI, 122
Holbrooke, Richard: Special Envoy for Af-Pak, 309
Humayan: Great Emperor of Mughal Empire, 25
Husain, Ishrat: former governor of State Bank, 67

India: 37, 41, 185, 281, 286, 296, 300, 303, 306; and Afghanistan, 315; and Balochistan, 342, 345; and Bangladesh, 287; and Hinduism, 10–11, 114; and Russian Federation, 302; and UK, 61; and USA, 6, 12, 270, 290, 341, 346; Bombay, 31; conflict with Pakistan, 5–6, 9, 11–13, 16, 18–19, 33, 38–9, 61, 79, 93, 268, 298–9, 303–4, 313, 319, 323, 325, 329–30, 339, 343–4, 347; defence spending in, 85; Delhi, 31, 61; economy of, 42, 203, 210; education system of, 253; exports from, 217; first nuclear explosive device test (1972), 269; independence of (1947), 10, 82; military of, 279, 295; Mumbai, 111, 281, 319, 338, 340–1; Muslim population of, 10, 33, 47, 81, 113; national identity of, 38, 40; New Delhi, 6, 12, 18, 112, 288–9, 293, 297, 323–4, 326–8, 330, 341–2, 345, 347; nuclear tests (1998), 16, 270–1; occupation of Kargil heights (1999), 16, 98, 274, 295, 323, 327; Parliament attack (2001), 273, 294; part of BRIC, 203, 300; part of G-3, 300; partition (1947), 84; presence in Afghanistan, 18; support for BLA, 287; suppression of Kashmiri population by, 303; territorial claims of, 18, 115
Indian Congress Party: 52; affiliation with Aligarh tradition, 114; led by Sonia Gandhi, 330
Indonesia: 185, 352; economy of, 86; military of, 85
Indus River: flooding of (2010), 1, 46, 110, 196, 199, 202, 212, 227–8
Integrated Energy Planning (IEP): 240–1, 245–8, 250; examples of, 243; origins of, 242; process of, 242

Jamaat-ud-Dawa (JuD): 340

Jamali, Mir Zafarullah Khan: and Atal Bihari Vajpayee, 329

Jamiat-e-Islami: led by Burhanuddin Rabbani, 120

Jamiat Ulema-e-Hind: founding of, 134

Jamiat Ulema-e-Islam (JUI): 133; and Asif Ali Zardari, 106; and ISI, 122; ideology of, 135; led by Maulana Fazl-ur-Rahman, 53; *madrassas* run by, 137; member of coalition in NWFP and Balochistan (1971), 135; member of MMA, 132; support for Taliban regime, 137

Jammu: 294

Japan: 40

Javed, General Hamid: presidential Chief of Staff, 69

Javed, Khawja: arrest of (2003), 144

Jinnah, Mohammad Ali: 3, 11, 27, 30–3, 114; broadcast to USA (1948), 28; death of, 22, 33, 52; family of, 22; first President of Pakistan, 23; invitation to Sir George Cunningham to return as Governor of North West Frontier Province, 29; nationalism of, 33; property in India, 31; rejection of original territory of Pakistan, 10; role in founding of Pakistan, 21–3, 25, 34, 283; use of Prophet Muhammad as role model in creation of Pakistan, 26, 28; Quad-i-Azam, 27, 80; vision of secular nation, 116

Jundullah: associates of, 144; founded by Ata-ur-Rehman, 142; members of, 143; presence in Karachi, 142

Junejo, Muhammad Khan: leader of Pakistan Muslim League, 104

Karakoram: 1

Karamat, General Jehangir: former Army Chief, 81, 97, 273

Karzai, Hamid: 306; administration of, 131, 286, 307, 309–10; accusation of Pakistani responsibility for Mumbai attack (2008), 339; potential rejection of Pakistani role in Afghanistan, 317

Kasab, Ajmal: interrogation report of, 341

Kashmir: 11, 18, 22, 82, 287, 293–4, 303, 323, 327, 345, 347; independence movement in, 295; Muslim population of, 84; occupation of Kargil heights by India (1999), 16, 98, 274, 295, 323, 327; population of, 294; presence of Lashkar-e-Taiba in, 125; source of conflict between India and Pakistan, 38, 51, 61, 79, 116, 124, 137, 268, 271, 273, 288, 295–6, 304, 324, 343; Pakistani controlled area of, 144; Uprising (1989), 294

Kayani, General Ashfaq Parvez: 92, 314; and Pervez Musharraf, 111; demeanour of, 93; given position of Chief of Army Staff (2007), 70–1, 80, 85, 90, 108; granted three-year extension by Gilani administration (2010), 110; head of ISI (2004), 111; media image of, 110; role in shaping policy focusing on India, 111–12

Khan, Abdul Qadeer: 277, 298; proliferation of nuclear secrets, 270, 272, 290; production of uranium centrifuges under, 269

Khan, General Ayub: accelerated economic growth under, 50, 170; Chief Martial law Administrator, 87; Defence Minister, 87; development of Islamic identity under, 117–20; regime of, 87, 104, 117;

model in creation of Pakistan, 26, 28

Mukherjee, Pranab: Minister for External Affairs, 339

*Mullah*: 13–14

Musharraf, Pervez: 49, 53–4, 85, 91, 97, 107, 177, 279, 308, 314, 328; accelerated economic growth under, 50–1; and Bush, George W., 306; and General Ashfaq Parvez Kayani, 111; and Tariq Aziz, 69; Army Chief (1998), 272; control over nuclear program, 270, 273, 276; forced from office (2008), 50, 66, 68, 70–1; issuing of National Reconciliation Ordinance (NRO) (2007), 105; media policies of, 50, 83; meetings with Mark Lyall Grant and Ryan Crocker, 68–9; regime of, 50, 58–60, 80–1, 88, 90, 98, 104, 124–5, 127, 141, 180, 338; rise to power (1999), 49, 82, 105; support for War on Terror, 125

Muslim: 12–13, 22, 34, 39, 64, 116–17, 132, 137, 282, 287, 297, 301, 303, 314; population of Bangladesh, 10; population of India, 10, 33, 47, 81, 113; population of Kashmir, 84; population of Pakistan, 10, 26–7; population of Punjab, 32

Muslim Brotherhood: founded by Hasan al Banna, 134, 144

Muslim League: 52, 54, 70, 77, 107; administration of, 50; affiliated with Deoband tradition, 114; and Asif Ali Zardari, 106; denial of share of power, 11; led by Mian Nawaz Sharif, 50, 70, 83, 101, 104, 339; resolution of (1940), 19; structure of, 53, 56

Muttahida Majlis-i-Amal (MMA): administration of, 134; growth

of, 133; members of, 132; polled (2002), 64

Muttahida Qaumi Movement (MQM): 107; and Asif Ali Zardari, 106; dominance in Sindh, 72; joined provincial government of Sindh (2008), 106; members of, 63; rise of, 63

Narayanan, M.K.: National Security Advisor for India, 339

National Accountability Bureau: establishment of, 165; questioning of impartiality and neutrality of, 154, 165

National Finance Commission (NFC): award, 37, 109, 157, 168, 198–9; purpose of, 63

Nazir, Mullah: 138; member of TTP, 138

Negroponte, John: visits to Pakistan (2007), 109; US Secretary of State, 109

Nehru, Jawaharlal: 13, 34

Netherlands: population of, 36

Niazi, General A. A. K.: 118

Nicaragua: conditional cash transfer programs, 263

Non-Aligned Movement: 13; Sharm-el-Sheikh Summit, 342

North Atlantic Treaty Organization (NATO): 111, 140, 305, 308; combat deaths, 310; members of, 6; military forces of, 16, 65, 307, 310; presence in Afghanistan, 65, 285–6

North Waziristan: 147, 293; Haqqani stronghold in, 311, 316

Obaidullah, Mullah: arrest of (2007), 308

Obama, Barack: 285, 293, 305, 344; administration of, 292, 302, 343; Afghanistan strategy of, 310; appointments of personnel,

309; ordering of escalation of
drone strikes, 140
Omar, Mullah: 311; in hiding, 308;
supporters of, 139
Orakzai: military operations in, 284
Organization of the Islamic Conference: second summit of (1974),
14
Overseas Development Institute:
research into determinants of
governance and development,
149

Pakistan: 2–3, 8, 31, 35, 46–7, 79,
95–7, 103, 150, 152–3, 166–7,
240–1, 266, 281, 288–9, 297–8,
300–1, 306, 349–52; air force,
280; Afghanistan opposition
to entry into UN (1947), 312;
Alternative Energy Development
Board, 244, 246; and USA, 5, 7,
12–14, 16, 19, 59, 62, 102–3,
111, 131, 178, 289, 293; and
USSR, 14; Auditor General, 164;
border of, 61, 316; Christian
minority population of, 28; coal
reserves in, 236–7; Competition
Commission of Pakistan (CCP),
187, 198; civil bureaucracy of,
4, 12, 100, 154–7; coal reserves,
206; Competitiveness Support
Fund, 220; conflict with India,
5–6, 9, 11–13, 16, 18–19, 33,
38–9, 61, 79, 93, 268, 298–9,
303–4, 313, 319, 323, 325,
329–30, 339, 343–4, 347;
Constituent Assembly, 23, 114;
Constitution (1973), 63; corruption in, 58, 161–2; defence
spending in, 85–6; economy of, 2,
37–8, 41–3, 57–8, 60, 67, 75, 85,
169–70, 175, 178, 186, 188, 190,
202–5, 207, 216, 221–3, 227–8,
235–6, 239, 261, 273; education
outcome rate in, 254; education

system of, 253–4; Eighteenth
Constitutional Amendment,
168; electoral outcome (2008),
107; energy sector, 231–4, 238;
Energy Yearbook 2009, 233;
Extended Fund Facility with IMF,
174; Faisalabad, 221; Federal
Court, 116; first free elections
in (1970), 47; Fiscal Deficit and
Debt Limitation Act (2003),
191, 225; Freedom of Information Act, 167; Gawadar, 206;
Hindu minority population of,
28, 32; independence of (1947),
3, 10–12, 20, 23, 33, 53, 80, 84,
113, 134; Infrastructure Project
Development Facility (IPDF),
212; Institute of Development
Economics, 170; involvement in
War on Terror, 49; Islamabad,
17–18, 59, 62, 126, 139, 190,
243, 270, 287, 291–2, 295, 302,
308, 315, 323–7, 329–30, 339,
341, 345, 347; Islamic identity
of, 13, 113, 115, 128; Karachi,
29–31, 37, 41, 177, 221, 248,
313; Lahore, 14, 33, 37, 101,
142, 221; literacy rate, 214;
member of CENTO, 13; member
of SEATO, 13; middle class of,
45–6, 74; military of, 1, 4–5, 12,
17–18, 41, 53–4, 63, 80–1, 84,
86, 88–9, 93–4, 97, 116, 131,
215, 273, 277, 284, 291, 295,
299, 307, 312, 315–16, 327;
Ministry of Finance, 225; Ministry of Food, Agriculture and
Livestock, 244, 246; Ministry
of Industries, 244; Ministry of
Labour and Manpower, 215;
Ministry of Law, 165; Ministry of Petroleum and Natural
Resources, 233, 244–5; Ministry
of Production, 244; Ministry
of Technology, 214; Ministry

of Urban Affairs, Forestry and Wildlife, 244, 246; Ministry for Water and Power, 244; Muslim population of, 10, 26–7; Naran, 41; National Assembly, 187, 191; National Command Authority, 270, 292; National Electric Power Regulatory Authority, 244; National Productivity Organization, 194, 220; National Professional Standards for Teachers, 264; National Vocational and Technical Education Commission (NAVTEC), 214; Nuclear Command Authority (NCA), 279–81; nuclear tests (1998), 16, 267; Objective Resolution (1949), 115; Official Secrets Act, 166; oil and gas discoveries in, 236–8; Oil and Gas Regulatory Authority, 244; Pakistan Atomic Energy Commission (PAEC), 155, 275–6; Pakistan Software Export Board (PSEB), 220; Pakistan Mineral Development Corporation, 244; Peshawar, 41; population growth, 201, 206, 211–12; poverty in, 41; recognition of Bangladesh (1974), 14; remittances received by (1975–85), 49; nationalism in, 9–10; nuclear tests (1998), 274; Police Order (2002), 160; population of, 2; poverty, 249; Public Sector Enterprises, 195; Private Power and Infrastructure Board, 244; School Management Committees (SMCs), 263; Securities and Exchange Commission, 164; Skardu, 41; Small and Medium Enterprise Authority (SMEDA), 220; Small and Medium Enterprise sector, 194, 216, 218–20, 227; State Bank (SBP), 87, 155, 164, 170, 172, 175, 177, 180, 191–2, 225; stock

market, 205, 223; Strategic Force Command (SFC), 280; Strategic Plans Division of the Army Headquarters, 83–4, 275, 279–80; Sufi culture, 129; support for Afghan resistance, 15; Supreme Court, 338; suspension of military and economic aid from USA (1990), 16; Taliban presence in, 8, 15, 21, 99, 124, 316; tax system reform in, 187–8, 192, 197–8, 211, 226; telecommunications sector, 67; territory of, 1, 206; textile industry, 217–18; trade corridor, 206, 240; urban sector, 75; Urdu as national language, 29; youth of, 35, 60, 82, 88, 261

Pakistan Afghan Transit Trade Agreement (PATTA): signing of (2010), 207

Pakistan Muslim League: led by Muhammad Khan Junejo, 104

Pakistan People's Party (PPP): 54, 68, 71, 100–1, 107, 109, 118, 157, 339; led by Asif Ali Zardari, 50; led by Benazir Bhutto, 50, 79, 83, 104–6; led by Zulfikar Ali Bhutto, 104, 172; strongholds of, 56

Pakistan Steel: 161; perception of corruption in sale of, 152

Palestine: and Israel, 302

Parsism: 29

Pashtun: 64, 313; military recruitment in, 89; militants in, 131, 315; territory of, 306, 314

Petraeus, General David: 92; commander of CENTCOM, 309

Pirzada, Abdus-Sattar: 29

Punjab: 11, 58, 175; language of, 36; LeT presence in, 316; military recruitment in, 89; Muslim population of, 32; non-elite private schools in, 263; Sikh uprising in Indian Punjab, 18; stronghold of